MY GRAMMAR COACH

내신기출 N제 중1

정답과 해설은 EBS 중학사이트(mid.ebs.co.kr)에서 다운로드 받으실 수 있습니다.

중학 내신 영어 해결사
MY COACH 시리즈

MY GRAMMAR COACH	기초편, 표준편
MY GRAMMAR COACH 내신기출 N제	중1, 중2, 중3
MY READING COACH	LEVEL 1, LEVEL 2, LEVEL 3
MY WRITING COACH 내신서술형	중1, 중2, 중3
MY VOCA COACH	중학 입문, 중학 기본, 중학 실력

MY GRAMMAR COACH

내신기출 N제 중1

이 책의 **구성과 특징**

＼첫째,

13종 교과서의 문법 요목 및 전국 중학교 시험 문제를 분석하여 구성 (p. 5~8 교과서 문법 연계표 참고)

＼둘째,

단원별 세분화된 요목으로 최대한 간단하게 문법 설명 제시

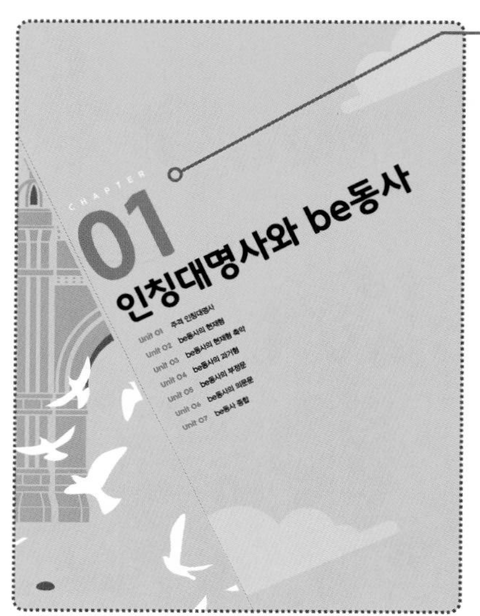

❶ 챕터별 세분화된 문법 요목

종합적인 이해에 앞서 세분화된 각각의 문법 요목에 대한 충분한 학습이 이루어지도록 유닛이 구성되었습니다.

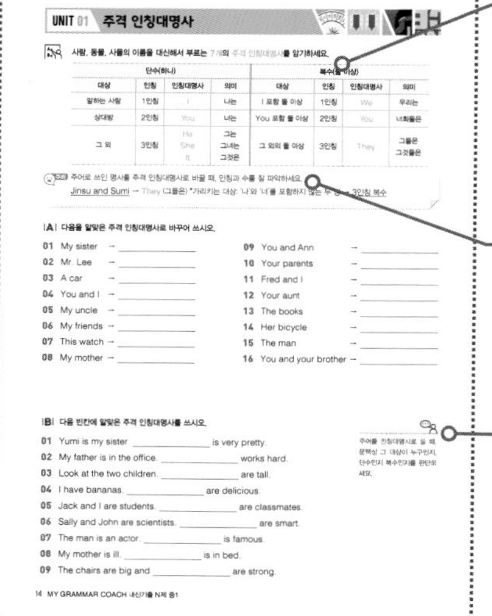

❷ 학습 지시 및 문법 핵심 정리

문법에 관한 긴 설명을 배제하고 어떻게 학습해야 하는지가 간단하게 제시되고, 해당 문법의 핵심만 한눈에 볼 수 있도록 정리되어 있습니다.

❸ 주의 및 참고

핵심 문법 정리만으로 부족할 수 있는 참고 사항 및 주의 사항이 세심하게 제시되어 있습니다.

❹ 문제 풀이 팁

막상 문제를 풀 때는 배운 내용이 기억나지 않거나, 배운 내용을 적용하기 힘든 경우들이 있습니다. 이를 위해 Coaching Tip을 통해 다시 한번 문법 설명이 제공됩니다.

셋째,
주관식 위주의 풍부한 드릴 문제 및 세심한 코칭

넷째,
서술형 비율을 높인 중간고사 · 기말고사 실전문제

다섯째,
추가 연습할 수 있는 워크북 제공

여섯째,
문제 해결의 단서와 주의 포인트를 짚을 수 있는 정답과 해설

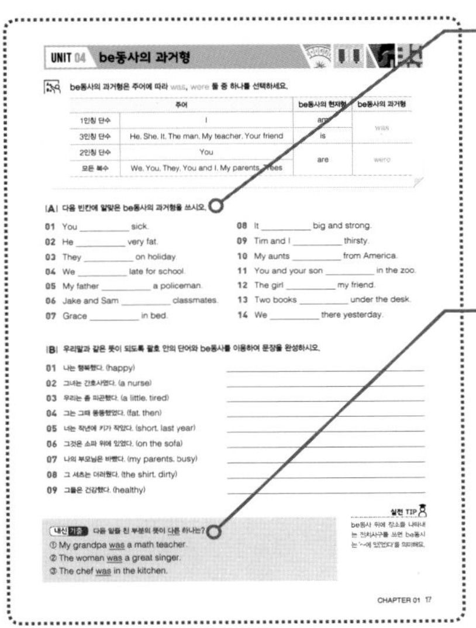

UNIT 04 be동사의 과거형

be동사의 과거형은 주어에 따라 was, were 둘 중 하나를 선택하세요.

주어		be동사의 현재형	be동사의 과거형
1인칭 단수	I	am	was
3인칭 단수	He, She, It, The man, My teacher, Your friend	is	
2인칭 단수	You	are	were
모든 복수	We, You, They, You and I, My parents, Trees		

|A| 다음 빈칸에 알맞은 be동사의 과거형을 쓰시오.

01 You ________ sick.
02 He ________ very fat.
03 They ________ on holiday.
04 We ________ late for school.
05 My father ________ a policeman.
06 Jake and Sam ________ classmates.
07 Grace ________ in bed.
08 It ________ big and strong.
09 Tim and I ________ thirsty.
10 My aunts ________ from America.
11 You and your son ________ in the zoo.
12 The girl ________ my friend.
13 Two books ________ under the desk.
14 We ________ there yesterday.

|B| 우리말과 같은 뜻이 되도록 괄호 안의 단어와 be동사를 이용하여 문장을 완성하시오.

01 나는 행복했다. (happy)
02 그녀는 간호사였다. (a nurse)
03 우리는 좀 피곤했다. (a little, tired)
04 그는 그때 통통했었다. (fat, then)
05 너는 작년에 키가 작았다. (short, last year)
06 그것은 소파 위에 있었다. (on the sofa)
07 나의 부모님은 바빴다. (my parents, busy)
08 그 셔츠는 더러웠다. (the shirt, dirty)
09 그들은 건강했다. (healthy)

내신 기출 다음 밑줄 친 부분의 뜻이 다른 하나는?
① My grandpa was a math teacher.
② The woman was a great singer.
③ The chef was in the kitchen.

실전 TIP
be동사 뒤에 장소를 나타내는 전치사구를 쓰면 be동사는 '~에 있었다'를 의미해요.

CHAPTER 01 17

❺ 주관식 위주의 드릴 문제

해당 문법에 대한 집중적인 연습 및 완벽한 이해를 위해 해당 문법 요목에 가장 효과적인 주관식 위주의 연습 문제가 제시됩니다.

❻ 내신 기출 맛보기

챕터 끝에서 종합적인 실전 문제를 풀기 전에, 배운 내용을 바로 바로 실전형으로 풀어 볼 수 있게 구성되었습니다. 해당 문법이 내신 문제화 되었을 때 어떻게 나올 수 있는지를 미리 만나 보며, 학습에 대한 동기 부여가 될 수 있습니다.

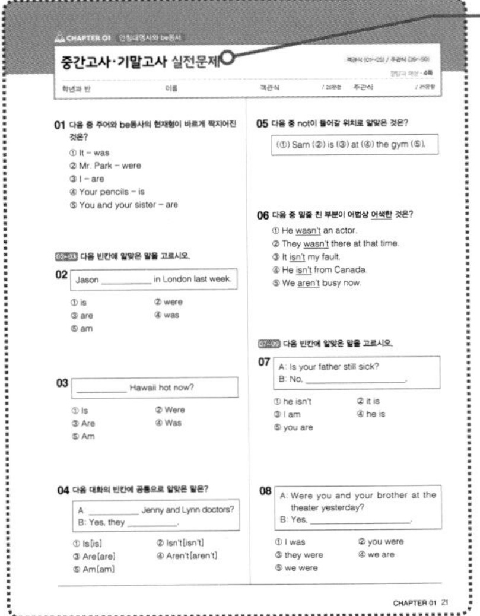

CHAPTER 01 인칭대명사와 be동사

중간고사·기말고사 실전문제

학년과 반 이름 객관식 / 25문항 주관식 / 25문항

01 다음 중 주어와 be동사의 현재형이 바르게 짝지어진 것은?
① It – was
② Mr. Park – were
③ I – are
④ Your pencils – is
⑤ You and your sister – are

[02~03] 다음 빈칸에 알맞은 말을 고르시오.

02 Jason ________ in London last week.
① is ② were ③ are ④ was ⑤ am

03 ________ Hawaii hot now?
① Is ② Were ③ Are ④ Was ⑤ Am

04 다음 대화의 빈칸에 공통으로 알맞은 말은?
A: ________ Jenny and Lynn doctors?
B: Yes, they ________.
① Is[is] ② Isn't[isn't] ③ Are[are] ④ Aren't[aren't] ⑤ Am[am]

05 다음 중 not이 들어갈 위치로 알맞은 것은?
(①) Sam (②) is (③) at (④) the gym (⑤).

06 다음 중 밑줄 친 부분이 어법상 어색한 것은?
① He wasn't an actor.
② They wasn't there at that time.
③ It isn't my fault.
④ He isn't from Canada.
⑤ We aren't busy now.

[07~09] 다음 빈칸에 알맞은 말을 고르시오.

07 A: Is your father still sick?
B: No, ________________.
① he isn't ② it is ③ I am ④ he is ⑤ you are

08 A: Were you and your brother at the theater yesterday?
B: Yes, ________________.
① I was ② you were ③ they were ④ we are ⑤ we were

CHAPTER 01 21

❼ 챕터별 중간고사 · 기말고사 실전문제

세분화된 유닛들로 충분한 학습을 한 후에 종합적으로 챕터별 실전문제를 풀 수 있습니다. 교과서별 중간고사 · 기말고사 시험 범위를 확인하여 시험 대비에도 도움이 될 것입니다. (객관식 25문항 + 주관식 25문항)

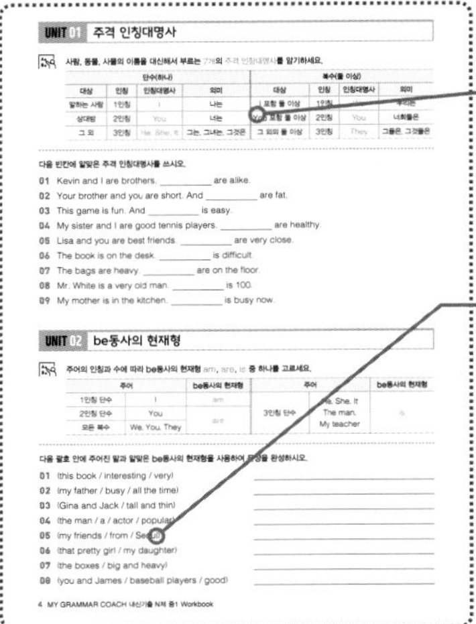

UNIT 01 주격 인칭대명사

01 Kevin and I are brothers. ________ are alike.
02 Your brother and you are short. And ________ are fat.
03 This game is fun. And ________ is easy.
04 My sister and I are good tennis players. ________ are healthy.
05 Lisa and you are best friends. ________ are very close.
06 The book is on the desk. ________ is difficult.
07 The bags are heavy. ________ are on the floor.
08 Mr. White is a very old man. ________ is 100.
09 My mother is in the kitchen. ________ is busy now.

UNIT 02 be동사의 현재형

01 (this book / interesting / very)
02 (my father / busy / all the time)
03 (Gina and Jack / tall and thin)
04 (the man / a / actor / popular)
05 (my friends / from / Seoul)
06 (that pretty girl / my daughter)
07 (the boxes / big and heavy)
08 (you and James / baseball players / good)

4 MY GRAMMAR COACH 내신기출 N제 중1 Workbook

워크북

❽ 유닛별 문법 요약

본문에서 배웠던 각 유닛의 문법을 요약하여 배운 내용을 상기해 볼 수 있습니다.

❾ 유닛별 추가 연습 문제

유닛별 추가 연습 문제를 통해 부족했던 부분들을 확실하게 보충할 수 있습니다.

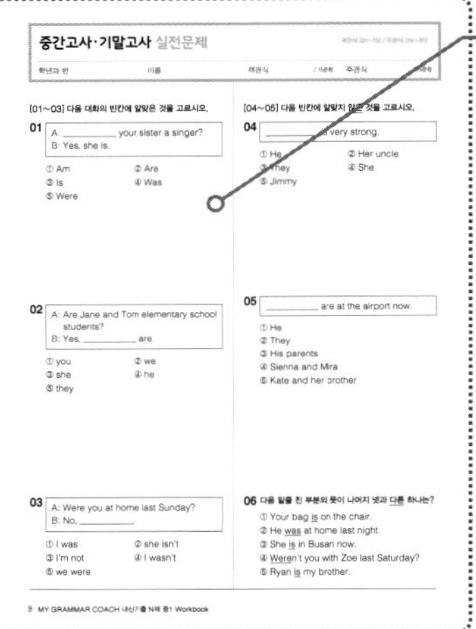

중간고사·기말고사 실전문제

01 A: ________ your sister a singer? B: Yes, she is.
① Am ② Are ③ Is ④ Was ⑤ Were

02 A: Are Jane and Tom elementary school students? B: Yes, ________ are.
① you ② we ③ she ④ he ⑤ they

03 A: Were you at home last Sunday? B: No, ________.
① I was ② she isn't ③ I'm not ④ I wasn't ⑤ we were

04 ________ very strong.
① He ② Her uncle ③ They ④ She ⑤ Jimmy

05 ________ are at the airport now.
① He ② They ③ His parents ④ Sienna and Mira ⑤ Kate and her brother

06
① Your bag is on the chair.
② He was at home last night.
③ She is in Busan now.
④ Weren't you with Zoe last Saturday?
⑤ Ryan is my brother.

8 MY GRAMMAR COACH 내신기출 N제 중1 Workbook

❿ 챕터별 중간고사 • 기말고사 실전문제

종합적인 문제 풀이를 할 수 있도록 워크북에도 추가적인 챕터별 실전문제가 수록되어 있습니다. 교과서별 중간고사 · 기말고사 시험 범위를 확인하여 시험 대비에도 도움이 될 것입니다. (객관식 15문항 + 주관식 15문항)

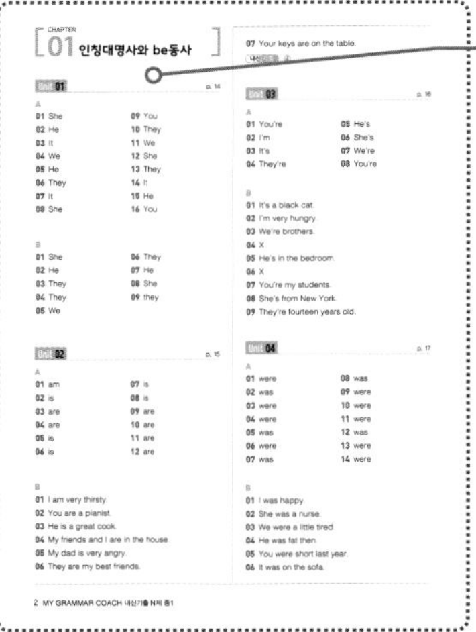

CHAPTER 01 인칭대명사와 be동사

2 MY GRAMMAR COACH 내신기출 N제 중1

⓫ 정답과 해설

정답과 함께, 문제 해결에 필요한 필수 문법 및 주의할 포인트를 확인 학습할 수 있습니다.

중1 영어 교과서 문법 연계표

YBM(박)		GRAMMAR COACH	
단원	문법	Chapter	Unit
1	be동사의 긍정문	1	2
	be동사의 부정문	1	5
	be동사의 의문문	1	6
2	일반동사의 긍정문	2	2
	일반동사의 부정문	2	6
	일반동사의 의문문	2	7
S1	현재진행형	3	7
	명령문	9	1
3	과거시제	3	2
	감각동사 + 형용사	10	3
4	will	3	3
	can	4	1
5	to부정사의 명사적 용법	11	1
	감탄문	9	7
6	동명사	11	7
	비교급	7	12
S2	to부정사의 부사적 용법(목적)	11	5
	수여동사 (4형식)	10	5
7	이유 접속사 because	13	4
	부가 의문문	9	3
8	시간 접속사 when	13	3
	5형식 동사 make	10	7

YBM(송)		GRAMMAR COACH	
단원	문법	Chapter	Unit
1	be동사의 긍정문	1	2
	be동사의 부정문	1	5
	be동사의 의문문	1	6
	일반동사의 긍정문	2	2
2	일반동사의 3인칭 단수변화	2	1
	일반동사의 부정문	2	6
	일반동사의 의문문	2	7
3	There is/are	5	9
	can	4	1
4	과거시제	3	2
	will	3	3
5	현재진행형	3	7
	감각동사 + 형용사	10	3
6	명령문	9	1
	시간 접속사 when	13	3
7	to부정사의 명사적 용법	11	1
	동명사	11	7
8	비교급	7	12
	이유 접속사 because	13	4
	전치사 because of	13	4
9	수여동사 (4형식)	10	5
	감탄문	9	7

천재(정)		GRAMMAR COACH	
단원	문법	Chapter	Unit
1	일반동사의 긍정문	2	2
	일반동사의 부정문	2	6
	일반동사의 의문문	2	7
	will	3	3
2	현재진행형	3	7
	to부정사의 명사적 용법	11	1
3	과거시제	3	2
	부가 의문문	9	3
4	수여동사(4형식)	10	5
	to부정사의 부사적 용법(목적)	11	5
5	재귀대명사	6	2
	원급 비교	7	11
6	must	4	5
	동명사	11	7
7	과거진행형	3	11
	최상급	7	14
8	감탄문	9	7
	시간 접속사 when	13	3

천재(이)		GRAMMAR COACH	
단원	문법	Chapter	Unit
1	be동사의 긍정문	1	2
	be동사의 부정문	1	5
	be동사의 의문문	1	6
2	일반동사의 긍정문	2	2
	일반동사의 부정문	2	6
	일반동사의 의문문	2	7
3	현재진행형	3	7
	will	3	3
4	There is/are	5	9
	can	4	1
5	과거시제	3	2
	동명사	11	7
6	to부정사의 명사적 용법	11	1
	should	4	7
7	to부정사의 부사적 용법(목적)	11	5
	시간 접속사 when	13	3
8	수여동사(4형식)	10	5
	비교급	7	12

동아(이)		GRAMMAR COACH	
단원	문법	Chapter	Unit
1	be동사의 긍정문	1	2
	be동사의 부정문	1	5
	be동사의 의문문	1	6
	일반동사의 긍정문	2	2
	일반동사의 부정문	2	6
2	현재진행형	3	7
	명령문	9	1
	감탄문	9	7
3	can	4	1
	의문사 의문문	8	1
4	과거시제	3	2
	재귀대명사	6	2
5	will	3	3
	수량형용사 a few, many	7	4
6	to부정사의 명사적 용법	11	1
	시간 접속사 when	13	3
7	수여동사(4형식)	10	5
	have to	4	6
8	동명사	11	7
	비교급	7	12

동아(윤)		GRAMMAR COACH	
단원	문법	Chapter	Unit
1	be동사의 긍정문	1	2
	be동사의 부정문	1	5
	일반동사의 긍정문	2	2
	일반동사의 부정문	2	6
2	be동사, 일반동사의 의문문	2	7
	현재진행형	3	7
3	명령문	9	1
	can	4	1
	will	3	3
4	과거시제	3	2
	There is/are	5	9
5	동명사	11	7
	비인칭주어 it	6	5
6	to부정사의 명사적 용법	11	1
	감각동사 + 형용사	10	3
7	be going to	3	5
	비교급	7	12
	최상급	7	14
8	접속사 that	13	5
	접속사 when, before, after	13	3

능률(김)		GRAMMAR COACH	
단원	문법	Chapter	Unit
1	be동사의 긍정문	1	2
	be동사의 부정문	1	5
	일반동사의 긍정문	2	2
	일반동사의 부정문	2	6
2	현재진행형	3	7
	will	3	3
	can	4	1
3	과거시제	3	2
	동명사	11	7
4	수여동사 (4형식)	10	4
	to부정사의 명사적 용법	11	1
5	비교급	7	12
	접속사 that	13	5
6	to부정사의 부사적 용법(목적)	11	5
	시간 접속사 when	13	3
7	감탄문	9	7
	5형식 동사 make	10	7

YBM(박)		GRAMMAR COACH	
단원	문법	Chapter	Unit
1	동명사	11	7
2	be going to	3	5
	to부정사의 명사적 용법	11	1
3	접속사 that	13	5
	must	4	5
4	to부정사의 부사적 용법(목적)	11	5
	감탄문	9	7
5	등위 접속사 and	13	1
	시간 접속사 when	13	3
6	부사 too	7	10
	수여동사 (4형식)	10	5
7	과거진행형	3	11
	부가 의문문	9	3
8	최상급	7	14
	부정대명사 one	6	6

미래엔(최)		GRAMMAR COACH	
단원	문법	Chapter	Unit
1	be동사의 긍정문	1	2
	be동사의 부정문	1	5
	일반동사의 긍정문	2	2
	일반동사의 부정문	2	6
2	현재진행형	3	7
	can	4	1
3	동명사	11	7
	감각동사 + 형용사	10	3
	There is/are	5	9
4	과거시제	3	2
	will	3	3
5	be going to	3	5
	to부정사의 명사적 용법	11	1
6	접속사 that	13	5
	to부정사의 부사적 용법(목적)	11	5
	수여동사 (4형식)	10	5
7	have to	4	6
	should	4	7
	시간 접속사 when	13	3
8	비교급	7	12
	최상급	7	14

다락원(강)		GRAMMAR COACH	
단원	문법	Chapter	Unit
1	인칭대명사와 be동사	1	1
	재귀대명사	6	2
	동명사	11	7
2	일반동사 현재시제	3	1
	목적어와 부사구	7	6
	감탄문	9	7
3	일반동사 과거시제	3	2
	There was/were	5	9
	to부정사 – 명사적 용법	11	1
4	명령문	9	1
	to부정사 – 부사적 용법	11	5
	부가의문문	9	3
5	수여동사	10	5
	명사절을 이끄는 that	13	5
	부사절을 이끄는 when	13	3
6	과거 진행 시제	3	11
	수동태	2권	3-1
	any	7	3
7	조동사 should	4	7
	문장 전체 수식 부사	7	6
	화법	2권	14-5
8	to부정사 – 형용사적 용법	11	4
	조건 부사절을 이끄는 if	13	4
	반전의 접속부사 however	3권	8-9

비상(김)		GRAMMAR COACH	
단원	문법	Chapter	Unit
1	be동사의 긍정문	1	2
	be동사의 의문문	1	6
	일반동사의 긍정문	2	2
	일반동사의 의문문	2	7
2	명령문	9	1
	현재진행형	3	7
3	과거시제	3	2
	감각동사 + 형용사	10	3
4	will	3	3
	수여동사 (4형식)	10	5
5	비교급	7	12
	최상급	7	14
6	to부정사의 명사적 용법	11	1
	부가 의문문	9	3
7	to부정사의 부사적 용법(목적)	11	5
	접속사 that	13	5
8	동명사	11	7
	시간 접속사 when	13	3

지학사(민)		GRAMMAR COACH	
단원	문법	Chapter	Unit
1	현재시제	3	1
	과거시제	3	2
	미래시제	3	3
2	현재진행형	3	7
	to부정사의 명사적 용법	11	1
3	to부정사의 형용사적 용법	11	4
	동명사	11	7
4	시간 접속사 when	13	3
	should	4	7
5	to부정사의 부사적 용법(목적)	11	5
	부가 의문문	9	3
6	비교급	7	12
	최상급	7	14
7	접속사 that	13	5
	수여동사 (4형식)	10	5

금성(최)		GRAMMAR COACH	
단원	문법	Chapter	Unit
1	일반동사의 긍정문	2	2
	일반동사의 부정문	2	6
	일반동사의 의문문	2	7
2	현재진행형	3	7
	will	3	3
	can, may	4	1
	should	4	7
3	과거시제	3	2
	감탄문	9	7
4	감각동사 + 형용사	10	3
	시간 접속사 when	13	3
5	to부정사의 명사적 용법	11	1
	빈도부사	7	9
6	접속사 that	13	5
	to부정사의 부사적 용법(목적)	11	5
7	수여동사 (4형식)	10	5
	5형식 동사 make	10	7
8	동명사	11	7
	비교급	7	12
	최상급	7	14

이 책의 **차례**

연계표를 확인하여 나의 영어 교과서에 나오는 문법을 체크(✔)하고, 그 부분을 집중적으로 공부하세요.

CHAPTER	UNIT	GRAMMAR	PAGE	MY TEXTBOOK
CHAPTER 01 인칭대명사와 be동사	1	주격 인칭대명사	014	✔ .... 단원
	2	be동사의 현재형	015	.... 단원
	3	be동사의 현재형 축약	016	.... 단원
	4	be동사의 과거형	017	.... 단원
	5	be동사의 부정문	018	.... 단원
	6	be동사의 의문문	019	.... 단원
	7	be동사 종합	020	.... 단원
CHAPTER 02 일반동사	1	일반동사의 현재형 1	030	.... 단원
	2	일반동사의 현재형 2	031	.... 단원
	3	일반동사의 과거형 규칙 변화 1	033	.... 단원
	4	일반동사의 과거형 규칙 변화 2	034	.... 단원
	5	일반동사의 과거형 불규칙 변화	035	.... 단원
	6	일반동사의 부정문	037	.... 단원
	7	일반동사의 의문문	038	.... 단원
	8	일반동사 종합	039	.... 단원
CHAPTER 03 시제	1	현재시제	048	.... 단원
	2	과거시제	049	.... 단원
	3	미래시제 1: will의 긍정문과 축약형	050	.... 단원
	4	미래시제 2: will의 부정문과 의문문	051	.... 단원
	5	미래시제 3: be going to	052	.... 단원
	6	시제 판단	054	.... 단원
	7	진행형 만드는 법	055	.... 단원
	8	현재진행형의 긍정문	057	.... 단원
	9	현재진행형의 부정문	058	.... 단원
	10	현재진행형의 의문문	059	.... 단원
	11	과거진행형의 긍정문	060	.... 단원
	12	과거진행형의 부정문과 의문문	061	.... 단원

CHAPTER	UNIT	GRAMMAR	PAGE	MY TEXTBOOK
CHAPTER 04 조동사	1	can	070	.... 단원
	2	be able to	071	.... 단원
	3	may	072	.... 단원
	4	can과 바꿔 쓸 수 있는 조동사	073	.... 단원
	5	must	074	.... 단원
	6	have to	075	.... 단원
	7	should	077	.... 단원
CHAPTER 05 명사와 관사	1	셀 수 있는 명사와 부정관사 a(n)	086	.... 단원
	2	셀 수 있는 명사의 규칙 복수형 1	087	.... 단원
	3	셀 수 있는 명사의 규칙 복수형 2	088	.... 단원
	4	셀 수 있는 명사의 불규칙 복수형	089	.... 단원
	5	셀 수 없는 명사	090	.... 단원
	6	셀 수 없는 명사의 수량 표현	091	.... 단원
	7	정관사 the	092	.... 단원
	8	관사의 생략	093	.... 단원
	9	There is/are	094	.... 단원
	10	There is/are의 부정문과 의문문	095	.... 단원
CHAPTER 06 대명사	1	인칭대명사의 격변화	104	.... 단원
	2	재귀대명사	105	.... 단원
	3	지시대명사	106	.... 단원
	4	지시형용사	107	.... 단원
	5	비인칭대명사 it	108	.... 단원
	6	부정대명사 1	109	.... 단원
	7	부정대명사 2	110	.... 단원
	8	부정대명사 3	111	.... 단원

CONTENTS

CHAPTER	UNIT	GRAMMAR	PAGE	MY TEXTBOOK
CHAPTER 07 형용사와 부사의 비교 표현	1	형용사	120	.... 단원
	2	형용사의 역할	121	.... 단원
	3	수량형용사 1: some, any	122	.... 단원
	4	수량형용사 2: many, much, a lot of	123	.... 단원
	5	수량형용사 3: (a) few, (a) little	124	.... 단원
	6	부사의 역할	125	.... 단원
	7	부사의 형태 1	126	.... 단원
	8	부사의 형태 2	127	.... 단원
	9	빈도부사	128	.... 단원
	10	too, either	129	.... 단원
	11	비교급과 최상급 만드는 방법	130	.... 단원
	12	원급 비교	133	.... 단원
	13	비교급	134	.... 단원
	14	최상급	135	.... 단원
	15	비교 표현 종합	136	.... 단원
CHAPTER 08 의문사 의문문	1	의문사 & who(m) 의문문	146	.... 단원
	2	what 의문문	147	.... 단원
	3	when/where 의문문	148	.... 단원
	4	why/how 의문문	149	.... 단원
	5	〈how+형용사/부사〉 의문문	150	.... 단원
	6	〈what/which/whose+명사〉 의문문	152	.... 단원
CHAPTER 09 문장의 종류	1	명령문	160	.... 단원
	2	청유문	161	.... 단원
	3	부가의문문 1	162	.... 단원
	4	부가의문문 2	163	.... 단원
	5	부정의문문	164	.... 단원
	6	선택의문문	165	.... 단원
	7	what으로 시작하는 감탄문	166	.... 단원
	8	how로 시작하는 감탄문	167	.... 단원

CHAPTER	UNIT	GRAMMAR	PAGE	MY TEXTBOOK
CHAPTER 10 문장의 형식	1	문장의 요소	176	.... 단원
	2	1형식/2형식 문장	177	.... 단원
	3	감각동사+형용사	178	.... 단원
	4	3형식 문장	179	.... 단원
	5	4형식 문장	180	.... 단원
	6	3형식 ↔ 4형식 문장 전환	181	.... 단원
	7	5형식 문장의 목적격보어 1	183	.... 단원
	8	5형식 문장의 목적격보어 2	184	.... 단원
	9	5형식 문장의 목적격보어 3	185	.... 단원
CHAPTER 11 to부정사와 동명사	1	to부정사의 명사적 용법 1	194	.... 단원
	2	to부정사의 명사적 용법 2	195	.... 단원
	3	to부정사의 명사적 용법 3	196	.... 단원
	4	to부정사의 형용사적 용법	198	.... 단원
	5	to부정사의 부사적 용법 1	199	.... 단원
	6	to부정사의 부사적 용법 2	200	.... 단원
	7	동명사의 역할 1	201	.... 단원
	8	동명사의 역할 2	202	.... 단원
	9	동명사 목적어 vs. to부정사 목적어	203	.... 단원
	10	동명사의 관용표현	205	.... 단원
CHAPTER 12 전치사	1	시간 전치사 1	214	.... 단원
	2	시간 전치사 2	215	.... 단원
	3	장소 전치사	216	.... 단원
	4	위치 전치사	217	.... 단원
	5	방향 전치사	218	.... 단원
	6	주요 전치사	219	.... 단원
CHAPTER 13 접속사	1	등위접속사 1: and, but	228	.... 단원
	2	등위접속사 2: or, so	229	.... 단원
	3	종속접속사 1: when, before, after	230	.... 단원
	4	종속접속사 2: because, if	231	.... 단원
	5	종속접속사 3: that	232	.... 단원

CHAPTER

01 인칭대명사와 be동사

Unit 01 주격 인칭대명사
Unit 02 be동사의 현재형
Unit 03 be동사의 현재형 축약
Unit 04 be동사의 과거형
Unit 05 be동사의 부정문
Unit 06 be동사의 의문문
Unit 07 be동사 종합

UNIT 01 주격 인칭대명사

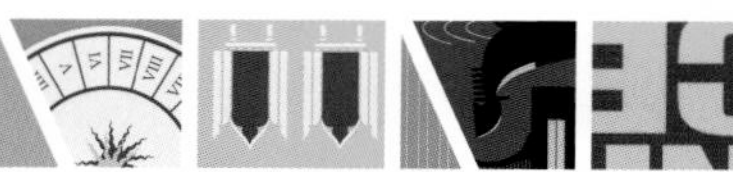

사람, 동물, 사물의 이름을 대신해서 부르는 7개의 주격 인칭대명사를 암기하세요.

단수(하나)				복수(둘 이상)			
대상	인칭	인칭대명사	의미	대상	인칭	인칭대명사	의미
말하는 사람	1인칭	I	나는	I 포함 둘 이상	1인칭	We	우리는
상대방	2인칭	You	너는	You 포함 둘 이상	2인칭	You	너희들은
그 외	3인칭	He She It	그는 그녀는 그것은	그 외의 둘 이상	3인칭	They	그들은 그것들은

주의 주어로 쓰인 명사를 주격 인칭대명사로 바꿀 때, 인칭과 수를 잘 파악하세요.
Jinsu and Sumi → They (그들은) *가리키는 대상: '나'와 '너'를 포함하지 않는 두 명 → 3인칭 복수

|A| 다음을 알맞은 주격 인칭대명사로 바꾸어 쓰시오.

01 My sister → ________
02 Mr. Lee → ________
03 A car → ________
04 You and I → ________
05 My uncle → ________
06 My friends → ________
07 This watch → ________
08 My mother → ________
09 You and Ann → ________
10 Your parents → ________
11 Fred and I → ________
12 Your aunt → ________
13 The books → ________
14 Her bicycle → ________
15 The man → ________
16 You and your brother → ________

|B| 다음 빈칸에 알맞은 주격 인칭대명사를 쓰시오.

주어를 인칭대명사로 쓸 때, 문맥상 그 대상이 누구인지, 단수인지 복수인지를 판단하세요.

01 Yumi is my sister. ________ is very pretty.
02 My father is in the office. ________ works hard.
03 Look at the two children. ________ are tall.
04 I have bananas. ________ are delicious.
05 Jack and I are students. ________ are classmates.
06 Sally and John are scientists. ________ are smart.
07 The man is an actor. ________ is famous.
08 My mother is ill. ________ is in bed.
09 The chairs are big and ________ are strong.

UNIT 02 be동사의 현재형

주어의 인칭과 수에 따라 be동사의 현재형 am, are, is 중 하나를 고르세요.

주어		be동사의 현재형
1인칭 단수	I	am
2인칭 단수 & 모든 복수	You	are
	We, You, They	
	You and I, My parents	
3인칭 단수	He, She, It	is
	The man, My teacher	

참고 be동사의 의미 '~(명사)이다', '~(형용사)하다', '~(장소에) 있다'를 기억하세요.

|A| 다음 빈칸에 알맞은 be동사의 현재형을 쓰시오.

01 I ______________ a teacher.
02 She ______________ from Canada.
03 They ______________ happy.
04 We ______________ friends.
05 Ben ______________ in my class.
06 My name ______________ Junsu.
07 My sister ______________ ten years old.
08 Your book ______________ in my bag.
09 Bill and I ______________ students.
10 You and Jina ______________ beautiful.
11 Two pens ______________ on the desk.
12 My parents ______________ in Korea now.

|B| 괄호 안의 단어와 be동사의 현재형을 이용하여 문장을 완성하시오.

01 (I, very, thirsty) → ______________________________
02 (you, a pianist) → ______________________________
03 (he, a great cook) → ______________________________
04 (my friends and I, in, the house) → ______________________________
05 (my dad, very angry) → ______________________________
06 (they, my best friends) → ______________________________
07 (your keys, on, the table) → ______________________________

내신 기출 다음 빈칸에 들어갈 수 없는 말은?

______________ is very honest and polite.

① The student ② My friend ③ Jenny
④ He and she ⑤ The little boy

실전 TIP
be동사 is를 보고 주어가 될 수 있는 것과 없는 것을 판단하세요.

UNIT 03 be동사의 현재형 축약

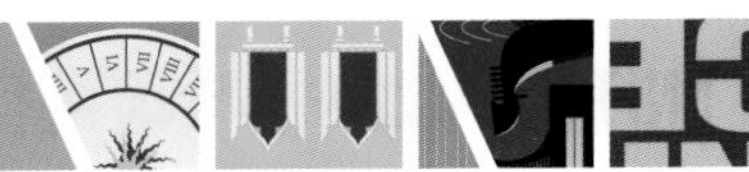

〈인칭대명사+be동사의 현재형〉만 줄여 쓸 수 있다는 점에 유의하세요.

주어		be동사의 현재형	축약형
1인칭 단수	I	am	I'm
2인칭 단수	You	are	You're
모든 복수	We, You, They		We're, You're, They're
	You and I, My parents		축약 ×
3인칭 단수	He, She, It	is	He's, She's, It's
	The man, My teacher		축약 ×

|A| 다음 밑줄 친 부분을 축약해서 쓰시오.

01 <u>You are</u> tall. → ____________

02 <u>I am</u> a singer. → ____________

03 <u>It is</u> a red pen. → ____________

04 <u>They are</u> very kind. → ____________

05 <u>He is</u> my teacher. → ____________

06 <u>She is</u> thirsty. → ____________

07 <u>We are</u> in the garden. → ____________

08 <u>You are</u> my best friends. → ____________

|B| 다음 밑줄 친 부분을 축약해서 문장을 다시 쓰시오. (단, 축약할 수 없는 경우에는 ×표시할 것)

01 <u>It is</u> a black cat. → ____________________

02 <u>I am</u> very hungry. → ____________________

03 <u>We are</u> brothers. → ____________________

04 <u>My father is</u> a doctor. → ____________________

05 <u>He is</u> in the bedroom. → ____________________

06 <u>You and I are</u> friends. → ____________________

07 <u>You are</u> my students. → ____________________

08 <u>She is</u> from New York. → ____________________

09 <u>They are</u> fourteen years old. → ____________________

〈인칭대명사+be동사〉만 축약이 가능하고, 그 외의 경우는 축약할 수 없다는 데 유의하세요.

UNIT 04 be동사의 과거형

be동사의 과거형은 주어에 따라 was, were 둘 중 하나를 선택하세요.

주어		be동사의 현재형	be동사의 과거형
1인칭 단수	I	am	was
3인칭 단수	He, She, It, The man, My teacher, Your friend	is	
2인칭 단수	You	are	were
모든 복수	We, You, They, You and I, My parents, Trees		

|A| 다음 빈칸에 알맞은 be동사의 과거형을 쓰시오.

01 You __________ sick.

02 He __________ very fat.

03 They __________ on holiday.

04 We __________ late for school.

05 My father __________ a policeman.

06 Jake and Sam __________ classmates.

07 Grace __________ in bed.

08 It __________ big and strong.

09 Tim and I __________ thirsty.

10 My aunts __________ from America.

11 You and your son __________ in the zoo.

12 The girl __________ my friend.

13 Two books __________ under the desk.

14 We __________ there yesterday.

|B| 우리말과 같은 뜻이 되도록 괄호 안의 단어와 be동사를 이용하여 문장을 완성하시오.

01 나는 행복했다. (happy) ______________________

02 그녀는 간호사였다. (a nurse) ______________________

03 우리는 좀 피곤했다. (a little, tired) ______________________

04 그는 그때 뚱뚱했었다. (fat, then) ______________________

05 너는 작년에 키가 작았다. (short, last year) ______________________

06 그것은 소파 위에 있었다. (on the sofa) ______________________

07 나의 부모님은 바빴다. (my parents, busy) ______________________

08 그 셔츠는 더러웠다. (the shirt, dirty) ______________________

09 그들은 건강했다. (healthy) ______________________

내신 기출 다음 밑줄 친 부분의 뜻이 다른 하나는?

① My grandpa was a math teacher.
② The woman was a great singer.
③ The chef was in the kitchen.

실전 TIP

be동사 뒤에 장소를 나타내는 전치사구를 쓰면 be동사는 '~에 있(었)다'를 의미해요.

UNIT 05 be동사의 부정문

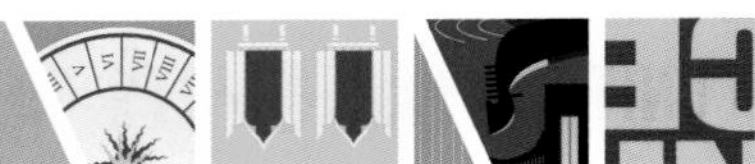

be동사의 부정은 be동사 뒤에 not을 써야 해요.

be동사의 현재형 부정		축약	be동사의 과거형 부정		축약
am	+not	×	was	+not	wasn't
is		isn't			
are		aren't	were		weren't

참고 am not은 축약하지 않아요. 또한, 〈인칭대명사+be동사의 과거형(was, were)〉도 축약하지 않아요.

|A| |보기|와 같이 부정형을 축약형으로 쓰시오.

|보기|
it is → it isn't[it's not]

01 I am → ______________

02 you are → ______________

03 he is → ______________

04 she is → ______________

05 they are → ______________

06 we are → ______________

07 the boy is → ______________

08 Jessie is → ______________

09 you were → ______________

10 he was → ______________

11 she was → ______________

12 it was → ______________

13 they were → ______________

14 we were → ______________

15 the woman was → ______________

16 Tom and I were → ______________

|B| 다음 문장을 부정문으로 바꾸어 쓰시오.

01 I am hungry. → ______________

02 You are hardworking. → ______________

03 She was a ballerina. → ______________

04 He is my teacher. → ______________

05 This bag is heavy. → ______________

06 You were six years old. → ______________

07 It is my cellphone. → ______________

08 They were in the classroom. → ______________

09 I was sick yesterday. → ______________

〈인칭대명사+be동사+not〉은 각각 〈인칭대명사+be동사〉의 축약형+not 또는 인칭대명사+〈be동사+not〉의 축약형, 이렇게 두 가지 방법으로 축약할 수 있음을 알아두세요.

UNIT 06 be동사의 의문문

be동사로 질문할 때는 be동사를 주어 앞에 쓰는 어순이 된다는 것을 기억하세요.

be동사의 의문문	긍정의 대답	부정의 대답
Be동사 + 주어 ~?	Yes, 인칭대명사 + be동사	No, 인칭대명사 + be동사 + not
Are you ~?	Yes, I am.	No, I am not.
Was Jinho ~?	Yes, he was.	No, he was not[wasn't]

참고 대답할 때는 인칭대명사를 이용하고, 부정의 대답은 축약해서 쓸 수 있어요.

A 다음 대화의 빈칸에 알맞은 말을 쓰시오.

01 A: ______________ you busy now? B: Yes, ______________ am.

02 A: ______________ he a cook now? B: No, he ______________.

03 A: ______________ your mother at home? B: Yes, ______________ is.

04 A: ______________ the cats in the basket? B: No, ______________ aren't.

05 A: ______________ it your computer? B: Yes, ______________ was.

06 A: ______________ they late yesterday? B: No, they ______________.

07 A: ______________ the flowers pretty? B: Yes, ______________ were.

08 A: ______________ she sick last week? B: No, she ______________.

현재인지 과거인지는 질문과 대답을 참고하거나 질문에 나오는 부사가 현재인지 과거인지 확인해 보세요.

B 다음 문장을 의문문으로 바꾸어 쓰시오.

01 You are fourteen years old. → ______________________________

02 He is a famous dancer. → ______________________________

03 They are in the library. → ______________________________

04 Kathy was a good swimmer. → ______________________________

05 The dishes were clean. → ______________________________

06 The movie is boring. → ______________________________

07 Mina and I are free now. → ______________________________

08 Lisa and Kevin were your classmates. → ______________________________

09 They were very close last year. → ______________________________

UNIT 07 be동사 종합

문장이 평서문, 부정문 또는 의문문인지를 판단하여 알맞은 be동사를 사용하세요.

평서문	주어에 따라, 현재형은 am, are, is, 과거형은 was, were	She was tired.
부정문	be동사 뒤에 not을 쓴다. 부정형은 축약 가능	She wasn't tired.
의문문	be동사를 주어 앞으로 이동	Was she tired?

|A| 다음 문장에서 어법상 어색한 부분에 밑줄 긋고 바르게 고치시오.

01 My brother and I are police officers. They are brave. → ______

02 He was a bus driver. His sisters was nurses. → ______

03 I am a doctor. I isn't a teacher. → ______

04 Lisa and Jack were actors. They wasn't famous. → ______

05 Mr. Brown is in bed. Was he sick? → ______

06 Your shoes are nice. Is it new? → ______

07 A: Are your pens black? B: Yes, you are. → ______

08 A: Were Linda and her sister tired? B: No, she wasn't. → ______

|B| 다음 문장을 괄호 안의 지시대로 바꾸어 쓰시오.

01 I am good at swimming. (부정문으로) → ______

02 My daughter is in hospital. (과거형으로) → ______

03 You are thirsty and hungry. (의문문으로) → ______

04 They are best friends. (부정문으로) → ______

05 Peter was a basketball player. (의문문으로) → ______

06 The new car is very expensive. (부정문으로) → ______

07 We were busy yesterday. (부정문으로) → ______

08 The games are very interesting. (의문문으로) → ______

09 She is a good dentist. (의문문으로) → ______

내신기출 다음 질문에 대한 대답으로 옳은 것은?

> Is your elder sister a famous YouTuber?

① Yes, he is. ② No, she isn't. ③ Yes, I am.
④ No, she is. ⑤ Yes, you are.

실전 TIP

대답할 때는 질문에서의 주어를 알맞은 인칭대명사로 바꾸어야 하며, 그에 따른 알맞은 be동사를 선택해요.

중간고사·기말고사 실전문제

객관식 (01~25) / 주관식 (26~50)

정답과 해설 • 4쪽

학년과 반 　 이름 　 객관식 　 / 25문항 　 주관식 　 / 25문항

01 다음 중 주어와 be동사의 현재형이 바르게 짝지어진 것은?

① It – was
② Mr. Park – were
③ I – are
④ Your pencils – is
⑤ You and your sister – are

02~03 다음 빈칸에 알맞은 말을 고르시오.

02

Jason ___________ in London last week.

① is　② were
③ are　④ was
⑤ am

03

___________ Hawaii hot now?

① Is　② Were
③ Are　④ Was
⑤ Am

04 다음 대화의 빈칸에 공통으로 알맞은 말은?

A: ___________ Jenny and Lynn doctors?
B: Yes, they ___________.

① Is[is]　② Isn't[isn't]
③ Are[are]　④ Aren't[aren't]
⑤ Am[am]

05 다음 중 not이 들어갈 위치로 알맞은 것은?

(①) Sam (②) is (③) at (④) the gym (⑤).

06 다음 중 밑줄 친 부분이 어법상 어색한 것은?

① He wasn't an actor.
② They wasn't there at that time.
③ It isn't my fault.
④ He isn't from Canada.
⑤ We aren't busy now.

07~09 다음 빈칸에 알맞은 말을 고르시오.

07

A: Is your father still sick?
B: No, ___________.

① he isn't　② it is
③ I am　④ he is
⑤ you are

08

A: Were you and your brother at the theater yesterday?
B: Yes, ___________.

① I was　② you were
③ they were　④ we are
⑤ we were

09

A: Was he ready for the show?
B: Yes, ______________.

① she was
② they were
③ he wasn't
④ she were
⑤ he was

10 다음 밑줄 친 was의 뜻이 나머지와 다른 것은?

① It was sunny yesterday.
② The firefighter was very brave.
③ His father was very tall.
④ She was at home last night.
⑤ He was great on the stage yesterday.

11 다음 대화 중 어법상 어색한 것은?

① A: Is your mother in the office now?
B: Yes, she is.
② A: Is it his car?
B: Yes, it is.
③ A: Were Linda and her husband happy at the news?
B: Yes, she was.
④ A: Is the boy a new student?
B: No, he isn't.
⑤ A: Was Emma absent from school?
B: Yes, she was.

12~13 다음 중 어법상 어색한 문장은?

12 ① This is an old violin. I like it.
② We are not high school students.
③ His son were a lawyer at that time.
④ He isn't fat at all.
⑤ Were you and your son sad yesterday?

13 ① It was my choice.
② We were upset about the news.
③ The sandwiches was delicious.
④ The magazine was helpful.
⑤ My mother was sick yesterday.

14 다음 중 어법상 올바른 문장은?

① Laura and I am good friends.
② Your sister are in my garden.
③ He was free at that time.
④ They wasn't from Paris.
⑤ That are my new scarf.

15 다음 빈칸에 들어갈 말이 나머지와 다른 것은?

① __________ he in Japan last year?
② I __________ lucky last night.
③ Your hairpin __________ in my bag yesterday.
④ Mary __________ a cheerleader last year.
⑤ Jisu and Laura __________ the same age.

16~17 다음 우리말을 영어로 바르게 옮긴 것은?

16

내 여동생과 나는 축구 팬이 아니다.

① My sister and I am not soccer fans.
② My sister and I wasn't soccer fans.
③ My sister and I are soccer fans.
④ My sister and me was soccer fans.
⑤ My sister and I are not soccer fans.

17

내가 가장 좋아하는 과목은 영어와 과학이다.

① My favorite subjects is English and science.
② My favorite subject were English and science.
③ My favorite subjects am English and science.
④ My favorite subjects are English and science.
⑤ My favorite subjects was English and science.

18 괄호 안에 알맞은 말이 바르게 짝지어진 것은?

(a) Jiho (is / are) brave and honest.
(b) I (am not / not am) a great cook.
(c) Sujin and I (am / are) the same age.

	(a)	(b)	(c)
①	is	not am	am
②	are	amn't	are
③	is	am not	are
④	are	am not	am
⑤	is	am not	am

19 다음 중 어법상 올바른 문장을 모두 고른 것은?

(a) Are Brian from Australia?
(b) He were not hungry.
(c) She was at the movie theater.
(d) I not am a soccer player.
(e) Charlie and I are good friends.

① (a), (b) ② (c), (e)
③ (d) ④ (d), (e)
⑤ (a), (c), (d)

20 다음 중 빈칸에 들어갈 수 없는 말은?

____________ are very brave.

① You
② They
③ Minsu
④ The soldiers
⑤ You and your sister

21 다음 질문에 대한 대답으로 가장 알맞은 것은?

Is Sophia an office worker?

① Yes, she isn't. ② Yes, she is.
③ Yes, you are. ④ Yes, is she.
⑤ Yes, there is.

22~23 다음 그림을 보고, 빈칸에 들어갈 말이 순서대로 바르게 짝지어진 것은?

22

> The gray cat ________ inside the house. ________ is outside the house with a brown dog.

① is – It　　② is – They
③ isn't – It　　④ aren't – They
⑤ is – She

23

> The weather ________ sunny, but the children ________ sad. They happily play in the puddles.

① is – is　　② are – are
③ isn't – are　　④ aren't – are
⑤ isn't – aren't

24~25 다음 표를 보고, 질문에 답하시오.

	job	favorite food	age
Grace	nurse	*kimchi*	30
Jason	soccer player	spaghetti	32

24 다음 대화의 빈칸에 알맞은 말은?

> Grace: Jason, is *kimchi* your favorite food?
> Jason: ________________.

① Yes, it is.　　② Yes, he was.
③ No, he isn't.　　④ Yes, they are.
⑤ No, it isn't.

25 위의 표의 내용과 일치하는 문장은?

① Grace is 32 years old.
② Jason isn't a soccer player.
③ Grace and Jason are the same age.
④ Grace is a nurse.
⑤ Jason is 30 years old.

26~28 인칭대명사와 be동사를 이용하여 다음 대화를 완성하시오.

26

> A: Is her room cold?
> B: No, ________________.

27

> A: Are you and your brother elementary school students?
> B: No, ________________.

28

A: Was Sam a science teacher?
B: Yes, ______________________.

29~30 다음 문장을 축약형을 이용하여 부정문으로 바꾸시오.

29 Brian was in China in 2020.

→ ______________________

30 Peter and I were late for school.

→ ______________________

31~32 밑줄 친 be동사의 쓰임이 같은 것을 |보기|에서 골라 그 번호를 쓰시오.

|보기|
ⓐ He is hungry.
ⓑ Kelly is a lawyer.
ⓒ My hairpins are in my bag.

31 My sister and I are high school students.

____

32 His dog is under the tree.

____

33~34 괄호 안의 말을 이용하여 다음 대화를 완성하시오.

33

A: ______________________ in the sink? (the dishes)
B: Yes, they are.

34

A: ______________________ at home? (your father)
B: Yes, he is.

35 A에 대한 B의 대답을 지시대로 바꿔 쓰시오. (단, 부정문은 축약형으로 쓸 것)

A: Are Amy and Grace are close friends?
B: (1) 긍정 → ______________________
(2) 부정 → ______________________

36~38 다음 우리말과 같은 뜻이 되도록 괄호 안의 말을 바르게 배열하시오.

36

그 신부는 어제 아름다웠다.
(beautiful / was / the / bride)

______________________ yesterday.

37

Tom과 그의 남동생은 지난 주말에 해변에 있었다.
(Tom / and / were / his / brother / the beach / at)

______________________ last weekend.

38

이 가방은 한 달 전에 할인 중이었다. (was / on / sale / this / bag)

______________________________ a month ago.

39~40 다음 문장을 우리말로 바르게 옮기시오.

39

You and John are my classmates.

→ ______________________________

40

We were members of the tennis team.

→ ______________________________

41 다음 글을 읽고, 질문에 답하시오. (단, 부정문은 축약형으로 쓸 것)

A cat is on the table. It is gray. A ball is under the table. The ball is yellow.

A: Is the ball gray?

B: __________, ______________________.

42~43 어법상 어색한 부분을 찾아 바르게 고치시오.

42 The new jacket are not warm.

______________ → ______________

43 Stella and her sister is thirsty.

______________ → ______________

44~45 다음 문장에서 어법상 어색한 부분을 찾아 바르게 고쳐 완전한 문장으로 다시 쓰시오.

44

This computer game not is interesting.

→ ______________________________

45

Was Roy and Tom at the shop?

→ ______________________________

46 다음 표를 보고, 빈칸에 알맞은 말을 쓰시오.

	age	job	personality
Kate	25	teacher	kind
Daniel	25	actor	funny

Kate and Daniel __________ best friends. They __________ the same age. Kate is a __________. She __________ very kind to her students. Daniel is an __________. He is funny.

47~48 다음 글을 읽고, 대화를 완성하시오.

Sarah is a middle school student. She is 14 years old. She is from England. She is a good badminton player.

47 A: Is Sarah a soccer player?

B: ____________, ________________________.

She is a badminton player.

48 A: Is Sarah from England?

B: ____________, ________________________.

49~50 다음 우리말을 주어진 |조건|에 맞게 영어로 바르게 쓰시오.

49 그의 생일은 지난주 일요일이었다.

|조건|
1. His로 시작할 것
2. 단어 birthday, Sunday, last를 사용할 것
3. 5 단어로 쓸 것

____

50 Daisy와 Zoe는 5년 전에 간호사가 아니었다.

|조건|
1. Daisy로 시작할 것
2. 단어 nurses, ago, years를 사용할 것
3. 8 단어로 쓸 것

____

내가 가장 취약한 부분에 대해
요점 정리를 해 보세요.

CHAPTER

02 일반동사

Unit 01 일반동사의 현재형 1
Unit 02 일반동사의 현재형 2
Unit 03 일반동사의 과거형 규칙 변화 1
Unit 04 일반동사의 과거형 규칙 변화 2
Unit 05 일반동사의 과거형 불규칙 변화
Unit 06 일반동사의 부정문
Unit 07 일반동사의 의문문
Unit 08 일반동사 종합

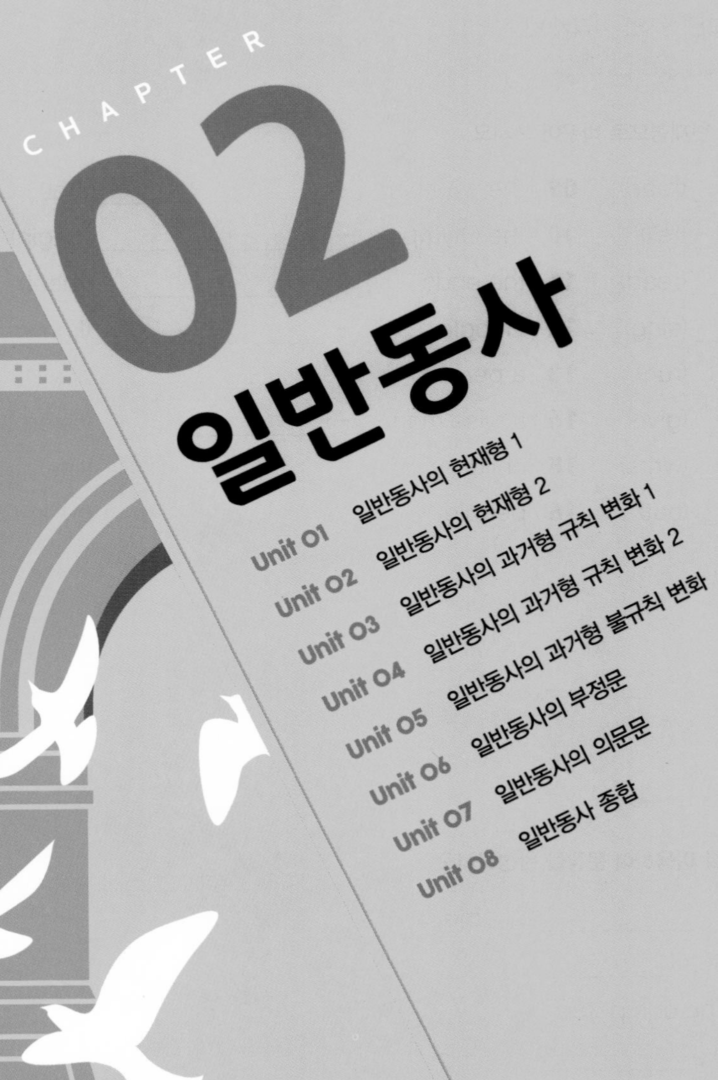

UNIT 01 일반동사의 현재형 1

일반동사의 현재형은 동사원형을 쓰지만, 주어가 3인칭 단수일 때는 동사원형에 -s를 붙이는 것에 유의하세요.

일반동사 현재형			
일반적인 주어 (1·2인칭 단·복수, 3인칭 복수)	동사원형	3인칭 단수 주어	동사원형+-s
I like English.		She likes English.	

참고 일반동사는 be동사와 조동사를 제외한 모든 동사를 가리키며, 주어의 동작 또는 상태를 나타내요.

|A| 다음 주어를 보고 괄호 안의 동사를 알맞은 현재형으로 바꾸어 쓰시오.

01 Jimin – ______________ (read)

02 time – ______________ (tell)

03 teachers – ______________ (read)

04 the birds – ______________ (sing)

05 the dog – ______________ (run)

06 the tree – ______________ (give)

07 my friends – ______________ (write)

08 women – ______________ (eat)

09 the weather – ______________ (get)

10 the Olympics – ______________ (begin)

11 the ends – ______________ (meet)

12 Google – ______________ (know)

13 a person – ______________ (walk)

14 a wise man – ______________ (listen)

15 children – ______________ (like)

16 people – ______________ (make)

|B| 우리말과 같은 뜻이 되도록 괄호 안의 단어를 이용하여 문장을 완성하시오.

01 나는 그 게임을 즐긴다. I ______________ the game. (enjoy)

02 수미는 대구에 산다. Sumi ______________ in Daegu. (live)

03 그 컴퓨터는 잘 작동한다. The computer ______________ fine. (work)

04 우리는 밤에 책을 읽는다. We ______________ a book at night. (read)

05 그는 카메라를 원한다. He ______________ a camera. (want)

06 그녀와 나는 영화를 사랑한다. She and I ______________ movies. (love)

07 그들은 학교에 걸어간다. They ______________ to school. (walk)

08 너는 K-pop을 듣는구나. You ______________ to K-pop. (listen)

09 Tom과 너는 서로를 안다. Tom and you ______________ each other. (know)

UNIT 02 일반동사의 현재형 2

3인칭 단수 주어의 일반동사 현재형을 만들 때, 주의해야 할 점을 알아 두세요.

대부분의 동사	-s	drink – drinks (마시다)	sing – sings (노래하다)
-o, -s, -x, -sh, -ch로 끝나는 동사	-es	do – does (하다) catch – catches (잡다)	finish – finishes (마치다) mix – mixes (섞다)
자음+y로 끝나는 동사	y를 없애고 -ies	cry – cries (울다) study – studies (공부하다)	try – tries (해 보다) worry – worries (걱정하다)
모음+y로 끝나는 동사	-s	play – plays (놀다) enjoy – enjoys (즐기다)	buy – buys (사다) stay – stays (머무르다)
불규칙	have	have – has (가지다, 먹다)	

|A| 다음 동사의 3인칭 단수 현재형을 쓰면서 외우시오.

01 do – ______________

02 buy – ______________

03 cry – ______________

04 have – ______________

05 mix – ______________

06 go – ______________

07 watch – ______________

08 study – ______________

09 say – ______________

10 finish – ______________

11 pass – ______________

12 fly – ______________

13 fix – ______________

14 play – ______________

15 worry – ______________

16 teach – ______________

17 enjoy – ______________

18 push – ______________

19 touch – ______________

20 try – ______________

|B| 괄호 안의 동사를 빈칸에 알맞은 현재형으로 쓰시오.

〈자음+y〉로 끝나는 동사와 〈모음+y〉로 끝나는 동사의 일반동사 현재형이 다름에 유의하세요.

01 I ______________ tennis with my friends. (play)

02 He ______________ to school early. (go)

03 She ______________ English very hard. (study)

04 My mother ______________ the dishes. (wash)

05 My sister ______________ beautiful blue eyes. (have)

06 John ______________ his homework in the evening. (do)

07 Kate ______________ cooking. (enjoy)

08 My father ______________ the news at 7. (watch)

09 My parents ______________ many things for us. (do)

|C| 다음 문장에서 어법상 어색한 부분에 밑줄 긋고 바르게 고치시오.

01 My baby sister crys all the time. → ____________

02 They enjoys their jobs. → ____________

03 The earth go around the sun. → ____________

04 Jake and Gina has dinner at six. → ____________

05 Jenny washs her hands before meals. → ____________

06 My brother and I plays basketball after school. → ____________

07 Ben have a bath every day. → ____________

08 He carrys her photo in his wallet. → ____________

|D| 다음 빈칸에 알맞은 말을 |보기|에서 골라 현재형으로 쓰시오.

|보기|

go　have　worry　play　do　catch　study　wash

01 She ____________ dark hair and brown eyes.

02 My sister ____________ the piano very well.

03 We ____________ English for two hours every day.

04 Sally often ____________ to the movies with her friends.

05 The early bird ____________ the worm.

06 Mr. Kim ____________ about his daughter.

07 The teacher ____________ the same thing every day.

08 He ____________ the car on Sundays.

내신기출 다음 빈칸에 알맞은 말은?

____________ works very hard for the future.

① I
② You
③ The ant
④ Ants
⑤ The ant and its friends

실전 TIP

동사 works가 쓰였으므로, 〈동사원형+-s〉를 쓸 수 있는 주어를 찾아야 해요.

UNIT 03 일반동사의 과거형 규칙 변화 1

일반동사의 과거형은 동사원형 뒤에 -ed를 붙이세요.

일반동사의 현재형 규칙 변화		일반동사의 과거형 규칙 변화	
일반적인 주어	동사원형	모든 주어	동사원형+-ed
3인칭 단수 주어	동사원형+-s		

주의 동사의 과거형은 주어에 따라 변하지 않아요.

|A| 빈칸에 다음 동사의 과거형을 쓰시오.

01 call – ______

02 play – ______

03 watch – ______

04 cook – ______

05 talk – ______

06 open – ______

07 work – ______

08 enjoy – ______

09 clean – ______

10 listen – ______

11 visit – ______

12 help – ______

13 look – ______

14 start – ______

15 want – ______

16 finish – ______

|B| 다음 빈칸에 괄호 안의 동사를 과거형으로 바꾸어 쓰시오.

01 I ______ my teeth after dinner. (brush)

02 He ______ the show yesterday. (watch)

03 She ______ in a bank last year. (work)

04 They ______ here two years ago. (visit)

05 We ______ the party last night. (enjoy)

06 My friends and I ______ basketball after school. (play)

07 The movie ______ at nine o'clock. (finish)

08 They ______ around the lake. (walk)

09 He ______ this book last week. (start)

UNIT 04 일반동사의 과거형 규칙 변화 2

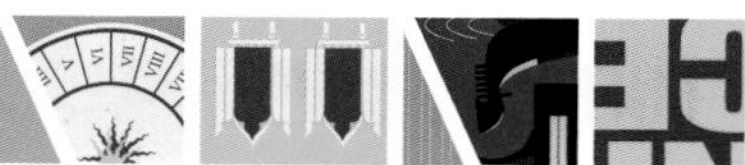

일반동사의 과거형을 만들 때 주의할 점을 알아 두세요.

대부분	-ed	accept – accepted (받아들이다) add – added (더하다)	listen – listened (듣다) enter – entered (들어가다)
-e로 끝나는 동사	-d	agree – agreed (동의하다) close – closed (닫다)	believe – believed (믿다) die – died (죽다)
단모음+단자음으로 끝나는 동사	마지막 자음 하나 더 쓰고 -ed	beg – begged (간청하다) drop – dropped (떨어뜨리다)	plan – planned (계획하다) stop – stopped (멈추다)
자음+y로 끝나는 동사	y를 없애고 -ied	copy – copied (복사하다) marry – married (결혼하다) try – tried (해 보다)	cry – cried (울다) study – studied (공부하다) worry – worried (걱정하다)
모음+y로 끝나는 동사	-ed	enjoy – enjoyed (즐기다) play – played (놀다)	destroy – destroyed (파괴하다) stay – stayed (머무르다)

빈칸에 다음 동사의 과거형을 쓰면서 외우시오.

01 accept (받아들이다) – ______

02 add (더하다) – ______

03 agree (동의하다) – ______

04 beg (간청하다, 빌다) – ______

05 believe (믿다) – ______

06 borrow (빌리다) – ______

07 collect (수집하다) – ______

08 copy (복사하다) – ______

09 cover (덮다) – ______

10 cry (울다) – ______

11 decide (결정하다) – ______

12 depend (의존하다) – ______

13 die (죽다) – ______

14 drop (떨어뜨리다) – ______

15 enjoy (즐기다) – ______

16 enter (~에 들어가다) – ______

17 fail (실패하다) – ______

18 finish (끝내다) – ______

19 happen (발생하다) – ______

20 hurry (서두르다) – ______

21 laugh (웃다) – ______

22 learn (배우다) – ______

23 marry (결혼하다) – ______

24 need (필요로 하다) – ______

25 pass (통과하다) – ______

26 plan (계획하다) – ______

27 pull (당기다) – ______

28 push (밀다) – ______

29 raise (올리다) – ______

30 remember (기억하다) – ______

31 save (구하다, 아끼다) – ______

32 smell (냄새 맡다, 냄새 나다) – ______

33 sound (소리가 나다) – ______

34 stay (있다, 머무르다) – ______

35 stop (멈추다, 그만두다) – ______

36 study (공부하다) – ______

37 touch (만지다) – ______

38 try (노력하다, 시도하다) – ______

39 watch (보다) – ______

40 worry (걱정하다) – ______

UNIT 05 일반동사의 과거형 불규칙 변화

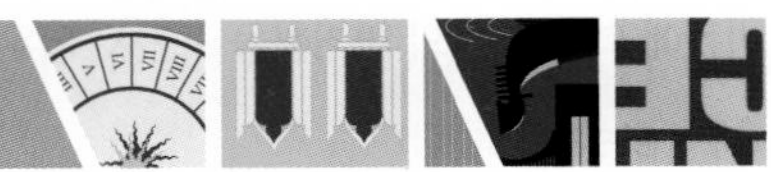

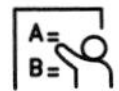 일반동사의 과거형 중에 형태가 불규칙하게 바뀌는 경우는 암기하세요.

정해진 규칙 없이 변하는 동사의 과거형	become – became (~이 되다)	begin – began (시작하다)
	bind – bound (묶다)	bite – bit (물다)
	bleed – bled (피를 흘리다)	blow – blew (입으로 불다)
	break – broke (깨뜨리다)	bring – brought (가져오다)
	build – built (짓다)	buy – bought (사다)
	catch – caught (잡다)	choose – chose (선택하다)
	come – came (오다)	do – did (하다)
	draw – drew (그리다)	drink – drank (마시다)
	drive – drove (운전하다)	eat – ate (먹다)
	fall – fell (떨어지다)	feed – fed (먹이를 주다)
	feel – felt (느끼다)	fight – fought (싸우다)
	find – found (발견하다)	fly – flew (날다, 날리다)
	forget – forgot (잊다)	forgive – forgave (용서하다)
	get – got (얻다)	give – gave (주다)
	go – went (가다)	grow – grew (자라다)
	have – had (가지다, 먹다)	hear – heard (듣다)
	hold – held (잡다)	keep – kept (유지하다)
	know – knew (알다)	lead – led (이끌다)
	leave – left (떠나다)	lend – lent (빌려주다)
	lose – lost (지다, 잃다)	make – made (만들다)
	mean – meant (의미하다)	meet – met (만나다)
	pay – paid (지불하다)	ride – rode (타다)
	ring – rang (울리다)	rise – rose (떠오르다)
	run – ran (달리다)	say – said (말하다)
	see – saw (보다)	sell – sold (팔다)
	send – sent (보내다)	shoot – shot (쏘다)
	sing – sang (노래하다)	sit – sat (앉다)
	sleep – slept (자다)	speak – spoke (말하다)
	spend – spent (시간이나 돈을 쓰다)	stand – stood (일어서다)
	steal – stole (훔치다)	swim – swam (수영하다)
	take – took (가지고 가다)	teach – taught (가르치다)
	tell – told (말하다)	think – thought (생각하다)
	throw – threw (던지다)	understand – understood (이해하다)
	wake – woke (일어나다)	wear – wore (입다)
	win – won (이기다)	write – wrote (쓰다)
현재형과 과거형이 같은 동사	bet – bet (내기를 걸다)	cost – cost (비용이 들다)
	cut – cut (자르다)	hit – hit (치다)
	hurt – hurt (아프다, 다치게 하다)	let – let (~하게 하다)
	put – put (두다, 놓다)	read [riːd] – read [red] (읽다)
	shut – shut (닫다)	spread – spread (펼치다, 펴다)

빈칸에 다음 동사의 과거형을 쓰면서 외우시오.

01 steal (훔치다) – ________
02 swim (수영하다) – ________
03 sit (앉다) – ________
04 sleep (자다) – ________
05 speak (말하다) – ________
06 spend (시간이나 돈을 쓰다) – ________
07 drink (마시다) – ________
08 leave (떠나다) – ________
09 lend (빌려주다) – ________
10 lose (지다, 잃다) – ________
11 make (만들다) – ________
12 mean (의미하다) – ________
13 think (생각하다) – ________
14 read [ri:d] (읽다) – ________
15 spread (펼치다, 펴다) – ________
16 throw (던지다) – ________
17 bring (가져오다) – ________
18 build (짓다) – ________
19 buy (사다) – ________
20 catch (잡다) – ________
21 choose (선택하다) – ________
22 come (오다) – ________
23 do (하다) – ________
24 draw (그리다) – ________
25 go (가다) – ________
26 grow (자라다) – ________
27 have (가지다, 먹다) – ________
28 hear (듣다) – ________
29 keep (유지하다) – ________
30 know (알다) – ________
31 lead (이끌다) – ________
32 take (가지고 가다) – ________
33 teach (가르치다) – ________
34 meet (만나다) – ________
35 pay (지불하다) – ________

36 ride (타다) – ________
37 ring (울리다) – ________
38 rise (떠오르다) – ________
39 run (달리다) – ________
40 get (얻다) – ________
41 give (주다) – ________
42 let (~하게 하다) – ________
43 put (두다, 놓다) – ________
44 say (말하다) – ________
45 see (보다) – ________
46 sell (팔다) – ________
47 send (보내다) – ________
48 sing (노래하다) – ________
49 drive (운전하다) – ________
50 eat (먹다) – ________
51 fall (떨어지다) – ________
52 feed (먹이를 주다) – ________
53 feel (느끼다) – ________
54 fight (싸우다) – ________
55 understand (이해하다) – ________
56 wake (일어나다) – ________
57 become (~이 되다) – ________
58 begin (시작하다) – ________
59 break (깨다) – ________
60 wear (입다) – ________
61 win (이기다) – ________
62 write (쓰다) – ________
63 cost (비용이 들다) – ________
64 cut (자르다) – ________
65 hit (치다) – ________
66 hurt (아프다, 다치게 하다) – ________
67 find (발견하다) – ________
68 fly (날다, 날리다) – ________
69 forget (잊다) – ________
70 forgive (용서하다) – ________

UNIT 06 일반동사의 부정문

일반동사의 부정문은 〈조동사 do/does/did+not〉을 동사원형 앞에 써야 해요.

일반동사의 현재 부정문			일반동사의 과거 부정문	
일반적인 주어	do not [don't]	+동사원형	모든 주어	did not [didn't] + 동사원형
3인칭 단수 주어	does not [doesn't]			

주의 현재시제는 주어에 따라 조동사 do/does를 쓰고, 과거시제는 주어에 상관없이 did를 사용해요.

주의 be동사의 부정문은 현재형 am/are/is나 과거형 was/were 뒤에 not을 붙인다는 점에 유의하세요.

|A| 다음 문장의 밑줄 친 부분을 바르게 고쳐 쓰시오. (단, 부정문은 축약형으로 쓸 것)

01 I not have an umbrella now. → ______

02 He plays not tennis every morning. → ______

03 I don't watch TV last night. → ______

04 We doesn't go to the movies on Saturdays. → ______

05 She didn't came with her sister yesterday. → ______

06 Bill and Jane doesn't stay up late every night. → ______

07 I saw Sally, but I don't saw Jason. → ______

08 My mother drinks tea, but she don't drink coffee. → ______

|B| 다음 문장을 부정문으로 바꾸어 쓰시오.

01 I like this car. → ______

02 She cooks well. → ______

03 We had a good time. → ______

04 They worked today. → ______

05 My sister rides a bike. → ______

06 Jenny finished her homework. → ______

07 He knows my number. → ______

08 I went to the restaurant. → ______

09 You won the game. → ______

UNIT 07 일반동사의 의문문

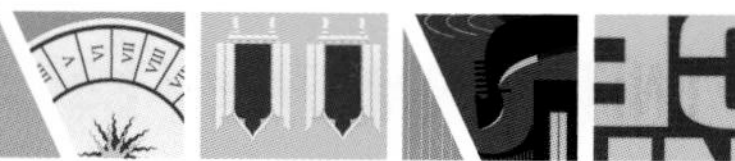

일반동사의 의문문은 조동사 Do/Does/Did를 주어 앞에 쓰세요.

일반동사의 현재 의문문			일반동사의 과거 의문문	
Do	+ 일반적인 주어	+ 동사원형 ~?	Did	+ 모든 주어 + 동사원형 ~?
Does	+ 3인칭 단수 주어			

주의 be동사의 의문문은 현재형 Am/Are/Is나 과거형 Was/Were를 주어 앞에 쓴다는 점에 유의하세요.

|A| 다음 문장을 의문문으로 바꾸어 쓰시오.

01 You like chocolate. → ____________________

02 She lives near here. → ____________________

03 Your mother called you. → ____________________

04 Kevin has two brothers. → ____________________

05 She cleans her room. → ____________________

06 He studied math. → ____________________

07 They have breakfast at seven. → ____________________

08 Sam stayed at home. → ____________________

|B| 우리말과 같은 뜻이 되도록 괄호 안의 단어를 이용하여 의문문을 만들고 알맞은 대답을 완성하시오.

01 너는 공포 영화를 좋아하니? (like, horror movies)

____________________ – __________, I do.

02 너의 아빠는 은행에서 일하시니? (your dad, work, a bank, at)

____________________ – No, __________.

03 그녀는 숙제를 끝냈니? (her homework, finish)

____________________ – __________, she did.

04 Jen과 Sam은 파티에 갔었니? (go, the party, to)

____________________ – Yes, __________.

05 너는 너의 엄마를 도와드리니? (help, your mom)

____________________ – __________, I don't.

06 너와 너의 남동생은 조깅을 즐기니? (enjoy, jogging)

____________________ – No, __________.

UNIT 08 일반동사 종합

문장이 평서문, 부정문 또는 의문문인지를 판단하여 알맞은 일반동사를 사용하세요.

평서문	현재형은 동사원형으로 쓰거나 동사 뒤에 -s를 붙이세요.	She likes movies.
	과거형은 동사원형 뒤에 -ed를 붙이세요.	She liked movies.
부정문	주어 + do / does / did + not + 동사원형의 어순으로 쓰세요.	She didn't like movies.
의문문	Do / Does / Did + 주어 + 동사원형 ~?의 어순으로 써야 해요.	Did she like movies?

주의 일반동사 현재형과 과거형의 규칙 변화 및 불규칙 변화 동사를 꼭 암기하세요.

|A| 다음 문장의 밑줄 친 부분을 어법상 바르게 고치시오.

01 Do your aunt live in New York now? → ____________

02 My parents buyed a bicycle last month. → ____________

03 Did she has a good summer vacation? → ____________

04 We don't went to the beach yesterday. → ____________

05 Henry sleeped for ten hours last night. → ____________

06 I don't like Andy and Andy don't like me. → ____________

07 I walk to school but my brother took a bus. → ____________

08 He gets up late and was late for school today. → ____________

|B| 다음 문장을 괄호 안의 지시대로 바꾸어 쓰시오.

01 She knows the song. (의문문으로) → ____________

02 We go to school together. (부정문으로) → ____________

03 They help each other. (의문문으로) → ____________

04 Did she make this cake? (평서문으로) → ____________

05 The teacher teaches music. (과거형으로) → ____________

06 They went to the park. (의문문으로) → ____________

07 She read the book yesterday. (부정문으로) → ____________

과거형과 현재형의 형태가 같은 동사는 부사구를 보고 시제를 판단해야 해요.

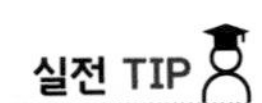

실전 TIP

Did로 질문했으니, 대답도 〈Yes/No, 주어+did/didn't.〉로 해야 해요.

내신 기출 다음 질문에 대한 대답으로 옳은 것은?

Did Jimin and you go to the library last week?

① No, I do. ② Yes, they did. ③ Yes, we did.
④ No, you didn't. ⑤ Yes, we do.

중간고사·기말고사 실전문제

객관식 (01~25) / 주관식 (26~50)

학년과 반 이름 객관식 / 25문항 주관식 / 25문항

01 다음 중 동사의 3인칭 단수 현재형이 어법상 어색한 것은?

① go – goes
② throw – throws
③ catch – catches
④ mix – mixs
⑤ solve – solves

02 다음 빈칸에 알맞은 말이 순서대로 짝지어진 것은?

• My grandmother ________ to church on Sundays.
• The bus ________ every 30 minutes.

① go – run ② gos – runs
③ goes – runs ④ goes – runes
⑤ gone – run

03~04 다음 빈칸에 알맞은 말을 고르시오.

03

________ they know your best friend?

① Is ② Does
③ Are ④ Do
⑤ Aren't

04

________ keeps a diary every day.

① Susan and I ② They
③ You ④ The students
⑤ My teacher

05 다음 밑줄 친 부분이 어법상 어색한 것은?

A: ⓐ Does David ⓑ looks ⓒ happy now?
B: Yes, ⓓ he ⓔ does.

① ⓐ ② ⓑ
③ ⓒ ④ ⓓ
⑤ ⓔ

06~07 다음 중 동사의 과거형이 어법상 어색한 것을 고르시오.

06 ① jump – jumped
② plan – planned
③ visit – visitted
④ cross – crossed
⑤ arrive – arrived

07 ① drive – drove
② stand – stood
③ mean – meaned
④ feed – fed
⑤ cost – cost

08 다음 문장을 부정문으로 바르게 바꾼 것은?

Emma envies her sister.

① Emma isn't envy her sister.
② Emma don't envy her sister.
③ Emma not do envy her sister.
④ Emma doesn't envies her sister.
⑤ Emma doesn't envy her sister.

09 다음 빈칸에 Does가 들어갈 수 없는 문장은?

① ________ he teach English?
② ________ Bomi practice the violin every day?
③ ________ your sisters like your grandparents?
④ ________ this bus go to Daegu?
⑤ ________ your brother drive his car carefully?

10~11 다음 질문에 대한 대답으로 알맞은 것을 고르시오.

10

> Did you make Mexican food for your mother yesterday?

① Yes, I did.
② Yes, I do.
③ No, I wasn't.
④ Yes, you did.
⑤ No, I don't.

11

> Does Rachel have a bicycle?

① No, I don't.
② Yes, I do.
③ No, she does.
④ No, she doesn't.
⑤ Yes, she is.

12 다음 대화의 빈칸에 공통으로 알맞은 말은?

> A: Does your brother ________ glasses?
> B: No, he doesn't. But my sisters ________ glasses.

① wears
② wore
③ worn
④ wear
⑤ wearing

13~14 우리말을 영어로 바르게 옮긴 것을 고르시오.

13

> Jason은 버스를 타고 학교에 가니?

① Is Jason go to school by bus?
② Was Jason go to school by bus?
③ Have Jason go to school by bus?
④ Do Jason go to school by bus?
⑤ Does Jason go to school by bus?

14

> Timothy와 Paul은 김 선생님을 알지 못한다.

① Timothy and Paul doesn't know Mr. Kim.
② Timothy and Paul Know Mr. Kim.
③ Timothy and Paul don't know Mr. Kim.
④ Timothy and Paul are not know Mr. Kim.
⑤ Timothy and Paul not does know Mr. Kim.

15~17 다음 중 어법상 어색한 문장을 고르시오.

15 ① Jenny hurt her feet yesterday.
② Minho read the book last year.
③ My uncle builds this house three years ago.
④ Mr. Park worked for the company in 2010.
⑤ Sienna and her husband took a walk an hour ago.

16 ① He swam very fast.
② Brian spend much money on shoes.
③ The students understood the questions.
④ She doesn't play the piano before her friends.
⑤ My father bought a new car a month ago.

17 ① I carried many books in my bag.
② James find a dollar under his bed.
③ I had a headache last night.
④ My teacher gave us lots of homework.
⑤ I sang a song at the festival.

18~19 다음 대화의 빈칸에 알맞은 말을 고르시오.

18

A: ______________________________
B: No, I didn't. I studied at home yesterday.

① Do you study at the library yesterday?
② Does you study at the library yesterday?
③ Did you study at the library yesterday?
④ Did I study at the library yesterday?
⑤ Did you studied at the library yesterday?

19

A: ______________________________
B: Yes, they do. They worry a lot about the test.

① Does Seho and Tom worry about the final test?
② Did Seho and Tom worry about the final test?
③ Do Seho and Tom worry about the final test?
④ Are Seho and Tom worry about the final test?
⑤ Is Seho and Tom worry about the final test?

20 다음 문장을 지시대로 바꾼 것 중 어법상 <u>어색한</u> 것은?

① Her mother buys a chocolate cake. (과거형)
→ Her mother bought a chocolate cake.
② Sam went there yesterday. (부정문)
→ Sam didn't go there yesterday.
③ The bus stops at Sejong Street. (과거형)
→ The bus stopping at Sejong Street.
④ Samantha likes classical music. (의문문)
→ Does Samantha like classical music?
⑤ Grace and Jisu take the same class. (과거형)
→ Grace and Jisu took the same class.

21 다음 중 어법상 올바른 문장의 개수는?

(a) His watch do not work.
(b) He tried his best at that time.
(c) Bomi keeped her photos in the cabinet.
(d) We sold cheese and milk at the flea market.

① 1개 ② 2개
③ 3개 ④ 4개
⑤ 0개

22 괄호 안의 동사를 어법상 바르게 고친 것끼리 바르게 짝지어진 것은?

(a) Stella (live) in Dubai three years ago.
(b) Mark (lose) his violin yesterday.
(c) Borris (go) to school by bus every day.

	(a)	(b)	(c)
①	lives	loses	went
②	live	lost	went
③	lived	lost	went
④	lived	lost	goes
⑤	lived	lost	go

23 다음 중 어법상 어색한 곳을 바르게 고치지 않은 것은?

① Aiden speak French very well.
→ Aiden speaks French very well.
② Mia was not write an email to him.
→ Mia did not write an email to him.
③ He lied on the grass.
→ He layed on the grass.
④ I fight with my brother yesterday.
→ I fought with my brother yesterday.
⑤ The elevator stoped at the second floor.
→ The elevator stopped at the second floor.

24 다음 중 어법상 어색한 문장은?

(A) A farmer went out and planted seeds. (B) He puts them into the ground. (C) They grew healthy and strong. (D) At harvest time, he had lots of crops. (E) He felt happy.

① (A) ② (B)
③ (C) ④ (D)
⑤ (E)

25 다음 글의 밑줄 친 부분이 어법상 어색한 것은?

Dear Daisy,

How are you? Our family ⓐ spent the weekend at the beach. It ⓑ was sunny and very hot. We ⓒ swimming in the sea. My brother and I ⓓ made sand castles. My little sister ⓔ flew a kite with my father. We had a great time. See you soon.

Your friend,
Clara

① ⓐ ② ⓑ
③ ⓒ ④ ⓓ
⑤ ⓔ

26 다음 동사의 3인칭 단수형을 쓰시오.

(1) eat – ________
(2) catch – ________
(3) fly – ________
(4) practice – ________

27~29 괄호 안의 단어를 빈칸에 알맞은 형태로 쓰시오.

27 Tim ________ black hair. (have)

28 Carrie and her father ________ tennis every Monday. (play)

29 Minsu ________ his teeth every morning. (brush)

30 다음 동사의 과거형을 쓰시오.

(1) drop – ________
(2) obey – ________
(3) leave – ________
(4) draw – ________

31~32 다음 문장을 주어진 지시대로 바르게 고쳐 쓰시오.

Lucas plays soccer twice a week.

31 부정문으로 고쳐 쓰시오.

→ ______________________

32 의문문으로 고쳐 쓰고, 부정의 대답을 쓰시오.

A: ______________________

B: ______________________

33 다음 빈칸에 알맞은 말을 넣어 대화를 완성하시오.

A: ________ ________ ________ ________ ________ early?
B: Yes, she does. My grandmother gets up early every day.

34~35 다음 괄호 안의 동사를 이용하여 문장을 완성하시오. (단, 과거형으로 쓸 것)

34 Bomi ________ a trip to Australia. (plan)

35 Jane ________ her water bottle. (drop)

36 다음 괄호 안에서 알맞은 말을 고르시오.

(1) He (raise / raised) his hand high.

(2) The South Korean team (wins / won) the game last week.

37~38 우리말과 같은 뜻이 되도록 괄호 안의 단어를 이용하여 문장을 완성하시오.

37

Kate와 Ben은 지난주 도쿄에 머물러 있지 않았다. (stay)

Kate and Ben ______________________ in Tokyo last week.

38

우리 할아버지는 지난주 호수에서 큰 물고기를 잡으셨다. (catch)

My grandfather ____________ a big fish in the lake last week.

39~40 다음 중 어법상 어색한 것을 골라 그 번호를 쓰고, 바르게 고치시오.

39

The leaves ⓐ fell. Winter ⓑ was on its way. A squirrel ⓒ searched for food for the winter. It ⓓ looked up into the trees and under the bushes. But it ⓔ didn't found any food.

________ → ________

40

Yesterday ⓐ <u>was</u> Jake's birthday. He ⓑ <u>invited</u> his friends. He received many gifts. After lunch, he ⓒ <u>went</u> to the beach with his friends. It ⓓ <u>wasn't take</u> a long time to get there. They ⓔ <u>had</u> a great time at the beach.

________ → ____________

41~42 Mandy의 지난 주말 일과표를 보고, 다음 대화를 완성하시오.

	Saturday	Sunday
hike the mountain	○	×
go to the library	×	○
play tennis	○	○

41 A: Did Mandy hike the mountain last Sunday?

B: ________, ____________.

42 A: Did Mandy play tennis last weekend?

B: ________, ____________.

43 Stella와 Aiden이 좋아하는 음식에 대한 표를 보고, 동사 like를 이용하여 다음 글을 완성하시오.

	spaghetti	soup	salad
Stella	○	×	○
Aiden	○	○	×

Stella and Aiden ________ spaghetti. Stella ____________ soup, but Aiden ________ soup. Aiden ____________ salad.

44~45 우리말과 같은 뜻이 되도록 괄호 안의 단어를 이용하여 문장을 완성하시오.

44

새 한 마리가 둥지에서 떨어졌다.
(fall, its nest, from)

____

45

나는 새 가방을 샀다. (buy, a new bag)

____

46~47 다음 문장을 우리말로 바르게 해석하시오.

46

My parents climb a mountain twice a month.

→ ______________________

47

Susan had a stomachache last night.

→ ______________________

48 다음 문장의 주어를 my brother로 바꾸어 다시 쓰시오.

I sleep late every Saturday.

→ ______________________

49~50 다음 글을 읽고, 어법상 어색한 곳을 2군데 찾아 바르게 고치시오.

49

Amy runs to the top of the mountain yesterday morning. She saw the sky. The sun rises in the east at that time. It was amazing.

(1) ________ → ________

(2) ________ → ________

50

I like fall. Fall came after summer. The air becomes cool. Leaves turns red, yellow and orange. Animals get ready for winter.

(1) ________ → ________

(2) ________ → ________

CHAPTER

03 시제

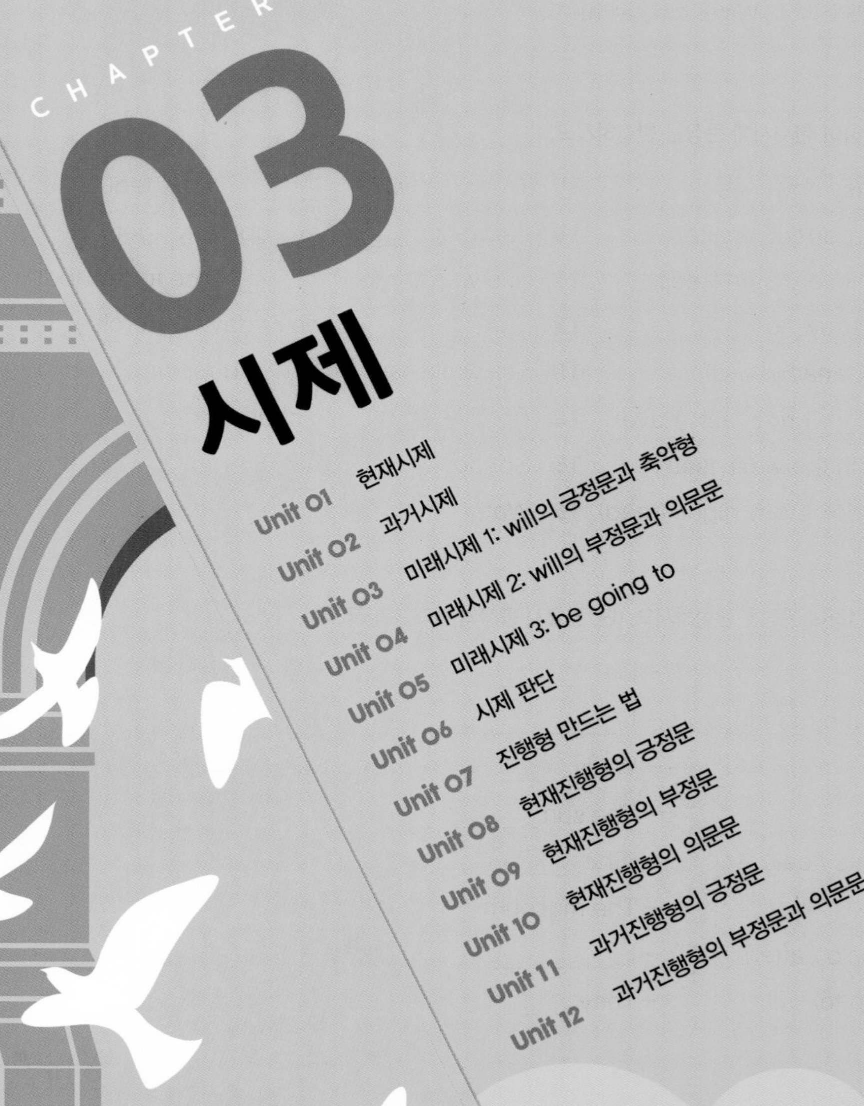

Unit 01 현재시제
Unit 02 과거시제
Unit 03 미래시제 1: will의 긍정문과 축약형
Unit 04 미래시제 2: will의 부정문과 의문문
Unit 05 미래시제 3: be going to
Unit 06 시제 판단
Unit 07 진행형 만드는 법
Unit 08 현재진행형의 긍정문
Unit 09 현재진행형의 부정문
Unit 10 현재진행형의 의문문
Unit 11 과거진행형의 긍정문
Unit 12 과거진행형의 부정문과 의문문

UNIT 01 현재시제

어떤 상황에서 현재시제를 써야 하는지 파악하세요.

현재시제를 써야 할 때	예문	
현재의 상태	He looks so sad now.	She is not my teacher.
반복적인 행동이나 습관	He goes there on Sundays.	I don't read every day.
속담 및 격언	Time is gold.	Every couple is not a pair.
과학적인 사실이나 진리	Water boils at 100℃.	Iron doesn't burn.

A 다음 괄호 안의 단어를 이용하여 현재시제 문장을 완성하시오.

01 I __________ very busy now. (be)

02 Practice __________ perfect. (make)

03 He __________ diary every day. (keep)

04 He __________ so happy. (look)

05 They __________ in Canada. (live)

06 Tom always __________ breakfast. (have)

07 The sun __________ in the west. (set)

08 Paul __________ a book every night. (read)

09 Two plus two __________ four. (equal)

10 I always __________ up early. (get)

11 The weather __________ nice today. (be)

12 She __________ on Fridays. (exercise)

13 Still waters __________ deep. (run)

14 He __________ to church. (go)

15 Spring __________ after winter. (come)

16 Water __________ at 0℃. (freeze)

B 괄호 안의 단어를 바르게 배열하여 문장을 완성하시오. (단, 필요시 동사의 형태를 바꿀 것)

01 (be / his twenties / in) → He ______________________.

02 (at seven / get up / in the morning) → I ______________________.

03 (have / ears) → Walls ______________________.

04 (the morning / rise / in) → The sun ______________________.

05 (every day / her parents / call) → She ______________________.

06 (close / at / six) → The museum ______________________.

07 (dinner / listen to / music / after) → I ______________________.

08 (by subway / work / go to) → They ______________________.

내신기출 다음 밑줄 친 부분 중 어법상 어색한 곳을 찾아 바르게 고치시오.

Light(①) traveled(②) in(③) a straight line.

실전 TIP

과학적 사실은 현재시제로 표현해야 해요.

UNIT 02 과거시제

다음의 과거 시간 부사(구)와 함께 이미 끝난 일이나 역사적 사실을 말할 때는 과거시제를 써야 해요.

과거 시간 부사(구)	예문	과거 시간 부사(구)	예문
last ~ (지난 ~에)	He came last week.	~ ago (~ 전에)	He came 3 days ago.
yesterday (어제)	He called yesterday.	the other day (얼마 전)	He called the other day.
then (그때)	He was busy then.	in+과거 연도 (~년에)	He was sick in 2000.

참고 CHAPTER 02의 UNIT 03~05에서 동사의 과거형을 다시 확인하세요.

|A| 다음 문장을 과거시제 문장으로 바꾸어 쓰시오.

01 I am very tired now. → ______________ yesterday.

02 The boys are in the yard now. → ______________ then.

03 Do you sleep well at night? → ______________ last night?

04 He drinks milk every morning. → ______________ this morning.

05 They build the Eiffel Tower. → ______________ in 1889.

06 I meet my friends every week. → ______________ the other day.

07 Mom makes cookies every day. → ______________ two hours ago.

08 They visit their grandpa. → ______________ last Sunday.

|B| 우리말과 같은 뜻이 되도록 괄호 안의 단어를 바르게 배열하여 문장을 완성하시오. (단, 필요시 동사의 형태를 변경할 것)

01 Jenny와 나는 어제 소풍을 갔다. (go on a picnic / yesterday / Jenny and I)

____

02 그가 1년 전에 이 집을 샀나요? (buy / a year ago / he / this house / did)

____

03 지난주에 날씨가 좋았니? (good / be / last week / the weather)

____

04 James는 어젯밤 돌아오지 않았다. (come back / didn't / James / last night)

____

05 Alexander Graham Bell은 1876년에 전화기를 발명했다.
(Alexander Graham Bell / in 1876 / the telephone / invent)

____

UNIT 03 미래시제 1: will의 긍정문과 축약형

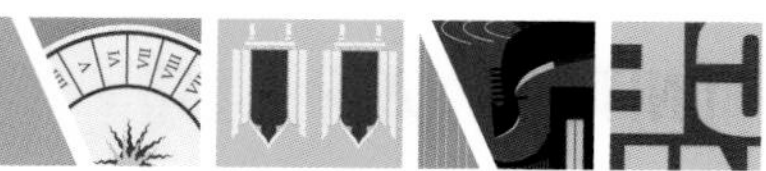

조동사 will은 미래의 계획이나 주어의 의지를 나타내며, 〈조동사 will+동사원형〉의 형태로 써야 해요.

구분	현재	과거	미래
be동사	am, are, is	was, were	will+동사원형
일반동사	동사원형(+-s) / 불규칙 변화	동사원형+-ed/불규칙 변화	
의미	~이다, ~(에) 있다, ~하다	~였다, ~(에) 있었다, ~했다	~일 것이다, ~할 것이다

주의 주어의 인칭이나 수에 따라 조동사의 형태가 바뀌지는 않으며, 조동사 뒤에는 항상 동사원형이 와야 해요.

참고 〈주격 인칭대명사+will〉은 축약해서 쓸 수도 있어요.
I'll / You'll / She'll / He'll / It'll / We'll / They'll

[A] 우리말과 같은 뜻이 되도록 괄호 안의 동사를 이용하여 문장을 완성하시오.

01 나는 내일 그녀를 만날 것이다. (meet) I ____________ her tomorrow.
02 그는 학교에 걸어갈 것이다. (walk) He ____________ to school.
03 Jenny는 늦을 것이다. (be) Jenny ____________ late.
04 그녀는 그 시험을 칠 것이다. (take) She ____________ the exam.
05 그 소년은 자전거를 살 것이다. (buy) The boy ____________ a bicycle.
06 Bill은 내년에 그들을 방문할 것이다. (visit) Bill ____________ them next year.
07 그는 그녀와 테니스를 칠 거다. (play) He ____________ tennis with her.

[B] 다음 괄호 안의 단어와 조동사 will을 이용하여 미래시제 문장을 완성하시오. (단, 가능하면 축약형으로 쓸 것)

01 (I, go, to the library) → ____________
02 (he, at home, be, today) → ____________
03 (open, the store, next month) → ____________
04 (soon, be, Tom, with us) → ____________
05 (the train, in five minutes, arrive) → ____________
06 (come back, they, tomorrow) → ____________
07 (take, a trip, next week, we) → ____________
08 (she, wash, her car, this Sunday) → ____________

내신기출 다음 빈칸에 들어갈 수 없는 말은?

We'll eat hamburgers for lunch ____________.

① last night ② today ③ soon

실전 TIP
미래시제는 과거를 나타내는 부사구와 함께 쓸 수 없어요.

UNIT 04 미래시제 2: will의 부정문과 의문문

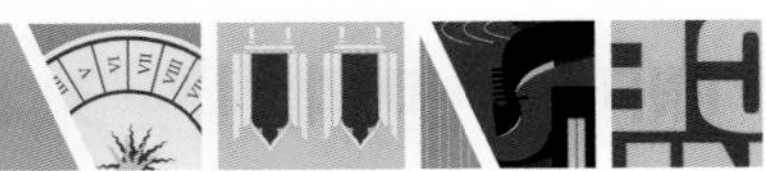

부정문과 의문문은 동사원형은 그대로 두고 조동사 will을 사용해야 해요.

구분	긍정문	부정문	의문문
어순	will+동사원형	will not+동사원형	Will+주어+동사원형 ~?
예문	He will be home tonight.	He will not be home tonight.	Will he be home tonight?
축약	He'll be home tonight.	He'll not be home tonight. He won't be home tonight.	–

참고 의문문에 대한 대답은 Yes, 주어+will. / No, 주어+won't.와 같이 해야 해요.

A 어법상 어색한 부분을 찾아 바르게 고치시오.

01 He will not visits his uncle tomorrow. ____________ → ____________

02 The bus will leave not in five minutes. ____________ → ____________

03 Will do you walk to school today? ____________ → ____________

04 Will he watches the movie tonight? ____________ → ____________

05 Jenny washs her hands before meals. ____________ → ____________

06 I not will play the guitar for them soon. ____________ → ____________

07 A: Will you join us? B: Sure, I do. ____________ → ____________

08 A: Will he buy it? B: No, he willn't. ____________ → ____________

B 다음 문장을 괄호 안의 지시대로 바꾸어 쓸 때 빈칸에 알맞은 말을 쓰시오.

01 She will be here soon.

→ (부정문) She ____________ here soon.

→ (의문문) ____________ here soon? – Yes, ____________.

02 Jack will read the book tomorrow.

→ (부정문) Jack ____________ the book tomorrow.

→ (의문문) ____________ the book tomorrow? – No, ____________.

03 He will make a vacation plan.

→ (부정문) He ____________ a vacation plan.

→ (의문문) ____________ a vacation plan? – No, ____________.

04 Your idea will work.

→ (부정문) Your idea ____________.

→ (의문문) ____________? – Yes, ____________.

UNIT 05 미래시제 3: be going to

'~할 예정이다'와 같이 계획된 미래의 일은 〈be going to+동사원형〉으로 쓰세요.

구분	긍정문	부정문	의문문
어순	be going to+동사원형	be동사+not+going to +동사원형	Be동사+주어+going to +동사원형 ~?
예문	He is going to be home.	He is not going to be home.	Is he going to be home?
축약	He's going to be home.	He's not going to be home. He isn't going to be home.	–

주의 be동사는 주어의 인칭과 수, 시제에 따라 바뀌며, to 뒤에는 항상 동사원형이 온다는 데 유의하세요.

참고 의문문에 대한 대답은 Yes, he is. / No, he isn't.와 같이 be동사만으로 대답해요.

|A| 다음 문장을 be going to를 이용하여 미래시제 문장으로 바꾸어 쓰시오.

01 I am a singer. → ______________________

02 We don't clean the kitchen. → ______________________

03 Do you have a math exam? → ______________________

04 He visits Europe. → ______________________

05 We aren't late for the concert. → ______________________

06 I finished my homework. → ______________________

07 She arrived here at nine. → ______________________

08 My dad watches TV. → ______________________

09 We met him at the mall. → ______________________

10 Do they play soccer? → ______________________

|B| 다음 문장을 괄호 안의 지시대로 바꾸어 쓸 때 빈칸에 알맞은 말을 쓰시오.

01 It is going to be sunny.

→ (부정문) It ______________________.

→ (의문문) ______________________? – No, ____________.

02 We are going to arrive early.

→ (부정문) We ______________________.

→ (의문문) ______________________? – Yes, ____________.

03 We are going to learn English.

→ (부정문) We ______________________________.

→ (의문문) ______________________________? – No, ______________.

04 She is going to sing for us.

→ (부정문) She ______________________________.

→ (의문문) ______________________________? – No, ______________.

|C| 다음 문장을 be going to를 이용하여 바꾸어 쓰시오. (단, 가능하면 축약형으로 쓸 것)

01 I'll leave for Europe this Saturday. → ______________________ this Saturday.

02 She will be back next week. → ______________________ next week.

03 He won't go out tonight. → ______________________ tonight.

04 We will paint the desk next Sunday. → ______________________ next Sunday.

05 Will you visit me next month? → ______________________ next month?

06 Will she be home tomorrow? → ______________________ tomorrow?

07 He will see Mr. Kim tomorrow. → ______________________ tomorrow.

|D| |보기|의 동사와 be going to를 이용하여 문장을 완성하시오.

보기
stay send take close visit eat buy

01 I ______________________ a taxi home.

02 Chris ______________________ Korea on his vacation.

03 I ______________________ a sandwich for lunch.

04 Jessica and I ______________________ the tickets.

05 We ______________________ the windows.

06 She ______________________ home today.

07 They ______________________ this letter by mail.

내신기출 다음 밑줄 친 부분 중 어법상 어색한 곳을 찾아 바르게 고치시오.

Look(①) at those black clouds(②)! It is going to(③) raining(④) this afternoon(⑤).

______________ → ______________

실전 TIP

미래를 나타내는 will이나 be going to 뒤에는 항상 동사원형을 써야 해요.

UNIT 06 시제 판단

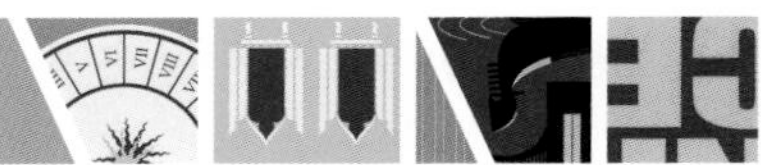

동사의 형태는 문맥과 시간 부사(구)로 시제를 판단하여 결정하세요.

현재시제	과거시제	미래시제
현재 상태, 반복적 동작, 불변의 진리 등	과거에 국한된 일, 역사적 사실 등	미래의 상태, 할 일, 벌어질 일 등
내용과 문맥으로 판단	과거 시간 부사(구) last ~, ~ ago, yesterday, the other day, then, in+과거 연도 등	미래 시간 부사(구) tomorrow, next ~, ~ later, in+미래 연도 등

참고 만약, 현재 시제라면 주어에 따라 동사의 형태를 다시 결정해야 해요.

|A| 괄호 안의 단어를 빈칸에 알맞은 형태로 쓰시오.

01 The earth ___________ around the sun. (go)

02 The Korean War ___________ in 1953. (end)

03 She ______________________ tomorrow. (not, come)

04 Tom ______________________ last year. (not, tall)

05 We ______________________ the class next year. (take)

06 ___________ she ___________ upset last night? (look) – Yes, ____________________.

07 ___________ you ___________ a letter these days? (write) – No, ____________________.

08 ___________ he ___________ a phone next month? (go to, buy) – No, ____________________.

|B| 다음 문장을 괄호 안의 지시대로 바꾸어 쓰시오.

01 It'll cost a lot of money. (과거 긍정문) → ______________________________

02 He had breakfast at eight. (현재 긍정문) → ______________________________

03 The meeting ended at five. (미래 긍정문) → ______________________________

04 They ate Italian food. (과거 의문문) → ______________________________

05 He didn't like the game. (현재 부정문) → ______________________________

06 I read the book all night. (과거 부정문) → ______________________________

07 Was he in the library? (미래 의문문) → ______________________________

동사 cost와 read는 현재형과 과거형의 형태가 같으니 유의하세요.

내신 기출 다음 중 어법상 어색한 것은?

① Susan won't go swimming next week.
② Susan went swimming two days ago.
③ Susan doesn't go swimming last week.

실전 TIP

부사구 last week는 과거시제 문장에 어울려요.

UNIT 07 진행형 만드는 법

'~하고 있다'와 같이 진행 중인 동작을 나타낼 때는 진행형 〈be동사+동사-ing〉로 써야 해요.

	현재형	현재진행형
형태	동사원형(+-s)	be동사+동사-ing
의미	~이다, ~한다	~하고 있다, ~하는 중이다
예문	We often play basketball. 우리는 자주 농구를 한다.	We are playing basketball. 우리는 농구를 하고 있다.

동사원형에 -ing를 붙이는 규칙을 알아 두세요.

대부분의 동사	동사원형+-ing	call (부르다, 전화하다) – calling bring (데려오다, 가져오다) – bringing
-e로 끝나는 동사	e를 빼고+-ing	make (만들다) – making come (오다) – coming
-ie로 끝나는 동사	ie를 y로 바꾸고+-ing	die (죽다) – dying lie (거짓말하다) – lying tie (묶다) – tying
1음절이며, 단모음+단자음으로 끝나는 동사	마지막 자음을 하나 더 쓰고+-ing	get (얻다) – getting put (놓다) – putting swim (수영하다) – swimming run (달리다) – running sit (앉다) – sitting shop (쇼핑하다) – shopping win (이기다) – winning cut (자르다) – cutting stop (멈추다) – stopping
2음절이지만 단모음+단자음으로 끝나고, 강세가 뒤에 있는 동사		begin (시작하다) – beginning forget (잊다) – forgetting regret (후회하다) – regretting

빈칸에 다음 동사의 -ing형을 쓰면서 외우시오.

01 arrive (도착하다) – ________
02 bake (굽다) – ________
03 begin (시작하다) – ________
04 believe (믿다) – ________
05 bring (가지고 오다) – ________
06 call (부르다, 전화하다) – ________
07 camp (야영하다) – ________
08 climb (오르다) – ________
09 close (닫다) – ________
10 come (오다) – ________
11 control (통제하다) – ________
12 dance (춤추다) – ________
13 die (죽다) – ________
14 drink (마시다) – ________
15 drive (운전하다) – ________
16 enter (들어가다) – ________
17 fly (날다, 날리다) – ________
18 get (얻다) – ________
19 give (주다) – ________
20 go (가다) – ________
21 have (가지다, 먹다) – ________
22 lie (눕다, 거짓말하다) – ________
23 listen (듣다) – ________
24 love (사랑하다) – ________
25 make (만들다) – ________
26 open (열다) – ________
27 play (놀다, 연주하다) – ________
28 put (놓다, 두다) – ________
29 read (읽다) – ________
30 ride (타다) – ________
31 run (뛰다) – ________
32 save (아끼다) – ________
33 say (말하다) – ________
34 shop (쇼핑하다) – ________
35 sing (노래하다) – ________
36 sit (앉다) – ________
37 smile (미소 짓다) – ________
38 start (출발하다) – ________
39 stop (멈추다) – ________
40 study (공부하다) – ________
41 swim (수영하다) – ________
42 take (가지고 가다) – ________
43 teach (가르치다) – ________
44 visit (방문하다) – ________
45 win (이기다) – ________
46 write (쓰다) – ________

내신기출 다음 중 동사의 -ing형이 틀린 것은?

① run – running
② drive – driving
③ win – wining
④ believe – believing
⑤ begin – beginning

실전 TIP

1음절 동사 win은 〈단모음+단자음〉으로 끝나는 점에 유의하세요.

UNIT 08 현재진행형의 긍정문

현재 진행 중인 일을 나타내는 현재진행형은 〈be동사의 현재형+동사-ing〉의 형태로, be동사는 주어의 인칭과 수에 맞춰 쓰세요.

현재형	I have breakfast.	She goes to school.
현재진행형	I am[I'm] having breakfast now.	She is[She's] going to school now.

주의 소유나 상태를 나타내는 동사(have, want, know 등)는 진행형으로 쓸 수 없어요.
하지만 have가 '먹다'라는 의미일 때는 진행형이 가능하다는 데에 유의하세요.

주의 She is going to school. 〈현재진행형〉 She is going to go to school. 〈미래〉

|A| 다음 문장을 현재진행형 문장으로 바꾸어 쓰시오.

01 I listen to music. → ______
02 He writes a letter. → ______
03 She talks on the phone. → ______
04 You wash the dishes. → ______
05 I do my homework. → ______
06 They have lunch. → ______
07 The girls sit on the sofa. → ______
08 We swim in the pool. → ______

|B| 다음 괄호 안의 단어를 이용하여 현재진행형 문장을 완성하시오. (단, 가능하면 주어와 be동사를 축약할 것)

주어가 인칭대명사가 아닌 경우, 〈주어+be동사〉를 축약할 수 없어요.

01 (I, read, a book) → ______
02 (he, a picture, draw) → ______
03 (on the grass, they, play) → ______
04 (fly, high, a bird) → ______
05 (lie, she, on the bed) → ______
06 (my brother, breakfast, have) → ______
07 (the man, at the map, look) → ______
08 (Mina and I, a song, sing) → ______

내신 기출 다음 밑줄 친 부분의 쓰임이 다른 하나는?

① She is going to watch the movie.
② She is going to the library with her friends.
③ She is going to help her mom in the kitchen.

실전 TIP

〈be going to+동사원형〉은 '~할 예정이다'라는 의미이고, 〈be going to+명사〉는 '~로 가는 중이다'라는 의미가 돼요.

UNIT 09 현재진행형의 부정문

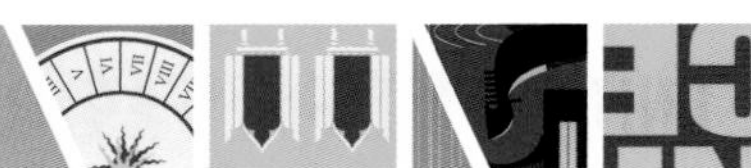

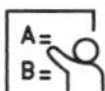

'~하고 있지 않다'를 의미하는 현재진행형의 부정문은 be동사 뒤에 not을 붙이세요.

현재진행형의 긍정문	They're having breakfast now.	She's going to school now.
현재진행형의 부정문	They're not[They aren't] having breakfast now.	She's not[She isn't] going to school now.

A 다음 문장을 현재진행형의 부정문으로 바꾸어 쓰시오.

01 I study math. → ______________________

02 He took a shower. → ______________________

03 Mike watches TV. → ______________________

04 She's playing the piano. → ______________________

05 They take a walk. → ______________________

06 You're exercising. → ______________________

07 My father washed his car. → ______________________

08 The mouse is eating cheese. → ______________________

B 우리말과 같은 뜻이 되도록 괄호 안의 단어를 이용하여 문장을 완성하시오. (단, be동사와 not은 축약할 것)

01 그들은 지금 그 문제에 대해 토론하고 있지 않다. (discuss, the problem)

They ______________________ now.

02 그는 지금 자전거를 타고 있지 않다. (ride, a bicycle)

He ______________________ right now.

03 그 남자는 자동차를 수리하고 있지 않다. (fix, the car)

The man ______________________.

04 우리는 지금 저녁 식사를 하고 있지 않다. (have, dinner)

We ______________________ now.

05 Ann은 이를 닦고 있지 않다. (brush, her teeth)

Ann ______________________.

06 나는 지금 자리를 찾고 있지 않다. (look for, a seat)

I ______________________ now.

UNIT 10 현재진행형의 의문문

'~하는 중이니?'라는 현재진행형의 의문문은 be동사만 주어 앞에 쓰세요.

현재진행형의 긍정문	They're having breakfast now.	She's going to school now.
현재진행형의 의문문	Are they having breakfast now? – Yes, they are. – No, they aren't[they're not].	Is she going to school now? – Yes, she is. – No, she isn't[she's not].

|A| 다음 괄호 안의 단어를 이용하여 현재진행형의 대화를 완성하시오.

01 A: ________ you ________ your homework? (do) B: Yes, I ____________.

02 A: ________ they ________ their friends? (help) B: Yes, they ____________.

03 A: ________ I ________ too fast? (speak) B: No, you ____________.

04 A: ________ Tom and his son ________ lunch? (eat) B: Yes, they ____________.

05 A: ________ Kathy ________ a dress? (wear) B: Yes, she ____________.

|B| 다음 괄호 안의 단어를 이용하여 현재진행형의 대화를 완성하시오.

01 A: ______________________________? (he, run, to school)
B: Yes, ____________________.

02 A: ______________________________? (she, make, a sandwich)
B: No, ____________________.

03 A: ______________________________? (you, look at, the pictures)
B: Yes, ____________________.

04 A: ______________________________? (Sam, wait for, the train)
B: No, ____________________.

05 A: ______________________________? (your mom, talk, on the phone)
B: No, ____________________.

06 A: ______________________________? (they, use, the computer)
B: No, ____________________.

내신 기출 다음 대화의 빈칸에 알맞은 말을 고르시오.

A: ____________________
B: Yes, she is. My sister loves to dance.

① Is your sister dancing? ② Does your sister dance?
③ Can your sister dance now?

실전 TIP
Yes, she is.로 대답하려면 질문에 be동사를 사용한 문장이 있어야 해요. 따라서 Does/Can your sister~?와 같은 문장은 올 수 없어요.

UNIT 11 과거진행형의 긍정문

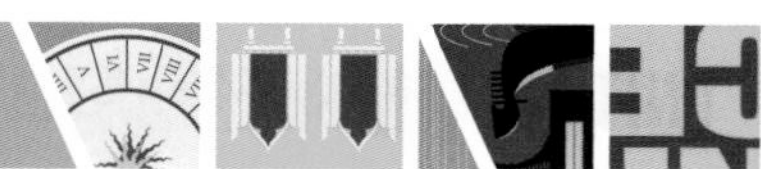

과거의 특정 시점에 진행되고 있던 동작은 be동사만 과거형으로 써서 과거진행형으로 만드세요.

현재진행형	She is having breakfast now.	They are going to school now.
과거진행형	She was having breakfast at that time.	They were going to school that day.

참고 과거의 특정 시점을 나타내는 부사(구)를 참고하세요.
at the[that] time 당시에, ~ ago ~ 전에, when+과거 ~했을 때, then 그때, at+시간 ~시에

A 다음 문장을 과거진행형으로 바꾸어 쓰시오.

01 She ran at the park. → ______

02 I went to the library. → ______

03 He put on his jacket. → ______

04 You walked to school. → ______

05 They played the violins. → ______

06 Kate drank some juice. → ______

07 We traveled to Paris. → ______

08 John took pictures of his family. → ______

run, put의 진행형을 만드는 방법에 유의하세요.

B 우리말과 같은 뜻이 되도록 괄호 안의 동사를 이용하여 빈칸에 알맞은 말을 쓰시오.

01 나는 1시간 전에 책을 읽고 있었다. (read)
I ______ a book an hour ago.

02 그녀는 그 파티에서 하얀 바지를 입고 있었다. (wear)
She ______ white pants at the party.

03 그는 당시에 이메일을 쓰고 있었다. (write)
He ______ an email at that time.

04 내가 전화했을 때 준수와 미나는 점심을 먹고 있었다. (have)
Junsu and Mina ______ lunch when I called.

05 친구들과 나는 그때 축구 경기를 보고 있었다. (watch)
My friends and I ______ the soccer game then.

06 태양은 빛나고 새들은 노래하고 있었다. (shine, sing)
The sun ______ and the birds ______.

UNIT 12 과거진행형의 부정문과 의문문

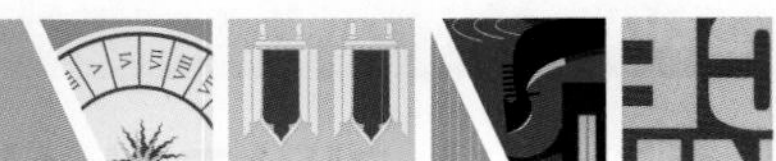

과거진행형의 부정문과 의문문도 모두 be동사의 과거형을 사용하는 것을 기억하세요.

구분	긍정문	부정문	의문문
어순	be동사의 과거형+동사-ing	be동사의 과거형+not+동사-ing	Be동사의 과거형+주어+동사-ing ~?
예문	He was eating.	He was not[wasn't] eating.	Was he eating? – Yes, he was. – No, he wasn't.

A 다음 밑줄 친 부분을 바르게 고쳐 과거진행형 문장을 완성하시오.

01 I was having not breakfast at the time. → ______________________

02 She not was washing some clothes then. → ______________________

03 Did your parents ateing dinner? → ______________________

04 He isn't sending an e-mail. → ______________________

05 Were your mother making a cake? → ______________________

06 We wasn't studying English when you called. → ______________________

07 My uncle weren't working an hour ago. → ______________________

08 Was you sleeping when they came? → ______________________

B 다음 문장을 괄호 안의 지시대로 바꾸어 쓸 때 빈칸에 알맞은 말을 쓰시오.

01 You were making a pizza.

→ (부정문) You ______________________ a pizza.

→ (의문문) ______________________ a pizza? – Yes, ______________.

02 She was crossing the road.

→ (부정문) She ______________________ the road.

→ (의문문) ______________________ the road? – Yes, ______________.

03 He was watching the movie.

→ (부정문) He ______________________ the movie.

→ (의문문) ______________________ the movie? – No, ______________.

04 The children were taking a bath then.

→ (부정문) The children ______________________ a bath then.

→ (의문문) ______________________ a bath then? – No, ______________.

중간고사·기말고사 실전문제

객관식 (01~25) / 주관식 (26~50)

학년과 반 이름 객관식 / 25문항 주관식 / 25문항

01~02 다음 빈칸에 알맞은 말을 고르시오.

01 Stella ________ hiking next Saturday.

① go ② going
③ went ④ is going
⑤ will go

02 The Earth ________ around the Sun.

① moved ② will move
③ moves ④ move
⑤ is going to move

03~04 다음 빈칸에 알맞은 말을 고르시오.

03 Jason will leave his hometown ________.

① last weekend ② yesterday
③ at that time ④ next Monday
⑤ an hour ago

04 Aiden arrives at school early ________.

① 2 hours ago ② every day
③ yesterday ④ last night
⑤ next Sunday

05 다음 중 동사의 진행형이 어법상 <u>어색한</u> 것은?

① cheer – cheering
② stay – staying
③ enter – enterring
④ move – moving
⑤ sit – sitting

06 다음 빈칸에 들어갈 말이 순서대로 짝지어진 것은?

• King Sejong ________ Hangeul.
• Mary ________ on a trip to England next year.

① creates – goes
② creates – went
③ will create – will go
④ created – will go
⑤ is going to create – went

07~08 다음 대화의 빈칸에 알맞은 말을 고르시오.

07
A: Are you taking a walk at the park?
B: ________ I am having lunch with my friends now.

① Yes, I am. ② Yes, I was.
③ No, I am not. ④ No, I wasn't.
⑤ No, you aren't.

08

A: Was Rose cooking dinner an hour ago?
B: ______________ She was cooking fish and chips.

① Yes, she is. ② Yes, she were.
③ Yes, she was. ④ No, she wasn't.
⑤ No, she isn't.

09~10 다음 빈칸에 들어갈 수 없는 말을 고르시오.

09

Jenny ______________ Mr. Brown.

① knew ② knows
③ didn't know ④ doesn't know
⑤ was knowing

10

Minsu __________ an expensive bike.

① bought ② is wanting
③ rode ④ will buy
⑤ found

11~12 다음 대화의 빈칸에 알맞은 말을 고르시오.

11

A: ______________?
B: Yes, she was exercising at the gym.

① Was Amy exercising then?
② Did Amy like the movie?
③ What will Amy do this weekend?
④ Is Amy going to visit her parents?
⑤ Does Amy exercise at the gym every day?

12

A: ______________
B: Yes, he is going to study in the library.

① Was Jason jogging with his friends?
② Did Jason study hard at home?
③ Is Jason studying history?
④ Does Jason go to the library every day?
⑤ Is Jason going to study for an exam tonight?

13 다음 빈칸에 공통으로 알맞은 말은?

• My father __________ smiling at me.
• __________ it raining at this time yesterday?

① will[Will] ② is[Is]
③ are[Are] ④ was[Was]
⑤ were[Were]

14 다음 우리말과 같은 뜻이 되도록 괄호 안의 말을 배열할 때, 세 번째에 올 단어는?

Lynn은 이번 주말에 캠핑을 가지 않을 것이다.
(Lynn / camping / will / go / this weekend / not)

① will ② camping
③ go ④ not
⑤ this

15~16 다음 우리말을 영어로 바르게 옮긴 것을 고르시오.

15

이 선생님은 내년에 프랑스어를 가르치지 않을 것이다.

① Mr. Lee doesn't teach French next year.
② Mr. Lee will teach French next year.
③ Mr. Lee not was teaching French next year.
④ Mr. Lee wasn't teaching French next year.
⑤ Mr. Lee isn't going to teach French next year.

16

내 컴퓨터는 어제 작동하지 않고 있었다.

① My computer is not working yesterday.
② My computer does not work yesterday.
③ My computer won't work yesterday.
④ My computer was not working yesterday.
⑤ My computer didn't working yesterday.

17 다음 빈칸에 들어갈 말이 순서대로 짝지어진 것은?

> • A bird ____________ flying over the tree at that time.
> • ____________ the children jumping on the bed now?

① is – Are　② was – Were
③ was – Are　④ will – Will
⑤ was – Is

18 다음 문장을 괄호 안의 지시대로 바꾼 것 중 어법상 어색한 것은?

The baby takes a nap.

① (미래시제로) The baby will take a nap.
② (과거시제로) The baby took a nap.
③ (현재진행시제로) The baby is taking a nap.
④ (과거진행시제로) The baby was takes a nap.
⑤ (부정문으로) The baby doesn't take a nap.

19~21 다음 중 어법상 올바른 문장을 고르시오.

19 ① The Second World War ends in 1945.
② Spring comes after winter.
③ Water freeze at zero degree Celsius.
④ She was hungry now.
⑤ Are they enjoying the party yesterday?

20 ① The shop opened at 10 a.m. tomorrow.
② Whales were mammals.
③ Seoul is the capital of South Korea.
④ Jake is sick last night.
⑤ Cathy visited Madrid next year.

21 ① It is not going to snow yesterday.
② Kyle is having a beautiful house on the hill.
③ Ben is going to practicing the violin tomorrow.
④ Kim Yuna won the gold medal in 2010.
⑤ Samantha always drink a cup of coffee after lunch.

22 다음 대화의 빈칸에 알맞은 말은?

> A: Were you and your brother making cookies?
> B: No, we weren't.
> ____________________

① We are playing basketball.
② We play basketball.
③ We were playing basketball.
④ We will play basketball.
⑤ We are going to play basketball.

23 다음 글의 ①~⑤ 중에서 어법상 어색한 문장은?

> ① Rose went on a trip to Europe. ② She arrived in Paris yesterday. ③ She went to the Eiffel Tower last night. ④ She will visit the Louvre Museum this afternoon. ⑤ She is going take a cruise on the Seine tomorrow.

24 다음 중 어법상 올바른 문장끼리 바르게 짝지어진 것은?

> (A) Jenny and Amy is going to take subway.
> (B) Minho was going cut his hair soon.
> (C) Alice not will wear that jacket today.
> (D) Is Jake going to buy some flowers for his mom this afternoon?
> (E) She will not goes to school tomorrow.
> (F) Jessica was taking a cello lesson then.

① (A), (D)　② (C), (D), (F)
③ (A)　④ (D), (F)
⑤ (A), (B)

25 다음 빈칸에 들어갈 말이 순서대로 짝지어진 것은?

> • My father ________ a kite for my sister a few days ago.
> • David ________ fishing with his brother this weekend.
> • Cathy and Susan ________ chatting on the phone then.

①	makes	goes	are
②	made	went	were
③	made	will go	was
④	makes	go	was
⑤	made	will go	were

26~27 다음 문장을 be going to를 이용하여 바꿔 쓰시오.

26

> Kate and Ben will sell their toys.

→ ____________________

27

> Tom won't walk to school tomorrow.

→ ____________________

28~29 괄호 안의 단어를 이용하여 현재진행형 문장을 완성하시오.

28 Young mothers and their children ____________ on the grass. (sit)

29 Catherine ____________ a wedding cake for her sister. (bake)

30 다음 문장을 의문문으로 바꾸시오.

She is going to leave for London soon.

→ ____________

31 빈칸에 공통으로 알맞은 말을 동사 make를 이용하여 쓰시오.

> A: What are you ____________?
> B: I am ____________ a doll for my sister.
> A: It is so pretty.

32~33 괄호 안의 단어를 빈칸에 알맞은 형태로 쓰시오.

32 The restaurant ____________ at 11 a.m. tomorrow. (open)

33 The train ____________ at 6 p.m. yesterday. (arrive)

34~35 아래 그림을 보고 괄호 안의 단어를 이용하여 주어진 질문에 답하시오.

34 What are the children doing? (make a sand castle)

→ ____________

35 Is their mother swimming?

→ ________, ____________.
She is reading a book.

36~38 우리말과 같은 뜻이 되도록 괄호 안의 단어를 이용하여 문장을 완성하시오.

36 Cathy의 고양이는 벤치 위에서 뛰고 있다.
(Cathy's cat, on the bench, jump)

____

37 너희 아버지는 한 시간 전에 욕실을 청소하고 계셨니?
(your father, an hour ago, clean, the bathroom)

____

38 Lauren은 내년에 중학생이 될 것이다.
(Lauren, next year, a middle school student, be)

____

39~40 밑줄 친 단어를 어법상 바르게 고치시오.

39 Jake <u>is</u> a famous baseball player someday.

→ ________________

40 Mr. Park <u>plays</u> golf last Sunday.

→ ________________________

41 다음 글에서 밑줄 친 말을 어법상 바르게 고치시오.

> Jenny (1) <u>is</u> sick two years ago. She was in hospital at that time. But, she is healthy now. She (2) <u>go</u> jogging every morning nowadays.

(1) ________________
(2) ________________

42~43 Ted의 내일 일정표를 보고, 다음 질문에 알맞은 답을 쓰시오.

8 a.m.	go to the library
12 p.m.	have lunch with Sam
3 p.m.	play basketball
6 p.m.	go to the shopping mall

42 What is Ted going to do at 12 p.m. tomorrow?

→ ________________________________

43 Will Ted go to the shopping mall at 3 p.m. tomorrow?

→ No, he won't. He ____________________
________________________________.

44 다음 그림을 보고, 괄호 안의 단어를 빈칸에 알맞은 형태로 쓰시오.

> Emily and her family __________ (go) camping yesterday. Her father was making lunch at noon. Her mother __________ __________ (drink) a cup of coffee. Her brother __________ __________ __________ __________ (fly, a kite). Emily __________ (stop) and got off her bike. She enjoyed the beautiful view.

45 괄호 안의 단어를 빈칸에 알맞은 형태로 써서 다음 글을 완성하시오.

> Jake ________ (be) in Hawaii last year. He ________ (take) a surfing class there. He practiced surfing very hard. He ________ (be) good at surfing now. He ____________ (take) part in the surfing competition next year.

46~48 우리말과 같은 뜻이 되도록 괄호 안의 단어를 이용하여 문장을 완성하시오.

46

> Peter는 새 차를 사지 않을 것이다.
> (be going to, a new car, buy)

____

47

> Jane은 매해 여름마다 해변에 간다.
> (the beach, go to, every summer)

____

48

> Tom은 지금 아빠의 사무실로 가고 있는 중이니?
> (go to, now, his dad's office)

____

49~50 다음 글을 읽고, 질문에 답하시오.

> Emma ⓐ <u>is</u> seven years old. She ⓑ <u>likes</u> chocolate so much. She ⓒ <u>eat</u> chocolate chip cookies yesterday. Now, she ⓓ <u>is making</u> hot chocolate with her sister. She is going to ⓔ <u>baking</u> chocolate muffins tomorrow.

49 ⓐ~ⓔ 중 어법상 <u>어색한</u> 곳을 두 군데 찾아 바르게 고치시오.

(1) ________ → ____________

(2) ________ → ____________

50 What is Emma making with her sister now?

→ ____________________

CHAPTER

04 조동사

Unit 01 can
Unit 02 be able to
Unit 03 may
Unit 04 can과 바꿔 쓸 수 있는 조동사
Unit 05 must
Unit 06 have to
Unit 07 should

UNIT 01 can

조동사 can은 '~할 수 있다'라는 의미 말고도 다양한 의미를 나타낼 수 있음을 기억하세요.

능력	I can swim.	요청	Can you wait?
가능	I can help you.	추측	He can be busy.
허가	You can stay here.	금지	You cannot stay here.

주의 can의 부정형은 cannot 또는 can't로 써야 해요. *cann't (×)

참고 can의 의문문은 〈Can+주어+동사원형 ~?〉의 어순으로 표현해요.

|A| 다음 문장의 밑줄 친 can(not)의 의미를 |보기|에서 골라 그 번호를 쓰시오.

|보기|
ⓐ 능력 ⓑ 가능 ⓒ 허가 ⓓ 요청 ⓔ 추측 ⓕ 금지

01 I can speak English. ________

02 I can take care of it. ________

03 You can use my pen. ________

04 Can you turn off the TV? ________

05 She can play the piano. ________

06 You can go now. ________

07 Mike can jump high. ________

08 You cannot use your phone today. ________

09 Can you open the door? ________

10 You cannot park a car here. ________

11 It can be difficult. ________

12 Can you pass me the salt? ________

13 It can be dangerous. ________

14 We can wait for you. ________

|B| 괄호 안의 동사와 can 또는 can't를 이용하여 다음 문장을 완성하시오.

01 I'm very tried, but I ________________. (sleep)

02 My brother is studying in America. He ________________ English. (speak)

03 You ________________ the desk alone. I'll help you. (move)

04 I'm sorry. I ________________ to your party. (come)

05 ____________ you ____________ the window? (open)

06 ____________ I ____________ the menu? (see)

07 Be careful! The soup ________________ very hot. (be)

내신기출 다음 중 밑줄 친 Can의 의미가 다른 하나는?

① Can I try on this skirt?
② Can he speak English?
③ Can you play soccer well?

실전 TIP
Can I ~?는 '내가 ~해도 될까?'의 의미로 사용할 수 있어요.

UNIT 02 be able to

능력이나 가능을 나타내는 〈be able to+동사원형〉은 조동사 can과 바꾸어 쓸 수 있어야 해요.

긍정문	현재	I am able to swim.	→ I can swim.
	과거	I was able to swim.	→ I could swim.
	미래	I will be able to swim.	–
부정문		I am not able to swim.	→ I cannot[can't] swim.
의문문		Are you able to swim?	→ Can you swim?

참고 be는 주어의 인칭과 수에 맞추고, to 뒤에는 항상 동사원형을 써야 해요.

주의 can을 be able to로 바꿀 때, 주어의 인칭 및 시제에 맞게 be동사를 고쳐 써야 해요.

|A| 다음 두 문장이 같은 뜻이 되도록 be able to를 이용하여 빈칸에 알맞은 말을 쓰시오.

01 I can dance. = I ______________________.

02 She can play the violin. = She ______________________ the violin.

03 He can't drive a car. = He ______________________ a car.

04 Can you speak Spanish? = ______________________ Spanish?

05 The little boy can read. = The little boy ______________________.

06 Can you come early? = ______________________ early?

07 You can't win the game. = You ______________________ the game.

08 Can she solve this problem? = ______________________ this problem?

|B| 다음 문장을 괄호 안의 지시대로 바꾸어 쓰시오.

01 We will be able to catch the bus. (의문문으로) → ______________________

02 She is able to finish it. (미래시제로) → ______________________

03 The baby is able to walk. (부정문으로) → ______________________

04 He is able to fix it. (can을 이용한 의문문으로) → ______________________

05 I will be able to do it. (부정문으로) → ______________________

06 Are you able to get it? (과거시제로) → ______________________

UNIT 03 may

조동사 may의 3가지 의미를 기억해 두세요.

추측	~일지도 모른다	The story may be true. The story may not be true.
허가	~해도 된다, ~해도 될까요?	You may come in. May I borrow your umbrella?
금지	~하면 안 된다	You may not come in.

주의 may의 부정형은 may not으로 쓰고, 축약하지 않아요.

|A| 다음 문장의 밑줄 친 may (not)이 추측, 허가, 금지 중 어떤 의미인지 쓰시오.

01 May I come in? ____________

02 She may be sick. ____________

03 You may come by 7. ____________

04 He may be angry. ____________

05 You may not park here. ____________

06 Sam may be busy. ____________

07 You may not watch TV. ____________

08 May I ask a question? ____________

09 He may be 14 years old. ____________

10 May I use your umbrella? ____________

11 It may be true. ____________

12 Jenny may go out. ____________

13 You may not sit here. ____________

14 He may not be home. ____________

15 You may borrow the book. ____________

16 It may rain or snow today. ____________

|B| 다음 우리말과 같은 뜻이 되도록 괄호 안의 단어와 may를 이용하여 문장을 완성하시오.

01 너는 집에 일찍 가도 된다. (go home, early) ____________

02 제가 당신의 펜을 사용해도 될까요? (use, your pen) ____________

03 내일은 추울지도 모른다. (be cold) ____________

04 그는 오늘 오지 않을지도 모른다. (come) ____________

05 이 고양이는 배가 고플지도 모른다. (be hungry) ____________

06 제가 오늘 밤에 외출해도 될까요? (go out, tonight) ____________

07 그녀는 그녀의 방에 있을지도 모른다. (be in her room) ____________

08 너는 내 전화기를 사용해서는 안 된다. (use, my phone) ____________

09 제가 창문을 좀 열어도 될까요? (open, the window) ____________

UNIT 04 can과 바꿔 쓸 수 있는 조동사

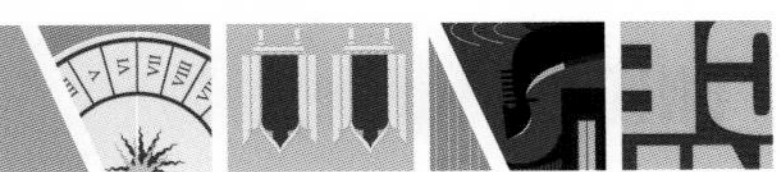

조동사 can은 조동사 may 또는 be able to와 바꾸어 쓸 수 있어야 해요.

추측	~일 수 있다	can=may	The story can be true.
	~일지도 모른다		The story may be true.
허가	~할 수 있다	can=may	You can come in.
	~해도 된다		You may come in.
금지	~할 수 없다	cannot=may not	You cannot come in.
	~하면 안 된다		You may not come in.
능력/가능	~할 수 있다	can=be able to	I can swim. I am able to swim.

A 다음 문장의 밑줄 친 부분의 의미를 |보기|에서 골라 그 번호를 쓰시오.

|보기|
ⓐ 추측　ⓑ 허가　ⓒ 금지　ⓓ 능력 / 가능

01 You can't leave now. ________
02 She may be wrong. ________
03 You may not sit here. ________
04 He may have the answer. ________
05 My sister is able to play tennis. ________
06 You may not go outside. ________
07 Can you reach the shelf? ________
08 Are they able to read it? ________
09 It can be chilly. ________
10 You may sit down now. ________

B 다음 문장의 밑줄 친 can 또는 can't를 may 또는 be able to를 이용하여 바꾸어 쓸 시오.

01 She can sing really well. → ____________________
02 You can ride my bike. → ____________________
03 They can't eat here. → ____________________
04 It can rain this afternoon. → ____________________
05 You can't lift it alone. → ____________________
06 Can I use your computer? → ____________________
07 It can be a real story. → ____________________

내신기출 다음 중 밑줄 친 부분의 의미가 다른 하나는?

① You can go home now.
② You may use the bathroom.
③ The train may arrive late.

실전 TIP

두 개의 문장은 '허가'의 의미로 사용되었지만, 다른 하나는 '추측'의 의미로 사용했어요.

UNIT 05 must

'~해야 한다'라는 의무나, '~임에 틀림없다'라는 강한 추측을 표현할 때 조동사 must를 쓰세요.

의무	~해야만 한다	We must follow the rules.
금지	~하면 안 된다	You must not tell lies.
강한 추측	~임에 틀림없다	She must be rich.

주의 부정의 강한 추측은 can't[cannot](~일 리가 없다)로 써요.
The story can't be true.

A 다음 문장의 밑줄 친 must (not)이 의무, 금지, 강한 추측 중 어떤 의미인지 쓰시오.

01 I must go there. ____________
02 He must be Paul. ____________
03 Must I wear this hat? ____________
04 You must do it again. ____________
05 You must be hungry. ____________
06 You must not enter. ____________
07 He must be there by 6. ____________
08 My father must be sick. ____________
09 He must be an actor. ____________
10 We must pass the test. ____________
11 You must not run here. ____________
12 You must wear a mask. ____________
13 It must be mine. ____________
14 The man must be busy. ____________
15 You must not touch it. ____________
16 We must be kind to others. ____________

B 다음 괄호 안의 단어와 must (not)을 이용하여 문장을 완성하시오.

must not과 cannot의 용도를 구별해야 해요.

01 He ____________ the exam. (take)
02 It's a red light! You ____________ the street. (cross)
03 She ____________ the book today. (return)
04 You ____________ the door when you go out. (lock)
05 He is waving at you. He ____________ your friend. (be)
06 You ____________ your phone in the theater. (turn on)
07 The engine is very old. It ____________ like this. (sound)
08 He gets up early. He ____________. (hardworking)
09 You ____________ your ID card in this building. (carry)

UNIT 06 have to

have/has to는 의미상 must와 바꾸어 쓰지만, 부정문은 서로 다른 의미인 것에 주의해야 해요.

	have to		must	
긍정문	We have to pay.	~해야 한다 〈의무〉	We must pay.	〈의무〉
부정문	We don't have to pay.	~해야 하는 건 아니다 〈불필요〉	We must not pay.	〈금지〉
의문문	Do we have to pay?	~해야 할까? 〈의무〉	Must we pay?	〈의무〉

주의 주어가 3인칭 단수면 has to로 써야 하며, 과거형(~했어야 했다)은 had to로 써요.

참고 must는 미래형과 과거형이 따로 없으므로, 각각 will have to와 had to로 나타내요.

|A| 우리말과 같은 뜻이 되도록 괄호 안의 단어와 have to를 이용하여 문장을 완성하시오.

01 나는 이 일을 끝내야 한다. (finish) → ______ this work.

02 네가 거기 가야 하는 건 아니다. (go) → ______ there.

03 내가 이 책을 읽어야 할까? (read) → ______ this book?

04 너는 장화를 신을 필요가 없다. (wear) → ______ rain boots.

05 그녀는 신발을 벗어야 했다. (take off) → ______ her shoes.

06 그는 거기 있을 필요가 없다. (be) → ______ there.

07 Tom은 스페인어를 배워야 한다. (learn) → ______ Spanish.

|B| 다음 문장에서 어법상 어색한 곳을 찾아 바르게 고쳐 쓰시오.

01 Do I must go out now?

______ → ______

02 Sam has to arrived here last week.

______ → ______

03 Jenny will has to plan her future.

______ → ______

04 My brother must to lose weight.

______ → ______

05 Jason don't has to be home tonight.

______ → ______

06 He will must answer this question someday.

______ → ______

미래의 의무를 나타낼 때는 will have to를 쓰는데, will은 조동사이므로 주어가 3인칭 단수일 때에도 have의 형태가 바뀌지 않음을 알아두세요.

|C| 우리말과 같은 뜻이 되도록 괄호 안의 단어를 바르게 배열하여 문장을 완성하시오.

01 우리는 2시에 기차를 타야만 한다. (the train / have to / catch)

We ______________________ at two o'clock.

02 너는 지금 당장 거기에 가지 않아도 된다. (don't / go / there / have to)

You ______________________ right now.

03 우리는 의사를 불러야 했다. (the doctor / call / had to)

We ______________________.

04 Bill은 책을 몇 권 사야 한다. (buy / some books / has to)

Bill ______________________.

05 그녀는 오늘 회의에 참석할 필요가 없다. (attend / doesn't / have to / the meeting)

She ______________________ today.

06 Judy는 다시 시험을 봐야 할 것이다. (will / take / have to / the test)

Judy ______________________ again.

|D| 다음 빈칸에 알맞은 말을 |보기|의 단어와 (don't) have to를 이용하여 알맞은 형태로 쓰시오.

|보기|

study work go change make take finish buy

01 I can't meet you today. I ______________________ in the office.

02 You ______________________ a mask. I'll give you one.

03 Today is Sunday. She ______________________ to school.

04 His shirt is dirty. He ______________________ it.

05 It is raining. We ______________________ an umbrella.

06 You ______________________ dinner. We'll go out for dinner.

07 I have a test tomorrow. I ______________________ tonight.

08 Jason is busy. He ______________________ his homework.

내신기출 밑줄 친 must 중 have/has to로 바꿔 쓸 수 없는 것은?

① A nurse must wear a uniform.

② You must be home by 9 p.m.

③ Jessica must be tired by now.

실전 TIP

must가 의무의 의미인지 추측의 의미인지 확인해 보세요.

UNIT 07 should

조동사 should는 '~해야 한다'라는 뜻으로 충고나 제안을 할 때 써요.

긍정문	~해야 한다, ~하는 게 좋겠다	You should wash your hands.
부정문	~하면 안 된다, ~하지 않는 게 좋겠다	You should not[shouldn't] play games too much.
의문문	~해야 하나?, ~하는 게 좋을까?	Should I take the bus? – Yes, you should. / No, you shouldn't.

|A| 다음 문장의 밑줄 친 부분을 어법상 바르게 고치시오.

01 My son should passes the exam. → ______________________

02 You should speak not so loud. → ______________________

03 She shoulds read many books. → ______________________

04 Should the girl wears a skirt? → ______________________

05 He shouldn't goes to bed so late. → ______________________

06 Do we should get there by 6 o'clock? → ______________________

07 We should not are late for class. → ______________________

08 Should I doing my homework by tomorrow? → ______________________

|B| 우리말과 같은 뜻이 되도록 괄호 안의 단어와 should를 이용하여 문장을 완성하시오.

조동사 should 뒤에는 항상 동사원형을 써야 해요.

01 우리는 다른 사람들에게 친절해야 한다. (be kind)

We ______________________ to other people.

02 너는 도서관에서 떠들면 안 된다. (make a noise)

You ______________________ in the library.

03 Jenny는 졸리다. 그녀는 자야 한다. (go)

Jenny is sleepy. She ______________________ to bed.

04 밖이 너무 춥다. 너는 코트를 입어야 한다. (wear)

It's too cold outside. You ______________________ your coat.

05 시간은 금이다. 너는 그것을 낭비해서는 안 된다. (waste)

Time is gold. You ______________________ it.

06 A: 그녀는 다른 일자리를 찾아야 하나요? B: 아니요, 그렇지 않아요. (look for)

A: ______________ another job? B: No, ______________.

중간고사·기말고사 실전문제

객관식 (01~25) / 주관식 (26~50)

학년과 반 | 이름 | 객관식 / 25문항 | 주관식 / 25문항

01~03 우리말과 같은 뜻이 되도록 빈칸에 알맞은 말을 고르시오.

01

그 동물은 암벽을 오를 수 있다.
The animal ________ climb up the rock face.

① is ② must
③ will ④ should
⑤ can

02

너는 쉽게 포기하지 않는 게 좋겠다.
You ________ give up easily.

① must ② may
③ shouldn't ④ cannot
⑤ don't have to

03

내가 숙제하는 것 좀 도와줄 수 있니?
________ you help me with my homework?

① Can ② May
③ Should ④ Have to
⑤ Must

04~05 다음 빈칸에 들어갈 수 없는 말을 고르시오.

04

Tom must ________ for his health.

① take a walk ② eat vegetables
③ get some rest ④ see a doctor
⑤ exercises more

05

My brother ________ apologize to me.

① must ② have to
③ should ④ can
⑤ may

06~07 다음 밑줄 친 말과 바꿔 쓸 수 있는 말을 고르시오.

06

They could reach the finish line.

① had to ② are able to
③ should ④ were able to
⑤ was able to

07

He must be nice to his classmates.

① can ② have ③ will
④ have to ⑤ has to

08~10 다음 우리말을 영어로 바르게 옮긴 것을 고르시오.

08

내가 그에게 먼저 전화하는 게 좋을까?

① May I call him first?
② Should I call him first?
③ Can I call him first?
④ Do I call him first?
⑤ Could I call him first?

09

그 남자아이는 중학생이 아닐지도 모른다.

① The boy isn't a middle school student.
② The boy mays not be a middle school student.
③ The boy doesn't may be a middle school student.
④ The boy may not be a middle school student.
⑤ The boy must not be a middle school student.

10

그 회사는 목표를 달성할 수 있을 것이다.

① The company will achieve the goal.
② The company can achieve the goal.
③ The company will can achieve the goal.
④ The company will able to achieve the goal.
⑤ The company will be able to achieve the goal.

11~12 다음 대화의 빈칸에 알맞은 말을 고르시오.

11

A: It is going to rain.
B: You __________ take an umbrella.

① don't ② cannot
③ should ④ may not
⑤ don't have to

12

A: My best friend moved to China.
B: You __________ miss her very much.

① must ② should
③ have to ④ can't
⑤ must not

13~14 다음 빈칸에 공통으로 알맞은 말을 고르시오.

13

• She isn't in her room. She __________ be on the second floor.
• You look sick today. You __________ have a break.

① have to ② may
③ should ④ must not
⑤ will be able to

14

• The man always wears expensive clothes. He __________ be rich.
• I have a test tomorrow. I __________ study tonight.

① may not ② have to
③ could ④ must
⑤ cannot

15 다음 중 빈칸에 may[May]를 쓸 수 없는 것은?

① The man __________ be my new teacher.
② __________ you lend me your pencil?
③ It __________ not be a bad suggestion.
④ You __________ not come to school today.
⑤ The boys __________ be very excited.

16 다음 밑줄 친 부분을 어법상 바르게 고친 것으로 알맞지 않은 것은?

① He must angry because of me. (→ must be angry)
② We should not taking pictures here. (→ take)
③ Children has to read a lot of books. (→ have to)
④ The engineer will can fix the machine. (→ will able to)
⑤ My brother can solves the difficult problem. (→ solve)

17~19 다음 중 어법상 어색한 것을 고르시오.

17 ① Is he able to lift the sofa?
② Could you bring me some water?
③ He doesn't must go there tomorrow.
④ They may attend the meeting.
⑤ You shouldn't lie to your teacher.

18 ① She cannot drive a car.
② May I use your computer?
③ We must come back home.
④ You can visit the palace on weekdays.
⑤ He should cleans his room.

19 ① My brother can speak English well.
② He must checks his email.
③ The teacher may not know the answer.
④ Can you turn off the light?
⑤ You should be quiet in the classroom.

20~21 다음 중 밑줄 친 부분의 쓰임이 다른 것을 고르시오.

20 ① Can I have some water?
② You can wear my shirt.
③ He can read Chinese characters well.
④ He can get some rest in my room.
⑤ Can we have some more?

21 ① Jane has a problem. She must talk to her teacher.
② She often wears something black. She must like black.
③ I must go now. My sister is waiting for me.
④ You broke the vase. You must pay for it.
⑤ Jim can't join us today. He must study late.

22 다음 중 밑줄 친 can을 is able to로 바꿔 쓸 수 없는 것은?

① A cat can see well in the dark.
② He can lift the desk with one hand.
③ The man can run 100m in ten seconds.
④ You can stay with us a little longer.
⑤ She can stay under water for five minutes.

23 다음 중 밑줄 친 must를 have/has to로 바꿔 쓸 수 없는 것은?

① The players must stand in line.
② You must stop at the red light.
③ Bill must wash the dishes tonight.
④ I must return these books to the library.
⑤ He must feel terrible because of a headache.

24 다음 중 어법상 어색한 문장의 개수는?

- She is able to speaks Italian well.
- We don't have to go to the hospital.
- You should not play soccer today.
- The boy and the girl has to take an entrance exam.

① 없음　② 1개
③ 2개　④ 3개
⑤ 4개

25 어법상 올바른 문장끼리 바르게 짝지어진 것은?

(a) Susan must practice the piano for the test.
(b) He can sing well, but he can't dances.
(c) Could you please bring my book?
(d) May I use this phone? – I'm sorry, you may.
(e) Should I sit here? – No, you shouldn't.

① (a), (c)　② (b), (c)
③ (c), (d), (e)　④ (a), (b), (d)
⑤ (a), (c), (e)

26~28 다음 문장에서 어법상 어색한 부분을 찾아 바르게 고치시오.

26 The boy cannot does his homework for himself.

__________ → __________

27 Does she has to follow the rules?

__________ → __________

28 Amber mays be hungry and tired.

__________ → __________

29~30 다음 대화의 빈칸에 알맞은 말을 쓰시오.

29

A: I'd like to ask you something. ________ ________ ________ ________ tonight?
B: Yes, you may. I will wait for your call.

30

A: ________ ________ ________ red?
B: No, they can't. Dogs can see only yellow and blue.

31~33 우리말과 같은 뜻이 되도록 조동사와 괄호 안의 단어를 이용하여 문장을 완성하시오.

31

그는 그의 약속을 잊어서는 안 된다. (forget)

He ________________ his promise.

32

너는 아침 식사를 준비할 필요가 없다. (prepare)

You ________________ breakfast.

33

James는 Tom보다 더 빨리 뛸 수 있니? (run)

Is James ________________ faster than Tom?

34~35 다음 대화의 빈칸에 알맞은 말을 괄호 안의 단어를 이용하여 쓰시오.

34

A: It's already eight o'clock. It's time to go to school.
B: Today is a holiday. You ________________ to school. (have to, go)

35

A: Are you going to throw a party for Jane?
B: Yes, but you ________________ her. It's a surprise party. (must, tell)

36~37 다음 두 문장이 같은 뜻이 되도록 빈칸에 알맞은 말을 쓰시오.

36

She must be kind to customers.

= She ________________ kind to customers.

37

They could play in the finals last year.

= They ________________ in the finals last year.

38~40 **우리말과 같은 뜻이 되도록 괄호 안의 단어를 바르게 배열하시오.**

38
> 제가 여러분께 제 소개를 해도 될까요?
> (can / myself / I / introduce)

______________________ to you?

39
> 너는 이 건물 앞에 주차해서는 안 된다.
> (park / you / not / in front of / must)

______________________ this building.

40
> 그는 전화를 잘못 걸었을지도 모른다.
> (the wrong number / have / may)

He ______________________________.

41~43 **다음 표를 보고, 대화를 완성하시오.**

	Tony	Becky
the flute	○	×
the violin	×	○
the guitar	○	○

41 A: What musical instrument can Tony play?
B: He ________________________.

42 A: Can Becky play the flute?
B: __________, she __________.

43 A: Who can play the guitar?
B: ____________________ the guitar.

44~45 **우리말과 같은 뜻이 되도록 괄호 안의 단어를 이용하여 문장을 완성하시오.**

44
> 아이들은 이 구역에 들어오면 안 됩니다.
> (into, come, may, children)

____________________ this area.

45
> 우리가 파티에 가야 할까?
> (have to, go, we)

____________________ to the party?

46~48 **다음 글을 읽고, 어법상 <u>어색한</u> 부분을 <u>세 군데</u> 찾아 바르게 고치시오.**

> Tom and I are going to go swimming this Saturday. I thought I should checking the pool safety rules before we go. So I looked them up on the Internet.
> 1. We should take a shower before entering the pool.
> 2. We not must run on the slippery floor.
> 3. We must not dive into the pool.
> 4. We can to use the kickboards for free.

46 ____________ → ____________

47 ____________ → ____________

48 ____________ → ____________

49~50 **다음 우리말을 주어진 |조건|에 맞게 영어로 바르게 쓰시오.**

49 고객들은 다음 주에 그 신형 스마트폰을 살 수 있을 것이다.

|조건|
1. Customers로 시작할 것
2. 단어 will, buy, the new smartphone을 사용할 것
3. 9 단어로 쓸 것

→ ________________________________

next week.

50 우리는 그 상점을 방문할 필요가 없었다.

|조건|
1. We로 시작할 것
2. 단어 the store, visit, have to를 사용할 것
3. 7 단어로 쓸 것

→ ________________________________

CHAPTER

05 명사와 관사

Unit 01 셀 수 있는 명사와 부정관사 a(n)
Unit 02 셀 수 있는 명사의 규칙 복수형 1
Unit 03 셀 수 있는 명사의 규칙 복수형 2
Unit 04 셀 수 있는 명사의 불규칙 복수형
Unit 05 셀 수 없는 명사
Unit 06 셀 수 없는 명사의 수량 표현
Unit 07 정관사 the
Unit 08 관사의 생략
Unit 09 There is/are
Unit 10 There is/are의 부정문과 의문문

UNIT 01 셀 수 있는 명사와 부정관사 a(n)

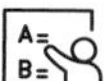

셀 수 있는 명사가 하나(단수 명사)면, 명사 앞에 부정관사 a(n)를 붙여야 해요.

	a+첫 발음이 자음인 명사	an+첫 발음이 모음인 명사	주의
부정관사 +명사	a house a week [wiːk] a university [jùːnəvə́ːrsəti]	an eraser an umbrella an hour [aʊər]	명사의 첫 발음에 맞춤
부정관사 +형용사+명사	a white [wait] eraser a red umbrella	an honest [ɑ́nist] boy an old movie	명사를 수식하는 형용사의 첫 발음에 맞춤

참고 a(n)의 의미를 알아 두세요.
1. 막연한 하나: He is a doctor.
2. 하나의 (one): She has a dog and two cats.
3. ~마다 (per): I go swimming twice a week.

|A| 다음 빈칸에 알맞은 부정관사를 쓰시오.

01 ______________ car
02 ______________ egg
03 ______________ umbrella
04 ______________ desk
05 ______________ orange
06 ______________ black cat
07 ______________ apple
08 ______________ old horse
09 ______________ house
10 ______________ hour
11 ______________ honest person
12 ______________ white shirt

|B| 우리말과 같은 뜻이 되도록 괄호 안의 단어와 알맞은 부정관사를 이용하여 문장을 완성하시오.

01 우리는 영어 수업이 일주일에 다섯 번 있다. (week)
We have five English classes ______________.

02 버스 정류장에 여자가 한 명 있다. 그녀는 버스를 기다리고 있다. (woman, bus)
There is ______________ at the bus stop. She is waiting for ______________.

03 코끼리는 동물이다. 그것은 큰 동물이다. (elephant, big animal)
______________ is an animal. It's ______________.

04 우리 가족은 한 달에 한 번 영화를 보러 갔다. (month)
My family went to the movies once ______________.

05 나는 내 방에 작은 침대 한 개와 오래된 책상 한 개가 있다. (small bed, old desk)
I have ______________ and ______________ in my room.

06 소파 위에 고양이 한 마리가 있다. 그것은 어린 고양이다. (cat, young cat)
There is ______________ on the sofa. She is ______________.

UNIT 02 셀 수 있는 명사의 규칙 복수형 1

셀 수 있는 명사가 둘 이상(복수 명사)이면, 부정관사 a(n)를 빼고 명사 뒤에 -s를 써서 복수형으로 만드세요.

단수 명사				복수 명사			
a chair	a house	a book	a picture	chairs	houses	books	pictures
an ant	an orange	an hour	an artist	ants	oranges	hours	artists

|A| 우리말과 같은 뜻이 되도록 괄호 안의 단어와 알맞은 부정관사를 이용하여 빈칸에 알맞은 말을 쓰시오.

01 계란들 (egg) ________________

02 나무 한 그루 (tree) ________________

03 책들 (book) ________________

04 별들 (star) ________________

05 의자 하나 (chair) ________________

06 연필들 (pencil) ________________

07 차 한 대 (car) ________________

08 학생들 (student) ________________

09 개미들 (ant) ________________

10 집 한 채 (house) ________________

11 한 시간 (hour) ________________

12 그림들 (picture) ________________

13 책상들 (desk) ________________

14 새들 (bird) ________________

15 소녀들 (girl) ________________

16 동물 한 마리 (animal) ________________

|B| 괄호 안의 단어를 빈칸에 알맞은 형태로 쓰시오.

> 명사 앞에 수량을 나타내는 표현이 있으면, 〈명사+-s〉 형태의 복수 명사로 써야 해요.

01 I took a lot of ________________ there. (picture)

02 New ________________ are very expensive. (car)

03 I know a kind ________________. (teacher)

04 My mom baked some sweet ________________. (cookie)

05 Sam gave me ten ________________ on my birthday. (rose)

06 Mr. Kim saw three ________________ in the playground. (girl)

07 There is ________________ at the bus stop. (student)

08 She has to finish the work in two ________________. (hour)

09 He has two ________________ and a ________________. (son, daughter)

10 We have a ________________, two eyes, two ________________, and a mouth. (nose, ear)

11 I had a ________________ and two ________________ for lunch. (hamburger, apple)

12 I bought an ________________ and two ________________. (eraser, pencil)

UNIT 03 셀 수 있는 명사의 규칙 복수형 2

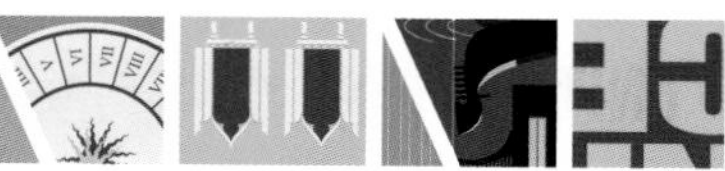

명사의 복수형을 만드는 다음의 규칙을 알아 두세요.

대부분의 명사	-s	kitchen – kitchens	building – buildings
-s, -x, -ch, -sh로 끝나는 명사	-es	bus – buses bench – benches	box – boxes dish – dishes
자음+o로 끝나는 명사	-es	potato – potatoes (예외) piano – pianos	hero – heroes photo – photos
자음+y로 끝나는 명사	y를 없애고 -ies	baby – babies country – countries	city – cities story – stories
-f, -fe로 끝나는 명사	f(e)를 v로 바꾸고 -es	wolf – wolves knife – knives (예외) roof – roofs	shelf – shelves leaf – leaves chef – chefs

다음 명사의 복수형을 쓰면서 외우시오.

01 piano (피아노) – ____________

02 story (이야기) – ____________

03 bus (버스) – ____________

04 clock (시계) – ____________

05 roof (지붕) – ____________

06 guitar (기타) – ____________

07 basket (바구니) – ____________

08 dish (접시) – ____________

09 tomato (토마토) – ____________

10 box (상자) – ____________

11 leaf (나뭇잎) – ____________

12 finger (손가락) – ____________

13 brush (붓) – ____________

14 shelf (책꽂이) – ____________

15 watch (손목시계) – ____________

16 key (열쇠) – ____________

17 knife (칼) – ____________

18 class (수업) – ____________

19 store (가게) – ____________

20 fox (여우) – ____________

21 zoo (동물원) – ____________

22 dress (드레스) – ____________

23 wolf (늑대) – ____________

24 photo (사진) – ____________

25 hero (영웅) – ____________

26 knife (칼) – ____________

27 baby (아기) – ____________

28 chicken (닭) – ____________

29 fly (파리) – ____________

30 potato (감자) – ____________

31 city (도시) – ____________

32 radio (라디오) – ____________

33 horse (말) – ____________

34 bench (벤치) – ____________

35 chef (요리사, 주방장) – ____________

36 church (교회) – ____________

UNIT 04 셀 수 있는 명사의 불규칙 복수형

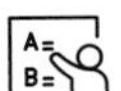 명사의 복수형이 불규칙인 경우에는 무조건 외워야 해요.

단 · 복수 형태가 다른 명사	man – men tooth – teeth child – children	woman – women foot – feet mouse – mice	person – people goose – geese ox – oxen
단 · 복수 형태가 같은 명사	sheep – sheep	deer – deer	salmon – salmon

|A| 다음 명사의 복수형을 쓰면서 외우시오.

01 sheep (양) – ____________

02 woman (여자) – ____________

03 goose (거위) – ____________

04 child (아이) – ____________

05 ox (황소) – ____________

06 foot (발) – ____________

07 deer (사슴) – ____________

08 mouse (쥐) – ____________

09 tooth (이, 치아) – ____________

10 man (남자) – ____________

11 salmon (연어) – ____________

12 person (사람) – ____________

|B| 다음 우리말과 같은 뜻이 되도록, 어법상 어색한 부분을 찾아 바르게 고치시오.

01 The movie has three different story. (그 영화는 세 개의 다른 이야기들을 가지고 있다.)

____________ → ____________

02 Some presents were in the box. (상자들 안에는 선물들이 몇 개 있었다.)

____________ → ____________

03 Girls are different from boy. (여자아이들은 남자아이들과는 다르다.)

____________ → ____________

04 The farmer has many sheeps in his farm. (그 농부는 농장에 양들이 많다.)

____________ → ____________

05 Chefs usually make the dish with some potato. (요리사들은 주로 감자 몇 개로 그 요리를 만든다.)

____________ → ____________

06 Many family spend time outside in summer. (많은 가족들이 여름에 밖에서 시간을 보낸다.)

____________ → ____________

내신 기출 다음 중 어법상 어색한 것은?

His two foot were dirty after the long walk.
① two foot ② dirty ③ after ④ the long walk

실전 TIP
명사 앞에 two가 있으므로 복수 명사가 따라와야 해요.

UNIT 05 셀 수 없는 명사

셀 수 없는 명사는 부정관사 a(n)를 붙이지 않고, 항상 단수형으로 쓴다는 데에 유의하세요.

추상명사	형체 없이 추상적인 개념 또는 감정	love, hope, advice, information, peace, beauty, truth 등
고유명사	사람, 지명, 월, 요일 등 고유의 이름	BTS, Tom, Suji, Korea, Seoul, April, Sunday 등
물질명사	나누어 셀 수 없는 물질	water, air, snow, rain, coffee, cheese, butter, bread, paper, flour, sugar, salt, pepper, rice, hair 등

주의 고유명사의 첫 글자는 항상 대문자로 써야 해요.

|A| 다음 중 셀 수 없는 명사를 골라 동그라미 하시오.

01	love	car	Korea	bird	help	water
02	cat	Jack	peace	father	job	honesty
03	chair	girl	Seoul	book	advice	truth
04	flower	tree	Emily	sugar	coffee	America
05	snow	paper	pencil	class	house	beauty
06	sister	man	April	family	rain	joy
07	Paris	student	air	money	time	rose
08	bread	hair	child	hat	wallet	information

|B| 다음 문장에서 어법상 어색한 부분에 밑줄 긋고 바르게 고치시오.

01 I'll give you an information. → ____________________

02 Would you like some coffees? → ____________________

03 My mother needs flours for cookies. → ____________________

04 My hometown is a Seoul. → ____________________

05 He bought some sugars yesterday. → ____________________

06 Tony drinks waters in the morning. → ____________________

07 My brother likes a cheese very much. → ____________________

08 The woman is a Jessica. → ____________________

09 Sally and I believe in a true love. → ____________________

UNIT 06 셀 수 없는 명사의 수량 표현

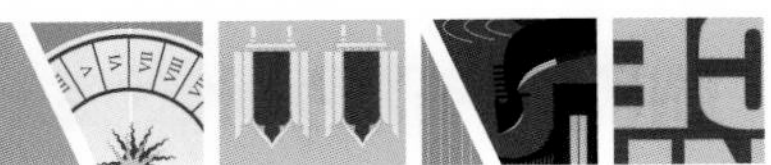

셀 수 없는 명사는 용기나 단위를 이용하여 셀 수 있다는 점을 알아 두세요.

a piece of	~ 한 조각	cake, pizza, bread, paper, advice, information, furniture
a glass of	~ 한 잔	water, juice, milk (주로 찬 음료)
a cup of	~ 한 컵	tea, coffee (주로 따뜻한 음료)
a slice of	~ (얇게 썬) 한 조각	cheese, bread, meat
a bottle of	~ 한 병	water, juice, milk
a bowl of	~ 한 그릇	rice, salad

주의 2개 이상일 경우, 용기나 단위를 나타내는 명사를 복수형으로 만들어야 해요.
two pieces of paper 종이 두 장 / three glasses of milk 우유 세 잔

참고 항상 복수로 쓰는 두 개가 한 쌍을 이루는 명사는 pair로 셀 수 있어요.
a pair of shoes, two pairs of glasses, three pairs of pants, some pairs of gloves

|A| 우리말과 같은 뜻이 되도록 빈칸에 알맞은 말을 쓰시오.

01 물 한 잔 ______________ water

02 신발 한 켤레 ______________ shoes

03 주스 한 병 ______________ juice

04 밥 한 그릇 ______________ rice

05 커피 네 컵 ______________ coffee

06 피자 세 조각 ______________ pizza

07 얇은 햄 한 조각 ______________ ham

08 수프 두 그릇 ______________ soup

|B| 우리말과 같은 뜻이 되도록 괄호 안의 단어와 |보기|의 말을 이용하여 문장을 완성하시오.

pair, cup, glass, bottle, piece의 복수형을 알아 두세요.

|보기|
pair　　cup　　glass　　bottle　　piece

01 너는 차 한 컵 마시고 싶니? (tea)
Do you want ______________________?

02 그가 나에게 양말 다섯 켤레를 주었다. (socks)
He gave ______________________ to me.

03 식탁 위에 치즈 케이크 두 조각이 있다. (cheese cake)
There are ______________________ on the table.

04 그녀는 오렌지 주스 세 병을 주문했다. (orange juice)
She ordered ______________________.

05 Jessica는 보통 아침에 토스트 한 조각을 먹는다. (toast)
Jessica usually eats ______________________ in the morning.

UNIT 07 정관사 the

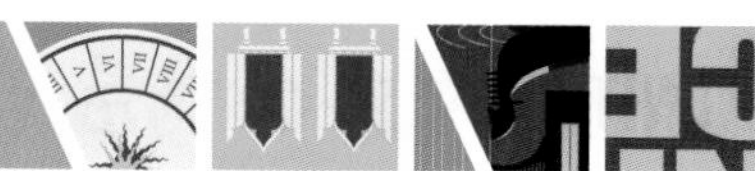

특정한 것을 가리킬 때는 명사 앞에 '그'라는 의미의 정관사 the를 쓰세요.

앞에 나왔던 명사를 가리킬 때	I have a pen. The pen is red.
서로 무엇을 말하는지 알고 있을 때	Could you open the door?
수식을 받아 무엇인지 분명할 때	The flowers on the table are roses.
관용적으로 the를 붙이는 경우	the sun, the moon, the earth, the sky, the Internet

참고 태양, 달 등 단 하나뿐인 것 앞에는 the를 붙여요.

|A| 다음 빈칸에 a(n)이나 the 중 알맞은 말을 쓰시오.

01 Will you open __________ window?

02 Can I use __________ blanket on the sofa?

03 The earth moves around __________ sun.

04 He is __________ baseball player and his sister is __________ artist.

05 She bought a new coat. __________ coat was very warm.

|B| 다음 문장의 밑줄 친 the의 쓰임과 같은 것을 |보기|에서 골라 그 번호를 쓰시오.

|보기|
ⓐ I have a dog. The dog is black and white.
ⓑ The sun rises in the east.
ⓒ The vase on the desk is from China.
ⓓ Will you close the window?

01 The chocolates in the box are very delicious. __________

02 Turn off the light and close the door. __________

03 I bought a book this morning. The book is in my bag. __________

04 We looked up at the stars in the sky. __________

05 We live in an old house. The house has a garden. __________

06 The moon is full now. It's beautiful. __________

내신 기출 다음 빈칸에 들어갈 말이 다른 하나는?

① I have a cat. __________ cat is very cute.
② I keep a diary four times __________ week.
③ __________ man on the bench is my father.

실전 TIP
부정관사가 들어가야 할지, 정관사가 들어가야 할지 파악하세요.

UNIT 08 관사의 생략

다음의 경우에는 명사 앞에 아무 관사도 쓰지 않아야 해요.

식사, 운동 종목, 과목	breakfast, lunch, dinner / soccer, basketball / math, history have breakfast / play soccer / learn history
교통수단	by car / by bus / by subway / on foot
본래의 용도대로 이용	go to bed 잠자리에 들다 / go to school 등교하다 / go to work 출근하다

A 다음 빈칸에 a(n)이나 the 중 알맞은 말을 쓰고, 관사가 필요하지 않으면 ×를 쓰시오.

01 I play ________ baseball every Saturday.

02 Many people use ________ Internet.

03 She had a sandwich for ________ lunch.

04 Do you have ________ pet at home?

05 I didn't go to ________ school yesterday.

06 He went to school by ________ bus.

07 I had ________ breakfast.

08 We came here on ________ foot.

09 We eat out once ________ week.

10 I like this hotel. ________ hotel is clean.

11 Judy studies ________ math every day.

12 Please pass me ________ salt.

B 다음 문장에서 어법상 어색한 부분을 찾아 밑줄 긋고 바르게 고치시오.

01 Could you pass me sugar? → ________

02 Jason didn't go to the work because of a high fever. → ________

03 The students go to school on the feet. → ________

04 Jessica likes to play a piano. → ________

05 My parents went out for a dinner. → ________

06 He wants to buy MP3 player. → ________

07 She is good at the tennis. → ________

08 I had three classes; the music, history, and math. → ________

09 You have to go to a university for four years. → ________

교통수단을 의미할 때는 전치사 뒤에 단수 명사가 오는 점에 유의해야 해요.

실전 TIP

관사를 쓰지 않는 경우는 셀 수 없는 명사, 식사, 운동 종목, 과목, 교통수단, 본래의 용도대로 쓸 때예요.

내신기출 다음 중 빈칸에 관사를 필요로 하는 것은?

① I will get there by ________ taxi.

② She goes to ________ bed at ten.

③ My uncle is ________ English teacher.

UNIT 09 There is/are

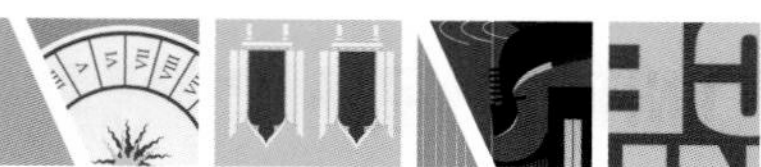

There is/are ~는 '~가/들이 있다'라는 표현으로, 뒤에 쓰는 명사의 수에 맞춰 is 또는 are를 선택하세요.

There is	+ 단수 명사	There is a computer in my room.	현재(~가 있다)
There was		There was water in the bottle.	과거(~가 있었다)
There are	+ 복수 명사	There are some books on your desk.	현재(~들이 있다)
There were		There were many trees in the garden.	과거(~들이 있었다)

주의 셀 수 없는 명사는 항상 단수 취급하므로 There is/was ~로 써야 해요.

|A| 괄호 안에서 알맞은 말을 고르시오.

01 There (is / are) a teddy bear.

02 There (is / are) two cats.

03 There was (salt / a salt).

04 There (was / were) some birds.

05 There (was / were) a newspaper.

06 There (is / are) a dog and a cat.

07 There (was / were) ten eggs.

08 There was some (water / waters).

09 There (was / were) some flowers.

10 There (was / were) useful information.

|B| 다음 우리말과 같은 뜻이 되도록 괄호 안의 단어를 이용하여 문장을 완성하시오.

01 냉장고에 우유가 많이 있다. (much, milk)

____________________ in the refrigerator.

02 도로 위에는 자동차들이 많이 있다. (many, car)

____________________ on the road.

03 땅 위에는 눈이 많이 있었다. (a lot of, snow)

____________________ on the ground.

04 그 집에는 방들이 많이 있었다. (many, room)

____________________ in the house.

05 일 년에는 4계절이 있다. (season)

____________________ in a year.

milk, snow 등의 물질명사는 셀 수 없으므로 단수 취급한다는 점에 유의해야 해요.

내신기출 다음 문장의 빈칸에 들어갈 수 없는 말은?

There are __________ in the kitchen.

① some cups ② some flour ③ some children

실전 TIP

There are ~이므로 빈칸에 단수 명사는 올 수 없어요.

UNIT 10 There is/are의 부정문과 의문문

There is/are ~의 부정문과 의문문은 모두 be동사만 이용하세요.

	형태	예문	참고
긍정문	There+be동사+명사	There was water in the bottle.	
부정문	There+be동사+not+명사	There were not many trees here.	be동사 뒤에 not 추가
의문문	Be동사+there+명사?	Was there a plan B? – Yes, there was. – No, there wasn't.	be동사를 문두에 씀

|A| 괄호 안에서 알맞은 말을 고르시오.

01 There aren't many (apple / apples) in the box.

02 There (isn't / aren't) much sugar in the bottle.

03 There (wasn't / weren't) two birds in the cage.

04 There (wasn't / weren't) a cloud in the sky.

05 A: Is there (a park / parks) near my house? B: Yes, (there is / there are).

06 A: (Is / Are) there four classes in the morning? B: No, (there isn't / there aren't).

07 A: (Was / Were) there a toy on the bed? B: Yes, (there was / there is).

08 A: (Was / Were) there a lot of people in the park? B: No, (there wasn't / there weren't).

|B| 다음 문장을 괄호 안의 지시대로 바꾸시오.

01 There were many eggs in the refrigerator. (부정문으로)

→ ______________________ in the refrigerator.

02 There was a soccer game yesterday. (의문문으로)

→ ______________________ yesterday?

03 Was there a post office near here? (평서문으로)

→ ______________________ near here.

04 There is a lot of snow on the mountain. (과거시제 부정문으로)

→ ______________________ on the mountain.

05 There is an elephant in this zoo. (의문문으로)

→ ______________________ in this zoo?

06 There were many people in the museum. (의문문으로)

→ ______________________ in the museum?

중간고사·기말고사 실전문제

객관식 (01~25) / 주관식 (26~50)

학년과 반 이름 객관식 / 25문항 주관식 / 25문항

01 다음 중 명사의 단수형과 복수형이 바르게 짝지어진 것은?

① boy – boyes
② bench – benchies
③ photo – photos
④ wolf – wolfes
⑤ chef – chefes

02~04 다음 빈칸에 알맞은 말을 고르시오.

02

Where can I buy an ___________?

① ruler ② oranges
③ eraser ④ paintbrush
⑤ green umbrella

03

There are ___________ in the farm.

① goose ② farmer
③ cheese ④ ox
⑤ sheep

04

Jane always carries a ___________ of gloves in her bag.

① slice ② glass ③ piece
④ pair ⑤ bowl

05 다음 대화의 빈칸에 들어갈 말이 순서대로 짝지어지지 않은 것은?

A: Do you have a ___________?
B: Yes, I have two ___________.

① pencil – pencils
② dish – dishes
③ tomato – tomatoes
④ baby – babyes
⑤ knife – knives

06~08 다음 빈칸에 들어갈 수 없는 말을 고르시오.

06

He bought two ___________ at the grocery.

① eggs ② salmon
③ chickens ④ apples
⑤ cheese

07

My brother likes to play the ___________.

① soccer ② game
③ piano ④ flute
⑤ guitar

08

She gave her daughter a ___________.

① candy ② love
③ book ④ bag
⑤ dress

11

• There are ___________ in the room.
• Brush your ___________ three times a day.

① a fly – tooths ② flys – teeth
③ flys – tooths ④ flies – teeth
⑤ flies – tooths

09 다음 중 빈칸에 a가 들어갈 수 있는 문장은?

① I practice ___________ piano every day.
② My husband is working as ___________ teacher.
③ You should not skip ___________ breakfast.
④ ___________ moon is shining in the night.
⑤ ___________ boy on the bench is my classmate.

12~14 밑줄 친 ①~⑤ 중 어법상 어색한 것을 고르시오.

12

The girl(①) and(②) the boy laughed(③) out with(④) happinesses(⑤).

13

Do(①) the(②) boys(③) go to school(④) on the(⑤) foot?

10~11 다음 빈칸에 들어갈 말이 순서대로 짝지어진 것을 고르시오.

10

• Three ___________ stepped on the stage.
• The ___________ are drawing pictures.

① man – child
② mans – childs
③ mans – children
④ men – childs
⑤ men – children

14

People didn't(①) believe(②) that earth(③) is round(④) at(⑤) first.

15~17 다음 우리말을 영어로 바르게 옮긴 것을 고르시오.

15 사슴들이 풀을 뜯어 먹고 있다.

① Deer is feeding on grass.
② Deers is feeding on grass.
③ Deers are feeding on grass.
④ Deer was feeding on grass.
⑤ Deer are feeding on grass.

16 아이들은 농장에서 양 세 마리와 쥐 두 마리를 보았다.

① The children saw three sheep and two mouse in the farm.
② The children saw three sheepes and two mouses in the farm.
③ The children saw three sheep and two mice in the farm.
④ The children saw three sheepes and two mice in the farm.
⑤ The children saw three sheeps and two mices in the farm.

17 그 여자들은 커피 세 컵을 주문했다.

① The woman ordered three cup of coffee.
② The women ordered three cups of coffee.
③ The womans ordered three cups of coffee.
④ The women ordered three cups of coffees.
⑤ The womens ordered three cups of coffees.

18 다음 밑줄 친 부분을 어법상 바르게 고친 것으로 알맞지 않은 것은?

① This book is about the heros of myths. (→ heroes)
② Our hands and foot are freezing. (→ foots)
③ Children should go to the bed early. (→ go to bed)
④ I drank much milks. (→ milk)
⑤ Please get me three piece of cakes from the bakery. (→ three pieces of cake)

19~20 빈칸에 들어갈 말이 나머지와 다른 것을 고르시오.

19 ① Tom is ________ honest boy.
② Why don't we see ________ movie?
③ I will buy ________ backpack.
④ My uncle can drive ________ car very well.
⑤ He goes fishing twice ________ month.

20 ① I am able to play ________ violin.
② Can you please open ________ door?
③ ________ hat in the closet is my father's.
④ Let's go on ________ picnic this Saturday.
⑤ Please hand in your report to ________ teacher.

21~23 다음 중 어법상 어색한 문장을 고르시오.

21 ① I have six classes today.
② There are three sheep in the cage.
③ Can you bring me a piece of paper?
④ We need three bowls of rice.
⑤ I bought two slice of meats at the store.

22 ① They are from London.
② We are going to meet in a March.
③ The room has many pieces of furniture.
④ They put some sugar in their coffee.
⑤ I went to see a doctor because of a headache.

23 ① All I want is love and peace.
② How about eating out for dinner?
③ We can get there by bus in a hour.
④ How many children are there in the playground?
⑤ My uncle and his son often play baseball.

24 다음 중 어법상 어색한 문장의 개수는?

- I am a big fan of BTS.
- He gave me a lot of good advices.
- There is a desk in her room.
- The cheves look so busy in the kitchen.

① 없음 ② 1개
③ 2개 ④ 3개
⑤ 4개

25 어법상 올바른 문장끼리 바르게 짝지어진 것은?

(a) My favorite subject is the science.
(b) Korea is a country famous for *kimchi.*
(c) The special burger has three slices of cheese.
(d) Can you please pass me a salt?
(e) There are three pairs of pant in the washing machine.

① (a), (c) ② (b), (c)
③ (c), (d), (e) ④ (a), (b), (d)
⑤ (a), (c), (e)

26~28 다음 빈칸에 a(n) 또는 the 중에서 알맞은 말을 쓰시오.

26 ___________ spaghetti on the table looks delicious.

27 We go on a field trip twice ___________ year.

28 ________ sun is hot and bright.

29~31 다음 괄호 안에서 알맞은 말을 고르시오.

29 The princess has long and curly (hair / hairs).

30 I saw a dog in the park. (A / The) dog was chasing a cat.

31 There (is / are) some butter in the refrigerator.

32~34 다음 밑줄 친 말을 어법상 바르게 고치시오.

32

The writer wrote a lot of fun <u>story</u> for children.

→ ________

33

There are five <u>ox</u> in his painting.

→ ________

34

My grandpa has some old <u>radio</u>.

→ ________

35~37 다음 문장에서 어법상 어색한 부분을 찾아 바르게 고치시오.

35 There is an university in this city.

________ → ________

36 Will you go there by a subway?

________ → ________

37 I have to get a X-ray tomorrow.

________ → ________

38~40 다음 우리말과 같은 뜻이 되도록 괄호 안의 단어를 바르게 배열하시오.

38

그녀는 케이크 두 조각을 먹었다.
(two / cake / of / pieces)

She ate ______________________.

39

그는 새 안경을 하나 새로 맞춰야 한다.
(pair / glasses / new / of / a)

He needs to get ______________________.

40

연어들은 매년 그 강을 헤엄쳐 오른다.
(river / the / swim up / salmon)

____
every year.

41~42 다음 빈칸에 공통으로 알맞은 말을 쓰시오.

41

- My teacher is wearing a __________ of blue pants.
- There is a __________ of shoes on the shelf.

42

- She is going to buy a __________ of furniture.
- I'd like to give him a __________ of information.

43~45 다음 대화의 빈칸에 알맞은 관사를 쓰고, 관사가 필요 없으면 X를 쓰시오.

43

A: Did you have fun at __________ party last weekend?
B: Yes, I did. It was great.

44

A: This game is not interesting.
B: Let's play __________ different game.

45

A: Thank you for coming. How did you get here?
B: I came by __________ bike.

46~48 다음 글에서 어법상 어색한 곳을 세 군데 찾아 바르게 고치시오.

> I got up at seven this morning. I had a fried egg, a cup of milk and two bananas for breakfast. I go to school by a school bus. When I left home to catch the school bus, my grandma gave me a scarf. I love a scarf because it has many color. I said "Thank you," to her.

46 ____________ → ____________

47 ____________ → ____________

48 ____________ → ____________

49~50 다음 우리말을 주어진 |조건|에 맞게 영어로 바르게 쓰시오.

49 우리는 그 공원에서 많은 사람들과 사슴들을 볼 수 있다.

|조건|
1. We로 시작할 것
2. 단어 many, deer, at을 사용하되 필요시 단어의 형태를 바꿀 것
3. 10 단어로 쓸 것

→ ______________________

50 상자 안에 물 다섯 병이 있다.

|조건|
1. There로 시작할 것
2. 단어 bottle, in, box, be를 사용하되 필요시 단어의 형태를 바꿀 것
3. 9 단어로 쓸 것

→ ______________________

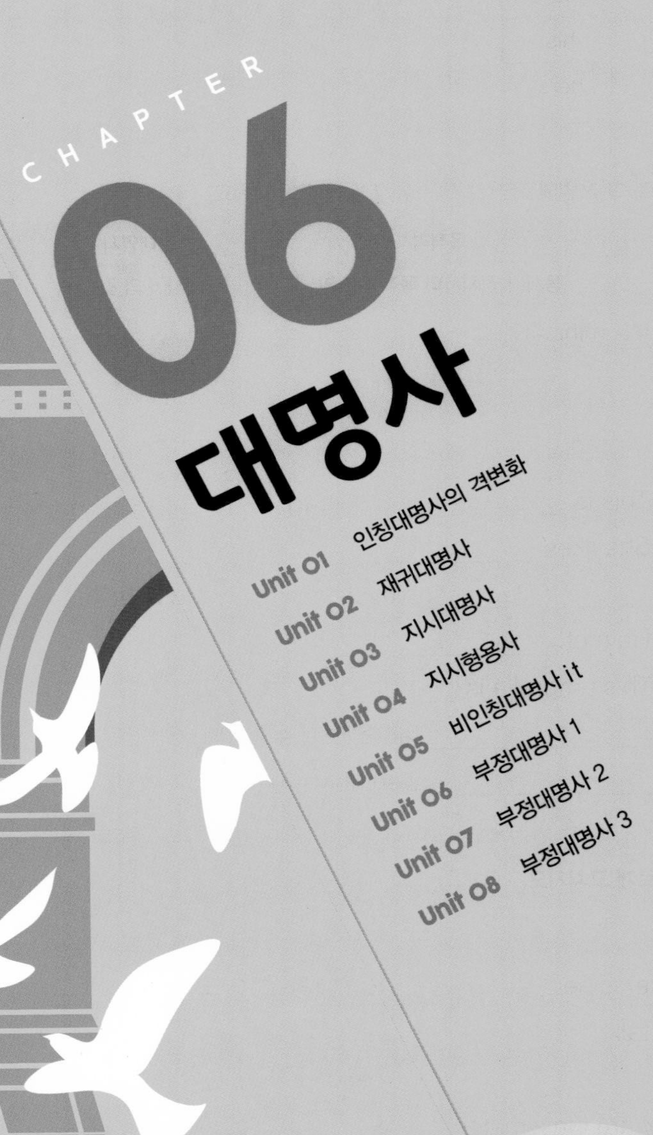

CHAPTER 06

대명사

Unit 01 인칭대명사의 격변화
Unit 02 재귀대명사
Unit 03 지시대명사
Unit 04 지시형용사
Unit 05 비인칭대명사 it
Unit 06 부정대명사 1
Unit 07 부정대명사 2
Unit 08 부정대명사 3

UNIT 01 인칭대명사의 격변화

격에 따른 인칭대명사의 변화를 확인하세요.

	단수				복수			
	주격	소유격	목적격	소유대명사	주격	소유격	목적격	소유대명사
1인칭	I	my	me	mine	we	our	us	ours
2인칭	you	your	you	yours	you	your	you	yours
3인칭	he	his	him	his	they	their	them	theirs
	she	her	her	hers				
	it	its	it	×				

참고 인칭대명사란 사람이나 사물을 가리키는 대명사로, 그 쓰임에 따라 주격, 소유격 등과 같이 나눠요.

격	주격	소유격	목적격	소유대명사
쓰임	주어 자리	명사 앞	동사나 전치사의 목적어 자리	명사(~의 것)

〈소유격+명사〉 = 소유대명사: my book 나의 책 = mine 나의 것

|A| 밑줄 친 말을 알맞은 인칭대명사로 바꾸시오.

01 This is my brother's bag. → This is ________ bag.

02 She likes Tom and me. → She likes ________.

03 Sally's bicycle is strong and light. → ________ bicycle is strong and light.

04 He met Mina and Mike this morning. → He met ________ this morning.

05 This is her umbrella. → This umbrella is ________.

06 The cat's tail is long and black. → ________ tail is long and black.

07 Bill and Sam went there by bus. → ________ went there by bus.

|B| 다음 문장에서 어법상 어색한 부분에 밑줄 긋고 바르게 고치시오.

01 Sally has a cat. The cats name is Tom. → ________

02 The woman is a tennis player. This racket is her. → ________

03 The man over there is Bills uncle. He is tall. → ________

04 This book is yours, not me. → ________

05 Kevin and I go to the same school. They are classmates. → ________

06 We moved into a new house. It's roof is red. → ________

07 I'm going out. You can come with mine. → ________

08 Where is Jessica? I'm looking for she. → ________

not이나 and 등의 접속사 앞뒤로는 같은 격의 단어가 와야 해요.

UNIT 02 재귀대명사

'나 자신', '그녀 자신'과 같은 재귀대명사의 형태를 알아 두세요.

주어		재귀대명사(~ 자신)	주어		재귀대명사(~들 자신)
단수	I	myself	복수	we	ourselves
	you	yourself		you	yourselves
	he	himself		they	themselves
	she	herself			
	it	itself			

재귀대명사를 어떤 경우에 사용하는지 파악하세요.

재귀	주어와 같은 목적어일 때	I love myself. (○) I love me. (×)	목적어이므로 생략 불가
강조	'직접'이라는 의미를 강조할 때	We made the cake (ourselves). We (ourselves) made the cake.	강조 역할로 생략 가능

|A| 다음 우리말과 같은 뜻이 되도록 빈칸에 알맞은 말을 쓰시오.

01 나는 직접 내 방을 청소했다. I ________ cleaned my room.

02 너는 직접 그것을 해야 한다. You must do it ________.

03 그는 혼잣말을 했다. He talked to ________.

04 나는 종종 나 자신을 그린다. I often draw ________.

|B| 다음 문장의 밑줄 친 부분의 쓰임과 같은 것을 |보기|에서 골라 그 번호를 쓰시오.

|보기|
ⓐ She herself went there. ⓑ He likes himself a lot.

01 Mary made the dress herself. ________

02 The cat will look after itself. ________

03 He himself fixed the chair. ________

04 Jason wrote this book himself. ________

05 Let me introduce myself. ________

내신 기출 다음 중 밑줄 친 부분을 생략할 수 없는 것은?

① They talked about themselves.

② We solved the problem ourselves.

③ Did you make this sandwich yourself?

실전 TIP
재귀대명사가 없어도 말이 되는지 안 되는지 확인해 보세요.

UNIT 03 지시대명사

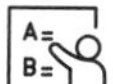

'이것', '저 사람들'과 같이 사람이나 사물을 가리킬 때는 지시대명사를 쓰세요.

가까이 있는 사물이나 사람		멀리 있는 사물이나 사람	
this	these	that	those
이것, 이쪽, 이분	이것들, 이 사람들, 이분들	저것, 저쪽, 저분	저것들, 저 사람들, 저분들
This is a leaf. (이것) This is my teacher. (이분) These are leaves. (이것들)		That is a bird. (저것) Those are birds. (저것들) Those are my friends. (저 사람들)	

A 우리말과 같은 뜻이 되도록 빈칸에 알맞은 말을 쓰시오.

01 이것은 나의 카메라이다. ________ is my camera.

02 저것은 그들의 학교이다. ________ is their school.

03 이것들은 너의 생일 선물들이다. ________ are your birthday presents.

04 저것들은 내 신발들이 아니다. ________ are not my shoes.

05 저 사람은 내 남동생 준호다. ________ is my brother, Junho.

06 이분은 Brown 선생님이시다. ________ is Mr. Brown.

07 저 사람들은 나의 사촌들이다. ________ are my cousins.

08 이것은 Tom의 자전거니? Is ________ Tom's bicycle?

B 우리말과 같은 뜻이 되도록 지시대명사와 괄호 안의 단어를 이용하여 문장을 완성하시오.

01 저것은 내 여행 가방이 아니다. (suitcase) ________

02 이것들이 너의 가족사진들이니? (family photos) ________

03 이것은 매우 맛있는 사과이다. (delicious) ________

04 저것들이 내 여동생의 장갑인가요? (gloves) ________

05 저것이 그의 오래된 재킷이니? (jacket) ________

06 저 사람은 내가 가장 좋아하는 가수예요. (favorite) ________

07 저 사람들이 너의 반 친구들이니? (classmates) ________

08 이것들은 나의 부모님으로부터 온 편지들이다. (letters) ________

09 이쪽은 저의 가장 친한 친구예요. (best friend) ________

UNIT 04 지시형용사

지시대명사는 명사를 수식하는 지시형용사로도 쓸 수 있다는 점 알아 두세요.

가까이 있는 사물이나 사람을 수식		멀리 있는 사물이나 사람을 수식	
this	these	that	those
이 ~	이 ~(들)	저 ~	저 ~(들)
This leaf is big. This man is my teacher. These leaves are colorful.		That bird is singing a song. Those birds are flying. Those children are my friends.	

주의 수식하는 명사의 수에 맞는 지시형용사를 쓰세요.

|A| 다음 문장의 밑줄 친 부분이 지시대명사이면 '대', 지시형용사이면 '형'이라고 쓰시오.

01 This is Tom's phone. ________

02 This phone is Tom's. ________

03 Is that girl your sister? ________

04 Is that your sister? ________

05 This is an interesting game. ________

06 This game is very interesting. ________

07 That house is very big. ________

08 That is a very big house. ________

09 Those are your pants. ________

10 Those pants are yours. ________

|B| 우리말과 같은 뜻이 되도록 지시형용사와 괄호 안의 단어를 이용하여 문장을 완성하시오.

01 이 남자는 친절하고 잘생겼다. (man) ________________ is kind and handsome.

02 저 상자는 크고 무겁다. (box) ________________ is big and heavy.

03 이 책들은 정말 재미있다. (book) ________________ are very interesting.

04 이 아름다운 꽃들을 봐라. (beautiful flower) Look at ________________.

05 너는 저 영화를 봤니? (movie) Did you see ________________?

06 저 신발들은 얼마니? (shoes) How much are ________________?

07 이 코트는 낡아 보인다. (coat) ________________ looks old.

08 그는 저 사람들을 잘 알고 있다. (people) He knows ________________ well.

09 이 꽃들은 당신을 위한 거예요. (flower) ________________ are for you.

shoes와 people은 항상 복수로 취급해야 해요.

실전 TIP

문장 안에서 단독으로 쓰였는지, 명사 앞에서 명사를 수식하는지 파악해야 해요.

내신 기출 다음 밑줄 친 부분의 쓰임이 다른 하나는?

① Are these your brand-new sneakers?
② Are those boys members of the national team?
③ Which do you like better, this one or that one?

UNIT 05 비인칭대명사 it

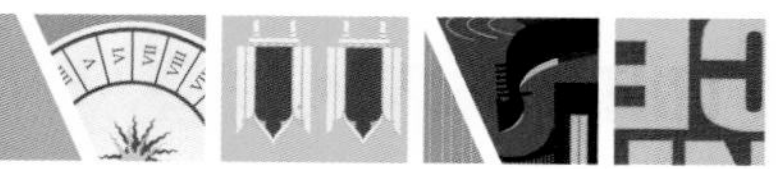

계절, 날짜, 요일 등에 사용하는 it은 가리키는 대상이 없고 해석하지 않는 점에 주의하세요.

it의 구분		예문	대상
비인칭대명사	계절	It is summer.	It = ×
	날짜	It is July 10th.	
	요일	It is Friday.	
	시간	It is nine o'clock.	
	날씨	It is hot today.	
	거리	How far is it from here to there?	
	명암	It is too dark here.	
인칭대명사	그것	This pencil is red. It is mine.	It = 연필

|A| 다음 질문에 알맞은 대답을 |보기|에서 골라 그 번호를 쓰시오.

01 A: What day is it today? B: ____________

02 A: What time is it? B: ____________

03 A: How was the weather yesterday? B: ____________

04 A: What is the date today? B: ____________

05 A: How long did it take to come here? B: ____________

06 A: How far is it from here to the library? B: ____________

|보기|
ⓐ It is ten o'clock.
ⓑ It is Monday.
ⓒ It is September 18th.
ⓓ It is about two kilometers.
ⓔ It was cold.
ⓕ It took thirty minutes.

|B| 다음 문장의 밑줄 친 It의 쓰임과 같은 것을 |보기|에서 골라 그 번호를 쓰시오.

|보기|
ⓐ It was a sunny day. ⓑ It is a new computer.

01 It is already spring. ____________

02 Get up. It is seven o'clock. ____________

03 She bought a new car. It was white. ____________

04 It is Wednesday. ____________

05 How far was it from here to the airport? ____________

06 Don't go out. It is dark outside. ____________

07 Don't do it again. ____________

08 What season is it in Korea now? ____________

09 How long does it take to get to work? ____________

UNIT 06 부정대명사 1

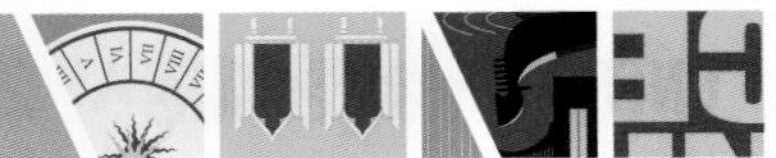

정해지지 않은 불특정한 사람이나 물건 또는 앞에 언급된 명사와 같은 종류를 언급할 때는 부정대명사 one을 사용해야 해요.

부정 대명사	정해지지 않은 것 앞에 언급한 명사	one	I need a shirt. I'll buy one. (정해지지 않은 셔츠)	단수
		ones	I need shoes. I'll buy these ones. (정해지지 않은 신발)	복수
인칭 대명사	정해진 것	it	I bought a shirt. I like it. (내가 산 그 셔츠)	단수
		they, them	I bought shoes. I like them. (내가 산 그 신발)	복수

|A| 다음 문장의 밑줄 친 부분을 어법상 바르게 고치시오.

01 I need an umbrella. Do you have it? → ________

02 He has a new bag, but I have an old it. → ________

03 Sally wants to adopt three cats. She likes these one. → ________

04 I lost my eraser. I have to buy it. → ________

05 You have a notebook. Can I use one? → ________

06 Sam ate big cookies and I ate small them. → ________

07 My mother bought me a watch. But I lost one. → ________

08 A: I don't have a pen. B: Then I can lend you it. → ________

|B| 다음 빈칸에 알맞은 말을 |보기|에서 골라 쓰시오.

|보기| it one ones they them

01 I don't have a pencil. Can you lend me ________?

02 My father bought a bike and gave ________ to me.

03 I like the purple grapes but not the green ________.

04 There is a magazine on the desk. I read ________.

05 I have two shirts but ________ are too small for me.

06 I have a white cap and three black ________.

07 My computer was old. I sold ________ and bought a new ________.

08 A: Where is my lunch? B: Your dad is preparing ________ now.

09 A: Are these your photo albums? B: Yes. Do you want to look at ________?

부정대명사 one은 앞에서 언급된 명사와 같은 종류의 불특정한 사람 · 사물을 가리키지만, 인칭대명사 it은 앞에서 언급된 특정한 명사를 가리켜요.

UNIT 07 부정대명사 2

정해진 범위 안에서 하나씩 가리킬 때 one, another, the other를 차례대로 써요.

구분	부정대명사	의미	수	예문
2개 중	one	하나	단수	One is red.
	the other	나머지 하나		The other is blue.
3개 중	one	하나		One is red.
	another	또 다른 하나		Another is blue.
	the other	나머지 하나		The other is yellow.

참고 other(그 밖의 다른, 그 밖의 다른 것) 앞에 the가 붙으면 특정한 것이 되므로 '나머지'라는 의미가 돼요.

|A| 다음 문장의 밑줄 친 부분을 어법상 바르게 고치시오.

01 This one is small. Please bring me <u>other</u>. → ______________

02 I want one of two. You can have <u>other</u>. → ______________

03 Mary has two dogs. One is white, and <u>another</u> is black. → ______________

04 One is white, <u>two</u> is blue and the other is red. → ______________

05 I don't like this jacket. Could you show me <u>the other</u>? → ______________

06 I have three bags. One is red, another is yellow, and <u>the others</u> is blue. → ______________

|B| 다음 우리말과 같은 뜻이 되도록 빈칸에 알맞은 말을 |보기|에서 골라 쓰시오.

|보기|

one　　another　　the other

01 이 수건은 더러워요. 다른 것을 주세요.

This towel is dirty. Give me ______________.

02 네가 그 나머지 하나를 가져갈 수 있다.

You can take ______________.

03 James가 하나를 먹었다. 너는 나머지 하나를 먹어라.

James had ______________. You can have the other.

04 그는 형이 두 명 있다. 한 명은 의사고 다른 한 명은 변호사다.

He has two brothers. ______________ is a doctor and ______________ is a lawyer.

05 한 명은 한국에서 왔고, 다른 한 명은 중국에서 왔으며, 나머지 한 명은 일본에서 왔다.

______________ is from Korea. ______________ is from China, and ______________ is from Japan.

UNIT 08 부정대명사 3

여러 개의 대상이 있는 상황에서 쓸 수 있는 대명사를 알아 두세요.

구분	부정대명사	의미	수	예문
여러 개 중	some	몇몇	복수	Some are red.
	others	다른 몇몇		Others are blue.
	the others	나머지 모두		The others are yellow.

|A| 다음 빈칸에 others 또는 the others 중 알맞은 말을 쓰시오.

01 Some people are kind, but ________________ are not.

02 Some boys like baseball, but ________________ like soccer.

03 I bought ten pens. Five are black, and ________________ are red.

04 Some people like the bus, but ________________ like the subway.

05 Some students like science, but ________________ don't.

|B| 다음 우리말과 같은 뜻이 되도록 괄호 안의 단어를 바르게 배열하시오.

01 어떤 사람들은 부지런하지만 다른 사람들은 게으르다. (people / hardworking / others / some / are / lazy / are / but)

____

02 바구니에 과일들이 많다. 일부는 사과지만 나머지는 오렌지다. (appels / oranges / some / the others / are / but / are)

There is a lot of fruit in the basket. ____

03 이 사람들 중 일부는 영어를 사용하지만 나머지 사람들은 한국어를 사용한다.

(these people / use / but / use / some / Korean / of / the others / English)

____

04 주차장에 차가 많이 있다. 몇 대는 검은색이고, 다른 몇 대는 흰색이지만, 나머지는 회색이다.

(black / white / are / but / gray / the others / are / some / others / are)

There are many cars in the parking lot. ____

내신 기출 다음 밑줄 친 부분의 쓰임이 어법상 올바른 것은?

① Some girls like roses, but the other do not.

② My mom's cellphone is broken. She has to buy another.

③ I have oranges. Some are fresh, but the other are not.

실전 TIP

another는 '또 다른 (것)'을 의미해요.

중간고사·기말고사 실전문제

객관식 (01~25) / 주관식 (26~50)

학년과 반 　　 이름 　　 객관식 　　 / 25문항 　 주관식 　　 / 25문항

01~03 다음 빈칸에 알맞은 말을 고르시오.

01

___________ met Jimmy in front of the building.

① He ② Her
③ Your ④ Its
⑤ Them

02

___________ birthday is May 2nd.

① It ② Him
③ You ④ His
⑤ Mine

03

The woman took care of ___________.

① they ② our
③ them ④ she
⑤ my

04 다음 밑줄 친 말을 대명사로 바꿔 쓴 것 중 어법상 어색한 것은?

① I live with my cat. (→ it)
② It is her doll. (→ her)
③ Bob is good at mathematics. (→ He)
④ I met the girl at the restaurant. (→ her)
⑤ My classmates and I are middle school students. (→ We)

05 다음 중 인칭대명사와 재귀대명사가 바르게 짝지어지지 않은 것은?

① I – myself
② he – himself
③ she – herself
④ they – themselves
⑤ we – ourself

06 다음 두 문장이 같은 뜻이 되도록 할 때 빈칸에 알맞은 말은?

The smartpad is hers. = It is ___________ smartpad.

① her ② she
③ him ④ his
⑤ she's

07~09 다음 빈칸에 들어갈 수 없는 말을 고르시오.

07 The baby likes ________ very much.

① me ② her
③ us ④ him
⑤ their

08 This ________ looks so wonderful.

① house ② computer
③ machine ④ shoes
⑤ pen

09 ________ watched themselves on TV.

① The children ② The boys
③ The women ④ Thomas and I
⑤ The students

10~11 다음 밑줄 친 말의 쓰임이 나머지와 다른 것을 고르시오.

10 ① What is it?
② What date is it?
③ It's sunny today.
④ It is three o'clock.
⑤ How far is it from here to the bank?

11 ① My mom baked these cookies.
② These women are from China.
③ The artist drew these pictures.
④ These are very important for us.
⑤ I think these words mean nothing.

12~14 다음 밑줄 친 ①~⑤ 중 어법상 어색한 것을 고르시오.

12 I'm going(①) to have a cheese burger(②). Do(③) you want it(④), too(⑤)?

13 She wants(①) to(②) introduce(③) her(④) to us(⑤).

14 This(①) gets(②) dark after(③) seven(④) in(⑤) the evening.

15~16 다음 빈칸에 들어갈 말이 순서대로 짝지어진 것을 고르시오.

15

• ___________ people are very kind.
• ___________ is my best friend.

① This – That ② Those – This
③ These – Those ④ Those –Those
⑤ This – This

16

• She helped ___________ yesterday.
• I often see ___________ in the mirror.

① me – me ② me – my
③ my – myself ④ myself – me
⑤ me – myself

17~19 다음 우리말을 영어로 바르게 옮긴 것을 고르시오.

17

저 신상품 가방은 그의 것이다.

① That brand-new bag is he's.
② Those brand-new bags are he's.
③ That brand-new bag is him.
④ Those brand-new bag is his.
⑤ That brand-new bag is his.

18

그가 어제 나에게 직접 전화를 걸었다.

① He called me yesterday.
② He called me myself yesterday.
③ He himself called me yesterday.
④ He called myself yesterday.
⑤ He himself called myself yesterday.

19

몇몇은 너무 작고, 나머지 것들은 낡았다.

① One is too small, and the other is old.
② Some are too small, and the others are old.
③ Ones are too small, and the others are old.
④ Some are too small, and others are old.
⑤ It is too small, and another is old.

20 다음 글의 빈칸 ⓐ와 ⓑ에 공통으로 알맞은 말은?

My name is Amanda. I'd like to introduce my little sister. _____ⓐ_____ name is Jina. She is five years old. She is cute and kind. Her hair is long and curly. I like _____ⓑ_____ very much.

① He[he] ② Him[him] ③ His[his]
④ Her[her] ⑤ She[she]

21~22 다음 빈칸에 들어갈 말이 나머지와 다른 것을 고르시오.

21 ① ________ was an interesting story.
② ________ is cloudy today.
③ What day is ________?
④ I have a cat. ________ legs are short.
⑤ I bought a shirt. ________ is so nice.

22 ① My bag is old. I need a new ________.
② I watched a comedy movie. ________ was funny.
③ My pencil is too short. Can you lend me ________?
④ I lost my notebook. I have to buy ________.
⑤ I don't like this color. Can you show me a different ________?

23 다음 중 밑줄 친 부분을 생략할 수 없는 것은?
① He himself made a sandwich.
② Jane fixed the computer herself.
③ I'm looking at myself in the mirror.
④ Did you answer the phone yourself?
⑤ My sister herself finished her homework.

24~25 다음 중 어법상 어색한 문장을 고르시오.

24 ① It was early in the morning.
② That is rainy today.
③ These are my clothes.
④ That computer is mine.
⑤ Look at those dogs.

25 ① Brian is in his room.
② I have five members in my family.
③ The woman is your teacher.
④ The men and women are our guests.
⑤ He sometimes borrowed me book.

26~27 다음 괄호 안에서 알맞은 말을 고르시오.

26 The beautiful dress is (her / hers).

27 We shouldn't blame (us / ourselves).

28~30 다음 빈칸에 it[It] 또는 one[One] 중에 알맞은 말을 쓰시오.

28 My cell phone doesn't work. I have to buy ___________.

29 I lost my umbrella. ___________ is big and yellow.

30 This bus is full. Let's wait for next ___________.

31~32 다음 두 문장이 같은 뜻이 되도록 빈칸에 알맞은 대명사를 쓰시오.

31

Today is October 17th.

→ ___________ is October 17th.

32

She has a cute doll.

→ ___________ doll is cute.

33~35 다음 글의 밑줄 친 ⓐ~ⓒ를 대명사로 바꿔 쓰시오.

I have a best friend. ⓐ My friend's name is Lucy. Lucy lives in New York. She has a sister. Her name is Angela. ⓑ Lucy and Angela sometimes send me a letter. I miss ⓒ Lucy and Angela so much.

33 ⓐ → ___________

34 ⓑ → ___________

35 ⓒ → ___________

36~38 다음 문장에서 어법상 어색한 부분을 찾아 바르게 고치시오.

36 How far is that from here to the airport?

___________ → ___________

37 I should change these tickets. I bought it online.

___________ → ___________

38 James and you can be proud of yourself.

_______________ → _______________

39~41 다음 우리말과 같은 뜻이 되도록 괄호 안의 단어를 바르게 배열하시오.

39

Mike의 형은 고등학생이다.
(is / high school / brother / student / a / Mike's)

____

40

하나는 길고, 나머지 하나는 짧다.
(the / is / short / other / and / long, / one / is)

____

41

이 책들은 내 것이다.
(books / are / these / mine)

____

42~43 다음 빈칸에 공통으로 알맞은 말을 쓰시오.

42

- _______________ was hot today.
- _______________ is seven o'clock.

43

- My pencil case is old. I want to buy a new _______________.
- I have two pens. _______________ is black, and the other is blue.

44 다음 밑줄 친 yours가 가리키는 것을 대화에서 찾아 두 단어로 쓰시오.

A: Wow, your dress is so beautiful.
B: Thank you.
A: I also want to wear a long dress like yours.

→ _______________

45 어법상 올바른 문장을 모두 골라 그 번호를 쓰시오.

(a) This is our school.
(b) They are nice to he.
(c) Are you and yours sister students?
(d) Those are the famous painter's paintings.
(e) It is a perfect day for hiking.

→ _______________

46~48 다음 글에서 어법상 어색한 부분을 세 군데 찾아 바르게 고치시오.

> Today, I talked about pets with my classmates. One students have cats, and others have dogs. There are three dogs in my house. One is a bulldog, other is a Jindo and the other is a poodle. I love it so much.

46 __________ → __________

47 __________ → __________

48 __________ → __________

49~50 다음 우리말을 주어진 |조건|에 맞게 영어로 바르게 쓰시오.

49 어제 내가 직접 그녀에게 이메일을 보냈다.

|조건|
1. 재귀대명사를 이용할 것
2. 단어 an email, sent, her를 사용할 것
3. 6 단어로 쓸 것

→ ______________________ yesterday.

50 오늘 저녁에 비가 올 것이다.

|조건|
1. 비인칭주어 it을 이용할 것
2. 단어 rain, will, this evening을 사용할 것
3. 5 단어로 쓸 것

→ ______________________

CHAPTER

07 형용사와 부사의 비교 표현

Unit 01 형용사

Unit 02 형용사의 역할

Unit 03 수량형용사 1: some, any

Unit 04 수량형용사 2: many, much, a lot of

Unit 05 수량형용사 3: (a) few, (a) little

Unit 06 부사의 역할

Unit 07 부사의 형태 1

Unit 08 부사의 형태 2

Unit 09 빈도부사

Unit 10 too, either

Unit 11 비교급과 최상급 만드는 방법

Unit 12 원급 비교

Unit 13 비교급

Unit 14 최상급

Unit 15 비교 표현 종합

UNIT 01 형용사

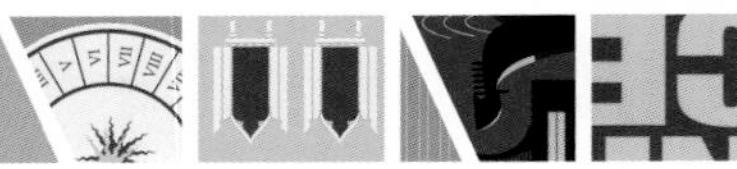

서로 반대되는 의미를 가진 형용사끼리 묶어서 암기하세요.

long 긴	↔ short 짧은	strong 강한	↔ weak 약한
pretty 예쁜	↔ ugly 못생긴	smart 똑똑한	↔ foolish 어리석은
old 늙은, 오래된	↔ young 젊은, 어린	sad 슬픈	↔ glad 기쁜
hungry 배고픈	↔ full 배부른	empty 비어 있는	↔ full 가득 찬
healthy 건강한	↔ sick 아픈	open 열린	↔ closed 닫힌
high 높은	↔ low 낮은	fast 빠른	↔ slow 느린
deep 깊은	↔ shallow 얕은	cold 차가운	↔ hot 뜨거운
heavy 무거운	↔ light 가벼운	thick 두꺼운	↔ thin 얇은
easy 쉬운	↔ difficult[hard] 어려운	bright 밝은	↔ dark 어두운
dry 마른	↔ wet 젖은	good 좋은	↔ bad 나쁜
fat 뚱뚱한	↔ skinny 마른	busy 바쁜	↔ free 한가한
polite 예의 바른	↔ rude 무례한	tall 키 큰	↔ short 키 작은
rich 부유한	↔ poor 가난한	dangerous 위험한	↔ safe 안전한
expensive 비싼	↔ cheap 싼	clean 깨끗한	↔ dirty 더러운

접두사 un- 을 붙여서 반대말을 만드는 형용사도 알아 두세요.

happy 행복한 ↔ unhappy 불행한	kind 친절한 ↔ unkind 불친절한
able 능력 있는 ↔ unable 능력 없는	wise 현명한 ↔ unwise 현명하지 못한

다음 형용사의 반대말을 쓰면서 외우시오.

01 able 능력 있는 ↔ __________ 능력 없는

02 bright 밝은 ↔ __________ 어두운

03 clean 깨끗한 ↔ __________ 더러운

04 dangerous 위험한 ↔ __________ 안전한

05 deep 깊은 ↔ __________ 얕은

06 open 열린 ↔ __________ 닫힌

07 dry 마른 ↔ __________ 젖은

08 easy 쉬운 ↔ __________ 어려운

09 empty 비어 있는 ↔ __________ 가득 찬

10 expensive 비싼 ↔ __________ 싼

11 happy 행복한 ↔ __________ 불행한

12 healthy 건강한 ↔ __________ 아픈

13 heavy 무거운 ↔ __________ 가벼운

14 high 높은 ↔ __________ 낮은

15 old 늙은, 오래된 ↔ __________ 젊은, 어린

16 polite 예의 바른 ↔ __________ 무례한

17 rich 부유한 ↔ __________ 가난한

18 smart 똑똑한 ↔ __________ 어리석은

19 strong 강한 ↔ __________ 약한

20 tall 키 큰 ↔ __________ 키 작은

21 thick 두꺼운 ↔ __________ 얇은

22 wise 현명한 ↔ __________ 현명하지 못한

UNIT 02 형용사의 역할

형용사는 명사를 수식하거나 보어 역할을 한다는 것을 알아 두세요.

명사 수식	They built the strong bridge.	튼튼한 다리
주격보어	This question is difficult.	문제가 어렵다 (주어 This question을 보충 설명)
목적격보어	She makes her mother happy.	어머니를 행복하게 (목적어 her mother를 보충 설명)

A 다음 문장의 밑줄 친 형용사가 수식하거나 보충 설명하는 말을 빈칸에 쓰시오.

01 This is a new shirt. ______________

02 The girl is pretty. ______________

03 My brother is tall. ______________

04 This is a red rose. ______________

05 It is an old book. ______________

06 She is kind. ______________

07 The house is new. ______________

08 He is an honest boy. ______________

09 Look at the white car. ______________

10 There is a big table. ______________

11 I have a little cat. ______________

12 The movie is interesting. ______________

13 These boxes are heavy. ______________

14 The woman is beautiful. ______________

B 다음 문장의 밑줄 친 말의 쓰임과 같은 것을 |보기|에서 골라 그 번호를 쓰시오.

형용사는 명사 앞에서 명사를 꾸며 주거나(ⓑ) 주어나 목적어를 보충 설명해 주는 보어(ⓐ)로 쓰여요.

|보기|
ⓐ She is smart. ⓑ She is a smart student.

01 You made me happy. __________

02 It is a cloudy day. __________

03 I want a new computer. __________

04 The soccer game was exciting. __________

05 My mother was busy yesterday. __________

06 Jessica is a famous dancer. __________

07 Sam and Mike look tired. __________

08 There is a tall tree in the garden. __________

내신 기출 다음 밑줄 친 말의 쓰임이 다른 하나는?

① These are my best friends.
② The news made me sad.
③ My little dog was sick last night.

실전 TIP
형용사가 명사를 수식하는지 보어로 쓰였는지 확인해 보세요.

UNIT 03 수량형용사 1: some, any

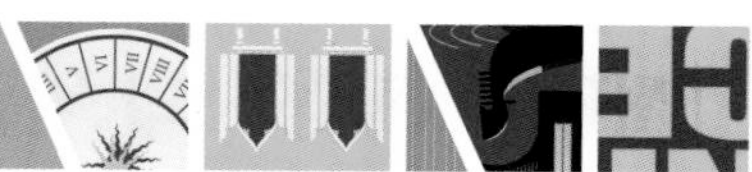

'약간, 얼마간의, 어떤'을 표현하고자 할 때는 some이나 any를 쓰세요.

some	주로 긍정문	There are some books.	약간의 책들 〈복수명사 앞〉
		She has some time.	약간의 시간 〈셀 수 없는 명사 앞〉
any	주로 부정문과 의문문	Are there any books?	책이 (어떤 것이라도) 있니?
		She doesn't have any time.	그녀는 약간의 시간도 없다.

주의 긍정의 대답을 기대하는 권유 또는 요청을 표현하는 의문문에는 any 대신 some을 써요.
Would you like some tea?

주의 '어느 ~든지'를 의미할 때는 긍정문에서도 any를 쓸 수 있음에 유의하세요.
You can call me any time.

|A| 우리말과 같은 뜻이 되도록 빈칸에 some이나 any 중 알맞은 말을 쓰시오.

01 그녀는 돈이 약간 있다. She has ________ money.
02 나는 돈이 조금도 없다. I don't have ________ money.
03 제게 물을 좀 가져다주세요. Bring me ________ water, please.
04 너는 형제가 있니? Do you have ________ brothers?
05 그녀는 약간의 치즈가 필요하다. She needs ________ cheese.
06 우리는 옷을 좀 살 것이다. We're going to buy ________ clothes.
07 냉장고에 우유가 조금도 없었다. There wasn't ________ milk in the fridge.
08 병 안에 약간의 사과 주스가 있다. There is ________ apple juice in the bottle.

|B| 빈칸에 some이나 any 중 알맞은 말을 쓰시오.

01 We don't have ________ homework today.
02 They heard ________ sad news last night.
03 Do you have ________ plans for this vacation?
04 I want ________ information about the hotel.
05 Tony doesn't have ________ money in his wallet.
06 I need ________ apples. Do you have ________?
07 She is going to the market. She wants ________ carrots.
08 She has ________ bread. But she doesn't have ________ butter.
09 A: Do you need ________ fruit? B: Yes. Give me ________ fruit.

UNIT 04 수량형용사 2: many, much, a lot of

'많은'이라는 뜻의 many, much, a lot of, lots of가 어떤 명사와 함께 쓰이는지 익히세요.

의미	수량형용사	+ 명사	예문
(수가) 많은	many	복수명사	There are many animals.
(양이) 많은	much	셀 수 없는 명사	There is not much time.
많은	a lot[lots] of	복수명사/셀 수 없는 명사	There are a lot of animals.

참고 much는 대개 부정문과 의문문에 쓰이고, 긍정문에는 a lot of나 lots of가 주로 쓰여요.

A 다음 밑줄 친 말을 many[Many] 또는 much[Much]로 바꾸어 쓰시오.

01 There are a lot of trees in the park. → ____________

02 I took lots of pictures there. → ____________

03 They didn't spend a lot of time together. → ____________

04 A lot of people like Internet shopping. → ____________

05 Does she have lots of homework to do? → ____________

06 You should not spend lots of money. → ____________

07 Do you have a lot of books? → ____________

08 We didn't have lots of snow this winter. → ____________

B 우리말과 같은 뜻이 되도록 |보기|의 말과 괄호 안의 단어를 이용하여 문장을 완성하시오.

명사가 셀 수 있는 명사인지 아닌지를 먼저 파악해야 해요. 셀 수 있다면 단 · 복수 여부도 정확히 파악해야 해요.

|보기|
many　much　a lot of　lots of

01 너는 하루에 물을 얼마나 마시니? (water)

How ____________ do you drink a day?

02 많은 사람들이 그 축구 경기를 TV로 본다. (people)

____________ watch the soccer game on TV.

03 그 남자는 많은 돈을 벌지는 못한다. (money)

The man doesn't make ____________.

04 너는 자매가 몇 명이니? (sister)

How ____________ do you have?

05 도서관에는 많은 책들이 있다. (book)

There are ____________ in the library.

06 너는 컴퓨터로 많은 정보를 찾을 수 있니? (information)

Can you find ____________ on the computer?

UNIT 05 수량형용사 3: (a) few, (a) little

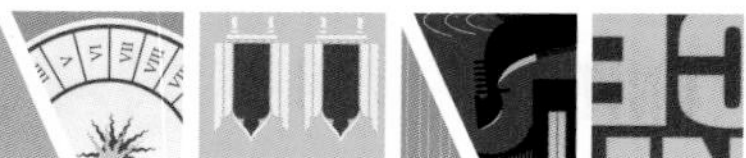

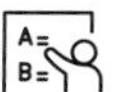

비슷해 보이지만 틀리기 쉬운 (a) few와 (a) little의 쓰임을 잘 구별해야 해요.

의미	수량형용사	+ 명사	예시	주의
조금/약간 있는	a few	복수명사	I have a few books.	긍정의 의미를 포함
	a little	셀 수 없는 명사	I have a little time.	
거의 없는	few	복수명사	I have few books.	부정의 의미를 포함
	little	셀 수 없는 명사	I have little time.	

주의 a를 뺀 few와 little은 부정의 뜻으로 '거의 없는'이라는 의미라는 데 주의하세요.

|A| 다음 괄호 안에서 알맞은 말을 고르시오.

01 There are (a few / a little) bananas on the table.

02 There is (a few / a little) water in the glass.

03 Sora added (a few / a little) salt to her soup.

04 (A few / A little) passengers are waiting for the bus.

05 The woman has (few / little) money.

06 There are (few / little) students in the classroom.

07 There is (few / little) milk in the bottle.

08 I have (a few / a little) close friends.

|B| 우리말과 같은 뜻이 되도록 |보기|의 말과 괄호 안의 단어를 이용하여 문장을 완성하시오.

|보기|
a few　　a little　　few　　little

01 이번 여름에는 비가 거의 오지 않았다. (rain)

There was ______________________ this summer.

02 오직 몇 명의 사람들만 내 이름을 안다. (people)

Only ______________________ know my name.

03 그는 피자를 만들기 위해 약간의 치즈가 필요하다. (cheese)

He needs ______________________ to make pizza.

04 그 아기는 말을 거의 못 한다. (word)

The baby speaks ______________________.

05 우리는 서둘러야 한다. 우리는 시간이 거의 없다. (time)

We have to hurry. We have ______________________.

UNIT 06 부사의 역할

수식하는 말에 따라 달라지는 부사의 위치를 파악하세요.

역할	위치	예문
형용사 수식	형용사 바로 앞	He is my very good friend.
다른 부사 수식	수식하는 부사 바로 앞	He speaks too slowly.
동사(구) 수식	주로 문장의 맨 뒤	Snails move slowly.
문장 전체 수식	문장의 맨 앞	Fortunately, there is a solution.

참고 부사는 위에 나열된 말을 수식하여 그 뜻을 분명하게 하거나 수식하는 말이에요.

|A| 다음 문장에서 밑줄 친 부사가 수식하는 말에 동그라미 하시오.

01 He is a very good neighbor.

02 The woman speaks English very well.

03 The train will start soon.

04 This problem is too difficult for me.

05 Finally, her daughter passed the exam.

06 Jenny plays the piano well.

07 That is a very high mountain.

08 Luckily, Tim got better after three days.

|B| 밑줄 친 부사의 역할을 |보기|에서 찾아 기호를 쓰시오.

|보기|
ⓐ 형용사 수식 ⓑ 다른 부사 수식 ⓒ 동사 수식 ⓓ 문장 전체 수식

01 Luckily, she found the lost bag. ________

02 This laptop notebook is very light. ________

03 Mr. Brown speaks kindly to the students. ________

04 Jenny goes to bed very late every night. ________

05 James walked slowly to school. ________

06 The car was too expensive. ________

내신 기출 다음 밑줄 친 very의 쓰임이 다른 하나는?

① The boy behaves very politely.
② The chicken soup tasted very sweet.
③ The little girl can climb very well.

실전 TIP

문장에서 형용사를 수식하는지 부사를 수식하는지 확인하세요.

UNIT 07 부사의 형태 1

부사는 very처럼 자체가 부사인 것도 있지만, 대부분 형용사에 -ly를 붙여 만들 수 있어요.

대부분의 경우	+ -ly	real → really safe → safely	usual → usually careful → carefully
자음+ -y로 끝나는 경우	y를 i로 바꾸고 + -ly	easy → easily heavy → heavily	happy → happily angry → angrily
-le로 끝나는 경우	e를 없애고 + -y	simple → simply	gentle → gently

주의 〈명사 + -ly〉는 형용사예요. → lovely 사랑스러운 / friendly 상냥한 / daily 매일의 / timely 시기적절한

|A| 다음 형용사를 부사로 바꾸어 쓰시오.

01 quick → ____________
02 slow → ____________
03 easy → ____________
04 happy → ____________
05 strange → ____________
06 usual → ____________
07 kind → ____________
08 simple → ____________
09 sad → ____________
10 real → ____________
11 angry → ____________
12 gentle → ____________
13 careful → ____________
14 lucky → ____________
15 safe → ____________
16 heavy → ____________

|B| 우리말과 같은 뜻이 되도록 괄호 안에서 알맞은 말을 고르시오.

01 그는 그녀의 이야기에 주의를 기울여 들었다.
He listened (careful / carefully) to her story.

02 Tony는 조용히 문을 닫고 자리에 앉았다.
Tony closed the door (quiet / quietly) and sat down.

03 좀 더 천천히 얘기해 줄래?
Can you speak more (slow / slowly)?

04 갑자기 모든 전등이 꺼졌다.
(Sudden / Suddenly), all the lights went out.

05 그 수학 문제는 쉬웠다. 나는 그것을 쉽게 풀었다.
The math problem was (easy / easily). I solved it (easy / easily).

06 나의 어머니는 항상 안전하게 운전하신다. 그녀는 안전하게 운전하는 분이다.
My mother always drives (safe / safely). She is a (safe / safely) driver.

UNIT 08 부사의 형태 2

형용사와 부사의 형태가 같은 단어에 유의하세요.

early	이른 / 일찍	high	높은 / 높이
late	늦은 / 늦게	hard	어려운, 딱딱한 / 열심히
fast	빠른 / 빠르게	near	가까운 / 가까이
long	긴 / 길게	pretty	예쁜 / 꽤

주의 -ly가 붙어 다른 뜻이 되는 단어에 유의하세요.
lately 최근에 / hardly 거의 ~않다 / highly 매우, 대단히 / nearly 거의 / closely 면밀히, 꼼꼼히

|A| 다음 밑줄 친 단어의 우리말 뜻을 쓰시오.

01 My flight was late. __________

02 He has to work late. __________

03 Lately, I feel happy. __________

04 She gets up early. __________

05 It blooms in early spring. __________

06 It was hard work. __________

07 He is studying hard. __________

08 I could hardly walk. __________

09 He can jump high. __________

10 How high is the mountain? __________

11 It was highly successful. __________

12 I'm pretty busy now. __________

13 She is a pretty girl. __________

14 Christmas is getting near. __________

15 His house is very near. __________

16 I nearly failed. __________

|B| 우리말과 같은 뜻이 되도록 괄호 안에서 알맞은 말을 골라 빈칸에 쓰시오.

01 여기에 도착하는 데 거의 두 시간이 걸렸다. (near / nearly)
It took __________ two hours to get here.

02 그녀는 최근에 그 소식을 들었다. (recent / recently)
She heard the news __________.

03 그것은 아주 중요한 문제이다. (high / highly)
That is a __________ important problem.

04 그 의자는 정말 딱딱하다. (hard / hardly)
The chair is really __________.

05 경찰은 그 고장 난 차를 꼼꼼히 살펴보았다. (close / closely)
The police officer looked at the broken car __________.

06 내 남동생은 거의 영어 공부를 하지 않는다. (hard / hardly)
My brother __________ studies English.

hardly는 '거의 ~하지 않다'라는 뜻으로, 이미 부정의 의미를 가지고 있으므로, 따로 not을 쓰지 않는다는 점에 유의하세요.

UNIT 09 빈도부사

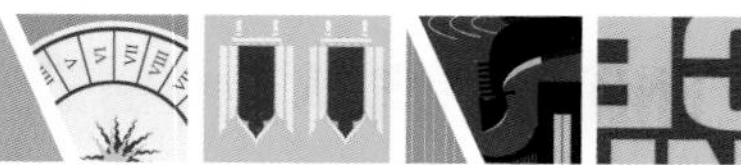

어떤 일이 얼마나 자주 일어나는지에 따라서 부사를 알맞게 선택해야 해요.

빈도	100%	80~90%	60%	30~40%	10%	0%
	←					
부사	always	usually	often	sometimes	hardly/seldom	never
	항상	보통, 대개	종종, 자주	가끔, 때때로	거의 ~않다	절대 ~않다

빈도부사를 쓰는 위치에 주의하세요.

be동사 뒤	She is never late.
일반동사 앞	She never comes late.
조동사가 있다면 조동사 뒤	She will never be late.

주의 hardly, seldom, never는 이미 부정의 의미가 있으므로, 따로 not을 쓰지 않는다는 점에 유의하세요.

A 다음 문장을 괄호 안의 빈도부사를 이용하여 다시 쓰시오.

01 My brother and I eat breakfast. (always) → ______

02 He goes to school by bus. (usually) → ______

03 Sally is late for school. (sometimes) → ______

04 We ride our bicycles on weekends. (often) → ______

05 We will forget you. (never) → ______

06 She goes swimming in the sea. (seldom) → ______

B 우리말과 같은 뜻이 되도록 괄호 안의 단어와 빈도부사를 이용하여 문장을 완성하시오.

01 나의 아버지는 절대 회사에 늦지 않으신다. (late, is)

My father ______ for work.

02 Sam과 Mike는 거의 책을 읽지 않는다. (books, read)

Sam and Mike ______.

03 그녀는 가끔 회의에 오지 않는다. (is, absent)

She ______ from the meeting.

04 우리는 보통 학교에 걸어간다. (go to, school)

We ______ on foot.

05 우리는 너의 미소와 따뜻한 마음을 항상 기억할 것이다. (remember, will)

We ______ your smile and warm heart.

UNIT 10 too, either

'또한, 역시'를 의미하며 동의나 공감을 나타낼 때, 긍정문에서는 too를, 부정문에서는 either를 사용해야 해요.

긍정의 동의 · 공감	A: I know him.	B: I know him, too.	= Me, too.
부정의 동의 · 공감	A: I'm not old.	B: I'm not old, either.	= Me, neither.

참고 부사 too는 형용사나 부사 앞에 와서 '너무'라는 약간 부정적인 뜻으로도 쓰여요.
These shoes look very good. But, they are too expensive. (너무 비싼)

참고 neither는 not ~ either를 의미해요.

|A| 다음 대화의 빈칸에 too나 either 중 알맞은 말을 쓰시오.

01 A: I like music. B: I like music, ___________.

02 A: Junho can't play the guitar. B: Mary can't play the guitar, ___________.

03 A: Judy passed the exam. B: I passed the exam, ___________.

04 A: I go to bed late at night. B: I go to bed late at night, ___________.

05 A: I don't like computer games. B: Aiden doesn't like computer games, ___________.

|B| 우리말과 같은 뜻이 되도록 too나 either를 이용하여 문장을 완성하시오.

01 John은 야구를 좋아한다. Tom 또한 그것을 좋아한다.
John likes baseball. Tom ___________________________.

02 내 남동생은 우유를 마시지 않는다. 나 또한 그것을 마시지 않는다.
My brother doesn't drink milk. I ___________________________.

03 나의 아버지는 주말에 낚시를 즐기신다. 나 또한 그것을 즐긴다.
My father enjoys fishing on weekends. I ___________________________.

04 진희는 고양이에게 먹이를 주지 않았다. 나 또한 주지 않았다.
Jinhee didn't feed the cat. I ___________________________.

05 James는 수영을 할 수 있다. Sally 또한 수영을 할 수 있다.
James can swim. Sally ___________________________.

내신 기출 다음 대화의 빈칸에 들어갈 말이 다른 것은?

① A: My brother is twelve years old.
B: My sister is twelve years old, ___________.

② A: I won't go to the party tonight.
B: I won't go to the party tonight, ___________.

③ A: He often plays soccer after school.
B: I often play soccer after school, ___________.

실전 TIP
동의하는 말이 긍정인지 부정인지 확인해 보세요.

UNIT 11 비교급과 최상급 만드는 방법

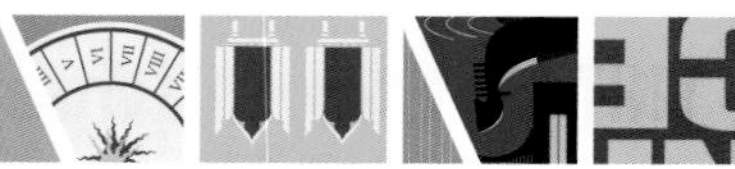

형용사나 부사의 비교급과 최상급을 만드는 방법을 알아 두세요.

형용사/부사의 형태		원급	비교급	최상급
대부분	+ -er / -est	tall	taller	tallest
-e로 끝남	+ -r / -st	nice	nicer	nicest
-y로 끝남	y를 삭제 + -ier / -iest	early	earlier	earliest
〈단모음+단자음〉으로 끝남	자음 추가 + -er / -est	hot	hotter	hottest
-ous, -ful, -ive, -ing, -less로 끝남	more / most + 원급	famous exciting	more famous more exciting	most famous most exciting
〈형용사+ly〉 부사		slowly	more slowly	most slowly
3음절 이상		difficult	more difficult	most difficult

비교급과 최상급의 불규칙 변화형은 암기해야 해요.

원급	비교급	최상급
good 좋은 / well 잘	better 더 좋은, 더 잘	best 가장 좋은, 가장 잘
bad 나쁜	worse 더 나쁜	worst 가장 나쁜
many 수가 많은 / much 양이 많은	more 더 많은	most 가장 많은
little 양이 적은	less 더 적은	least 가장 적은

다음 단어의 비교급과 최상급을 쓰면서 외우시오.

01 able 능력 있는 – ______ – ______

02 angry 화난 – ______ – ______

03 bad 나쁜 – ______ – ______

04 beautiful 아름다운 – ______ – ______

05 big 큰 – ______ – ______

06 boring 따분한 – ______ – ______

07 brave 용감한 – ______ – ______

08 bright 밝은 – ______ – ______

09 busy 바쁜 – ______ – ______

10 careless 부주의한 – ______ – ______

11 carefully 조심하여 – ______ – ______

12 cheap 싼 – ______ – ______

13 깨끗한 clean – ____________ – ____________
14 차가운 cold – ____________ – ____________
15 편안한 comfortable – ____________ – ____________
16 위험한 dangerous – ____________ – ____________
17 어두운 dark – ____________ – ____________
18 깊은, 깊게 deep – ____________ – ____________
19 맛있는 delicious – ____________ – ____________
20 어려운 difficult – ____________ – ____________
21 근면한 hardworking – ____________ – ____________
22 더러운 dirty – ____________ – ____________
23 쉽게 easily – ____________ – ____________
24 흥미로운 exciting – ____________ – ____________
25 비싼 expensive – ____________ – ____________
26 유명한 famous – ____________ – ____________
27 빠른, 빨리 fast – ____________ – ____________
28 뚱뚱한 fat – ____________ – ____________
29 어리석은 foolish – ____________ – ____________
30 신선한 fresh – ____________ – ____________
31 상냥한 friendly – ____________ – ____________
32 좋은 good – ____________ – ____________
33 훌륭한 great – ____________ – ____________
34 잘생긴 handsome – ____________ – ____________
35 행복한 happy – ____________ – ____________
36 어려운, 열심히 hard – ____________ – ____________
37 건강한 healthy – ____________ – ____________
38 무거운 heavy – ____________ – ____________
39 도움이 되는 helpful – ____________ – ____________
40 높은, 높게 high – ____________ – ____________
41 뜨거운 hot – ____________ – ____________
42 중요한 important – ____________ – ____________
43 재미있는 interesting – ____________ – ____________
44 친절한 kind – ____________ – ____________
45 큰, 넓은 large – ____________ – ____________
46 게으른 lazy – ____________ – ____________
47 가벼운 light – ____________ – ____________
48 양이 적은 little – ____________ – ____________

49 긴 long – ____________ – ____________
50 사랑스러운 lovely – ____________ – ____________
51 낮은, 낮게 low – ____________ – ____________
52 운이 좋은 lucky – ____________ – ____________
53 많은 many, much – ____________ – ____________
54 좋은 nice – ____________ – ____________
55 시끄러운 noisy – ____________ – ____________
56 나이 많은, 오래된 old – ____________ – ____________
57 예의 바른 polite – ____________ – ____________
58 인기 있는 popular – ____________ – ____________
59 예쁜 pretty – ____________ – ____________
60 빨리 quickly – ____________ – ____________
61 조용한 quiet – ____________ – ____________
62 부유한 rich – ____________ – ____________
63 무례한 rude – ____________ – ____________
64 슬픈 sad – ____________ – ____________
65 안전한 safe – ____________ – ____________
66 심각한, 진지한 serious – ____________ – ____________
67 얕은 shallow – ____________ – ____________
68 짧은 short – ____________ – ____________
69 천천히 slowly – ____________ – ____________
70 작은 small – ____________ – ____________
71 똑똑한 smart – ____________ – ____________
72 강한 strong – ____________ – ____________
73 화창한 sunny – ____________ – ____________
74 단 sweet – ____________ – ____________
75 키가 큰 tall – ____________ – ____________
76 맛있는 tasty – ____________ – ____________
77 끔찍한 terrible – ____________ – ____________
78 두꺼운 thick – ____________ – ____________
79 얇은 thin – ____________ – ____________
80 유용한 useful – ____________ – ____________
81 약한 weak – ____________ – ____________
82 넓은 wide – ____________ – ____________
83 현명한 wise – ____________ – ____________
84 어린, 젊은 young – ____________ – ____________

UNIT 12 원급 비교

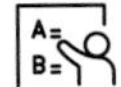 '~만큼 …한/하게'는 〈as+형용사/부사의 원급+as〉로 표현하세요.

형용사	She is	as	kind	as	him[he is].
부사	She can swim		well		him[he can].

부정문(~만큼 …하지 않다)에서는 〈not+as[so] 형용사/부사의 원급+as〉로 쓸 수 있어요.

형용사	She isn't	as[so]	kind	as	him[he is].
부사	She can't swim		well		him[he can].

|A| 다음 문장의 밑줄 친 부분을 우리말로 바르게 옮기시오.

01 I am as old as your brother. ______________________

02 John is as strong as James. ______________________

03 My brother is not as tall as you. ______________________

04 John's shoes are as expensive as Judy's. ______________________

05 Is your hair as long as your sister's? ______________________

06 Mina can swim as fast as Sora can. ______________________

07 Judy plays the piano as well as Mary does. ______________________

08 The desk is not as heavy as the table. ______________________

|B| 우리말과 같은 뜻이 되도록 괄호 안의 단어를 이용하여 문장을 완성하시오.

01 Jessica는 Lisa만큼 아름답다. (beautiful)

Jessica is ______________________ Lisa.

02 너의 자전거는 내 자전거만큼 좋다. (good)

Your bike is ______________________ mine.

03 그는 Jane만큼 예의 바르지 않다. (not, polite)

He is ______________________ Jane.

04 내 남동생은 너만큼 높이 뛸 수 있다. (high)

My brother can jump ______________________ you.

05 나는 사자처럼 용감해질 수 있다. (brave)

I can be ______________________ a lion.

06 너의 정원은 나의 정원만큼 넓지 않다. (not, large)

Your garden is ______________________ mine.

UNIT 13 비교급

비교 표현 '~보다 더 …한/하게'는 〈비교급+than ~〉의 형태로 써야 해요.

비교 포인트	예문	의미
형용사 비교급 + than	She is taller than her mom.	그녀는 그녀의 엄마보다 더 키가 크다.
부사 비교급 + than	She can run faster than her dad.	그녀는 그녀의 아빠보다 더 빠르게 달릴 수 있다.

참고 than은 '~보다'라는 의미의 전치사예요.

주의 비교급을 강조하여 '훨씬 더'라고 할 때, 비교급 앞에 much, even, far, still, a lot을 써요. 이때, very는 쓸 수 없음에 주의하세요.

|A| 다음 괄호 안에서 알맞은 말을 고르시오.

01 I can be (strong / stronger / strongest) than you.

02 This car is (big / bigger / biggest) than that one.

03 This summer is (hot / hotter / as hot) than last summer.

04 Two heads are (good / better / best) than one.

05 I'll get up as (early / earlier / more early) as my mom.

06 Today is (very / many / much) colder than yesterday.

07 This book is (many / more / most) interesting than that one.

08 This problem is as (difficult / more difficult / most difficult) as that one.

|B| 다음 그림을 보고 괄호 안의 단어를 이용하여 비교급 문장을 완성하시오.

01 ⓐ Mt. Everest is ______________ Mt. Baekdu. (high)

ⓑ Mt. Baekdu is ______________ Mt. Everest. (low)

02 ⓐ Mike is ______________ Jane. (heavy)

ⓑ Jane is ______________ Mike. (light)

03 ⓐ A soccer ball is ______________ a baseball. (big)

ⓑ A baseball is ______________ a soccer ball. (small)

04 ⓐ The red dress is ______________ the yellow one. (expensive)

ⓑ The yellow dress is ______________ the red one. (cheap)

UNIT 14 최상급

다음 최상급 표현의 쓰임을 알아 두세요.

형태	the+최상급	one of the+최상급+복수 명사
의미	가장 ~한/하게	가장 ~한 것들 중 하나
예문	Mina is the tallest student in the class. 반에서 키가 가장 큰 학생	Seoul is one of the busiest cities. 가장 바쁜 도시들 중 하나
	It's the most difficult of all the questions. 그 모든 문제들 중 가장 어려운	Math is one of the most difficult subjects. 가장 어려운 과목들 중 하나

참고 최상급 뒤에 〈in+단수 명사(장소나 집단)〉가 오면, '~에서 가장 …한'을 의미하고, 〈of+복수 명사〉가 오면 '~들 중에서 가장 …한'을 뜻해요.

|A| 다음 괄호 안에서 알맞은 말을 고르시오.

01 She is (tallest / the tallest) student in her class.

02 This is (most largest / the largest) lake in this country.

03 Tom is (the fastest / the most fastest) runner in the team.

04 A dolphin is (the smarter / the smartest) of all animals.

05 What is (the bigest / the biggest) city in England?

06 Mina is (the most young / the youngest) of us all.

07 His grandfather is (the oldest / more oldest) person in the town.

08 He's one of the richest (man / men) in the world.

|B| 우리말과 같은 뜻이 되도록 괄호 안의 단어를 이용하여 문장을 완성하시오.

〈one of the+최상급〉 뒤에는 반드시 복수 명사가 온다는 점에 유의하세요.

01 그는 모든 과목들 중에서 영어를 가장 좋아한다. (much)

He likes English ____________________ of all subjects.

02 가장 편안한 좌석들은 뒤에 있다. (comfortable, seat)

____________________ are at the back.

03 뉴욕은 세계에서 가장 바쁜 도시들 중 하나이다. (busy, city)

New York is one of ____________________ in the world.

04 한국에서 가장 긴 강은 무엇이니? (long, river)

What is ____________________ in Korea?

05 8월은 1년 중 가장 더운 달이다. (hot, month)

August is ____________________ of the year.

06 그녀는 미국에서 가장 유명한 가수들 중 한 명이다. (famous, singer)

She is one of ____________________ in America.

UNIT 15 비교 표현 종합

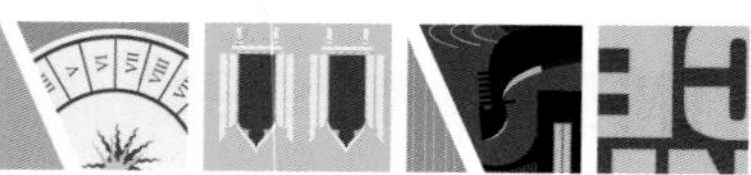

원급, 비교급, 최상급에 관한 기본 사항을 표에서 다시 확인한 후 종합해서 연습하세요.

구분	형태	의미	참고
원급	as ~ as ...	…만큼 ~한/하게	as ~ as 사이에 원급을 써요.
비교급	-er[more ~] than ...	…보다 더 ~한/하게	전치사 than과 함께 써요.
최상급	the -est[most ~] in/of ...	…에서/중에서 가장 ~한/하게	최상급 앞에 the를 붙여요.

A 다음 문장의 밑줄 친 부분을 어법상 바르게 고치시오.

01 Sumi can speak English as good as you. → ______

02 My room is as not dirty as your room. → ______

03 Jessica is the most young of my sisters. → ______

04 Good health is most important than money. → ______

05 James is the better student in my school. → ______

06 This car is one of the expensivest cars. → ______

B 우리말과 같은 뜻이 되도록 괄호 안의 단어를 이용하여 문장을 완성하시오.

01 그녀는 모든 소녀들 중에서 가장 아름답다. (beautiful)

She is ______ of all the girls.

02 이 책이 저 책보다 더 어렵다. (difficult)

This book is ______ that one.

03 이 파란 셔츠는 저 흰 셔츠만큼 싸다. (cheap)

This blue shirt is ______ that white shirt.

04 James는 그의 팀에서 최고의 축구 선수이다. (great, soccer player)

James is ______ in his team.

05 그 상자는 이 상자만큼 무겁지 않다. (not, heavy)

The box is ______ this box.

06 내 컴퓨터가 네 컴퓨터보다 훨씬 더 빠르다. (much, fast)

My computer is ______ yours.

내신기출 다음 중 밑줄 친 Very[very]가 어법상 어색한 것은?

① Very few people know the truth.
② She likes Van Gogh very better than Picasso.
③ They were very impressed with the fast delivery.

실전 TIP

very는 비교급을 강조하는 표현에 쓸 수 없어요.

중간고사·기말고사 실전문제

객관식 (01~25) / 주관식 (26~50)

정답과 해설 • 32쪽

학년과 반 이름 객관식 / 25문항 주관식 / 25문항

01 다음 중 형용사와 부사가 잘못 짝지어진 것은?

① strong – strongly
② bright – brightly
③ hard – hardly
④ gentle – gently
⑤ expensive – expensively

02~04 다음 빈칸에 알맞은 말을 고르시오.

02

We had __________ rain last week.

① many ② few
③ a lot ④ a few
⑤ little

03

__________, the light went on.

① Lucky ② Suddenly
③ Perfect ④ Surprising
⑤ Sure

04

You look __________ than before.

① good ② gooder
③ goodest ④ better
⑤ best

05 다음 ①~⑤ 중 usually가 들어갈 위치로 알맞은 곳은?

Peter ① and his brother ② go ③ to bed ④ before ⑤ midnight.

06 다음 중 원급-비교급-최상급이 잘못 짝지어진 것은?

① fat – fatter – fattest
② safe – safer – safest
③ well – weller – wellest
④ sunny – sunnier – sunniest
⑤ serious – more serious – most serious

07 다음 대화의 빈칸에 알맞은 말끼리 순서대로 짝지어 진 것은?

A: I'm __________ sorry. I couldn't understand this explanation.
B: Don't worry. I couldn't do it, _______.

① terrible – too
② terrible – either
③ terribly – too
④ terribly – either
⑤ terribly – so

08 다음 빈칸에 알맞은 말을 모두 고르면?

I cannot run ___________ fast as Jim.

① to ② for
③ as ④ too
⑤ so

09~11 다음 빈칸에 알맞지 않은 말을 고르시오.

09

There is ___________ salt in the bowl.

① some ② little
③ little ④ lots of
⑤ a few

10

This building is the most ___________ in the city.

① interesting ② important
③ complex ④ popular
⑤ large

11

She is ___________ more popular than him.

① very ② much
③ far ④ even
⑤ still

12 다음 밑줄 친 부분이 어법상 어색한 것은?

① The boy ate too many candies.
② He had too much homework.
③ Jessica wants to make a lot of money.
④ Why do you have much questions?
⑤ She put lots of sugar into her coffee.

13~14 다음 빈칸에 들어갈 말이 순서대로 짝지어진 것을 고르시오.

13

- This book is thinner ___________ that one.
- Chris is the smartest student ___________ his class.

① than – in ② as – in
③ than – of ④ as – of
⑤ the – of

14

- How ___________ water do you drink every day?
- How ___________ times a day do you brush your teeth?

① much – much ② many – many
③ much – many ④ many – a lot
⑤ lots of – a lot

15 다음 중 밑줄 친 부분을 어법상 바르게 고치지 못한 것은?

① Puppies are cutter than kitties. (→ cuter)
② It was the badest time of my life. (→ baddest)
③ Baseball is excitinger than basketball. (→ more exciting)
④ Judy is the friendlyest girl in my family. (→ friendliest)
⑤ Do you know that the cutting board is more dirty than the toilet? (→ dirtier)

16~18 다음 우리말을 영어로 바르게 옮긴 것을 고르시오.

16

나는 절대 밤에 뭔가를 먹지 않는다.

① I don't eat anything at night.
② I often eat something at night.
③ I never don't eat anything at night.
④ I never eat anything at night.
⑤ I sometimes don't eat anything at night.

17

Tom은 우리 반에서 가장 키가 큰 남자아이이다.

① Tom is tall boy in my class.
② Tom is taller boy in my class.
③ Tom is the tallest boy in my class.
④ Tom is tallest boy in my class.
⑤ Tom is the most tall boy in my class.

18

원숭이도 가끔 나무에서 떨어진다.

① Even a monkey sometimes falls from a tree.
② Even a monkey falls sometimes from a tree.
③ Even a monkey often falls from a tree.
④ Even a monkey never falls from a tree.
⑤ Even a monkey falls never from a tree.

19 다음 빈칸에 들어갈 말이 나머지와 다른 것은?

① Tom is the ________ hardworking boy in my town.
② The tiger is ________ dangerous than the fox.
③ Creativity is ________ important than knowledge.
④ The smartpad is ________ expensive than the laptop.
⑤ Children learn a new language ________ easily than adults.

20~21 다음 밑줄 친 ①~⑤ 중 어법상 어색한 것을 고르시오.

20

A little(①) students were(②) late(③) for school(④) in(⑤) the morning.

21

Seoul is(①) one of(②) the nicest(③) city(④) in the world(⑤).

22~23 다음 중 어법상 어색한 문장을 고르시오.

22 ① It was a very old house.
② The final test was so easily.
③ He always makes me happy.
④ Finally, I made contact with him.
⑤ You should listen carefully to your teacher.

23 ① I have a few friends.
② He gave me a little advice.
③ I know few English words.
④ She sang a few songs about peace.
⑤ There are a little cars on the roads.

24 다음 중 어법상 어색한 문장의 개수는?

- Do you have any pets?
- Can you speak more slowly?
- You should always be nice to others.
- This is very more difficult than that.

① 없음 ② 1개
③ 2개 ④ 3개
⑤ 4개

25 어법상 올바른 문장끼리 바르게 짝지어진 것은?

(a) I often drink coffee, either.
(b) Erin speaks Spanish better than Jane.
(c) Fortunate, he got well soon.
(d) January is the coldest month of the year.
(e) Horses have very strongly legs.

① (a), (c) ② (b), (d)
③ (d), (e) ④ (a), (b), (d)
⑤ (a), (c), (e)

26~28 다음 괄호 안에서 알맞은 말을 고르시오.

26 My teacher (always is / is always) kind and nice.

27 This year isn't so (hot / hotter) as last year.

28 I believe I can fly (high / highly) in the sky.

29~31 다음 빈칸에 many 또는 much 중에 알맞은 말을 쓰시오.

29 I don't spend __________ money on myself.

30 Do not have too __________ salt.

31 You can see __________ things under a microscope.

32~34 괄호 안의 단어를 빈칸에 알맞은 형태로 쓰시오.

32 The movie is the __________ (boring) in the world.

33 The man looks __________ (skinny) than before.

34 The castle is big and __________ (beauty).

35~37 다음 문장에서 어법상 어색한 부분을 찾아 바르게 고치시오.

35 I go sometimes shopping with my mom.

__________ → __________

36 His words made her angrily.

__________ → __________

37

She moved to another city a little days ago.

_______________ → _______________

38~40 우리말과 같은 뜻이 되도록 괄호 안의 단어를 바르게 배열하여 문장을 완성하시오. (단, 필요시 단어의 형태를 바꿀 것)

38

James는 그의 할머니를 자주 찾아뵙니?
(James / often / do / visit)

_______________ his grandmother?

39

여기가 이 호텔에서 가장 넓은 방들 중 하나이다.
(the / of / one / room / wide)

This is _______________ in this hotel.

40

그녀의 오빠는 그녀만큼 유명하다.
(her / famous / as / as)

Her brother is _______________.

41~42 다음 빈칸에 공통으로 알맞은 말을 쓰시오.

41

- Which animal do you like the _______?
- What is the _______ expensive watch in this store?

42

- We spend too _______ time on smartphone.
- It is _______ smaller than the guitar.

43~45 책에 대한 다음 표를 보고, 괄호 안의 단어를 빈칸에 알맞은 형태로 쓰시오.

	Book A	Book B	Book C
page	96	160	64
price	12,000	25,000	12,000
interesting	★★★	★★★★	★★★★★

43 Book B is _______________ than Book A. (thick)

44 Book A is _______________ Book C. (cheap)

45 Book C is _______________ of the three. (interesting)

46~48 다음 글에서 어법상 어색한 부분을 세 군데 찾아 바르게 고치시오.

> I make usually breakfast for my family on weekends. This morning, I found a little cheese, any bread, a lot of eggs, and a little onions in the fridge. So, I decided to make the tastiest toast and onion soup.

46 ________ → ________

47 ________ → ________

48 ________ → ________

49 Who is the tallest boy? Complete the sentence.

> Tom is not shorter than Jim.
> Bob is shorter than Mike.
> Tom is as tall as Brian.
> Mike is taller than Tom.

→ ________ is ________ ________ boy.

50 다음 우리말을 주어진 |조건|에 맞게 영어로 바르게 쓰시오.

> 행운은 절대 그에게 미소 짓지 않을 것이다.

|조건|
1. 빈도부사를 이용할 것
2. 단어 fortune, will, smile upon을 이용할 것
3. 6 단어로 쓸 것

→ ________________

내가 가장 취약한 부분에 대해
요점 정리를 해 보세요.

CHAPTER

08 의문사 의문문

Unit 01 의문사 & who(m) 의문문

Unit 02 what 의문문

Unit 03 when/where 의문문

Unit 04 why/how 의문문

Unit 05 〈how+형용사/부사〉 의문문

Unit 06 〈what/which/whose+명사〉 의문문

UNIT 01 의문사 & who(m) 의문문

 사람 또는 사물에 대한 구체적인 정보를 요구할 때 쓰는 의문사의 종류와 의미를 알아 두세요.

what	무엇	who	누구	when	언제
why	왜	where	어디, 어디에서	how	어떤, 어떻게

주의 의문사로 시작하는 의문문은 〈의문사+be동사/일반동사+주어 ~?〉 또는 〈의문사+조동사/do동사+주어+동사원형 ~?〉의 어순으로 쓰세요.

의문사 who가 문장에서 어떻게 쓰이는지 확인하세요.

의미	누구	누가	누구를
역할	보어	주어	목적어
예문	Who is she? 그녀는 누구니?	Who knows you? 누가 너를 아니?	Who(m) do you like? 너는 누구를 좋아하니?

주의 의문사가 주어 역할을 할 때에는 3인칭 단수로 취급하는 점에 유의하세요.

|A| 주어진 대답을 보고 빈칸에 알맞은 의문사를 쓰시오.

01 A: __________ is the man? B: He is my uncle.

02 A: __________ does he do? B: He is an engineer.

03 A: __________ do you get up? B: I get up at seven o'clock.

04 A: __________ does she work? B: She works at a bank.

05 A: __________ were you late? B: Because I got up late.

06 A: __________ do you go to school? B: I go to school by bus.

07 A: __________ did Jessie invite? B: She invited her classmates.

08 A: __________ will you go there? B: I will go there tomorrow morning.

|B| 우리말과 같은 뜻이 되도록 의문사 who(m)와 괄호 안의 단어를 이용하여 문장을 완성하시오.

01 너의 선생님은 누구시니? (your teacher) ____________________

02 누가 그 문을 닫았니? (close, the door) ____________________

03 그녀는 누구를 가르치니? (teach) ____________________

04 어제 누가 Tom과 같이 있었니? (be, with) ____________________

05 누가 이 집에 사니? (live in, this house) ____________________

06 Jessica는 누구를 좋아하니? (like) ____________________

07 누가 너의 부모님을 도와드리니? (help, your parents) ____________________

UNIT 02 what 의문문

의문사 what이 의문문에서 어떻게 쓰이는지 확인하세요.

의문사 who의 의미와 쓰임			의문사 what의 의미와 쓰임		
누구	보어	Who is she?	무엇	보어	What is this?
누가	주어	Who knows you?	무엇이	주어	What makes you mad?
누구를	목적어	Who(m) do you like?	무엇을	목적어	What do you like?

|A| 다음 대화의 빈칸에 알맞은 말을 |보기|에서 골라 그 번호를 쓰시오.

|보기|
ⓐ What do you do?
ⓑ What did she buy?
ⓒ What is your hobby?
ⓓ What are you doing?
ⓔ What did you have for breakfast?

01 A: ______________ B: I'm an engineer.

02 A: ______________ B: I'm cleaning my room.

03 A: ______________ B: My hobby is playing golf.

04 A: ______________ B: I had a sandwich.

05 A: ______________ B: She bought some books.

|B| 괄호 안의 단어를 바르게 배열하여 대화를 완성하시오.

01 A: ____? (what / she / does / have)
B: She has a teddy bear.

02 A: ____? (you / do / what / do / on Sundays)
B: I play tennis with my father.

03 A: ____? (that / what / there / is / over)
B: It is my birthday present.

04 A: ____? (what / talk about / did / John)
B: John talked about his vacation.

05 A: ____? (you / doing / are / now / what)
B: I'm playing computer games with my friends.

내신 기출 다음 대화의 빈칸에 들어갈 말이 다른 것은?

① A: ____________ does your father do?
B: He is a chef.
② A: ____________ did you meet?
B: I met my old friend.
③ A: ____________ is your name?
B: I'm Jessica Anderson. Call me Jessy.

실전 TIP
'누구'를 묻는지, '무엇'을 묻는지 확인해 보세요.

UNIT 03 when/where 의문문

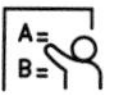

'언제'를 물을 때는 when, '어디'를 물을 때는 where를 써야 해요.

when	언제	When is the exam? When do you go to bed?	그 시험은 언제니? 너는 언제 잠자리에 드니?
where	어디에, 어디서	Where is the bathroom? Where do you study?	화장실은 어디니? 너는 어디서 공부하니?

참고 시간을 묻는 when은 what time으로 바꾸어 쓸 수 있어요.
When did she go to bed? = What time did she go to bed?

|A| When, What, Where 중 알맞은 말을 골라 다음 대화에 빈칸에 쓰시오.

01 A: ______________ is your birthday? B: It's on December 15th.

02 A: ______________ is your mother? B: She's in the living room.

03 A: ______________ are you from? B: I'm from Canada.

04 A: ______________ does the bus leave? B: It leaves at ten o'clock.

05 A: ______________ does she work? B: She works at a hospital.

06 A: ______________ time does he get up? B: He gets up at seven.

07 A: ______________ is the exam? B: It's on Monday.

08 A: ______________ will you meet her? B: I will meet her in the library.

|B| 우리말과 같은 뜻이 되도록 괄호 안의 단어와 알맞은 의문사를 이용하여 문장을 완성하시오.

01 너의 가방은 어디에 있니? (your bag) ______________

02 그 영화는 언제 시작하니? (the movie, begin) ______________

03 Judy는 어디에서 사니? (live) ______________

04 너는 언제 학교에 가니? (go, school) ______________

05 서점은 어디에 있니? (the bookstore) ______________

06 Sam과 Tom은 그곳에 언제 갈 거니? (go, there) ______________

07 그의 아버지는 언제 집에 오시니? (come, home) ______________

08 너는 어제 어디에 갔었니? (go, yesterday) ______________

09 병원은 몇 시에 문을 여니? (time, open, the hospital) ______________

UNIT 04 why/how 의문문

'왜'를 물을 때는 why, '어떤, 어떻게'를 물을 때는 how를 써야 해요.

why	왜	Why are you sad? Why do you like it?	너는 왜 슬프니? 너는 왜 그것을 좋아하니?
how	어떤 어떻게	How was your weekend? How do you go there?	너의 주말은 어땠니? 너는 어떻게 거기에 가니?

|A| Why와 How 중 알맞은 말을 골라 다음 대화의 빈칸에 쓰시오.

01 A: __________ are you angry? B: Because I lost my umbrella.

02 A: __________ is the weather today? B: It is snowing.

03 A: __________ did you run? B: Because I was late.

04 A: __________ was your holiday? B: It was great.

05 A: __________ are you today? B: I'm fine.

06 A: __________ did she go to bed early? B: Because she was sick.

07 A: __________ do you go to school? B: By bus.

08 A: __________ is your room so messy? B: Because I am very busy.

|B| 대화의 빈칸에 알맞은 말을 |보기|에서 골라 그 번호를 쓰시오.

01 A: Why is Judy so happy? B: ________

02 A: How can I help you? B: ________

03 A: How do I go to City Hall? B: ________

04 A: Why did you read this book? B: ________

05 A: Why can't we go on a picnic? B: ________

06 A: How was the party last night? B: ________

07 A: How did you like the food? B: ________

08 A: Why did you turn on the light? B: ________

09 A: Why did you stay home last weekend? B: ________

|보기|
ⓐ Take the subway.
ⓑ Because it was funny.
ⓒ Because today is her birthday.
ⓓ Because it will rain tomorrow.
ⓔ I'm looking for gloves.
ⓕ It was boring.
ⓖ Because it was dark in here.
ⓗ Because I was tired.
ⓘ It was really delicious.

UNIT 05 <how+형용사/부사> 의문문

'얼마나 ~한/하게'라고 물을 때는 〈how+형용사/부사〉로 만들어 하나의 의문사처럼 쓰세요.

의미	의문사	+형용사/부사	의문문
얼마나 자주	How	often	do you go there?
몇 살 (얼마나 오래된)		old	is your brother?
얼마나 긴(길게)		long	does it take?
얼마나 키가 큰		tall	is the building?
(수가) 얼마나 많이		many	do you have?
(가격/양이) 얼마(나 많이)		much	is a ticket?
얼마나 먼		far	is the market?

주의 How many/much 뒤에 명사를 쓸 수 있고, 〈How many/much+명사〉를 하나의 의문사로 취급해요.

How many books do you have? * many+셀 수 있는 명사

How much time do you have? * much+셀 수 없는 명사

|A| 우리말과 같은 뜻이 되도록 빈칸에 알맞은 말을 쓰시오.

01 너의 여동생은 몇 살이니? How ______________ is your sister?

02 너의 아버지는 키가 얼마나 크시니? How ______________ is your father?

03 그의 집은 얼마나 크니? How ______________ is his house?

04 너는 얼마나 자주 산책을 하니? How ______________ do you take a walk?

05 여기에서 병원까지 거리가 얼마나 되니? How ______________ is it from here to the hospital?

06 서울역까지 시간이 얼마나 걸리니? How ______________ does it take to Seoul Station?

07 거기에 얼마나 많은 학생들이 있었니? How ______________ students were there?

|B| 다음 대화의 빈칸에 알맞은 말을 쓰시오.

01 A: ______________ are you? B: I'm fourteen years old.

02 A: ______________ is Seoul Tower? B: It's 236.7m tall.

03 A: ______________ do you meet her? B: I meet her once a month.

04 A: ______________ cats does she have? B: She has two cats.

05 A: ______________ is the subway station from here? B: It's about two kilometers.

06 A: ______________ will you be on vacation? B: For two weeks.

07 A: ______________ salt do you need? B: I need two teaspoons of salt.

|C| 다음 대화의 빈칸에 알맞은 대답을 |보기|에서 골라 그 번호를 쓰시오.

01 A: How old are they? B: ________

02 A: How much is a ticket? B: ________

03 A: How tall is your daughter? B: ________

04 A: How many books did you buy? B: ________

05 A: How far is it from here to the bus stop? B: ________

06 A: How often do you go swimming? B: ________

07 A: How long will you be in New York? B: ________

08 A: How much water do you want? B: ________

|보기|
ⓐ I bought five books.
ⓑ Three times a week.
ⓒ She is 160 cm tall.
ⓓ It is thirty thousand won.
ⓔ I'll be here for a week.
ⓕ They are about 40 years old.
ⓖ Two glasses of water.
ⓗ It's about one kilometer.

|D| 우리말과 같은 뜻이 되도록 괄호 안의 단어를 이용하여 문장을 완성하시오.

01 너의 새 아파트는 얼마나 크니? (big, apartment)

____

02 너는 얼마나 오래 여기에서 기다려야 하니? (long, should, wait here)

____

03 63빌딩은 얼마나 높니? (tall, the 63 Building)

____

04 너는 얼마나 자주 이를 닦니? (often, brush your teeth)

____

05 그의 집에서 사무실까지 거리가 얼마나 되니? (far, his house, the office, it)

____

06 그 연주회에 얼마나 많은 사람들이 왔니? (many, there, were, at the concert)

____

실전 TIP

how much와 how many의 쓰임을 구별해야 해요.

내신 기출 다음 빈칸에 들어갈 말이 다른 하나는?

① How ________ is this bag?
② How ________ water is there in the cup?
③ How ________ books are there in your room?

UNIT 06 <what/which/whose+명사> 의문문

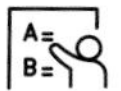

의문사 what, which, whose 뒤에 명사를 써서 하나의 의문사처럼 쓰는 법을 알아 두세요.

의미	의문사	+ 명사	+의문문	해석
무슨 ~	What	time	is it?	몇 시니?
		day	is it?	무슨 요일이니?
		color	do you like?	너는 무슨 색을 좋아하니?
어느 ~	Which	one	do you like better?	너는 어느 것을 더 좋아하니?
		subject	is more difficult?	어느 과목이 더 어렵니?
누구의 ~	Whose	bag	is this?	이것은 누구의 가방이니?
		shoes	are these?	이것은 누구의 신발이니?

참고 what은 정해지지 않은 대상 중에서 선택을 필요로 할 때 쓰는 반면, which는 정해진 대상 중에 선택할 때 쓴다는 점에 유의하세요.

A 우리말과 같은 뜻이 되도록 what, which, whose 중 알맞은 말을 골라 빈칸에 쓰시오.

01 어느 상자가 더 무겁니? ______________ box is heavier?

02 이것은 누구의 모자니? ______________ hat is this?

03 너는 무슨 간식을 먹고 싶니? ______________ snack do you want?

04 저것은 누구의 집이니? ______________ house is that?

05 이 카메라와 저 카메라 중 어느 것이 더 낫니? ______________ camera is better, this one or that one?

B 괄호 안의 단어를 바르게 배열하여 다음 대화를 완성하시오.

01 A: ______________________? (does / the movie / time / begin / what)
B: It begins at six thirty.

02 A: ______________________? (which / prefer / bag / you / do)
B: I like the black one better.

03 A: ______________________? (this / whose / is / umbrella)
B: It's mine.

04 A: ______________________? (color / what / your mother's car / is)
B: It is red.

05 A: ______________________? (it / today / day / is / what)
B: It is Saturday.

06 A: ______________________? (faster / which / is / bike)
B: This one.

중간고사·기말고사 실전문제

객관식 (01~25) / 주관식 (26~50)

정답과 해설 • 35쪽

학년과 반 　 이름 　 객관식 　 / 25문항 　 주관식 　 / 25문항

01~03 다음 빈칸에 알맞은 말을 고르시오.

01

_______ can I get Wi-Fi?

① How ② Who
③ What ④ Which
⑤ Whose

02

_______ will the train for Busan depart?

① Who ② When
③ Whose ④ Which
⑤ How far

03

_______ do you go to the theater?

① How far ② How much
③ How well ④ How often
⑤ How long

04~05 우리말과 같은 뜻이 되도록 빈칸에 알맞은 말을 고르시오.

04

_______ drank the juice on the table?
(누가 식탁 위에 있던 주스를 마셨니?)

① How ② Who
③ What ④ When
⑤ Where

05

_______ flower does your mother like?
(너희 엄마는 무슨 꽃을 좋아하시니?)

① Why ② How
③ Whom ④ What
⑤ Whose

06~07 다음 괄호 안의 단어들을 순서대로 배열할 때, 세 번째로 오는 단어를 고르시오.

06

_______, large or small?
(size / which / you / need / do)

① do ② you
③ size ④ need
⑤ which

07

_______ birthday party?
(people / many / came / how / to / your)

① how ② your
③ came ④ many
⑤ people

08~09 다음 빈칸에 공통으로 알맞은 말을 고르시오.

08

- _______ will Ms. Jeong meet us today?
- _______ is the nearest subway station?

① Why ② When
③ Where ④ What
⑤ Which

09

- ________ did you tell my secret to her?
- ________ is the market closed today?

① Why ② Who
③ What ④ Where
⑤ Which

10 다음 중 어법상 올바른 문장을 모두 고르면?

① What do you want to watch?
② When did Sophia got married?
③ How many sugar does he have?
④ Whose floor does Sora live on, 4 or 5?
⑤ How do I get to the Empire State Building?

11 다음 대화의 빈칸에 알맞은 말은?

A: ________ did you prepare for the presentation?
B: Almost a month.

① How old ② How many
③ How long ④ What time
⑤ Which one

12~14 다음 빈칸에 들어갈 말이 순서대로 짝지어진 것을 고르시오.

12

- ________ did John have for dinner?
- ________ did you meet on the bus?

① Who – Why ② What – Which
③ Whom – When ④ What – Whom
⑤ Whose – Where

13

- ________ phone is this on the sofa?
- ________ way is the exit, this way or that way?

① What – Who ② When – Which
③ How – When ④ Whose – What
⑤ Whose – Which

14

- ________ did they rebuild the building?
- ________ people attended the Busan International Film Festival?

① Why – How many
② Why – How much
③ What – How long
④ What – How often
⑤ Which – How far

15 다음 빈칸에 들어갈 말이 다른 것은?

① ________ did Mike hand in his report?
② ________ did you have some pizza?
③ ________ is your opinion on this subject?
④ ________ are you going to see your parents?
⑤ ________ does your brother go jogging every morning?

16~17 다음 대화의 밑줄 친 ①~⑤ 중 어법상 어색한 것을 고르시오.

16

A: ① Why ② Minho does ③ study English hard every day?
B: ④ Because he wants ⑤ to live in America.

17

A: ① How much time ② does you ③ need ④ to finish the work?
B: ⑤ I think I need two days.

18~19 다음 중 어법상 어색한 문장을 고르시오.

18 ① How wide is this river?
② What does this word mean?
③ How did you learn about our company?
④ Who will be the captain of the soccer team?
⑤ Which season do she like better, summer or winter?

19 ① Who hit you in the face?
② Which bus goes to Gangnam?
③ How often does he uses the taxi?
④ Why didn't you show up for the class?
⑤ What animal did the children see in the forest?

20~21 다음 우리말을 영어로 바르게 옮긴 것을 고르시오.

20

네 최신형 전화기는 얼마나 크니?

① How old is your latest phone?
② How tall is your latest phone?
③ How big is your latest phone?
④ How long is your latest phone?
⑤ How much is your latest phone?

21

그녀는 왜 그렇게 피곤해 보이니?

① Why she looks so tired?
② Why does she look so tired?
③ Why she does look so tiring?
④ Why does she looks so tired?
⑤ Why she does looks so tiring?

22 다음 빈칸에 들어갈 수 없는 말은?

- ________ did you meet at the coffee shop?
- ________ did Mr. Lee buy for his daughter?
- ________ do I upload a video to the website?
- ________ is a better exercise, running or swimming?

① Who ② How
③ What ④ Where
⑤ Which

23 다음 중 밑줄 친 부분을 묻는 의문문으로 알맞지 않은 것은?

① Chris lives in Seoul.
← Where does Chris live?
② She was in Brazil in 2018.
← When was she in Brazil?
③ My favorite fruit is the strawberry.
← What's your favorite fruit?
④ Jane's best friend is Jimin.
← Who is Jane's best friend?
⑤ He drinks water because he's thirsty.
← Which drink does he want?

24 다음 중 어법상 어색한 문장의 개수는?

- What movie does Sujin likes?
- How should I make my password?
- Why does she leave so early yesterday?
- Where did you heard the news about the famous singer?
- When are you going to have your homecoming party?

① 1개 ② 2개 ③ 3개 ④ 4개 ⑤ 5개

25 다음 짝지어진 대화 중 어법상 어색한 것은?

① A: Which ones do you want to buy?
B: I want to buy these light shoes.

② A: When did Ms. Smith have her first kid?
B: In 2010.

③ A: Why didn't you come? Everybody else was there.
B: Because I got up late.

④ A: Why do you make cupcakes?
B: First, mix some flour with some eggs, salt and water.

⑤ A: How many times does she go to the gym in a week?
B: She goes to the gym three times a week.

26~28 |보기|에서 알맞은 말을 골라 문장을 완성하시오.

보기		
Which	Whose	When
Why	How old	How many

26 ______________ is this building?

27 ______________ did you buy the groceries at the store?

28 ______________ was the Olympic Park crowded yesterday?

29~31 다음 대화에서 어법상 어색한 부분을 찾아 바르게 고치시오.

29

A: What are you think about your job?
B: I'm satisfied with my job.

______________ → ______________

30

A: Where you did buy these sunglasses?
B: I bought them at the department store.

______________ → ______________

31

A: How did Henry come to work early this morning?
B: Because he had some work to do.

______________ → ______________

32~34 |보기|에서 알맞은 말을 골라 대화를 완성하시오.

|보기|

How often	How many	How much
How old	How long	How far

32

A: ______________ were you when we first met?
B: I was 14 years old.

33

A: ______________ are there flights to Chicago?
B: Two times a day.

34

A: ______________ sugar do you want in your tea?
B: Just one teaspoon, please.

35~36 우리말과 같은 뜻이 되도록 다음 대화의 빈칸에 알맞은 말을 쓰시오.

35

A: ______________ are you listening to?
(너는 무슨 노래를 듣고 있니?)
B: I'm listening to "Stay."

36

A: ______________ do you think is more expensive?
(너는 어느 것이 더 비싸다고 생각하니?)
B: The blue one.

37~38 다음 빈칸에 공통으로 알맞은 의문사를 쓰시오.

37

- ______________ did you move to New York in 2020?
- ______________ did you decide to be a nurse?

38

- ______________ time do you usually eat dinner?
- ______________ time will you check in at our hotel?

39~41 우리말과 같은 뜻이 되도록 괄호 안의 말을 바르게 배열하시오.

39

너는 왜 회의에 늦었니?

____
the meeting? (were / why / you / late for)

40

너는 무엇을 볼 거니?

______________________________?
(watch / what / you / are / going to)

41

그녀는 얼마나 자주 사진을 찍니?

______________________________?
(how / does / she / often / take pictures)

42~43 다음 문장 중 어법상 어색한 부분을 두 군데 찾아 바르게 고치시오.

(a) What did you do last night?
(b) Why didn't you tell me anything?
(c) Where does Eric go to have lunch?
(d) Who want a cup of coffee during the break?
(e) When are we go to move to the new building?

42 ______________ → ______________

43 ______________ → ______________

44~45 우리말과 같은 뜻이 되도록 괄호 안의 단어를 이용하여 문장을 완성하시오.

44 제가 이 바지를 어디에서 입어 볼 수 있나요?

______________________ these pants? (can, try, on)

45 당신은 양복이 몇 벌이나 있나요?

______________________?
(suits, have)

46 다음 괄호 안의 단어를 바르게 배열하여 대화를 완성하시오.

A: Front desk. May I help you?
B: Can I check out a little later?
A: ______________________?
(time / want / do / check out / what / you / to)
B: Around 11:30? I have something to do early in the morning.
A: Okay, no problem.

47~49 다음 대화에서 어법상 어색한 부분을 세 군데 찾아 바르게 고치시오.

A: Are you ready for our trip this weekend?
B: Yes! When are we going to meet?
A: Let's meet in front of the school.
B: Okay. How we get to the airport?
A: We have two choices, by bus or by subway.
B: Whose one is faster?
A: The subway is faster than the bus.

47 ______________ → ______________

48 ______________ → ______________

49 ______________ → ______________

50 다음 문장을 주어진 |조건|에 맞게 영어로 바르게 쓰시오.

Mary and Tom knew the result of the test on <u>September 1st</u>.

|조건|
1. 의문사로 시작할 것
2. 밑줄 친 부분을 묻는 의문문이 될 것
3. 필요시 어법에 맞게 단어의 형태를 바꿀 것

→ ______________________

CHAPTER

09 문장의 종류

Unit 01 명령문
Unit 02 청유문
Unit 03 부가의문문 1
Unit 04 부가의문문 2
Unit 05 부정의문문
Unit 06 선택의문문
Unit 07 what으로 시작하는 감탄문
Unit 08 how로 시작하는 감탄문

UNIT 01 명령문

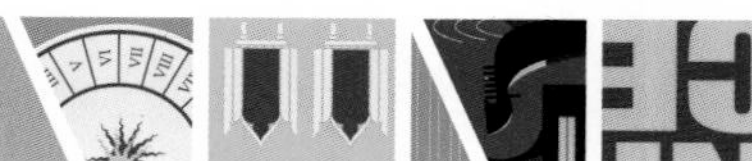

'~해라, ~하세요'와 같은 명령문은 주어 You를 없애고, 동사원형으로 문장을 시작해야 해요.

	긍정 명령문		부정 명령문	
be동사	Be	quiet.	Don't be	quiet.
일반동사	Close	the door.	Don't close	the door.

참고 공손한 요청은 명령문 앞뒤에 please를 넣고, '절대 하지 마라'라고 강조할 때는 Don't 대신 Never를 쓰면 돼요.
Be quiet, please. 조용히 해 주세요.
Never close the door. 절대 문을 닫지 마.

|A| 우리말과 같은 뜻이 되도록 괄호 안의 단어를 이용하여 문장을 완성하시오.

01 다른 사람들에게 친절해라. (kind) ________________ to others.

02 자, 여기에 이름을 쓰세요. (write) Please ________________ your name here.

03 돈을 낭비하지 마라. (waste) ________________ your money.

04 교실에서 조용히 해라. (quiet) ________________ in the classroom.

05 다시는 늦지 마라. (late) ________________ again.

06 매일 영어 공부를 해라. (study) ________________ English every day.

07 너무 빨리 달리지 마라. (run) ________________ too fast.

08 절대 약속을 어기지 마라. (never, break) ________________ a promise.

|B| 다음 문장을 |보기|와 같이 명령문으로 바꾸어 쓰시오.

|보기|
You should do your best. → Do your best.
You shouldn't take pictures here. → Don't take pictures here.

01 You should be honest all the time. → ________________

02 You shouldn't play soccer in the garden. → ________________

03 You should read a lot of books. → ________________

04 You should never lie. → ________________

05 You shouldn't make any noise in the library. → ________________

06 You should be a good student. → ________________

07 You should come back home by six. → ________________

08 You should turn off your phone during the show. → ________________

UNIT 02 청유문

'~하자'처럼 같이 하자고 제안을 할 때 〈Let's+동사원형〉으로 쓰세요.

	긍정 청유문		부정 청유문	
be동사	Let's be	quiet.	Let's not be	quiet.
일반동사	Let's close	the door.	Let's not close	the door.

주의 부정 청유문에서 not은 Let's와 동사원형 사이에 위치하는 점에 유의하세요.

|A| 우리말과 같은 뜻이 되도록 괄호 안의 단어를 이용하여 문장을 완성하시오.

01 영화 보러 가자. (go) ______________________ to a movie.

02 노래 부르자. (sing) ______________________ a song.

03 버스를 타지 말자. (take) ______________________ the bus.

04 이번 일요일에 소풍가자. (go on) ______________________ a picnic this Sunday.

05 학교에 걸어가자. (walk) ______________________ to school.

06 그 문제에 대해 그만 얘기하자. (talk about) ______________________ the problem.

07 테니스 동아리에 가입하자. (join) ______________________ the tennis club.

|B| 우리말과 같은 뜻이 되도록 어법상 어색한 부분에 밑줄 긋고 바르게 고치시오.

01 Let's does wash the dishes after dinner. (저녁 식사 후에 설거지를 하자.) → ______________________

02 Let write a letter to our parents. (부모님께 편지를 쓰자.) → ______________________

03 Let's are quiet in the library. (도서관에서 조용하자.) → ______________________

04 Let's not to tell this to Sandy. (이것은 Sandy에게 말하지 말자.) → ______________________

05 Let's be not late for school. (학교에 지각하지 말자.) → ______________________

06 Let's stop and has lunch. (그만하고 점심 먹자.) → ______________________

07 Let's not crossing the street here. (여기서 길을 건너지 말자.) → ______________________

08 Let's inviting her family to dinner. (그녀의 가족을 저녁 식사에 초대하자.) → ______________________

09 Let's to buy a birthday present for him. (그에게 줄 생일 선물을 사자.) → ______________________

실전 TIP

청유문과 명령문에 쓰이는 동사의 형태를 기억해 보세요.

내신 기출 다음 빈칸에 공통으로 알맞은 말은?

- Let's not ____________ out this evening.
- Don't ____________ the fish. It smells bad.

① eat ② eats ③ ate ④ eating ⑤ to eat

UNIT 03 부가의문문 1

평서문 뒤에 '그렇지?, 그렇지 않니?'라고 확인을 구하는 부가의문문의 사용법을 알아 두세요.

	평서문,	+ 부가의문문	예문
be동사	긍정	be동사의 부정형+주격 인칭대명사?	She is wise, isn't she?
	부정	be동사의 긍정형+주격 인칭대명사?	She isn't wise, is she?
일반동사	긍정	do동사의 부정형+주격 인칭대명사?	She has a bike, doesn't she?
	부정	do동사의 긍정형+주격 인칭대명사?	She doesn't have a bike, does she?

주의 대답은 긍정이면 무조건 Yes, 부정이면 무조건 No로 해야 해요.

A: She is wise, isn't she?

B: Yes, she is. (현명함) / No, she isn't. (현명하지 않음)

주의 부가의문문에서 am의 부정은 aren't로 한다는 것에 주의하세요.

I am too late, aren't I?

|A| 다음 문장의 밑줄 친 부분을 바르게 고치시오.

01 My sister is so cute, doesn't she? → ____________

02 She isn't busy now, isn't she? → ____________

03 He bought a bike, wasn't he? → ____________

04 It was a great party, didn't it? → ____________

05 Mike likes sports, isn't he? → ____________

06 You speak English well, aren't you? → ____________

07 They didn't visit him, did him? → ____________

|B| 빈칸에 알맞은 말을 써서 다음 부가의문문과 대답을 완성하시오.

01 A: This is your computer, ____________? B: Yes, ____________.

02 A: She has a pet, ____________? B: Yes, ____________.

03 A: They play basketball, ____________? B: No, ____________.

04 A: Tom and Bill were good friends, ____________? B: Yes, ____________.

05 A: My sister doesn't dance well, ____________? B: No, ____________.

06 A: They aren't students, ____________? B: Yes, ____________.

07 A: You were a doctor, ____________? B: No, ____________.

08 A: Jessica runs very fast, ____________? B: Yes, ____________.

09 A: Minseok didn't pass the exam, ____________? B: No, ____________.

부가의문문의 시제는 앞에 있는 평서문과 일치시켜야 해요.

UNIT 04 부가의문문 2

조동사가 있는 문장이나, 명령문, 청유문의 부가의문문을 만드는 방법에 유의하세요.

	평서문,	+ 부가의문문	예문
조동사	긍정	조동사의 부정형+주격 인칭대명사?	She can ride a bike, can't she?
	부정	조동사의 긍정형+주격 인칭대명사?	She can't ride a bike, can she?
명령문	긍정	will you?	Be quiet, will you?
	부정		Don't touch it, will you?
청유문	긍정	shall we?	Let's start the game, shall we?
	부정		Let's not do it, shall we?

A 다음 문장의 밑줄 친 부분을 바르게 고치시오.

01 Susan can speak Korean, can't Susan? → ______________________

02 Let's go to the movies, will we? → ______________________

03 Take a seat, shall we? → ______________________

04 Don't touch the picture, do it? → ______________________

05 Let's play soccer, shall you? → ______________________

06 It will rain tomorrow, doesn't it? → ______________________

B 다음 빈칸에 알맞은 부가의문문을 쓰시오.

01 Jason can drive, ______________________?

02 Turn left at the corner, ______________________?

03 Let's not go shopping this afternoon, ______________________?

04 Don't be late again, ______________________?

05 You will go hiking, ______________________?

06 Be kind to old people, ______________________?

07 Let's eat out tonight, ______________________?

08 Read a book every day, ______________________?

09 She should prepare for the test, ______________________?

내신 기출 다음 밑줄 친 부분이 어법상 어색한 것은?

① Tom can't play tennis well, can he?

② We shouldn't play games here, should we?

③ Kevin read the newspaper, doesn't he?

실전 TIP

부가의문문 앞에 있는 평서문의 동사가 과거인지 현재인지 구별해야 해요. 이때, 과거형의 불규칙 변화에 유의해야 해요.

UNIT 05 부정의문문

'~이지 않니?'와 같이 부정으로 질문할 때는 부정의문문을 쓰세요.

	긍정의문문	부정의문문
be동사	Were you angry?	Weren't you angry?
일반동사	Do you like music?	Don't you like music?
조동사	Can you speak English?	Can't you speak English?

주의 대답은 부가의문문처럼 긍정이면 무조건 Yes, 부정이면 무조건 No로 해야 해요.

|A| 다음 우리말과 같은 뜻이 되도록 빈칸에 알맞은 말을 쓰시오.

01 너는 학생이지 않니? ______________ a student?

02 그는 배고프지 않니? ______________ hungry?

03 그들은 스페인어를 말하지 않니? ______________ speak Spanish?

04 그녀는 고양이를 좋아하지 않니? ______________ like cats?

05 너는 어제 그녀를 만나지 않았니? ______________ meet her yesterday?

06 그들은 친한 친구지 않니? ______________ close friends?

07 너는 우리와 함께할 수 있지 않니? ______________ join us?

08 그녀는 우산을 가져가야 하지 않니? ______________ take an umbrella?

|B| 우리말과 같은 뜻이 되도록 괄호 안의 단어를 이용하여 다음 대화를 완성하시오.

01 A: 너는 지금 춥지 않니? (cold)
______________ now?
B: 아니, 안 추워. (not)
No, ______________.

02 A: 그는 그 소식을 알지 않니? (know)
______________ the news?
B: 아니, 그는 몰라. (doesn't)
No, ______________.

03 A: 너는 내일까지 보고서를 끝낼 수 있지 않니? (finish)
______________ the report tomorrow?
B: 아니, 그럴 수 없어. (can't)
______________.

04 A: 그녀는 어제 네게 전화했지 않니? (call)
______________ you yesterday?
B: 응, 전화했어. (did)
______________.

부정의문문은 부정어 not을 포함하는 의문문으로, 질문의 형태와 상관없이 대답의 내용이 긍정이면 Yes, 부정이면 No로 답해야 해요.

UNIT 06 선택의문문

둘 중 하나를 고르도록 묻고자 할 때는 or를 넣어 선택의문문으로 만드세요.

일반 의문문	선택의문문
Is this cap yours?	Is this cap yours or your brother's?
Who ate my pizza?	Who ate my pizza, Tom or Jerry?
What do you want?	Which do you want, tea or juice?

|A| 우리말과 같은 뜻이 되도록 빈칸에 알맞은 말을 쓰시오.

01 그는 의사니 아니면 선생님이니? ____________ he a doctor ____________ a teacher?

02 너는 그곳에 버스로 가니, 택시로 가니? ____________ you go there by bus ____________ by taxi?

03 Sam과 Mike 중 누가 더 어리니? ____________ is younger, Sam ____________ Mike?

04 너는 주스와 차 중 어느 것을 원하니? ____________ do you want, juice ____________ tea?

05 네 부모님은 서울에 계시니, 부산에 계시니? ____________ your parents in Seoul ____________ in Busan?

06 이것과 저것 중 어느 연필이 더 긴가? ____________ pencil is longer, this one ____________ that one?

07 그녀는 고양이를 키우니 아니면 개를 키우니? ____________ she have a cat ____________ a dog?

08 너는 여름과 겨울 중 어느 계절을 더 좋아하니?

____________ season do you like better, summer ____________ winter?

|B| 우리말과 같은 뜻이 되도록 괄호 안의 단어를 이용하여 문장을 완성하시오.

or의 앞과 뒤에 오는 말은 동일한 문장 성분이어야 해요.

01 저 남자는 너의 형이니 아니면 너의 삼촌이니? (that man, brother, uncle)

____

02 너는 창가 쪽 좌석을 원하니 아니면 통로 쪽 좌석을 원하니? (want, a window seat, an aisle seat)

____

03 Jessica와 Sally 중 누가 그 방을 청소했니? (clean, the room)

____

04 그녀는 책을 읽고 있니 아니면 잡지를 읽고 있니? (read, a book, a magazine)

____

05 너는 검정색과 흰색 중 어느 색을 더 좋아하니? (color, like, better, black, white)

____

06 금요일과 토요일 중 너는 언제 한가하니? (free, on Friday, on Saturday)

____

UNIT 07 what으로 시작하는 감탄문

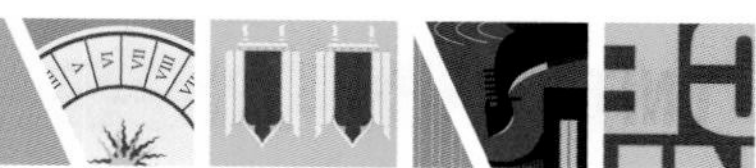

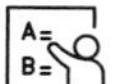

'정말[참] ~한 …이구나!'와 같이 명사에 대한 감탄을 나타낼 때는 what으로 시작하는 감탄문으로 써요.

감탄의 대상	어순					예문
셀 수 없는 명사	What	–	(형용사)	명사	(주어+동사)!	What big bread (it is)!
셀 수 있는 단수 명사		a(n)	(형용사)			What a wonderful world (it is)!
셀 수 있는 복수 명사		–	(형용사)			What fast boys (they are)!

주의 셀 수 있는 단수 명사에 대한 감탄문일 때만 부정관사 a(n)를 써요.

참고 what으로 시작하는 감탄문은 〈주어+동사〉를 생략하는 경우가 많아요.

|A| 다음 문장을 what으로 시작하는 감탄문으로 바꾸시오.

01 It is a nice dress. → ______________________

02 They have very old paintings. → ______________________

03 She is a very kind girl. → ______________________

04 They are very smart students. → ______________________

05 He is a very generous boy. → ______________________

06 It is a very interesting game. → ______________________

07 It was a very wonderful day. → ______________________

08 They are very good basketball players. → ______________________

|B| 우리말과 같은 뜻이 되도록 괄호 안의 단어를 바르게 배열하시오.

01 그것은 정말 높은 건물이구나! (a / building / is / what / it / tall)

____

02 이 집은 정말 큰 집이구나! (house / big / what / is / this / a)

____

03 그것은 정말 아름다운 정원이구나! (what / beautiful / a / is / it / garden)

____

04 정말 좋은 날씨구나! (weather / it / is / nice / what)

____

05 그는 정말 비싼 자동차를 가지고 있구나! (car / he / an / what / has / expensive)

____

06 그들은 정말 환상적인 여행을 했구나! (they / trip / had / a / what / fantastic)

____

UNIT 08 how로 시작하는 감탄문

'정말[참] ~하구나!'와 같이 형용사나 부사에 대한 감탄은 how로 시작하는 감탄문으로 표현하세요.

감탄의 대상	어순			예문
형용사	How	형용사	(주어+동사)!	How big (the apple is)!
부사		부사		How fast (the boys can run)!

참고 주어나 동사를 구체적으로 표현할 때가 아니라면, how로 시작하는 감탄문에서도 〈주어+동사〉를 생략하는 경우가 많아요.

|A| 다음 문장을 how로 시작하는 감탄문으로 바꾸시오.

01 This room is very large. → ______________________

02 The man walks very fast. → ______________________

03 The test was very easy. → ______________________

04 This dish is very delicious. → ______________________

05 The ring is very expensive. → ______________________

06 She gets up very early. → ______________________

07 The cat is very cute. → ______________________

|B| 우리말과 같은 뜻이 되도록 괄호 안의 단어를 바르게 배열하시오.

01 그 소년은 정말 용감했구나! (brave / how / was / the boy)

____

02 이 배낭은 정말 무겁구나! (this backpack / how / is / heavy)

____

03 이 꽃들은 정말 아름답구나! (how / these flowers / beautiful / are)

____

04 별이 정말 밝게 빛나는구나! (the stars / brightly / how / shine)

____

05 시간이 정말 빠르게 지나가는구나! (fast / how / goes by / time)

____

내신 기출 다음 문장을 밑줄 친 부분을 강조하는 감탄문으로 바꾸시오.

- The movie was sad. → ______________________
- It was a sad movie. → ______________________

실전 TIP

형용사나 부사를 강조할 때는 How, 명사를 강조할 때는 What을 사용한다는 것을 기억하세요.

중간고사·기말고사 실전문제

객관식 (01~25) / 주관식 (26~50)

학년과 반 이름 객관식 / 25문항 주관식 / 25문항

01~03 다음 빈칸에 알맞은 말을 고르시오.

01

_______ climb up the tree! It's dangerous.

① Do ② Don't
③ Let's ④ Be
⑤ Go

02

What a funny book _________!

① it is ② is it
③ they are ④ he is
⑤ are you

03

Don't forget to bring your ticket, _________?

① do you ② are you
③ will you ④ were you
⑤ can you

04 다음 두 문장의 뜻이 같도록 빈칸에 알맞은 말이 순서대로 짝지어진 것은?

_______ a beautiful house it is!
_______ beautiful the house is!

① How – What ② What – So
③ Very – So ④ How – Very
⑤ What – How

05 다음 대화의 빈칸에 알맞은 말은?

A: Aren't Jerry and Julia from England?
B: _________________ They are from America.
A: I got it.

① Yes, we are.
② Yes, they aren't.
③ No, you aren't.
④ No, they aren't.
⑤ No, they don't.

06~08 우리말과 같은 뜻이 되도록 빈칸에 알맞은 말을 고르시오.

06

_______ washed the dishes, Jinho or Jisu?
(진호와 지민이 중에 누가 설거지를 했니?)

① Where ② What
③ Who ④ When
⑤ How

07

_________ your cell phone during the meeting.
(회의 중에는 휴대 전화를 끄세요.)

① Turn off ② Turning off
③ Turns off ④ Turned off
⑤ Don't turn off

08

I'm tired of arguing with you. _________ _________ do it anymore.
(너와 말싸움하는 것에 지쳤어. 더 이상 하지 말자.)

① Let's ② Not
③ None ④ Let's not
⑤ Not let's

09 다음 괄호 안의 단어들을 순서대로 배열할 때, 여섯 번째로 오는 단어는?

"(is / and / how / beautiful / this / city / clean)!" he said.

① city ② is
③ this ④ how
⑤ clean

10 다음 우리말을 영어로 바르게 옮긴 것은?

너는 버스 타고 왔니, 아니면 택시 타고 왔니?

① Did you come by bus or by taxi?
② Can you come by bus or by taxi?
③ Are you coming by bus or by taxi?
④ Which do you prefer, a bus or a taxi?
⑤ Do you want to take a taxi rather than a bus?

11~12 다음 빈칸에 공통으로 알맞은 말을 고르시오.

11

• _________ pick the flowers in the garden.
• Mike and Judy practice singing for a contest, _________ they?

① Do[do] ② Don't[don't]
③ Didn't[didn't] ④ Can't[can't]
⑤ Won't[won't]

12

• This watch looks good, _________ it?
• _________ she go to school by bike?

① does[Does] ② did[Did]
③ doesn't[Doesn't] ④ don't[Don't]
⑤ isn't[Isn't]

13 다음 빈칸에 들어갈 말이 나머지와 다른 것은?

① _________ an amazing story!
② _________ long this tunnel is!
③ _________ short pencils they are!
④ _________ pretty toys the children have!
⑤ _________ a nice cellphone you bought!

14 다음 밑줄 친 부분 중 어법상 어색한 것은?

① Koalas only live in Australia, don't they?
② Tom and I made a great song, didn't he?
③ Jane was listening to the radio, wasn't she?
④ Mina and Subin are good friends, aren't they?
⑤ You know Picasso was a Spanish painter, don't you?

15 다음 빈칸에 들어갈 수 없는 말은?

- __________ not cross the street here, shall we?
- They don't like to try new foods, __________ they?
- __________ a busy day it is!
- Maria __________ take her medicine, shouldn't she?

① Do[do] ② Let's[let's]
③ Should[should] ④ What[what]
⑤ Does[does]

16~18 다음 중 어법상 어색한 문장을 고르시오.

16 ① Let's not make any noise.
② I'm not ready yet. Please wait for me.
③ It's freezing outside. Not let's go out.
④ Let's meet at one o'clock. Don't be late.
⑤ I don't want to talk to you. Leave me alone.

17 ① I'm a little late, aren't I?
② How beautiful these flowers are!
③ Mike watches TV a lot, doesn't he?
④ Didn't they take a walk after lunch?
⑤ Isn't Spain wonderful? Please visits Spain someday.

18 ① Let's have some cake, shall we?
② Don't take pictures here, do you?
③ Jennifer is a great athlete, isn't she?
④ Seho didn't like to play soccer, did he?
⑤ Your grandmother can speak English, can't she?

19 다음 중 어법상 올바른 문장을 모두 고르면?

① You feel thirsty, are you?
② She can ride a bike, will she?
③ Kihun isn't waiting for me, is he?
④ They don't want to travel to Europe, do they?
⑤ Donghun will bake cupcakes at home, does he?

20~22 다음 빈칸에 들어갈 말이 순서대로 짝지어진 것을 고르시오.

20

- You won't be late, __________?
- Tiffany loves her pet dog, __________?

① won't you – is she
② shall we – does she
③ will you – don't she
④ will you – doesn't she
⑤ will you – didn't she

21

> • ___________ your father a taxi driver?
> • ___________ you understand this question?

① Isn't – Can't
② Don't – Won't
③ Aren't – Can't
④ Weren't – Won't
⑤ Doesn't – Shouldn't

22

> • ___________ this spaghetti. It is so delicious.
> • ___________ up late at night. You have to get up early tomorrow.

① Take – Stay
② Take – Get
③ Have – Not stay
④ Try – Don't stay
⑤ Try – Doesn't stay

23 다음 중 어법상 어색한 문장의 개수는?

> • Let's go for a picnic, will you?
> • Don't you like the food at this restaurant?
> • Which would you like to have, rice or bread?
> • She wasn't there on Tuesday, didn't she?
> • Chris likes to play the guitar, doesn't he?

① 1개 ② 2개
③ 3개 ④ 4개
⑤ 5개

24 다음 평서문을 감탄문으로 바꾼 것 중 어법상 어색한 것은?

① It's a scary movie.
→ What a scary movie!
② The dog is so small.
→ How small the dog is!
③ It is a very old piano.
→ What an old piano it is!
④ She jumps very high.
→ How high she jumps!
⑤ These are very expensive shoes.
→ What an expensive shoes these are!

25 다음 짝지어진 대화 중 어법상 어색한 것은?

① A: They don't like cold weather, do they?
B: No, they don't.
② A: You didn't get the job, do you?
B: Yes, I did.
③ A: Jiho was very tired, wasn't he?
B: No, he wasn't.
④ A: We should protect wild animals, shouldn't we?
B: Yes, we should.
⑤ A: There is a yellow house over there, isn't there?
B: Yes, there is.

26~27 다음 빈칸에 What 또는 How 중에 알맞은 말을 쓰시오.

26 ____________ generous you are!

27 ____________ a great daughter she has!

28~30 다음 문장을 괄호 안의 단어를 이용하여 감탄문으로 바꾸시오.

28

Your blue dress is very pretty. (How, is)

→ ________________________________

29

She is a wonderful lady. (What, is)

→ ________________________________

30

He did it bravely. (How, it)

→ ________________________________

31~33 빈칸에 알맞은 말을 넣어 다음 대화를 완성하시오.

31

A: Minho can't solve the problem, can he?
B: __________, ____________________.
He is very smart.

32

A: You didn't clean up your room over the weekend, did you?
B: __________, ____________________.
I slept all day.

33

A: Jessy and Susan won't go to the wedding, will they?
B: __________, __________ __________.
They want to go to the wedding.

34~36 다음 괄호 안의 단어를 어법상 바르게 고치시오.

34

What are you going to do this weekend? Let's (going) for a drive.

→ ________________

35

I'm your best friend, (am) I? I hope our friendship lasts forever.

→ ______________

36

There were a lot of people on the train, (didn't they)?

→ ______________

37~38 다음 문장 중 어법상 <u>어색한</u> 문장을 <u>두 개</u> 찾아 바르게 고치시오.

(a) Let's buy not this bag.
(b) How wonderful the weather is!
(c) Don't be rude to old people.
(d) Didn't our kids go to school together?
(e) She put a knife on the table, doesn't she?

37 ______________ → ______________

38 ______________ → ______________

39~42 우리말과 같은 뜻이 되도록 괄호 안의 단어를 이용하여 문장을 완성하시오.

39

너는 멋진 정원을 가지고 있구나!
(nice, what, have)

______________!

40

저녁 먹기 전에 손 씻는 것을 잊지 마라.
(hands, wash, forget to)

______________ before dinner.

41

Jane은 매일 운동하지 않아, 그렇지?
(she, every day, exercise)

Jane ______________?

42

너는 음악과 미술 중 어느 과목이 더 좋니?
(which, or, like, better, subject)

______________?

43~45 다음 글에서 어법상 어색한 부분을 세 군데 찾아 바르게 고치시오.

Here are some tips for a healthy life.
1. Wears a mask.
2. Wash your hands with soap.
3. Not do touch your face without washing your hands.
4. Avoided crowded places.

43 ____________ → ____________

44 ____________ → ____________

45 ____________ → ____________

46~48 다음 대화의 빈칸에 알맞은 말을 쓰시오.

46
A: Your father had a car accident, ____________?
B: Yes, he did.
A: Then your father is in hospital, isn't he?
B: ________, ____________.
He didn't get hurt badly. He's at home.

47
A: You like flowers, ____________?
B: Yes, I do. Why do you ask?
A: Today is your birthday, ____________?
B: No, it isn't. My birthday was last month.

48
A: It is windy today, ____________?
B: Yes, it is. It is blowing hard.
A: So, you will stay at home, ____________?
B: Yes, I will. I will read these books.
A: They are comic books, ____________?
B: Yes, they are. I love comic books.

49~50 다음 우리말을 주어진 |조건|에 맞게 영어로 바르게 쓰시오.

49 Tina가 던지는 공은 얼마나 빠른지!

|조건|
1. What으로 시작할 것
2. 단어 fast, throw를 이용할 것
3. 6 단어로 쓰고, 필요시 어법에 맞게 단어의 형태를 바꿀 것

→ ____________

50 너는 수영과 테니스 중 어떤 스포츠를 더 좋아하니?

|조건|
1. Which로 시작할 것
2. 단어 sport, better를 이용할 것
3. 9 단어로 쓸 것

→ ____________

CHAPTER

10 문장의 형식

Unit 01 문장의 요소
Unit 02 1형식/2형식 문장
Unit 03 감각동사 + 형용사
Unit 04 3형식 문장
Unit 05 4형식 문장
Unit 06 3형식 ↔ 4형식 문장 전환
Unit 07 5형식 문장의 목적격보어 1
Unit 08 5형식 문장의 목적격보어 2
Unit 09 5형식 문장의 목적격보어 3

UNIT 01 문장의 요소

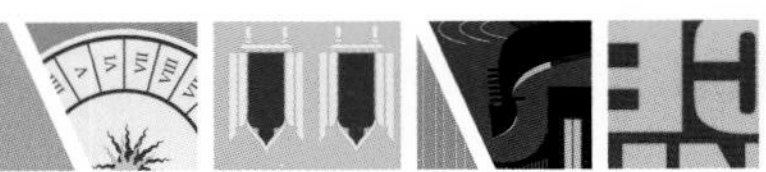

문장을 구성하는 5대 요소인 주어, 동사(서술어), 목적어, 보어, 수식어를 외워 두세요.

문장 구성 요소	역할	예문
주어	문장의 주체 (~은, 는, 이, 가)	The teacher teaches science.
동사	주어의 상태, 동작 서술 (~이다, ~하다)	The teacher teaches science.
목적어	동작의 대상 (~을, ~를, ~에게)	The teacher teaches us science.
보어	주어나 목적어 보충 설명	He is a teacher. The teacher makes us happy.
수식어	명사, 동사, 문장 수식	The new teacher teaches science in our school.

|A| 다음 밑줄 친 말의 문장 요소를 |보기|에서 찾아 빈칸에 그 약자를 쓰시오.

|보기|
주어: S (subject) 동사: V (verb) 보어: C (complement) 목적어: O (object) 수식어: M (modifier)

01 I am a student. ______

02 He sings very well. ______

03 She likes tennis. ______

04 I became a doctor. ______

05 She lives in Seoul. ______

06 Mary is kind. ______

07 They read books. ______

08 We are close friends. ______

09 She goes to school. ______

10 My dad bought me a bike. ______

11 He made them happy. ______

12 John writes a letter. ______

13 Sam and I play soccer. ______

14 We went to the party. ______

15 Wash your hands well. ______

16 The game was fun. ______

|B| |보기|와 같이 각 문장 요소에 밑줄 긋고 그 약자를 쓰시오.

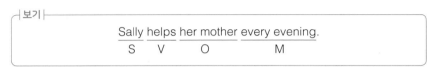

|보기|
Sally helps her mother every evening.
S V O M

〈조동사+동사원형〉은 하나의 덩어리로서, 서술어 역할을 한다는 점을 알아 두세요.

01 He is an English teacher.

02 She will go to Canada.

03 You look tired today.

04 The game made us excited.

05 She visited her parents yesterday.

06 Bill likes Jessica very much.

07 My father made me a kite.

08 Junsu is playing basketball.

UNIT 02 1형식 / 2형식 문장

〈주어 + 동사〉 뒤에 보어가 있는지 없는지에 따라 문장의 1형식 또는 2형식으로 구분하세요.

	문장 구성 요소	예문	참고
1형식	주어+동사	The train / arrived (on time).	주어와 동사만으로 완전한 문장
		She / is sleeping (on the sofa).	
2형식	주어+동사+보어	The train / is / (very) long.	보어가 없으면 불완전한 문장
		She / became / a nurse (in 2020).	

참고 부사, 전치사구와 같은 부사적 수식어는 구성 요소에서 제외해요.

|A| 다음 문장이 1형식이면 1, 2형식이면 2라고 쓰시오.

01 The baby smiled. ________

02 She looks sad today. ________

03 He is a computer engineer. ________

04 The rose smells sweet. ________

05 I go to school by bus. ________

06 We moved to a new office. ________

07 She became a writer. ________

08 They are in New York. ________

09 There are many stars in the sky. ________

10 The movie was so funny. ________

11 The students kept quiet. ________

12 There is no class on Saturday. ________

There is가 이끄는 문장도 1형식이라는 점에 유의하세요.

|B| |보기|와 같이 빈칸에 문장 형식을 쓴 뒤, 각 문장 요소에 밑줄 긋고 그 약자를 쓰시오.

|보기|

I became tired. ___1___
S V C

01 The sun rises in the east. ________

02 The earth moves around the sun. ________

03 This sandwich tastes good. ________

04 The singer became popular. ________

05 The game was exciting. ________

06 My sister and I felt cold. ________

07 He is waiting at the bus stop. ________

08 The boys are playing now. ________

내신 기출 다음 밑줄 친 부분의 역할이 다른 것은?

① The train arrived at the station.
② She's doing very well at school.
③ Your new jacket looks very nice.

실전 TIP

밑줄 친 부분이 없어도 문장이 성립하는지를 확인해 보세요.

UNIT 03 감각동사 + 형용사

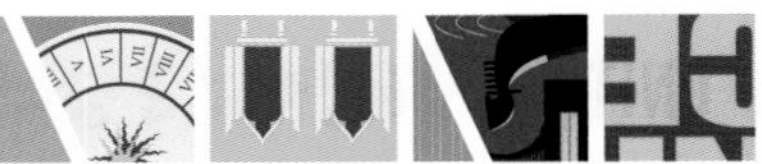

2형식 문장에는 be동사와 감각동사가 주로 사용돼요. be동사와 감각동사가 취하는 보어의 종류와 그 의미를 파악하세요.

보어를 취하는 동사		보어	의미
be동사	be, am, are, is, was, were	명사, 형용사	~이다, ~하다
감각동사	feel, look, sound, smell, taste	형용사	~하게 느끼다, ~해 보이다, ~한 소리가 나다, ~한 냄새가 나다, ~한 맛이 나다

참고 감각동사 뒤에 명사를 쓰려면 〈감각동사+like+(a/an+)명사〉로 쓰면 돼요.
He looks smart. → He looks like a smart person.

A 다음 문장에서 어법상 어색한 부분에 밑줄 긋고 바르게 고치시오.

01 He looked happily this morning. → ________
02 That sounds greatly. → ________
03 These candies smell sweetly. → ________
04 She looks an old lady. → ________
05 Tom really sounds like angry. → ________
06 This soup tastes badly. → ________
07 He looks a teacher. → ________
08 You look like sad and tired. → ________

B 우리말과 같은 뜻이 되도록 괄호 안의 단어를 바르게 배열하시오.

01 Amy의 전화 목소리가 이상하게 들렸다. (strange / Amy's voice / sounded / on the phone)

____

02 이 빵은 맛이 훌륭하다. (great / this bread / tastes)

____

03 이 옷감은 촉감이 부드럽고 매끄럽다. (feels / soft / smooth / and / this cloth)

____

04 James는 한국 사람처럼 보인다. (looks / Korean / James)

____

05 이 꽃은 예뻐 보이고 향기도 좋다. (looks / smells / this flower / pretty / good / and)

____

UNIT 04 3형식 문장

〈주어+동사〉 뒤에 보어(~이다)가 오면 2형식, 목적어(~을, ~를)가 오면 3형식 문장이라는 점을 꼭 알아두세요.

	문장 구성 요소	예문	참고
2형식	주어+동사+보어	The train / is / (very) long.	보어(~이다)가 없으면 불완전
		She / became / a nurse (in 2020).	
3형식	주어+동사+목적어	The train / takes / us (to Busan).	목적어(~을, ~를)가 없으면 불완전
		She / wants / juice.	

|A| |보기|와 같이 각 문장 요소에 밑줄 긋고 그 약자를 쓰시오.

|보기|
S: 주어 V: 동사 O: 목적어 M: 수식어

01 My sister has a guitar.

02 The woman sells flowers in the shop.

03 The boys look so funny.

04 Kites are flying in the sky.

05 Jason plays basketball well.

06 My father reads the news online.

|B| 우리말과 같은 뜻이 되도록 괄호 안의 단어를 바르게 배열하시오.

01 모든 학생들이 그녀를 좋아한다. (all / like / her / the students)

____

02 Jessica는 긴 드레스를 입을 것이다. (Jessica / a long dress / wear / will)

____

03 나의 엄마는 나무들과 꽃들을 좋아한다. (trees / flowers / my mother / and / likes)

____

04 나는 약간의 빵과 우유를 원한다. (want / milk / and / some / I / bread)

____

05 우리는 보통 7시에 저녁을 먹는다. (at seven / dinner / have / usually / We)

____

내신 기출 다음 중 문장 형식이 다른 하나는?

① She writes an email herself every day.
② We were looking at the menu to order lunch.
③ My mother often goes to the traditional market.

실전 TIP
동사 뒤에 수식어구가 오는지, 보어가 오는지, 목적어가 오는지 확인해야 해요.

UNIT 05 4형식 문장

목적어 두 개 '~에게'와 '~을'을 취하는 4형식 동사들을 알아 두세요.

	수여동사(~에게 …을 ~해주다)	간접목적어	직접목적어
4형식 동사	give, make, show, send, ask, tell, lend, get, bring, teach, buy, cook, bake 등	~에게	~을

주의 목적어가 1개 있으면 3형식, 목적어(간접목적어, 직접목적어)가 2개 있으면 4형식이에요.

주의 직접목적어가 대명사일 경우 4형식은 쓸 수 없고 3형식만 가능해요.
I gave her it. (×) I gave it to her. (○)

|A| 다음 문장에서 괄호 안의 문장요소를 찾아 빈칸에 쓰시오.

01 I showed her my pictures. (간접목적어) ______________________

02 My dad bought me a new computer. (직접목적어) ______________________

03 Mr. Brown teaches us English. (동사) ______________________

04 Mary and I will give him a birthday present. (주어) ______________________

05 She made her son a cake. (간접목적어) ______________________

06 Tom lent me his bicycle. (직접목적어) ______________________

07 He gave me a notebook yesterday. (수식어구) ______________________

08 My parents sent me some books. (직접목적어) ______________________

|B| 우리말과 같은 뜻이 되도록 괄호 안의 단어를 이용하여 4형식 문장을 완성하시오.

01 그는 아내에게 코트를 사 주었다. (buy, a coat, his wife)

He ______________________________.

02 Sandy는 그녀의 아버지에게 스웨터를 만들어 드렸다. (make, a sweater, her father)

Sandy ______________________________.

03 그녀는 나에게 이메일을 보냈다. (me, send, an e-mail)

She ______________________________.

04 나는 그에게 나의 새 시계를 보여 주었다. (show, my new watch, him)

I ______________________________.

05 저에게 사과를 좀 가져다주세요. (some apples, bring, me)

Please ______________________________.

06 Mike는 내게 그의 핸드폰을 빌려주었다. (his cell phone, lend, me)

Mike ______________________________.

4형식 문장은 〈주어+수여동사+간접목적어+직접목적어〉의 어순으로 나타내요.

UNIT 06 3형식 ↔ 4형식 문장 전환

4형식 문장은 3형식 문장으로 바꾸어 쓸 수 있는데, 이때 어순에 주의해야 해요.

4형식 어순	주어+동사+간접목적어(~에게)+직접목적어(~을)	I gave her water.
3형식 어순	주어+동사+직접목적어(~을)+전치사+간접목적어	I gave water to her.

4형식 문장을 3형식으로 바꿀 때, 동사에 따라 사용하는 전치사에 유의하세요.

3형식 어순	수여동사	직접목적어 (~을)	to	간접목적어 (~에게)
	get, make, buy, cook, bake, build, find		for	
	ask, inquire	a question, a favor	of	

|A| 다음 빈칸에 to, for, of 중 알맞은 말을 쓰시오.

01 He gave a soccer ball __________ his son.

02 I read the book __________ my grandmother.

03 Mom bought a new desk __________ me.

04 My uncle teaches science __________ students.

05 She asked some questions __________ Tom.

06 Mary made some soup __________ her mother.

07 My mother cooked a delicious dinner __________ us.

|B| 다음 문장을 괄호 안의 지시대로 바꾸시오.

01 I asked the librarian a favor. (3형식으로)

→ ______________________________

02 Mr. Kim taught tennis to us. (4형식으로)

→ ______________________________

03 Minho wrote her a birthday card. (3형식으로)

→ ______________________________

04 His mom made us a pizza. (3형식으로)

→ ______________________________

05 Mina brought a glass of water to me. (4형식으로)

→ ______________________________

06 She told her daughter an interesting story. (3형식으로)

→ ______________________________

|C| 다음 문장에서 어법상 어색한 부분에 밑줄 긋고 바르게 고치시오.

01 We made some food to them. → ______________________

02 You can send a card for her on her birthday. → ______________________

03 I'll show the concert ticket them. → ______________________

04 I told my secret for my parents. → ______________________

05 Tony gave his friend to a gift. → ______________________

06 The teacher asked a question for me. → ______________________

07 Jane made a scarf for I. → ______________________

08 He bought a camera his daughter. → ______________________

|D| 우리말과 같은 뜻이 되도록 괄호 안의 단어와 알맞은 전치사를 이용하여 3형식 문장을 완성하시오.

01 Tom은 그녀에게 반지를 사주었다. (a ring, bought, her)

Tom ______________________________________.

02 그녀는 우리에게 특별한 피자를 만들어 주었다. (made, us, a special pizza)

She ______________________________________.

03 김 선생님은 내게 기타를 가르쳐 주셨다. (me, taught, guitar)

Mr. Kim ______________________________________.

04 내 여동생이 나에게 우산을 가져다주었다. (an umbrella, me, brought)

My sister ______________________________________.

05 미나는 자주 그에게 이메일을 보낸다. (him, an e-mail, sends)

Mina often ______________________________________.

06 나는 너에게 생일 선물로 테니스 라켓을 줄 것이다. (racket, give, you)

I will ______________________________________ for your birthday.

내신 기출 다음 빈칸에 들어갈 말이 다른 하나는?

① He found the lost watch __________ her.

② The girl lent her umbrella __________ me.

③ I will show my new dress __________ you.

실전 TIP

동사 get, make, buy, cook, find 등을 3형식으로 쓸 때, 어떤 전치사를 쓰는지 상기해 보세요.

UNIT 07 5형식 문장의 목적격보어 1

목적어 뒤에 목적어를 설명하는 명사나 형용사 보어가 있는 5형식 문장을 알아 두세요.

	명사/형용사를 목적격보어로 쓰는 5형식 동사	목적어	목적격보어
5형식 어순	make, call, name, find, keep, elect, think, believe, consider 등	~을, ~이/가	명사, 형용사

참고 목적어와 목적격보어는 동격 관계예요.
She made him a doctor. *him = a doctor 그녀는 그를 의사로 만들었다.
She made him angry. *him = angry 그녀는 그를 화나게 만들었다.

|A| |보기|와 같이 각 문장 요소에 밑줄 긋고 그 약자를 쓰시오.

|보기| S: 주어 V: 동사 O: 목적어 OC: 목적격보어 M: 수식어

01 The news made me surprised.

02 They called him John.

03 She named her dog Happy.

04 Tony bought his friend a pretty hat.

05 He found the bank easily.

06 She keeps her room clean.

07 She made her son a pilot.

08 My brother made me angry.

|B| 우리말과 같은 뜻이 되도록 괄호 안의 단어를 바르게 배열하시오.

01 그는 그의 아들을 기술자로 만들었다. (his son / an engineer / he / made)

____

02 나는 그 상자가 비어 있다는 것을 발견했다. (I / the box / empty / found)

____

03 우리 가족은 우리 고양이를 Sally라고 부른다. (calls / Sally / our family / our cat)

____

04 태양은 우리를 따뜻하게 해 준다. (us / the sun / warm / keeps)

____

05 신선한 음식은 우리를 건강하게 만든다. (fresh food / us / makes / healthy)

____

06 그들은 Aiden을 회장으로 뽑았다. (Aiden / elected / they / president)

____

UNIT 08 5형식 문장의 목적격보어 2

목적격보어로 to부정사를 쓰는 동사들을 알아 두세요.

	to부정사를 목적격보어로 쓰는 5형식 동사	목적어	목적격보어
5형식 어순	want, ask, tell, expect, enable, encourage, allow, advise, order, get, permit, force 등	~에게, ~가	to부정사 (~하기를/~하라고)

참고 to부정사의 부정은 to앞에 not을 쓰면 돼요.

|A| 다음 문장의 밑줄 친 부분을 어법상 바르게 고치시오.

01 He asked me cleaning the car. → ____________

02 She wants her son be a teacher. → ____________

03 Father told me wash the dishes. → ____________

04 She wants you to doing the work. → ____________

05 My parents wanted me studied harder. → ____________

06 He advised me taking a rest. → ____________

07 I asked him return the books. → ____________

08 My mother told me not waiting. → ____________

|B| 우리말과 같은 뜻이 되도록 괄호 안의 단어를 이용하여 문장을 완성하시오.

01 그녀는 나에게 파티에 오라고 요청했다. (ask, come)

She ____________ to the party.

02 Sally는 내가 그녀의 부모님을 만나기를 바란다. (want, meet)

Sally ____________ her parents.

03 그는 그의 아들에게 게임을 그만하라고 말했다. (tell, stop)

He ____________ playing the game.

04 Tom은 내가 그와 쇼핑하러 가기를 바란다. (want, go shopping)

Tom ____________ with him.

05 그녀는 나에게 늦게 자지 말라고 충고했다. (advise, go)

She ____________ to bed late.

06 선생님은 우리에게 수업에 늦지 말라고 말씀하셨다. (tell, be late)

The teacher ____________ for class.

UNIT 09 5형식 문장의 목적격보어 3

사역동사(~에게 …하도록 시키다)는 목적격보어를 원형부정사로 쓰세요.

	원형부정사를 목적격보어로 쓰는 사역동사	목적어	목적격보어	의미
5형식 어순	make, have	~이/가	원형부정사	~가 …하게 만들다, 시키다
	let			~가 …하게 두다

참고 원형부정사란 to부정사에서 to가 없는 동사원형으로 쓰는 부정사를 말해요.

주의 help는 목적격보어로 to부정사와 원형부정사 모두를 쓰지만, get은 오직 to부정사만 써야 해요.

|A| 다음 문장에서 어법상 어색한 부분에 밑줄 긋고 바르게 고치시오.

01 Please let me to go now. → ______________________

02 She made me brushed my teeth. → ______________________

03 His father let him went there last night. → ______________________

04 The teacher made me to wait an hour. → ______________________

05 They had him carrying the box. → ______________________

06 We made her to sing a song. → ______________________

07 I helped my brother wrote his diary. → ______________________

08 He had me doing the dishes. → ______________________

|B| 우리말과 같은 뜻이 되도록 괄호 안의 단어를 바르게 배열하시오.

01 그녀의 어머니는 그녀를 집에 있게 했다. (her mother / her / at home / stay / made)

____

02 James는 그녀를 즉시 떠나게 했다. (her / leave / made / James / at once)

____

03 그의 아버지는 그를 일찍 일어나게 했다. (made / him / early / his father / get up)

____

04 나는 그가 편지를 네게 보내도록 하겠다. (I'll / him / you / to / send / have / a letter)

____

05 그들은 내가 새 가방을 사도록 했다. (a new bag / to buy / they / got / me)

____

06 Mary는 그녀의 엄마가 집을 청소하는 것을 도와 드렸다. (helped / her mother / the house / Mary / clean)

____

중간고사·기말고사 실전문제

객관식 (01~25) / 주관식 (26~50)

학년과 반 이름 객관식 / 25문항 주관식 / 25문항

01~02 다음 빈칸에 알맞은 말을 고르시오.

01

The villagers helped us ________ baseball there.

① plays ② played
③ playing ④ to play
⑤ to playing

02

This dress looks ________ on you. You look prettier.

① nicely ② good
③ greatly ④ neatly
⑤ bad

03~04 다음 빈칸에 들어갈 수 없는 말을 고르시오.

03

My brother ________ me do my art homework.

① let ② had
③ made ④ asked
⑤ helped

04

Steve ________ me to join the tennis club.

① told ② asked
③ let ④ wanted
⑤ allowed

05 다음 중 문장의 형식이 나머지와 다른 것은?

① She found his latest novel interesting.
② The telephone on my desk rang loudly.
③ Suji made her brother clean the bathroom.
④ They called him the most popular singer in Asia.
⑤ This coat keeps me warm from the cold winter winds.

06~07 밑줄 친 부분 중 어법상 어색한 것을 고르시오.

06 ① This candy tastes sweet.
② Julia felt so tiredly yesterday.
③ That onion soup smells delicious.
④ This ring looks tight on your finger.
⑤ Their words always sound strange to me.

07 ① Jeremy bought his daughter a big bag.
② We showed Tom some pictures of Paris.
③ I'm happy that my dad cooked to me it.
④ The girl lent her friend her new skateboard.
⑤ His students gave him a present when he retired.

08 다음 ①~⑤ 중 to가 들어가기에 알맞은 곳은?

The security guard (①) didn't (②) allow (③) them (④) swim (⑤) across the river.

09~10 우리말과 같은 뜻이 되도록 빈칸에 알맞은 말을 고르시오.

09

You ____________ a movie star.
(너는 영화배우처럼 보인다.)

① look ② show
③ feel like ④ sound like
⑤ look like

10

The clear blue sea makes me ____________.
(맑고 푸른 바다는 내가 행복하게 느끼게 해 준다.)

① feel happy ② to feel happy
③ feel happily ④ feeling happy
⑤ to feel happily

11~13 빈칸에 들어갈 말이 순서대로 짝지어진 것을 고르시오.

11

• She likes to show her postcard collection ________ her friends.
• Jinho always asks questions ________ the teacher after class.

① to – to ② to – for
③ to – of ④ of – to
⑤ for – of

12

• My cat was sick and I felt ________.
• They tried to keep the people ________.

① upset – quietly
② happy – angrily
③ nicely – excited
④ lonely – strangely
⑤ sad – quiet

13

• My brother ________ me study hard.
• Ms. Green ________ my dog stand up.

① wanted – had
② asked – made
③ allowed – had
④ helped – made
⑤ told – let

14~15 밑줄 친 ①~⑤ 중 어법상 어색한 것을 고르시오.

14

My grandfather ① didn't ② look health last week. I'm ③ very ④ worried about ⑤ him.

15

Yujin ① made a necklace ② to me as my birthday present. ③ I think the necklace ④ is beautiful and ⑤ looks great on me.

16~17 다음 괄호 안의 단어들을 순서대로 배열할 때, 빈칸에 네 번째로 오는 단어를 고르시오.

16

Mom wanted ____________.
(to / study / harder / me / make)

① to ② me
③ harder ④ make
⑤ study

17

We didn't ____________.
(Tom / expect / to / win / the car race)

① win ② Tom
③ to ④ the
⑤ expect

18 다음 중 어법상 올바른 문장을 모두 고르시오.

① Jonathan asked I to marry him.
② Your explanation sounds reasonably.
③ She told me to remembering the password.
④ This sauce makes the food hot and sweet.
⑤ The train arrived at Seoul Station.

19 다음 빈칸에 들어갈 말이 나머지와 다른 것은?

① I advised you ________ take your umbrella!
② My parents gave some money ________ me.
③ Are you making a pizza ________ your friend?
④ Julia allowed him ________ come to her party.
⑤ The teacher told us not ________ be late for school.

20~21 우리말을 영어로 바르게 옮긴 것을 고르시오.

20

나는 내 자전거를 내 이웃에게 주었다.

① I gave my bike to my neighbor.
② I gave my bike for my neighbor.
③ I gave my neighbor to my bike.
④ I gave my neighbor of my bike.
⑤ I gave my bike my neighbor.

21

우리는 그에게 조용히 말하라고 요청했다.

① We asked him speak quietly.
② We asked him to speak quiet.
③ We asked his speaking quietly.
④ We asked his to speak quietly.
⑤ We asked him to speak quietly.

22 다음 빈칸 ⓐ~ⓔ에 알맞지 않은 말은?

- Swallows ___ⓐ___ high in the sky.
- The trash can smells ___ⓑ___.
- The police ___ⓒ___ the bank robbers.
- Can money bring us ___ⓓ___?
- I told Jerry to ___ⓔ___ to Jimin.

① ⓐ fly　② ⓑ disgusting
③ ⓒ arrested　④ ⓓ happy
⑤ ⓔ go and talk

23 다음 빈칸 ⓐ~ⓒ에 들어갈 말이 순서대로 짝지어진 것은?

- The animation makes me ___ⓐ___.
- Mr. Kim let him ___ⓑ___ into the room.
- Mina expected Jim ___ⓒ___ the driving test on his first try.

	ⓐ	ⓑ	ⓒ
①	laugh	go	pass
②	laugh	go	to pass
③	laugh	going	to pass
④	to laugh	goes	passing
⑤	to laugh	to go	to pass

24 다음 중 어법상 어색한 문장의 개수는?

(a) I bought a magazine yesterday.
(b) I go to a study cafe before exams.
(c) Jessica feels guilty about something.
(d) Exercising makes me feeling healthily.
(e) The doctor often showed the visitors to the painting.

① 1개　② 2개
③ 3개　④ 4개
⑤ 5개

25 우리말을 영어로 바르게 옮긴 것을 모두 고르시오.

① John은 슈퍼 영웅처럼 보인다.
→ John looks a superhero.
② 나는 내 사촌에게 편지를 썼다.
→ I wrote a letter for my cousin.
③ 그는 주머니에 손을 넣었다.
→ He put his hands in his pockets.
④ 회의는 오후 4시에 끝났다.
→ The meeting ended at four in the afternoon.
⑤ 그 검은 옷이 진수를 말라보이게 했다.
→ The black suit made Jinsu to look thin.

26~28 다음 괄호 안에서 알맞은 말을 고르시오.

26 My father looks (old / young / strange) for his age. He looks about twenty years old.

27 Elizabeth sometimes lets her dog (sleep / sleeping / to sleep) on her bed.

28 Ms. Smith (made / had / expected) us to cut the grass.

29~30 다음 대화의 밑줄 친 단어를 어법에 맞게 고치시오.

29

A: You look happy. What's going on?
B: I bought a silk scarf. This scarf feels softly.

→ ______________

30

A: What's wrong with you?
B: I'm so sleepy. I think this medicine makes me feeling sleepy.

→ ______________

31~33 다음 문장에서 어법상 어색한 부분을 찾아 바르게 고치시오.

31

My doctor advised me drinking more water.

______________ → ______________

32

My parents don't allow me stay out late.

______________ → ______________

33

Minsu and Jane made I waited for an hour at the park.

______________ → ______________

34~36 우리말과 같은 뜻이 되도록 괄호 안의 단어를 바르게 배열하시오.

34

저 산에 있는 바위는 코끼리처럼 보인다.

The rock on that mountain ______________ ______________

(like / looks / an elephant)

35

네가 피곤할 때 내가 발 마사지해 줄게.

I'll ______________ when you are tired.

(you / give / a foot massage)

36

나는 너무 피곤해서 당신이 차를 운전해 주기를 원한다.

I'm really tired, so ______________ ______________.

(want / to / you / drive / I)

37~38 다음 문장을 목적어가 하나인 문장으로 바꾸시오.

37

May I ask you a question?

= May I ask ______________?

38

Sejin is planning to cook her friends some food.

= Sejin is planning to cook ______________ ______________.

39~40 다음 대화를 읽고, 주어진 문장을 완성하시오.

39

Mom: You have to finish your homework before going shopping.
Girl: Yes, I will.

→ My mom made ______________ before going shopping.

40

Jenny: Can you help me? I can't open the window.
Minsu: Sure, no problem.

→ Minsu will help ______________.

41~42 우리말과 같은 뜻이 되도록, 괄호 안의 단어를 이용하여 대화를 완성하시오.

41

A: What did your dad buy you for Christmas?
B: 아빠는 나에게 새 신발을 사 주셨어.
(my, buy, pair of)

____

42

A: How was the musical?
B: It was fantastic. 마지막 장면은 우리 모두를 울게 만들었어.
(cry, the last scene, make, all of us)

____

43~44 다음 대화에서 어법상 어색한 부분을 두 군데 찾아 바르게 고치시오.

A: Did you like the movie, *The Crazy City*?
B: Yes, it made me to laugh a lot.
A: Really? Was it that funny?
B: Yes, it was. By the way, how about sleeping over at Tony's house?
A: I'm afraid I can't. My parents won't let me staying somewhere overnight.

43 ______________ → ______________

44 ______________ → ______________

45 괄호 안의 단어를 바르게 배열하여 다음 글을 완성하시오.

I washed my father's car last weekend. ______________ on Saturday afternoon. (had / he / wash / me / his car) And then ______________. (he / some / gave / pocket money / me)

46~48 다음을 읽고, 우리말과 같은 뜻이 되도록 괄호 안의 단어를 이용하여 문장을 완성하시오.

Yesterday was Parents' Day. Suji, Minsu and Jina prepared something special for their parents.

46 수지는 그녀의 부모님께 꽃을 드렸다.
(give, some flowers)

(3형식) → ______

(4형식) → ______

47 민수는 그의 부모님께 컵케이크를 구워드렸다.
(bake, some cupcakes)

(3형식) → ______

(4형식) → ______

48 지나는 그녀의 부모님께 감사 편지를 썼다.
(write, a thank-you letter)

(3형식) → ______

(4형식) → ______

49~50 다음 우리말을 주어진 |조건|에 맞게 영어로 바르게 쓰시오.

49 선생님은 내가 내 책을 Jennie와 함께 보도록 하셨다.

|조건|
1. 단어 have, share, with를 사용할 것
2. 9 단어로 쓸 것
3. 필요시 어법에 맞게 단어의 형태를 바꿀 것

→ ______

50 Kate는 Aiden에게 방과 후에 자기를 도와달라고 부탁했다.

|조건|
1. 단어 ask, to, after school을 이용할 것
2. 8 단어로 쓸 것
3. 필요시 어법에 맞게 단어의 형태를 바꿀 것

→ ______

CHAPTER

11 to부정사와 동명사

Unit 01 to부정사의 명사적 용법 1
Unit 02 to부정사의 명사적 용법 2
Unit 03 to부정사의 명사적 용법 3
Unit 04 to부정사의 형용사적 용법
Unit 05 to부정사의 부사적 용법 1
Unit 06 to부정사의 부사적 용법 2
Unit 07 동명사의 역할 1
Unit 08 동명사의 역할 2
Unit 09 동명사 목적어 vs. to부정사 목적어
Unit 10 동명사의 관용 표현

UNIT 01 to부정사의 명사적 용법 1

동사를 명사(~하기, ~하는 것)처럼 사용하려면 〈to부정사 + 동사원형〉의 형태로 만들어야 해요. to부정사(구)가 주어 역할을 할 때는 '~하는 것은'으로 해석해요.

명사 역할 – 주어	주의
To become a scientist takes years. 과학자가 되는 것은 수년이 걸린다.	① to부정사는 뒤에 목적어나 부사구를 취할 수 있다. ② to부정사 주어는 3인칭 단수 취급한다. ③ to부정사의 부정은 to 앞에 not을 쓴다.

참고 부정사란 정해진 품사가 없다는 뜻으로 명사, 형용사, 부사로 쓰여요.

참고 to부정사(구) 주어(진주어)는 문장 뒤로 옮길 수 있는데, 이때 가(짜)주어 It을 주어 자리에 넣어야 해요.
It takes years to become a scientist.

|A| 우리말과 같은 뜻이 되도록 괄호 안의 단어를 이용하여 문장을 완성하시오.

01 영어를 배우는 것은 쉽지 않다. (learn) ______________ English is not easy.

02 너를 만나서 반가웠다. (see) It was nice ______________ you.

03 TV 보는 것은 아주 재미있다. (watch) ______________ TV is very interesting.

04 테니스 치는 것은 너를 건강하게 해 준다. (play) ______________ tennis makes you healthy.

05 바다에서 수영하는 것은 위험하다. (swim) It is dangerous ______________ in the sea.

06 거짓말을 하는 것은 나쁘다. (tell) It is wrong ______________ a lie.

07 자전거를 타는 것은 좋은 운동이다. (ride) ______________ a bike is good exercise.

08 사진을 찍는 것은 나의 취미다. (take) ______________ pictures is my hobby.

|B| 다음 문장을 |보기|와 같이 가주어 It으로 시작하는 문장으로 바꾸어 쓰시오.

to부정사 주어는 3인칭 단수 취급해야 해요.

|보기|
To study English is fun. → It is fun to study English.

01 To get up early is good for your health. → ______________

02 To do two jobs is not easy. → ______________

03 To watch the soccer game was exciting. → ______________

04 To make good friends is important. → ______________

05 To understand others is difficult. → ______________

06 To drive fast can be dangerous. → ______________

UNIT 02 to부정사의 명사적 용법 2

to부정사를 명사처럼 be동사 뒤에서 주격보어로 쓸 때는 '~하는 것(이다)'라고 해석해요.

명사 역할 – 주격보어	주의
My dream is to become a scientist. 나의 꿈은 과학자가 되는 것이다.	① to부정사는 뒤에 목적어나 부사구를 취할 수 있다. ② to부정사의 부정은 to 앞에 not을 쓴다.

참고 주격보어란 주어를 보충 설명하는 말로 〈주어 = 보어〉의 관계가 성립돼요.
my dream = to become a scientist

A 우리말과 같은 뜻이 되도록 괄호 안의 단어를 이용하여 문장을 완성하시오.

01 그의 꿈은 기술자가 되는 것이다. (become) His dream is ______________ an engineer.

02 나의 계획은 6시에 떠나는 것이다. (leave) My plan is ______________ at six.

03 나의 취미는 동전을 모으는 것이다. (collect) My hobby is ______________ coins.

04 그녀의 직업은 바이올린을 연주하는 것이다. (play) Her job is ______________ the violin.

05 그의 꿈은 학생들을 가르치는 것이다. (teach) His dream is ______________ students.

06 나의 소원은 자전거를 갖는 것이다. (have) My wish is ______________ a bicycle.

07 나의 목표는 유명한 가수가 되는 것이다. (become) My goal is ______________ a famous singer.

08 John의 계획은 한국어를 배우는 것이다. (learn) John's plan is ______________ Korean.

B 우리말과 같은 뜻이 되도록 괄호 안의 단어를 바르게 배열하시오.

01 그의 꿈은 세계를 여행하는 것이었다. (the world / his dream / was / travel / to)

____

02 그의 일은 책상과 의자를 만드는 것이다. (is / make / his work / desks and chairs / to)

____

03 그녀의 꿈은 훌륭한 피아니스트가 되는 것이다. (is / become / a great pianist / her dream / to)

____

04 Tom의 취미는 자동차 모형을 만드는 것이다. (a model car / to / is / Tom's hobby / make)

____

05 우리의 계획은 콘서트에 가는 것이다. (a concert / to / our plan / go to / is)

____

06 그녀의 바람은 외국에서 공부하는 것이다. (abroad / her hope / study / is / to)

____

UNIT 03 to부정사의 명사적 용법 3

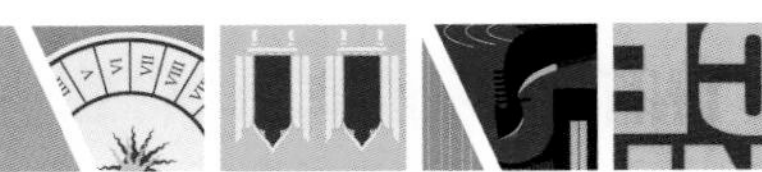

to부정사는 '~하는 것을'이라는 뜻으로 목적어 역할을 할 수 있어요. to부정사를 목적어로 쓰는 동사들을 파악하세요.

want, would like 원하다	hope 바라다	plan 계획하다	refuse 거절하다
wish 소망하다	promise 약속하다	choose 선택하다	fail 실패하다
expect 예상하다	agree 동의하다	decide 결정하다	need 필요가 있다

A 다음 문장에서 밑줄 친 to부정사의 역할을 |보기|에서 골라 빈칸에 쓰시오.

가주어 It이 이끄는 문장에서는 to부정사구가 진짜 주어인 점에 유의해야 해요.

|보기|
주어: S 보어: C 목적어: O

01 To walk in the morning is good. ________

02 His dream was to be a great scientist. ________

03 She wants to buy a new dress. ________

04 I hope to talk to my English teacher after class. ________

05 It is very interesting to study Korean. ________

06 Mina decided to go the party. ________

07 Sue failed to buy the ticket. ________

08 His hobby is to climb the mountain on Sundays. ________

B 우리말과 같은 뜻이 되도록 괄호 안의 단어를 이용하여 문장을 완성하시오.

01 나는 훌륭한 과학자가 되길 바란다. (become, hope)

I ________________ a great scientist.

02 우리는 볼링을 치고 싶다. (would like, play)

We ________________ bowling.

03 그녀는 내일 여행을 떠날 계획이다. (plan, take)

She ________________ a trip tomorrow.

04 Tom은 그 시험에 합격하기를 기대한다. (expect, pass)

Tom ________________ the exam.

05 우리는 다음 주에 그들을 만날 필요가 있다. (need, meet)

We ________________ them next week.

06 그들은 지하철로 그곳에 가기로 결정했다. (decide, go)

They ________ there by subway.

|C| 다음 문장에서 어법상 어색한 부분을 바르게 고치시오.

01 Jenny refused to helped us.

________ → ________

02 To stay up late are not good.

________ → ________

03 Jason wants be a movie star.

________ → ________

04 He hopes seeing her soon.

________ → ________

05 I plan go to the movie tonight.

________ → ________

06 She decided to cutting her long hair.

________ → ________

to부정사 주어는 3인칭 단수 취급한다는 점 꼭 기억해야 해요.

|D| 다음 밑줄 친 부분과 쓰임이 같은 것을 |보기|에서 골라 그 번호를 쓰시오.

|보기|
ⓐ I want to go to the zoo.
ⓑ To play soccer is my hobby.
ⓒ My hobby is to take a walk.

01 My brother doesn't like to clean his room. ________

02 My wish is to make a lot of money. ________

03 Jenny chose to wear a red dress. ________

04 I expect to be back soon. ________

05 She decided to go home late. ________

06 Judy hopes to be a nurse. ________

07 It is hard to find a job. ________

내신기출 다음 밑줄 친 부분의 쓰임이 다른 것은?

① I hope to see you tomorrow.
② It is very important to sleep well.
③ She promises to help her mother.

실전 TIP

to부정사가 문장에서 주어 역할을 하는지 목적어 역할을 하는지 확인하세요.

UNIT 04 to부정사의 형용사적 용법

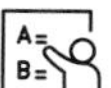

to부정사는 '~(해야) 할, ~하는'의 의미로 형용사처럼 명사를 꾸밀 수 있는데, 이때 어순에 주의하세요.

어순	형용사	명사	형용사	형용사 역할 to부정사
일반적인 명사의 경우	many	books		to read (읽어야 할, 읽을)
-thing / -one / -body의 경우		something	interesting	

|A| 밑줄 친 to부정사가 수식하는 말을 문장에서 찾아 빈칸에 쓰시오.

01 I have many things to do. ________________

02 They need something to eat. ________________

03 I bought a pen to write with. ________________

04 Please give me cold water to drink. ________________

05 Jenny wants something new to read. ________________

06 Mike needed a coat to wear. ________________

07 There are many places to visit. ________________

08 There is nothing to worry about. ________________

|B| 우리말과 같은 뜻이 되도록 괄호 안의 단어를 바르게 배열하시오.

01 Judy는 그녀를 도와줄 친구가 필요하다. (a friend / her / help / to)

Judy needs ________________.

02 도서관에는 읽을 책들이 많이 있다. (to / many / read / books)

There are ________________ in the library.

03 Jessica는 TV를 고칠 사람이 필요하다. (a person / the TV / fix / to)

Jessica needs ________________.

04 나는 네게 할 중요한 말이 있다. (tell / important / something / to)

I have ________________ you.

05 Sam은 일할 곳을 찾고 있다. (to / a place / work in)

Sam is looking for ________________.

06 그들은 먹을 음식이 충분하지 않다. (eat / food / to / enough)

They don't have ________________.

UNIT 05 to부정사의 부사적 용법 1

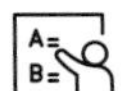

to부정사가 주어, 목적어, 보어가 아니라면, 부사의 역할을 하는 것으로 판단하세요.

부사적 to부정사의 의미	예문	
~하기 위해서(목적)	I exercise to lose weight.	몸무게를 줄이기 위해 운동한다.
~하게 되어, ~해서(감정의 원인)	I'm happy to see you again.	너를 다시 만나서 행복하다.

|A| 우리말과 같은 뜻이 되도록 괄호 안의 단어를 이용하여 문장을 완성하시오.

01 나는 당신을 만나서 반갑다. (meet) I'm glad ______________ you.

02 그녀는 우리를 도와주러 여기에 왔다. (help) She came here ______________ us.

03 나는 그 소식을 들으니 정말 행복하다. (hear) I'm so happy ______________ the news.

04 나는 그를 보러 병원에 갈 것이다. (see) I will go to the hospital ______________ him.

05 Amy는 올림픽 경기를 보기 위해 파리에 방문했다. (watch) Amy visited Paris ______________ the Olympics.

06 그는 카메라를 사기 위해 그곳에 갔다. (buy) He went there ______________ a camera.

07 우리는 공부하러 학교에 간다. (study) We go to school ______________.

08 나는 그 편지를 읽고 놀랐다. (read) I was surprised ______________ the letter.

|B| 다음 문장의 밑줄 친 부분의 쓰임과 같은 것을 |보기|에서 골라 그 번호를 쓰시오.

to부정사의 부사적 용법으로 ⓐ는 '목적'의 의미를, ⓑ는 '감정의 원인'을 나타내요.

|보기|
ⓐ Sally went out to meet him. ⓑ I was sad to hear the news.

01 I was surprised to meet her there. ____________

02 She went to the shop to get a magazine. ____________

03 Let's stop to watch the news. ____________

04 Mike is happy to help her. ____________

05 Bill went to the station to send off his friend. ____________

06 I had to wait for an hour to see a doctor. ____________

07 I'm really happy to have a friend like you. ____________

08 She needs a computer to do her homework. ____________

09 He was sorry to be late for the party. ____________

UNIT 06 to부정사의 부사적 용법 2

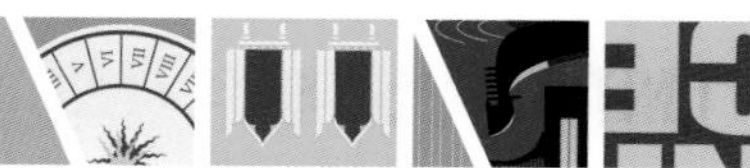

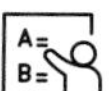

to부정사는 목적, 감정의 원인 이외에도 여러 의미로 쓰이므로 문맥에 맞게 해석해야 해요.

부사적 to부정사의 의미	예문	
~하기에 …한(형용사 수식)	This sentence is hard to understand.	이해하기에 어려운
~하다니 …한(판단의 근거)	She must be clever to think of such an idea.	생각하다니 영리한
~해서 (결국) …하다(결과)	The poor girl grew up to be a famous star. The sea turtle lived to be 188 years old. He left the town only to return soon.	자라서 스타가 됐다 188살까지 살았다 떠났지만 결국 돌아왔다

|A| 다음 밑줄 친 to부정사의 쓰임을 |보기|에서 골라 빈칸에 그 번호를 쓰시오.

|보기|
ⓐ 목적 ⓑ 감정의 원인 ⓒ 형용사 수식 ⓓ 판단의 근거 ⓔ 결과

01 She grew up to become a good doctor. ________

02 You are so kind to help others. ________

03 This book is difficult to understand. ________

04 He got up early to catch the first train. ________

05 My grandmother lived to be ninety. ________

06 The mountain is hard to climb. ________

07 Sora will be surprised to see him today. ________

08 Jason must be smart to solve this question. ________

|B| 우리말과 같은 뜻이 되도록 괄호 안의 단어를 바르게 배열하시오.

01 그의 아들은 커서 훌륭한 예술가가 되었다. (grew up / be / his son / a great artist / to)

____

02 이 새 핸드폰은 사용하기 쉽다. (use / easy / this new cell phone / is / to)

____

03 그녀는 열심히 공부했지만 시험에 떨어졌다. (she / studied hard / only to / the exam / fail)

____

04 이 음악은 듣기에 좋다. (this music / listen to / nice / is / to)

____

05 그 질문에 대답하다니 너는 매우 지혜롭구나. (you / are / to / very wise / the question / answer)

____

UNIT 07 동명사의 역할 1

동사를 명사처럼 쓸 때는 동사를 to부정사나 동명사로 만드세요. 동명사는 〈동사원형+-ing〉의 형태로, 문장에서 주어, 목적어, 보어로 써요.

구분	명사 역할 – 주어	명사 역할 – 보어
to부정사	To become a scientist takes years. 과학자가 되는 것은 수년이 걸린다.	My dream is to become a scientist. 나의 꿈은 과학자가 되는 것이다.
동명사	Becoming a scientist takes years. 과학자가 되는 것은 수년이 걸린다.	My dream is becoming a scientist. 나의 꿈은 과학자가 되는 것이다.

참고 동명사를 만드는 법은 진행형을 만드는 법과 같으므로, CHAPTER 03 UNIT 07을 참고하세요.

참고 주어와 보어 역할을 하는 to부정사와 동명사는 의미가 같아요.

|A| 우리말과 같은 뜻이 되도록 괄호 안의 단어를 동명사로 바꿔 문장을 완성하시오.

01 책을 읽는 것은 중요하다. (read) ______________ books is important.

02 나의 취미는 여행을 가는 것이다. (go) My hobby is ______________ on trips.

03 새로운 언어를 배우는 것은 쉽지 않다. (learn) ______________ a new language is not easy.

04 그녀의 꿈은 간호사가 되는 것이다. (become) Her dream is ______________ a nurse.

05 이메일을 보내는 것은 어렵지 않다. (send) ______________ an e-mail is not difficult.

06 좋은 친구를 사귀는 것은 중요하다. (make) ______________ good friends is important.

07 사진을 찍는 것은 그녀의 취미이다. (take) ______________ pictures is her hobby.

08 그의 일은 학생들에게 수학을 가르치는 것이었다. (teach) His job was ______________ math to students.

|B| 우리말과 같은 뜻이 되도록 괄호 안의 단어를 바르게 배열하시오.

01 영어로 일기를 쓰는 것은 재미있다. (a diary / is / interesting / keeping / in English)

____

02 제시간에 수업에 오는 것은 정말 중요하다. (on time / very / coming / important / is / to class)

____

03 그의 목표는 돈을 많이 저축하는 것이다. (saving / a lot of / his goal / is / money)

____

04 바다에서 수영하는 것은 쉽지 않다. (in the sea / not / swimming / easy / is)

____

05 밤에 운전하는 것은 위험하다. (dangerous / at night / driving / is)

____

06 그의 꿈은 훌륭한 축구 선수가 되는 것이다. (becoming / a great soccer player / his dream / is)

____

UNIT 08 동명사의 역할 2

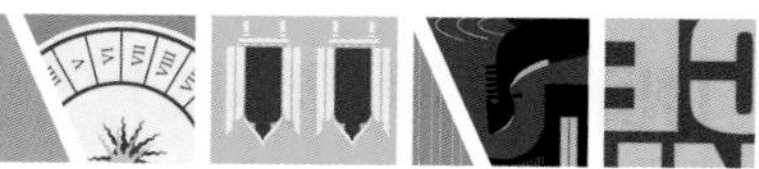

동명사가 동사의 목적어로 쓰일 때는 '~하는 것을'이라고 해석해야 해요. to부정사만 목적어로 쓸 수 있는 동사가 있듯이, 동명사만 목적어로 쓰는 동사를 파악하세요.

enjoy 즐기다	keep 계속 ~하다	imagine 상상하다	practice 연습하다
avoid 피하다	quit 그만 두다	deny 부정하다	give up 포기하다
finish 마치다	mind 신경 쓰다	suggest 제안하다	consider 고려하다

참고 동명사는 to부정사와 달리, 전치사의 목적어로도 쓸 수 있어요.
By donating your talent, you can make the world a better place. 재능을 기부함으로써

|A| 다음 문장에서 밑줄 친 동명사의 쓰임을 |보기|에서 골라 그 약자를 빈칸에 쓰시오.

|보기|
주어: S　　보어: C　　목적어: O

01 Watching TV is fun. ______
02 I like traveling alone. ______
03 I'm sorry for being late. ______
04 My hobby is collecting stamps. ______
05 He enjoyed playing basketball. ______
06 Thank you for helping me. ______
07 His job is selling a car. ______
08 I started reading a book. ______
09 She stopped crossing the street. ______
10 The baby began crying. ______
11 He finished cleaning his room. ______
12 Getting up early is not easy. ______

|B| 다음 문장에서 어법상 어색한 부분에 밑줄 긋고 바르게 고치시오.

01 My mother enjoys to taking a walk after dinner. → ______
02 Did you give up learn guitar? → ______
03 It kept rain for a week. → ______
04 Can you finish to paint the wall today? → ______
05 I should practice to dance. → ______
06 I'm considering buy a new car. → ______
07 Jenny is good at speak Korean. → ______
08 Do you mind to wash the dishes? → ______

내신 기출 다음 밑줄 친 부분의 쓰임이 다른 하나는?
① Her hobby is taking pictures with her friends.
② Did you enjoy watching the concert last night?
③ The children didn't give up climbing the mountain.

실전 TIP
밑줄 친 동명사가 '~하는 것을'로 해석될 수 있는지 없는지를 확인해 보세요.

UNIT 09 동명사 목적어 vs. to부정사 목적어

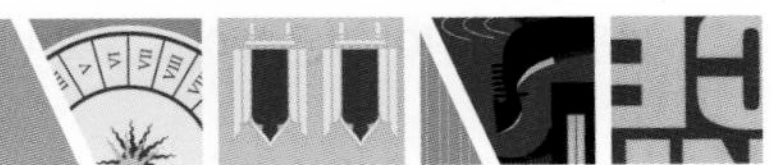

동사별로 목적어를 to부정사로 쓸지, 동명사로 쓸지, 아니면 둘 다 쓸 수 있는지를 파악하세요.

to부정사만 목적어로 취하는 동사	want, would like, wish, expect, hope, promise, agree, plan, choose, decide, refuse, fail, need
동명사만 목적어로 취하는 동사	enjoy, keep, imagine, practice, avoid, quit, deny, give up, finish, mind, suggest, consider
둘 다 목적어로 취하는 동사	like, love, hate, prefer, begin, start, continue

A 다음 괄호 안에서 알맞은 말을 고르시오.

01 I want (to go / going) to America.

02 He finished (to make / making) a model airplane.

03 We decided (to attend / attending) the meeting.

04 I gave up (to go / going) to the movies tonight.

05 Mike enjoys (to sing / singing) songs with his family.

06 Jina promised (to come / coming) back home early.

07 She hopes (to visit / visiting) her grandfather this summer vacation.

B 우리말과 같은 뜻이 되도록 괄호 안의 단어를 이용하여 문장을 완성하시오.

01 그 학생은 질문에 대답하기를 거절했다. (refuse, answer)

The student ______________________________ the question.

02 이 가방 좀 들어주시겠어요? (mind, carry)

Do you ______________________________ this bag for me?

03 그는 매일 농구 연습을 해야 한다. (need, practice)

He ______________________________ basketball every day.

04 우리는 내년에 유학을 갈 계획이다. (plan, study)

We are ______________________________ abroad next year.

05 나는 주말에 아빠와 배드민턴 치는 걸 즐긴다. (enjoy, play)

I ______________________________ badminton with my dad on weekends.

06 너는 왜 나를 계속 귀찮게 하는 거니? (keep, bother)

Why do you ______________________________ me?

|C| 다음 두 문장이 같은 뜻이 되도록 빈칸에 알맞은 말을 쓰시오.

01 I like swimming in the river.
= I like ________________ in the river.

02 Suddenly, it started to snow.
= Suddenly, it started ________________.

03 The baby began crying.
= The baby began ________________.

04 She will continue to work hard.
= She will continue ________________ hard.

05 My brother loves to draw pictures.
= My brother loves ________________ pictures.

06 Susan likes watching TV dramas.
= Susan likes ________________ TV dramas.

|D| 다음 문장의 밑줄 친 부분을 어법상 바르게 고치시오.

01 Do you <u>want reading</u> this book? → ________________

02 My father <u>finished to read</u> the newspaper. → ________________

03 Minho <u>started learned</u> English. → ________________

04 I <u>don't like talk</u> on the phone. → ________________

05 Jessica <u>decided staying</u> in Seoul this summer. → ________________

06 James <u>enjoyed to fish</u> on ice. → ________________

07 We <u>hope visit</u> Jeju Island this winter. → ________________

08 I'm so tired. Do you <u>mind to drive</u>? → ________________

내신기출 다음 중 어법상 <u>어색한</u> 문장은?

① My sister needs to go to see a doctor.
② I keep to tell him, but he won't listen.
③ James wants to buy a present for his friend.

실전 TIP
to부정사를 목적어로 취할 수 없는 동사를 찾아보세요.

UNIT 10 동명사의 관용 표현

동명사와 자주 쓰이는 관용 표현은 외워야 쓸 수 있어요.

go -ing	~하러 가다	be busy -ing	~하느라 바쁘다
How/What about -ing?	~하는 게 어때?	spend + 시간/돈 + -ing	시간/돈을 ~하는 데 쓰다

|A| 다음 문장에서 어법상 어색한 부분에 밑줄 긋고 바르게 고치시오.

01 How about have a surprise party for Joey? → ____________________

02 She is busy to write an e-mail now. → ____________________

03 Mike and Sam went to shop last Saturday. → ____________________

04 What about to taking a break? → ____________________

05 James spends a lot of time play computer games. → ____________________

06 How about to make a cake together? → ____________________

07 I want to go to hiking with my friends. → ____________________

08 Don't spend too much money to buy toys. → ____________________

|B| 우리말과 같은 뜻이 되도록 괄호 안의 단어를 이용하여 문장을 완성하시오.

01 Sally는 저녁 식사 후에 설거지를 하느라 바쁘다. (busy, do)

Sally ____________________ the dishes after dinner.

02 그는 주말마다 아들과 함께 등산하러 간다. (go, climb)

He ____________________ with his son on weekends.

03 우리는 지난밤에 시험공부를 하느라 바빴다. (busy, study)

We ____________________ for the exam last night.

04 그녀는 계획을 설명하는 데 많은 시간을 썼다. (a lot of, spend, explain, time)

She ____________________ the plan.

05 오늘 밤에 영화 보러 가는 게 어때? (how, go)

____________________ to a movie tonight?

06 나는 이번 방학에 바다에 수영하러 가고 싶다. (go, swim)

I want to ____________________ in the sea this vacation.

대부분의 동명사는 동사원형에 -ing를 붙이지만, swim처럼 예외의 경우도 있음에 주의하세요.

중간고사·기말고사 실전문제

객관식 (01~25) / 주관식 (26~50)

학년과 반 이름 객관식 / 25문항 주관식 / 25문항

01~03 다음 빈칸에 알맞은 말을 고르시오.

01

My plan was ___________ my homework by 8:00.

① finish ② to finish
③ finishes ④ finished
⑤ to finishing

02

The most important thing is ___________ our best in the present.

① do ② does
③ did ④ doing
⑤ to doing

03

Sera is busy ___________ for a trip to Bali.

① prepare ② prepares
③ prepared ④ to prepare
⑤ preparing

04~05 다음 빈칸에 알맞은 말을 모두 고르시오.

04

Karl started ___________ really fast.

① talking ② talk
③ talked ④ to talk
⑤ being talk

05

I like ___________ a glass of apple juice in the morning.

① drink ② to drink
③ drunk ④ to drinking
⑤ drinking

06~07 다음 밑줄 친 부분의 쓰임이 나머지와 다른 것을 고르시오.

06 ① Give me something to eat.
② I have no friend to play with.
③ I don't have any money to lend him.
④ She was surprised to know the fact.
⑤ Can I borrow a pencil to write with?

07 ① Jane's hobby is riding a bicycle.
② Tom enjoys cooking for his friends.
③ Sora doesn't like playing with dolls.
④ Are you interested in dancing with me?
⑤ Mr. Kim doesn't mind opening the door.

08 다음 중 어법상 어색한 문장은?

① He bought a ticket to see a movie.
② It was not easy to find her gold ring.
③ Tiffany has nothing special to do today.
④ He studied so hard in order to becoming a lawyer.
⑤ The most important thing is to study as hard as you can.

09 다음 중 어법상 올바른 것을 모두 고르면?

① It is good expressing your feelings.
② When does he begin teaching students?
③ I need someone to look after my cat.
④ Listening to loud songs aren't good for your ears.
⑤ Minho turned off the TV so as not to disturbed her.

10 다음 대화의 빈칸에 알맞은 말은?

A: Helen, what do you want?
B: I'm so bored. I want something fun ________________.

① to drink
② to clean
③ to borrow
④ to talk with
⑤ to play with

11~12 밑줄 친 ①~⑤ 중 어법상 어색한 것을 고르시오.

11

A police officer ① came ② to my house ③ so as to ④ asking me about ⑤ a neighbor.

12

① Do you ② have any questions ③ asking? If you don't, I will finish ④ my lesson ⑤ on climate change.

13~14 다음 괄호 안의 단어들을 순서대로 배열할 때, 빈칸에 세 번째로 오는 단어를 고르시오.

13

You spend ________________.
(playing / much / the computer games / time)

① time
② much
③ playing
④ games
⑤ computer

14

Sarah is going to ________________.
(to / continue / this website / manage)

① to
② this
③ website
④ manage
⑤ continue

15~17 다음 빈칸에 들어갈 말이 순서대로 짝지어진 것을 고르시오.

15

• I will buy something delicious ________.
• Is there something interesting ________?

① eat – read ② eats – reads
③ ate – read ④ eating – reading
⑤ to eat – to read

16

• Why don't we go ________ this weekend?
• Alex is always busy ________ ready for class.

① ski – get ② skied – got
③ skiing – getting ④ to ski – to get
⑤ skiing – to get

17

• ________ a diary every day is not easy.
• Minsu's dream is ________ an excellent announcer.

① Keep – become
② Keeping – became
③ Keeps – to become
④ Keeping – to become
⑤ To keep – to becoming

18~19 두 문장이 같은 뜻이 되도록 빈칸에 알맞은 말을 고르시오.

18

Jian was surprised because she saw Tom at the art gallery.
= Jian was surprised ________ Tom at the art gallery.

① see ② to see
③ seeing ④ saw
⑤ to seeing

19

We are so lucky because we have him as our captain.
= We are so lucky ________ him as our captain.

① has ② have
③ to have ④ having
⑤ to having

20~21 우리말을 영어로 바르게 옮긴 것을 고르시오.

20

우리는 앉을 의자가 많이 필요하다.

① We need many chairs to sit.
② We need many chairs to sit on.
③ We need many chairs to sitting.
④ We need many chairs sitting on.
⑤ We need many chairs to sit with.

21

> 그녀는 몸을 따뜻하게 하기 위해 겨울에 코트를 입는다.

① She wears a coat keep warm in winter.
② She wears a coat keeping warm in winter.
③ She wears a coat to keep warm in winter.
④ She wears a coat keeping warmly in winter.
⑤ She wears a coat to keep warmly in winter.

22 다음 문장의 밑줄 친 It과 쓰임이 같은 것은?

> It was a pleasure to talk with you.

① How is it going?
② This is my car. I like it.
③ It was windy at the beach.
④ It is 50 km from here to Mokpo.
⑤ It is dangerous to ride a bicycle without a helmet.

23 밑줄 친 부분의 쓰임이 같은 것끼리 짝지어진 것은?

> (a) My dad is cooking Chinese food.
> (b) Her biggest concern is getting a job.
> (c) Writing a letter to him is a good idea.
> (d) Semin enjoys drawing cartoons these days.
> (e) Jessy finished planting flowers in the garden.

① (a), (b) ② (a), (d)
③ (b), (c) ④ (c), (e)
⑤ (d), (e)

24 빈칸 ⓐ~ⓒ에 들어갈 말이 순서대로 짝지어진 것은?

> • We bought a big house ___ⓐ___.
> • Tony brought a notebook ___ⓑ___.
> • There is something interesting ___ⓒ___.

	ⓐ	ⓑ	ⓒ
①	living	writing	talking
②	to live	to write	to talk
③	living in	writing in	talking about
④	to live in	to write in	to talk about
⑤	to live on	to write with	to talk to

25 다음 글에서 밑줄 친 ⓐ~ⓔ를 어법상 바르게 고친 것은?

> Last Sunday, my dad finished ⓐ clean the backyard. My mom ⓑ spends a lot of time ⓒ to design clothes. I enjoyed ⓓ watch a movie with my sister. This Saturday, I want ⓔ go camping with my family.

① ⓐ clean → to clean
② ⓑ spends → spend
③ ⓒ to design → designing
④ ⓓ watch → to watching
⑤ ⓔ go → going

26~28 다음 괄호 안에서 알맞은 말을 고르시오.

26 There are many places (visit, visiting, to visit) in Korea.

27 (Climb, Climbing, To climbing) Mt. Everest was a big challenge for us.

28 Julia needs someone (to talk, to talk to, talking to).

29~30 괄호 안의 단어를 빈칸에 알맞은 형태로 쓰시오.

29 Were you excited ____________ your old friends? (meet)

30 Do you mind ____________ Tommy to school tomorrow? (take)

31~33 다음 문장에서 어법상 어색한 부분을 찾아 바르게 고치시오.

31 I'm freezing! I need warm something to wear.

____________ → ____________

32 I'm sorry, I missed your call. I was busy take caring of the children all day.

____________ → ____________

33 That is a good idea to play the piano at the birthday party.

____________ → ____________

34~36 우리말과 같은 뜻이 되도록 괄호 안의 단어를 이용하여 문장을 완성하시오.

34 그 수학 문제는 제 시간에 풀기에는 어려웠다. (solve)

The math problem was hard ____________ ____________ in time.

35

나는 이번에는 살 빼는 것을 포기하지 않을 것이다. (give up, lose)

I won't ________________ weight this time.

36

준수는 샌드위치를 만들기 위해 햄, 치즈와 채소를 샀다. (order, make)

Junsu bought ham, cheese and vegetables ________________ a sandwich.

37~38 다음 대화에서 어법상 어색한 부분을 찾아 바르게 고치시오.

37

A: I have a stomachache and it's getting worse.
B: How about go to see a doctor?
A: Okay, I will.

________________ → ________________

38

A: Andy, where would you like to travel to this vacation?
B: Well, I would like to traveling to Niagara Falls.
A: Sounds good.

________________ → ________________

39~40 다음 두 문장을 to부정사를 이용하여 하나의 문장으로 연결하시오.

39

• Mike has a lot of friends.
• They will help him.

→ Mike ________________.

39

• She has a dream.
• It is to have her own company.

→ She ________________.

41~42 우리말과 같은 뜻이 되도록 괄호 안의 단어를 바르게 배열하시오.

41

6학년을 마친 후에, 나는 혼자 프랑스로 갔다.

________________, I went to France by myself. (finishing / the sixth grade / after)

42

폭설에 운전을 하다니 그 남자는 미쳤음에 틀림없다.

The man ________________ in the heavy snow. (must / to / crazy / drive / be)

43~45 다음 글을 읽고, 어법상 어색한 부분을 세 군데 찾아 바르게 고치시오.

I have healthy habits in order to be in good shape. I enjoy to eat fresh vegetables and fruits. I like drinking lots of water. I also enjoy exercising. I walk more than 6,000 steps a day. Sometimes I go swim with my friends. I want being a healthy person.

43 ______________ → ______________

44 ______________ → ______________

45 ______________ → ______________

46~48 다음 글을 읽고, 괄호 안의 단어를 이용하여 빈칸에 알맞은 말을 쓰시오.

Next Thursday, we are going on a field trip to Olympic Park. Our homeroom teacher said there were a few things to remember.

46 It's going to be very windy. Don't forget to ______________________.
(your jacket, bring, wear)

47 You should bring ______________________.
(eat, something, for lunch)

48 Think of ______________________ with your friends. (do, interesting, some, things)

49~50 다음 우리말을 주어진 |조건|에 맞게 영어로 바르게 쓰시오.

49 밤에 혼자 거리를 걷는 것은 위험하다.

|조건|
1. 가주어 It으로 시작할 것
2. 단어 dangerous, alone, at, on the street를 이용할 것
3. 11 단어로 쓸 것

→ ______________________________.

50 Alex와 Judy는 과일을 사기 위해 시장에 갔어, 그렇지 않니?

|조건|
1. 부가의문문을 이용할 것
2. 단어 the market, some, they를 이용할 것
3. 13 단어로 쓸 것

→ ______________________________
____

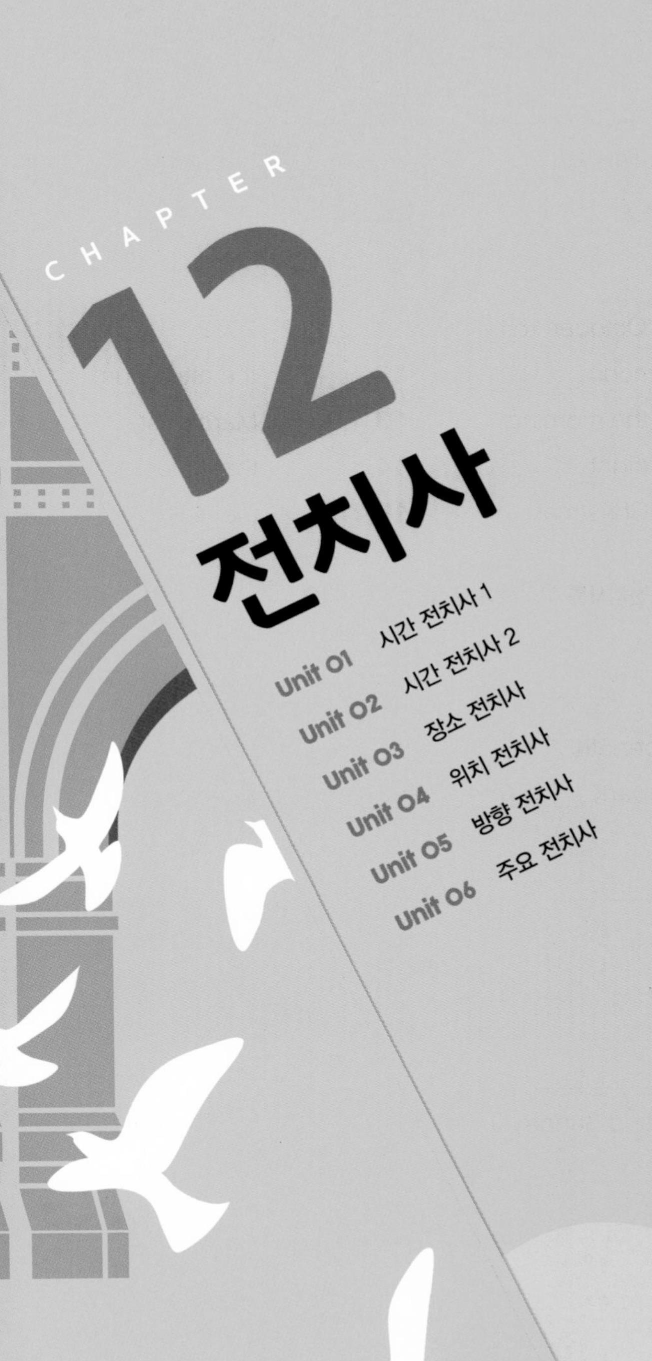

CHAPTER 12

전치사

Unit 01 시간 전치사 1
Unit 02 시간 전치사 2
Unit 03 장소 전치사
Unit 04 위치 전치사
Unit 05 방향 전치사
Unit 06 주요 전치사

UNIT 01 시간 전치사 1

'(언제) ~에'라는 표현은 시간을 나타내는 명사에 따라 전치사 in, on, at 중 하나를 쓰세요.

전치사	+ 시간 명사	예시
in	기간이 있는 시간(월, 오전, 오후, 년도)	in August, in the morning, in 2020
on	날짜, 요일(며칠, 무슨 요일, ~날)	on May 5th, on your birthday, on Sunday
at	정확한 시각(몇 시, 몇 시 몇 분)	at five o'clock, at 5:30, at noon(정오)

참고 전치사는 명사(구)나 대명사 앞에 위치한다는 점 잊지 마세요.

|A| 다음 빈칸에 알맞은 전치사를 쓰시오.

01 _______ eight o'clock
02 _______ winter
03 _______ 6:30
04 _______ Tuesday
05 _______ September
06 _______ October 15th, 2021
07 _______ noon
08 _______ the morning
09 _______ night
10 _______ Christmas
11 _______ 2022
12 _______ the afternoon
13 _______ March 1st
14 _______ that time
15 _______ the new year

|B| 우리말과 같은 뜻이 되도록 괄호 안의 단어와 알맞은 전치사를 이용하여 문장을 완성하시오.

01 그는 6시에 서울에 도착할 것이다. (six o'clock)
He will arrive in Seoul ________________________.

02 우리는 11월 5일에 놀이공원에 갈 계획이다. (November 5th)
We are planning to go to the amusement park ________________________.

03 나의 부모님은 아침에 산책을 하신다. (the morning)
My parents take a walk ________________________.

04 그때 그는 무엇을 하고 있었나요? (that moment)
What was he doing ________________________?

05 우리는 여름에 자주 해변에 간다. (summer)
We often go to the beach ________________________.

06 토요일과 일요일에는 피아노 수업이 없다. (Saturdays and Sundays)
There are no piano lessons ________________________.

내신기출 다음 빈칸에 들어갈 말이 다른 것은?

① _________ April 14th
② _________ the evening
③ _________ Children's Day

실전 TIP
전치사 뒤에 나오는 말이 날짜인지 기간인지 확인해 보세요.

UNIT 02 시간 전치사 2

전치사 in, on, at 이외의 시간을 나타내는 전치사를 알아 두세요.

시간 전치사		예시
before	~ 전에	before sunset, before lunch
after	~ 후에	after school, after lunch
for	~ 동안 (구체적 시간 동안)	for five hours, for three days
during	~ 동안 (특정 행사, 기간 동안)	during the class, during lunch
from ~ to...	~부터 …까지	from nine to six, from Monday to Friday

|A| 우리말과 같은 뜻이 되도록 빈칸에 알맞은 말을 쓰시오.

01 나는 어제 8시간 동안 잤다. I slept ___________ eight hours yesterday.

02 그녀는 방학 동안 캐나다에 있었다. She was in Canada ___________ the vacation.

03 1월은 12월 다음에 온다. January comes ___________ December.

04 너는 수영 전에 준비 운동을 해야 한다. You must warm up ___________ swimming.

05 우리는 9시부터 6시까지 일한다. We work ___________ nine ___________ six.

06 우리는 30분 동안 얘기했다. We talked ___________ thirty minutes.

07 그는 영화가 상영되는 동안 잠이 들었다. He fell asleep ___________ the movie.

|B| 괄호 안의 단어와 |보기|의 전치사를 이용하여 우리말과 같은 뜻이 되도록 문장을 완성하시오.

for 뒤에는 주로 구체적 시간을 나타내는 '숫자'가 나오는 점을 알아 두세요.

|보기|
for   during   before   after   from ~ to ...

01 Jessica는 어제 2시간 동안 공부했다. (hour)

Jessica studied ____________________________ yesterday.

02 너는 저녁 식사 전에 손을 씻어야 한다. (dinner)

You have to wash your hands ____________________________.

03 그 가게는 11시부터 8시까지 문을 연다. (eleven, eight)

The store is open ____________________________.

04 그는 몇 시간 후에 집에 돌아왔다. (a few)

He returned home ____________________________.

05 우리는 여행하는 동안 많은 사람들을 만났다. (the trip)

We met a lot of people ____________________________.

06 그 영화제는 1주일 동안 계속되었다. (a week)

The film festival lasted ____________________________.

UNIT 03 장소 전치사

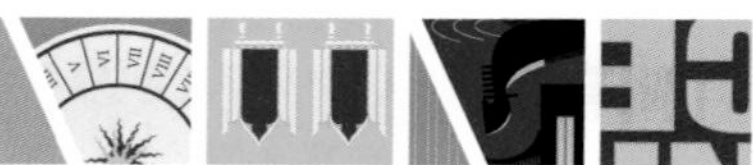

'(어디) ~에'라는 표현은 장소를 나타내는 명사에 따라 전치사 in, on, at 중 하나를 쓰세요.

전치사	+ 장소 명사	예시
in	어떤 공간이나 넓은 장소 안에(방, 건물, 도시, 나라)	in the city, in the room
on	면에 붙어 위에(바닥, 벽, 도로)	on the wall, on the road
at	공간이 없는 장소나 하나의 지점에(정류장, 공항)	at the bus stop, at the airport

|A| 우리말과 같은 뜻이 되도록 빈칸에 알맞은 말을 쓰시오.

01 그는 침대 위에 누워 있다. He is lying __________ the bed.

02 나는 역에서 그녀를 기다렸다. I waited for her __________ the station.

03. Judy는 작년에 한국에서 살았다. Judy lived __________ Korea last year.

04 Sam은 자기 방에서 공부하는 중이다. Sam is studying __________ his room.

05 잔디 위에 앉지 마라. Don't sit __________ the grass.

06 그녀는 책상에서 편지를 쓰고 있다. She is writing a letter __________ her desk.

|B| 다음 빈칸에 알맞은 말을 in, on, at 중에서 골라 쓰시오.

01 Finally, they arrived __________ home.

02 Put your package down __________ the table.

03 Turn to the right __________ the corner.

04 The dog was sleeping __________ the sofa.

05 I stayed __________ the Seoul Hotel this holiday.

06 She enjoyed swimming __________ the sea.

07 His office is __________ the third floor.

08 The stars are shining __________ the sky.

09 There is a picture __________ the wall __________ the living room.

내신 기출 다음 빈칸에 들어갈 말이 나머지와 다른 하나는?

① There is a fly __________ the ceiling.
② Let's go swimming __________ the river.
③ There are some pictures __________ the wall.

실전 TIP
'~안에서'인지 '~위에서'인지 확인해 보세요.

UNIT 04 위치 전치사

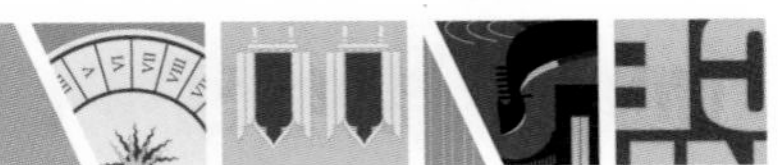

위치를 나타내는 다양한 전치사와 그 의미를 암기하세요.

near	~ 가까이	near my house	behind	~ 뒤에	behind the curtain
over	~ 위로	over the river	in front of	~ 앞에	in front of the store
under	~ 아래	under the table	next to	~ 옆에	next to the bank
between	~ 사이에	between the boxes	across from	~ 맞은편에	across from the library

참고 between은 주로 between A and B의 형태로, 'A와 B 사이에'를 나타내요.

|A| 우리말과 같은 뜻이 되도록 빈칸에 알맞은 말을 쓰시오.

01 그는 공항 근처에 살고 있다. He lives ____________ the airport.

02 나는 Tom과 Bill 사이에 앉았다. I sat ____________ Tom and Bill.

03 그 강 위에 다리가 하나 있다. There is a bridge ____________ the river.

04 그녀는 문 뒤에 숨어 있었다. She was hiding ____________ the door.

05 고양이가 탁자 아래에서 자고 있다. The cat is sleeping ____________ the table.

06 Sally는 거울 앞에 섰다. Sally stood ____________ the mirror.

07 내가 네 옆에 앉아도 되겠니? Can I sit ____________ you?

08 우리 집은 병원 맞은편에 있다. My house is ____________ the hospital.

|B| 다음 그림을 보고 빈칸에 알맞은 말을 |보기|에서 골라 쓰시오.

|보기| over under between in front of next to across from

01 There is a rainbow ____________ the mountain.

02 The girl is sitting ____________ the tree.

03 There is a bike ____________ the girl.

04 The dog is sitting ____________ the bench.

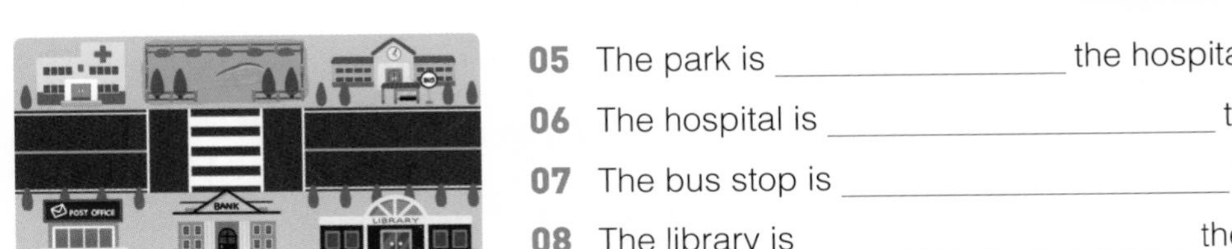

05 The park is ____________ the hospital and the school.

06 The hospital is ____________ the post office.

07 The bus stop is ____________ the school.

08 The library is ____________ the bank.

UNIT 05 방향 전치사

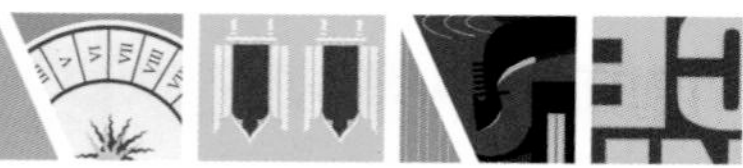

방향을 나타내는 주요 전치사와 그 의미를 암기하세요.

to	~로, ~까지	to school, to the river
from	~에서부터	from my house, from New York (~ 출신)
into	~ 안으로	into the room, into the pocket
out of	~ 밖으로	out of the room, out of the pocket
up	~ 위로	up the stairs, up the hill
down	~ 아래로	down the stairs, down the hill

|A| 다음 그림을 보고 빈칸에 알맞은 말을 쓰시오.

01

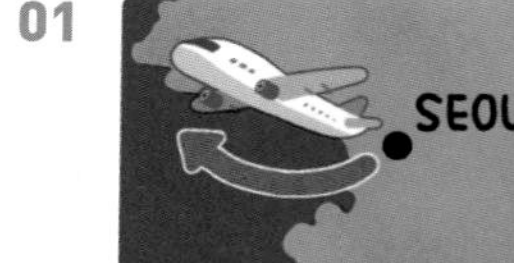

I'm _______ Seoul.

02

She went _______ Seoul.

03

We walked _______ the hill.

04

We walked _______ the hill.

05

The bird flew _______ the cage.

06

The bird flew _______ the cage.

|B| 우리말과 같은 뜻이 되도록 빈칸에 알맞은 말을 쓰시오.

01 나는 다음 주에 런던에 갈 예정이다.

I'm going to go ___________ London next week.

02 Tom은 건물에서 밖으로 달려 나와 택시를 탔다.

Tom ran ___________ the building and took a taxi.

03 나는 서점에서 나와 선물 가게로 들어왔다.

I went ___________ the bookstore and came ___________ this gift shop.

04 그 남자는 사다리를 올라가고 있다.

The man is climbing ___________ the ladder.

05 여기에서 너의 집은 얼마나 머니?

How far is it ___________ here ___________ your house?

UNIT 06 주요 전치사

시간 · 장소 · 위치 · 방향 전치사 외에 자주 쓰는 전치사의 쓰임과 의미를 알아 두세요.

about	~에 대해	about me, about K-pop
of	~의	a friend of Minsu, a member of the team
for	~을 위해	for you, for the exam
like	~처럼, ~ 같은	like a horse, like a model
with	~와, ~을 가지고	with her friends, with a knife
because of	~ 때문에	because of noise, because of stress

주의 전치사 because of 뒤에는 명사를 쓰고, 접속사 because 뒤에는 문장을 쓴다는 데 유의하세요.

|A| 우리말과 같은 뜻이 되도록 빈칸에 알맞은 전치사를 쓰시오.

01 그것에 대해 모두 내게 말해 주세요. Tell me all ________ it.

02 나는 칼로 스테이크를 잘랐다. I cut the steak ________ a knife.

03 그는 시험을 위해 영어를 공부했다. He studied English ________ the test.

04 Jason은 내 사촌의 친구이다. Jason is a friend ________ my cousin.

05 나는 자동차에 대해 많이 알지 못한다. I don't know much ________ cars.

06 Sue는 아기처럼 울고 있었다. Sue was crying ________ a baby.

07 나는 건강을 위해 매일 운동한다. I exercise every day ________ my health.

08 우리는 비 때문에 밖에 나가지 않았다. We didn't go outside ________ the rain.

|B| 빈칸에 알맞은 말을 |보기|에서 골라 다음 문장을 완성하시오.

|보기|
of for about like with because of

01 I'll work harder ________ my dream.

02 She usually writes a letter ________ a pen.

03 I like the color ________ her hair.

04 They are talking ________ the weather.

05 My mother can't smell ________ a cold.

06 The man was acting ________ a child.

07 My grandmother walks ________ a cane.

08 This road is ________ bikes. No cars!

중간고사·기말고사 실전문제

객관식 (01~25) / 주관식 (26~50)

학년과 반 이름 객관식 / 25문항 주관식 / 25문항

01~03 다음 빈칸에 알맞은 말을 고르시오.

01

My mom organized the books ________ the shelf.

① on ② for
③ like ④ down
⑤ about

02

Our coffee shop is open ________ Monday to Friday.

① for ② next
③ over ④ from
⑤ into

03

The airplane flies ________ Seoul and Paris.

① near ② under
③ behind ④ before
⑤ between

04~05 다음 대화의 빈칸에 알맞은 말을 고르시오.

04

A: When did you get your driver's license?
B: I got it ________ August.

① to ② in
③ at ④ for
⑤ during

05

A: Where is the bank?
B: It's ________ the clothing store.

① after ② from
③ next to ④ about
⑤ out of

06 다음 ①~⑤ 중 for가 들어갈 알맞은 곳은?

They (①) will not be (②) allowed (③) to use (④) their cellphone (⑤) an hour.

07~08 우리말과 같은 뜻이 되도록 빈칸에 알맞은 말을 고르시오.

07

Sujin spent her childhood ___________ California.
(수진이는 캘리포니아에서 그녀의 어린 시절을 보냈다.)

① in ② on
③ at ④ for
⑤ with

08

They complained to the restaurant manager ___________ the food.
(그들은 식당 매니저에게 음식에 대해 불평했다.)

① near ② with
③ for ④ about
⑤ like

09~10 밑줄 친 ①~⑤ 중 어법상 어색한 것을 고르시오.

09

Minsu ① went to the theater ② at noon ③ yesterday. But he ④ fell asleep ⑤ for the movie.

10

① When Susan was ② ten years old, she ③ had a terrible experience ④ because ⑤ an earthquake.

11~12 다음 괄호 안의 단어들을 순서대로 배열할 때, 네 번째로 오는 단어를 고르시오.

11

Is that basket ___________ yours?
(of / in / your / bicycle / front)

① in ② of
③ your ④ front
⑤ bicycle

12

This printer doesn't work ___________.
(of / missing / a / because / part)

① of ② the
③ part ④ missing
⑤ because

13~14 다음 중 어법상 어색한 문장을 고르시오.

13 ① He is running with his dog.
② There is a letter in the bottle.
③ My sister likes sweets like chocolate.
④ She's going to meet some friends after work.
⑤ We celebrated John's wedding during three days.

14 ① Yuna is standing behind her father.
② My classmate lives on the 19th floor.
③ How about meeting at the bus stop?
④ Mike yelled, "Let's dive over the water!"
⑤ The restaurant has its breaktime from three to five.

15 다음 중 어법상 올바른 문장을 모두 고르면?

① It's across for the gas station.
② The man climbed up the ladder.
③ The ceremony is scheduled in July 30.
④ Put the table between the sofa and the TV.
⑤ Alex and Jerry avoided the rain from a big tree.

16~18 다음 빈칸에 공통으로 알맞은 말을 고르시오.

16

- Jisu sat opposite him ____________ the meal.
- Please turn off your cellphones ____________ the conference.

① for ② under
③ during ④ about
⑤ behind

17

- Mr. Choi went on a business trip ____________ England.
- The film festival took place from September 10th ____________ 25th.

① to ② in
③ for ④ near
⑤ into

18

- I regularly exercise ____________ an hour after school.
- Ms. Smith often made some cookies ____________ her guests.

① to ② for
③ out of ④ with
⑤ during

19 우리말을 영어로 바르게 옮긴 것은?

물고기 두 마리가 어항 밖으로 나왔다.

① Two fish came out of the fish bowl.
② Two fish came next to the fish bowl.
③ Two fish came between the fish bowl.
④ Two fish came in front of the fish bowl.
⑤ Two fish came because of the fish bowl.

20~21 빈칸에 들어갈 말이 순서대로 짝지어진 것을 고르시오.

20

- The moon disappeared ____________ the clouds.
- Don't forget to bring a camera ____________ you.

① before – of ② near – like
③ over – from ④ under – about
⑤ behind – with

21

• I wash my hands ________ every meal.
• Vehicles must not park ________ the entrance.

① for – down ② in – with
③ about – from ④ before – in front of
⑤ next to – out of

22 다음 빈칸에 들어갈 말이 나머지와 다른 것은?

① Jane cut the paper ________ scissors.
② I am excited ________ my trip to Australia.
③ I don't know much ________ Italian history.
④ Some people don't talk ________ their work.
⑤ Did you see the program ________ global warming on TV?

23 다음 우리말을 영어로 바르게 옮긴 것을 모두 고르면?

① 그녀는 소파 위에 누웠다.
→ She lay down into the sofa.
② 나는 겨울에 썰매 타는 것을 좋아한다.
→ I like to ride in a sled in winter.
③ 세라는 동상 근처에 서 있다.
→ Sera is standing next to the statue.
④ 말이 울타리를 뛰어넘었다.
→ The horse jumped over the fence.
⑤ 군인들이 언덕 위로 걸어가고 있다.
→ The soldiers are walking down the hill.

24 빈칸 ⓐ~ⓒ에 들어갈 말이 순서대로 짝지어진 것은?

• Can you translate this letter ___ⓐ___ me?
• Julia arrived ___ⓑ___ a small town in Germany.
• They heard a noise ___ⓒ___ thunder.

	ⓐ	ⓑ	ⓒ
①	to	at	about
②	for	in	under
③	for	at	like
④	of	before	during
⑤	of	near	from

25 빈칸에 들어갈 말이 같은 것끼리 바르게 짝지어진 것은?

(a) I'm never bored ________ home.
(b) My birthday falls ________ February 6th.
(c) My family cleaned the house ________ three hours.
(d) The referee stopped the game ________ heavy snow.
(e) The bread plate is ________ the left of the place setting.

① (a), (b) ② (b), (c)
③ (b), (e) ④ (c), (d)
⑤ (d), (e)

26~28 |보기|에서 알맞은 말을 골라 다음 문장을 완성하시오.

|보기|

on	to	over
during	next to	out of

26 Excuse me, can I sit ______________ you?

27 She didn't know she left my passport ______________ the table.

28 They had a meeting ______________ their lunch break.

29~31 우리말과 같은 뜻이 되도록 다음 대화의 빈칸에 알맞은 말을 쓰시오.

29
A: Jim, where is your sister?
B: She is standing ______________ the woman in red.
(그녀는 빨간 옷을 입은 여자 앞에 서 있어.)

30
A: What time will you come back home?
B: I'll come back home ______________ midnight.
(자정 전에 집에 돌아올게.)

31
A: When did you eat fish and chips for the first time?
B: I first ate it ______________ my stay in England.
(나는 영국에 머무는 동안 그 음식을 처음 먹었어.)

32~34 다음 문장에서 어법상 어색한 부분을 찾아 바르게 고치시오.

32 Helen worked as a flight attendant during ten years.

______________ → ______________

33 Minho was rolling a pencil behind two fingers.

______________ → ______________

34 Many tourists sit over the steps in front of the museum.

______________ → ______________

35~37 |보기|에서 알맞은 말을 골라 다음 문장을 완성하시오.

|보기|

over	on	to
from	near	at
between	because of	for

35 There used to be a big strawberry farm ______ my house.

36 My family will visit Gangneung ______ Friday ______ Sunday.

37 Mr. Baker woke up ______ 3:00 ______ the time difference.

38~40 우리말과 같은 뜻이 되도록 괄호 안의 단어를 바르게 배열하시오.

38 당신은 이 길의 끝에서 오른쪽으로 돌아야 한다.

You should turn right ______________ ______________.

(this road / of / at / the end)

39 숙제 끝난 후에 나에게 전화해.

Call me ______________.

(finishing / homework / after / your)

40 한 남자가 감옥에서 탈출하기 위해 담을 넘었다.

A man climbed ______________ ______________ the prison.

(from / over / the wall / to escape)

41~42 우리말과 같은 뜻이 되도록 괄호 안의 단어를 이용하여 문장을 완성하시오.

41 몇몇 커플들이 공원에 있는 벤치에 앉아 있다.

Some couples are ______________ ______________.

(sit, the benches, the park)

42 물러서! 절벽의 끝 가까이에 가지 마.

Step back! Don't go ______________ ______________.

(the cliff, of, the edge)

43 괄호 안의 단어를 바르게 배열하여 다음 글을 완성하시오.

> Attention! Ladies and gentleman. The dance festival will be held ____ⓐ____.
> (7 p.m. / on / at / the 13th floor)
> of the Great Tower. This festival lasts ____ⓑ____ 20th to 24th.
> (for / from / five days / July)

44~45 다음 문장 중 어법상 어색한 부분을 두 군데 찾아 바르게 고치시오.

> (a) Did you make this burger for me?
> (b) I will go to see Mary at her birthday.
> (c) Who is the little girl behind the curtain?
> (d) The car accident happened before five o'clock.
> (e) My father can't chew because a toothache.

44 ________ → ________

45 ________ → ________

46~48 다음 글에서 어법상 어색한 부분을 세 군데 찾아 바르게 고치시오.

> My friends and I went out for dinner last Saturday. We ate on an Italian restaurant. When we got there, it was very crowded. So we put my name with the waiting list and we waited into the car.

46 ________ → ________

47 ________ → ________

48 ________ → ________

49~50 다음 우리말을 주어진 |조건|에 맞게 영어로 바르게 쓰시오.

49 그는 여기에 오기 위해 5시간 동안 운전했다.

|조건|
1. 단어 drive, hours, get을 이용할 것
2. 8 단어로 쓸 것
3. 필요시 어법에 맞게 단어를 변형할 것

→ ________

50 연습을 많이 한 후에 운전면허 시험을 치러라.

|조건|
1. 명령문으로 쓸 것
2. 단어 take, the driving test, practice, a lot을 사용할 것
3. 8 단어로 쓰고, 필요시 어법에 맞게 단어를 변형할 것

→ ________

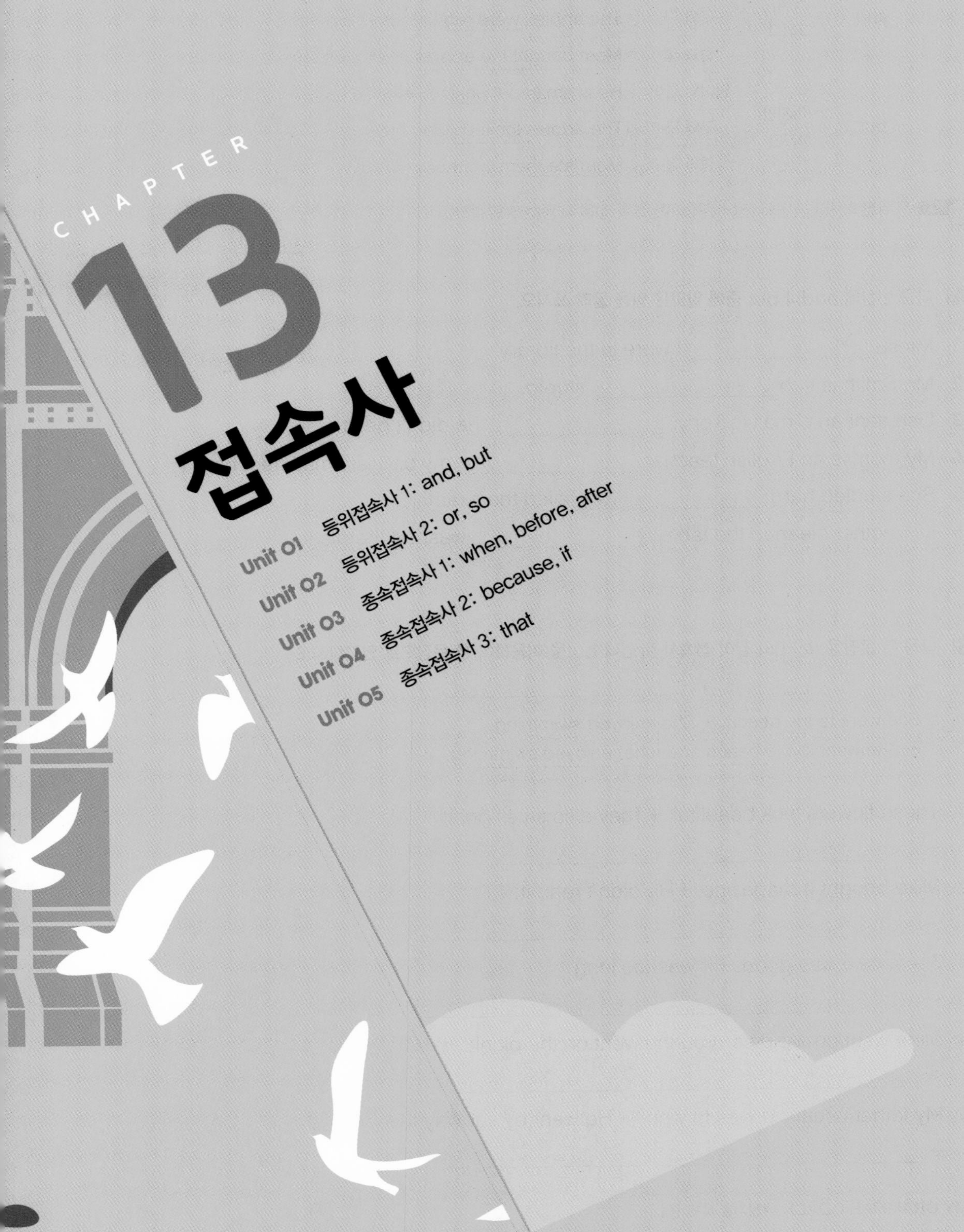

CHAPTER 13 접속사

Unit 01 등위접속사 1: and, but
Unit 02 등위접속사 2: or, so
Unit 03 종속접속사 1: when, before, after
Unit 04 종속접속사 2: because, if
Unit 05 종속접속사 3: that

UNIT 01 등위접속사 1: and, but

앞뒤 말을 파악하여 and(그리고) 또는 but(그러나)으로 연결하세요.

and	~와, 그리고	단어와 단어	Jane and Tom are friends. Jane과 Tom
		구와 구	The apples were red and looked delicious. 빨갰고, 맛있어 보였다
		절과 절	Mom bought the apples and I ate them. 엄마가 샀고, 나는 먹었다
but	~이지만, 하지만	단어와 단어	He is smart but unkind. 똑똑하지만 불친절한
		구와 구	The apples looked good but tasted bad. 좋아 보였지만, 맛이 나빴다
		절과 절	Mom ate them, but I didn't eat them. 엄마는 먹었지만, 난 안 먹었다

참고 등위접속사란 단어와 단어, 구와 구, 절과 절을 대등하게 연결하는 말이에요.

|A| 다음 빈칸에 and나 but 중에 알맞은 말을 골라 쓰시오.

01 Minsu ________________ I were in the library.

02 Mr. Smith is rich ________________ stupid.

03 Lisa sent an e-mail to Tony, ________________ he didn't get it.

04 My mom is an English teacher ________________ my dad is a math teacher.

05 She studied hard ________________ failed the exam.

06 My mother cleaned the table ________________ washed the dishes.

|B| 다음 두 문장을 |보기|와 같이 접속사 and나 but을 이용하여 한 문장으로 연결하시오.

보기
She went to the beach. + She enjoyed swimming.
→ She went to the beach and (she) enjoyed swimming.

절과 절을 등위접속사를 이용해서 연결할 때, 주어가 같으면, 뒤에 나오는 주어는 생략할 수 있음을 알아 두세요.

01 These flowers look beautiful. + They also smell good.

→ ________________________________

02 Mike bought a magazine. + He didn't read it.

→ ________________________________

03 The movie was good. + It was too long.

→ ________________________________

04 Mina went on a picnic. + Junho went on the picnic, too.

→ ________________________________

05 My father usually drives to work. + He went by subway this morning.

→ ________________________________

UNIT 02 등위접속사 2: or, so

앞뒤 말을 파악하여 or(또는) 또는 so(그래서)로 연결하세요.

or	또는, ~이거나	단어와 단어	Is it good or bad? 좋거나 나쁜
		구와 구	I can call her or visit her house. 그녀에게 전화하거나 집에 방문할 수 있다
		절과 절	I can call her or she can visit me. 내가 그녀에게 전화하거나, 그녀가 나를 방문할 수 있다
so	그래서, ~이므로	절과 절	I called her so she came. 내가 전화해서, 그녀가 왔다

주의 접속사 so는 절과 절만 연결하며, so 뒤에는 앞 절의 결과에 해당하는 말을 써요.

A 다음 빈칸에 or나 so 중에 알맞은 말을 골라 쓰시오.

01 You can eat the food here ________ take it out.

02 It was too hot ________ I had a cold shower.

03 The movie was very boring ________ I fell asleep.

04 Which shoes are hers, these ________ those?

05 You can go with your son ________ your daughter.

06 She was hungry ________ she had some bread and milk.

B 우리말과 같은 뜻이 되도록 괄호 안의 단어와 접속사를 이용하여 문장을 완성하시오.

01 너는 여름 또는 겨울 중에 어느 계절을 더 좋아하니? (better, summer, winter, like)

Which season do you ________________?

02 택시가 없어서 그는 버스를 타고 사무실에 갔다. (went to, by bus, the office, he)

There were no taxis ________________.

03 우리 영화 보러 갈까 아니면 집에 있을까? (go to, stay, the movies, at home)

Shall we ________________?

04 나는 감기에 걸려서, 의사의 진찰을 받으러 갔다. (I, a doctor, went, to see)

I caught a cold ________________.

실전 TIP

'그리고'인지, '하지만'인지, '또는'인지, '그래서'인지 앞뒤 문맥을 파악해 보세요.

내신기출 다음 빈칸에 and, but, or, so 중에 알맞은 말을 쓰시오.

- Did you go there by bus ________ by subway?
- My grandma gets up early ________ has breakfast.
- Sam did his English homework ________ Tom didn't.
- I missed the school bus ________ I was late for school.

UNIT 03 종속접속사 1: when, before, after

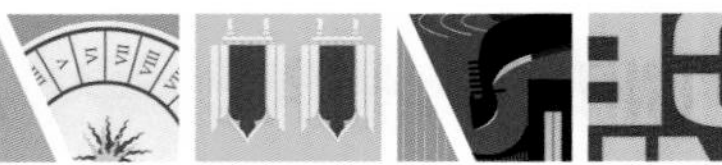

앞뒤 문맥에 맞게 시간을 나타내는 접속사를 사용하세요.

when	~할 때, ~하면	절과 절	She smiled when I said hi to her. 인사했을 때
before	~하기 전에	절과 절	Take off your shoes before you enter. 들어가기 전에
after	~한 후에	절과 절	After I got home, I took a nap. 집에 도착한 후

참고 부사절이 앞에 오면 부사절 뒤에 콤마(,)를 써서 연결하고, 부사절이 뒤에 올 때는 콤마(,) 없이 연결해요.

참고 부사절은 종속절이고도 부르는데, 주절에 내용을 보충하는 종속 관계이기 때문이에요.

|A| 다음 빈칸에 알맞은 말을 |보기|에서 골라 그 번호를 쓰시오.

01 I brush my teeth ___________.

02 He watched TV ___________.

03 Be polite and kind ___________.

04 Did she leave a message ___________?

05 Look both ways ___________.

06 We have to buy a ticket ___________.

07 Raise your hand ___________.

08 She always goes to the same city ___________.

|보기|
ⓐ when you have a question
ⓑ before she left
ⓒ before we get on the train
ⓓ when you talk to others
ⓔ after I eat meals
ⓕ after he finished his work
ⓖ when she goes on vacation
ⓗ before you cross the road

|B| 우리말과 같은 뜻이 되도록 괄호 안의 단어와 접속사를 이용하여 문장을 완성하시오.

01 어렸을 때 나는 뚱뚱했다. (young)

I was fat ___________________________.

02 당신이 출근하기 전에 나를 깨워 주세요. (go to work)

Wake me up ___________________________.

03 너희들은 식사를 끝낸 후에 밖에 나가서 놀아도 된다. (finish, eating)

You can play outside ___________________________.

04 너는 엄마가 돌아오시기 전에 숙제를 해야 한다. (come back)

You have to do your homework ___________________________.

05 내가 그 방에 들어갔을 때, 그녀는 저녁을 먹고 있었다. (enter, the room)

___________________________, she was having dinner.

06 내가 약간의 팝콘과 쿠키를 사고 난 후에 영화는 시작했다. (buy, drinks, popcorn)

The movie began ___________________________.

UNIT 04 종속접속사 2: because, if

앞뒤 문맥에 맞게 조건이나 이유를 나타내는 접속사를 사용하세요.

because	~하기 때문에	절과 절	She took a taxi because it rained. 비가 왔기 때문에
if	~한다면	절과 절	She will take a taxi if it rains. 비가 오면

주의 시간이나 조건을 나타내는 부사절에서는 현재시제가 미래시제를 대신해요.

주의 because/as/since는 접속사이므로 뒤에 문장을 쓰고, because of는 전치사이므로 뒤에 (동)명사를 써야 해요.
The roads were slippery because[as, since] it snowed. 눈이 내렸기 때문에
= The roads were slippery because of the snow. 눈 때문에

|A| 다음 빈칸에 because와 if 중에 알맞은 말을 골라 쓰시오.

01 ________________ I was very late, I took a taxi.

02 ________________ it rains, we will not go camping tomorrow.

03 She is healthy ________________ she jogs every morning.

04 Jason will come to see me ________________ he is free today.

05 ________________ I meet her, I will give a birthday present to her.

06 ________________ he was tired, he didn't go to the party last night.

|B| 다음 두 문장을 알맞은 접속사를 이용하여 한 문장으로 연결하시오.

01 My favorite season is winter. + I like skiing.
→ My favorite season is winter ____________________________.

02 You are hungry. + You can eat the spaghetti.
→ ____________________________, you can eat the spaghetti.

03 I like my English teacher. + He is kind.
→ ____________________________, I like him.

04 I was very busy today. + I couldn't have lunch.
→ I couldn't have lunch ____________________________.

05 He gets up early. + He won't be late.
→ He won't be late ____________________________.

내신 기출 다음 밑줄 친 부분 중 어법상 어색한 것을 찾아 바르게 고쳐 쓰시오.

Can I try this skirt on? I will buy the skirt if it will fit me.
① Can ② will buy ③ will fit

실전 TIP
if절이나 when절에서는 현재시제가 미래시제를 대신한다는 점 기억하세요.

UNIT 05 종속접속사 3: that

하나의 절 앞에 접속사 that(~하다는 것)을 붙여서 하나의 명사처럼 사용하세요.

that절	의미: 그가 늦게 일어난다는 것	주의
주어	That he gets up late is unbelievable.	that절은 단수 취급
목적어	No one knows (that) he gets up late.	목적어 that절의 that은 생략 가능
보어	The truth is that he gets up late.	

참고 that절이 주어 역할을 할 때에는 보통 가주어 It을 주어 자리에 쓰고, 진짜 주어인 that절은 문장 뒤로 옮길 수 있어요.
→ It is unbelievable that he gets up late.

|A| 다음 밑줄 친 부분의 역할이 주어이면 S, 보어이면 C, 목적어이면 O라고 쓰시오.

01 That he likes you is certain. ________
02 The problem is that we can't go out. ________
03 I didn't know that she was absent yesterday. ________
04 The fact is that we don't have enough money. ________
05 I think that you will like this bag very much. ________
06 It is true that she passed the exam. ________
07 Do you believe that the earth is round? ________
08 I think that Jiho broke the window. ________

|B| 우리말과 같은 뜻이 되도록 괄호 안의 단어와 접속사 that을 이용하여 문장을 완성하시오.

01 나는 네가 최선을 다했다고 생각한다. (do your best)
I think ________________________.

02 그가 제시간에 여기 오지 못할 것은 확실하다. (be, in time, will)
It is certain ________________________.

03 나는 네가 실수를 하지 않았다는 것을 알고 있다. (make a mistake)
I know ________________________.

04 사실은 그가 답을 알지 못한다는 것이다. (know, the answer)
The fact is ________________________.

05 김 선생님은 그 시험이 매우 어려웠다고 동의했다. (the exam, very difficult)
Mr. Kim agreed ________________________.

06 Sally는 요가를 배우고 있다고 말했다. (learn, yoga)
Sally said ________________________.

중간고사·기말고사 실전문제

객관식 (01~25) / 주관식 (26~50)

정답과 해설 • 53쪽

학년과 반 이름 객관식 / 25문항 주관식 / 25문항

01~03 다음 빈칸에 알맞은 말을 고르시오.

01

Semi usually listens to bright music ________ it rains.

① if ② so
③ or ④ but
⑤ that

02

The traffic was heavy ________ Ms. Kim was late for work.

① or ② so
③ when ④ that
⑤ before

03

________ I arrived at home, my mom was talking on the phone.

① But ② And
③ When ④ That
⑤ Because

04~05 다음 대화의 빈칸에 알맞은 말을 고르시오.

04

A: Do you know about Hermann Hesse?
B: Yes, he was a great poet ________ novelist.

① or ② so
③ but ④ and
⑤ when

05

A: Why are you laughing?
B: ________ this webtoon is so funny.

① That ② When
③ Before ④ After
⑤ Because

06~07 밑줄 친 ①~⑤ 중 어법상 어색한 것을 고르시오.

06

① Everyone ② can ③ visit my blog ④ and ⑤ watching my videos.

07

① If my parents ② will come home ③ early, I ④ will go ⑤ shopping with them.

08 다음 빈칸에 들어갈 수 없는 말은?

I feel happy ________________.

① when I eat delicious food
② when I play with my friends
③ when I wear some new clothes
④ when I go camping with my family
⑤ when I get a bad grade on my test

09~10 빈칸에 들어갈 말이 순서대로 짝지어진 것을 고르시오.

09

> • I think ________ I can pass the exam.
> • He told me to go there, ________ I didn't go there.

① when – but ② that – so
③ that – but ④ before – so
⑤ after – and

10

> • I will buy shoes ________ clothes for Julie's birthday.
> • Get out of my house ________ I call the police.

① or – so ② or – before
③ and – so ④ and – but
⑤ but – after

11 다음 우리말을 영어로 바르게 옮긴 것은?

> Tom은 저녁 식사를 끝낸 후에 외출했다.

① Tom finishes his dinner and goes out.
② If Tom finishes his dinner, he will go out.
③ Tom went out after he finished his dinner.
④ Before Tom finished his dinner, he went out.
⑤ Tom went out because he finished his dinner.

12~13 밑줄 친 부분의 쓰임이 나머지와 다른 것을 고르시오.

12 ① When does the school festival begin?
② When you go to school, do you walk?
③ When I watch movies, I always eat popcorn.
④ When they play badminton, they look so excited.
⑤ When Jinho feels sad, he takes a walk with his dog.

13 ① I will call you before I have lunch.
② We left for the airport before sunrise.
③ Shall we get some drinks before the movie starts?
④ Sora left a message with me before she went away.
⑤ Please take off your wet clothes before you catch a cold.

14~15 다음 빈칸에 공통으로 알맞은 말을 고르시오.

14

> • The noodles were spicy ________ delicious.
> • I bought a book, ________ I didn't read it.

① so ② and
③ but ④ before
⑤ after

15

> • ________ she reads many books is true.
> • The problem is ________ you don't have a car.

① If[if] ② That[that]
③ When[when] ④ After[after]
⑤ Because[because]

16~17 다음 중 어법상 어색한 문장을 고르시오.

16 ① Jenny believes that she will succeed.
② Peter is shy, so he doesn't talk much.
③ I checked the apples before I bought them.
④ Will you come to the party if he invite you?
⑤ My family moved to Ulsan when I was three years old.

17 ① Mike and Suji are coming to dinner.
② What do you do when are you bored?
③ It is certain that my mother loves me.
④ After you wash your face, get dressed.
⑤ She got wet because she didn't have an umbrella.

18~19 다음 괄호 안의 단어들을 순서대로 배열할 때, 세 번째로 오는 단어를 고르시오.

18

My father wears glasses ___________. (he / when / reads / the / newspaper)

① the ② he
③ reads ④ when
⑤ newspaper

19

___________________, you will catch a cold. (don't / if / you / wear / warm / clothes)

① you ② wear
③ don't ④ warm
⑤ clothes

20 다음 문장의 밑줄 친 that과 쓰임이 같은 것은?

We hope that we don't fail the test.

① That I had a fight with Seho was true.
② The fact is that she is older than me.
③ It is interesting that Olivia loves *kimchi*.
④ The good news is that we can go fishing.
⑤ Our visitors said that the services were not good.

21 다음 밑줄 친 부분 중 어법상 어색한 것은?
① Some birds have wings but can't fly.
② When winter comes, let's go sledding.
③ My teacher said that we would go on a picnic.
④ The food is delicious, so the restaurant is popular.
⑤ After finish your homework, you can play computer games.

22 다음 빈칸에 들어갈 말이 나머지와 다른 것은?
① Is today Monday __________ Tuesday?
② Which drink do you want, juice __________ coke?
③ Joey looks five __________ six years old.
④ Mary woke up at 6:00 __________ she left home at 8:00.
⑤ Is she Korean __________ Japanese?

23 다음 |보기|의 말이 빈칸에 알맞지 않은 문장은?

|보기|
if so but because

① The door opened ___________ she came in.
② Ms. Han succeeded ___________ she worked hard.
③ Leo wanted to come, ___________ he was busy.
④ My car ran out of gas, ___________ I stopped at a gas station.
⑤ ___________ I go to China, I will see the Great Wall.

24 빈칸에 들어갈 말이 같은 것끼리 바르게 짝지어진 것은?

(a) ___________ he goes camping, I will go with him.
(b) I go to bed ___________ I brush my teeth.
(c) ___________ I saw her, she was eating spaghetti.
(d) We finished our meal ___________ ordered dessert.
(e) ___________ they don't get here soon, we will leave without them.

① (a), (c) ② (a), (e)
③ (b), (d) ④ (b), (e)
⑤ (c), (d)

25 우리말을 영어로 바르게 옮긴 것을 모두 고르시오.

① 지훈은 샤워를 하고 TV를 봤다.
→ Jihun took a shower and watches TV.
② 우리 팀이 경기에서 이겼을 때 나는 행복했다.
→ I was happy when my team won the game.
③ 나는 배가 고파서 만두를 다 먹었다.
→ I was hungry, but I ate all the dumplings.
④ 나는 Chris가 그녀에게 편지를 썼다는 것을 알았다.
→ I knew that Chris wrote her a letter.
⑤ 피곤하면 잠시 앉으세요.
→ After you feel tired, please sit down for a while.

26~27 두 문장이 같은 뜻이 되도록 빈칸에 알맞은 말을 쓰시오.

26
I brush my teeth before I go to sleep.
= I go to sleep ___________ I brush my teeth.

27
It was very hot, so we turned on the air conditioner.
= We turned on the air conditioner ___________ it was very hot.

28~30 괄호 안의 단어를 빈칸에 알맞은 형태로 쓰시오.

28
Tiffany took many pictures and ___________ them to her family. (show)

29

If Lucas ___________ early tomorrow, I will plant a pine tree with him. (get up)

30

My sister is good at singing, dancing and ___________ the guitar. (play)

31~33 |보기|에서 알맞은 접속사를 골라 다음 대화를 완성하시오.

|보기|

and	but	so
that	when	because

31

A: Why are you studying at this late hour?
B: ___________ I have an English test.

32

A: Do you think Mr. Smith is guilty?
B: No. I believe ___________ he is innocent.

33

A: What did Jisu and her family do last weekend?
B: They cleaned the house, cut the grass ___________ watched a movie.

34~36 다음 문장에서 어법상 어색한 부분을 찾아 바르게 고치시오.

34

I call you immediately if I hear any news tomorrow.

_______________ → _______________

35

I don't like to listen to music and studied at the same time.

_______________ → _______________

36

When Jane gets home, the house was quiet and all the lights were out.

_______________ → _______________

37~39 우리말과 같은 뜻이 되도록 괄호 안의 단어를 바르게 배열하시오.

37

오늘 아침은 흐렸지만, 지금 하늘은 맑다.

It was cloudy this morning, ___________
_______________.
(but / is / clear / the sky / now)

38

나는 교실에서 나온 후에 내 휴대폰을 켠다.

I turn on my cell phone ___________
_______________.
(I / after / the classroom / out of / get)

39

Brown 선생님은 어제 커피를 많이 마셔서 지난 밤에 잠을 잘 수 없었다.

Mr. Brown drank a lot of coffee yesterday,
_______________.
(couldn't / he / so / sleep / well / last night)

40~42 다음 문장 중 어법상 어색한 문장을 세 군데 찾아 바르게 고치시오.

(a) Fish and swimming are my hobbies.
(b) He didn't like my opinion but accepted it.
(c) Julia likes him because of he has a warm heart.
(d) My dog won't bark at you if you give her a stick.
(e) The good news is when you don't have to go to school.

40 ______________ → ______________

41 ______________ → ______________

42 ______________ → ______________

43 우리말과 같은 뜻이 되도록 괄호 안의 단어를 바르게 배열하시오.

Things to do in the museum
1. 당신이 박물관에 있는 그림들을 볼 때, you must not take photos.
2. You must not eat food in the museum.

→ ______________________________
(you / see / when / in / the museum / the paintings)

44~45 다음 글에서 어법상 어색한 부분을 두 군데 찾아 바르게 고치시오.

I often forget things, so I always take notes.
• If I meet Susan tomorrow, I talk about our group project.
• If I will have some free time tomorrow, I will buy a present for my mom.

44 ______________ → ______________

45 ______________ → ______________

46~48 다음 두 문장을 알맞은 접속사를 이용하여 한 문장으로 바꾸시오.

46
• Mina went abroad to study medicine.
• Tom went abroad to study medicine, too.

→ ______________________________

47
• You take a shower.
• You should clean the bathroom.

→ ______________________________

48
• I went to a traditional market.
• I couldn't buy sweet potatoes.

→ ______________________________

49~50 다음 우리말을 주어진 |조건|에 맞게 영어로 바르게 쓰시오.

49 이번 연휴에 Henry는 수영을 하러 가거나 축구를 할 것이다.

|조건|
1. 접속사 or와 동명사를 이용할 것
2. 단어 go, this holiday를 이용할 것
3. 10 단어로 쓸 것

→ ______________________________

50 네가 도서관에 갈 때, 이 책을 반납해 줄 수 있니?

|조건|
1. 접속사 when으로 시작할 것
2. 단어 go, can, return을 이용할 것
3. 11 단어로 쓸 것

→ ______________________________

내가 가장 취약한 부분에 대해
요점 정리를 해 보세요.

내가 가장 취약한 부분에 대해
요점 정리를 해 보세요.

필독 중학 국어로 수능 잡기 시리즈

문학 – 비문학 독해 – 문법 – 교과서 시 – 교과서 소설

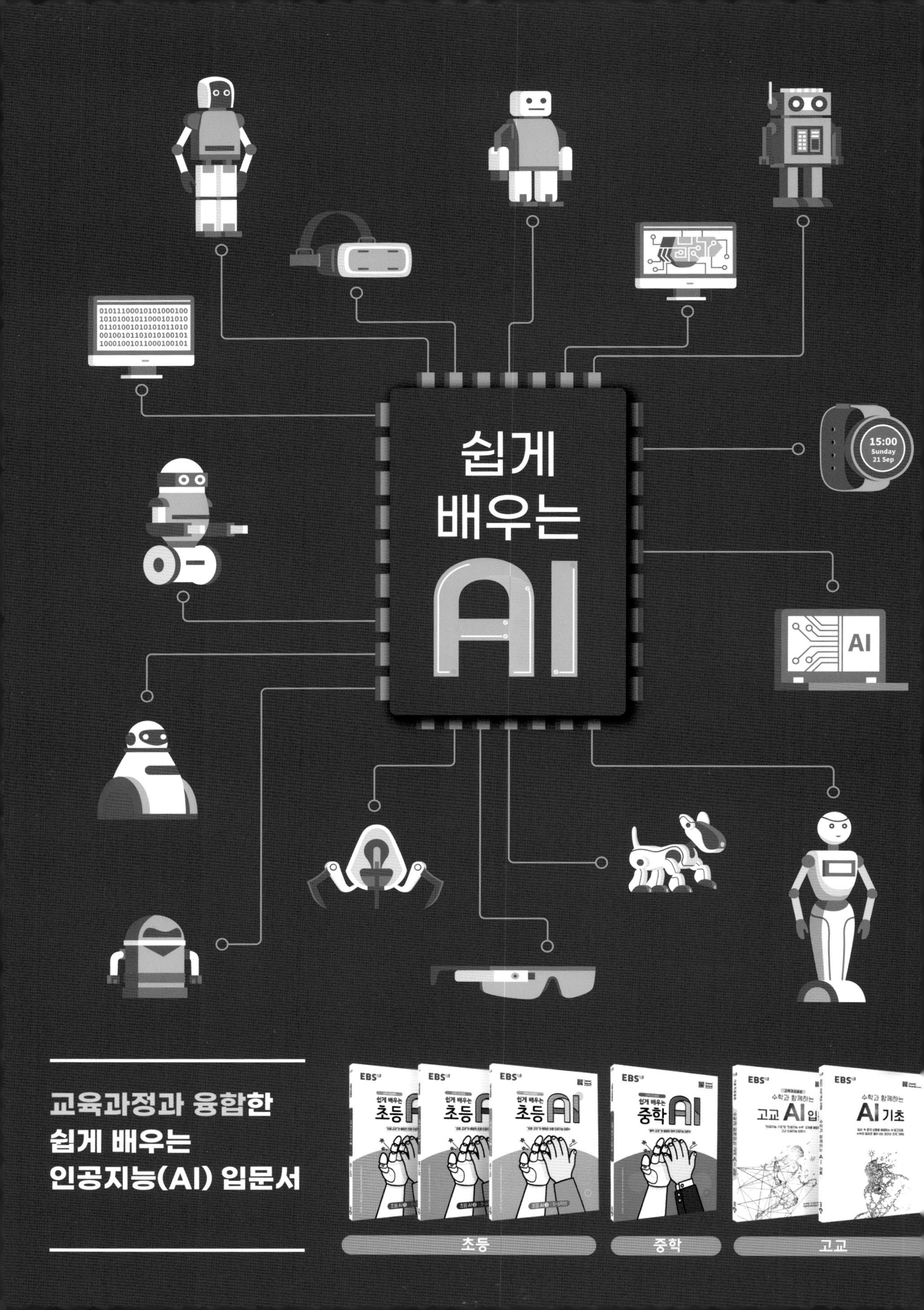

EBS

중 | 학 | 도 | 역 | 시 EBS

중학 내신 영문법의 결정판

MY GRAMMAR COACH

내신기출 N제

Workbook

Workbook

CHAPTER

01

인칭대명사와 be동사

UNIT 01 주격 인칭대명사

사람, 동물, 사물의 이름을 대신해서 부르는 7개의 주격 인칭대명사를 암기하세요.

단수(하나)				복수(둘 이상)			
대상	인칭	인칭대명사	의미	대상	인칭	인칭대명사	의미
말하는 사람	1인칭	I	나는	I 포함 둘 이상	1인칭	We	우리는
상대방	2인칭	You	너는	You 포함 둘 이상	2인칭	You	너희들은
그 외	3인칭	He, She, It	그는, 그녀는, 그것은	그 외의 둘 이상	3인칭	They	그들은, 그것들은

다음 빈칸에 알맞은 주격 인칭대명사를 쓰시오.

01 Kevin and I are brothers. __________ are alike.

02 Your brother and you are short. And __________ are fat.

03 This game is fun. And __________ is easy.

04 My sister and I are good tennis players. __________ are healthy.

05 Lisa and you are best friends. __________ are very close.

06 The book is on the desk. __________ is difficult.

07 The bags are heavy. __________ are on the floor.

08 Mr. White is a very old man. __________ is 100.

09 My mother is in the kitchen. __________ is busy now.

UNIT 02 be동사의 현재형

주어의 인칭과 수에 따라 be동사의 현재형 am, are, is 중 하나를 고르세요.

주어		be동사의 현재형	주어		be동사의 현재형
1인칭 단수	I	am	3인칭 단수	He, She, It The man, My teacher	is
2인칭 단수	You	are			
모든 복수	We, You, They				

다음 괄호 안에 주어진 말과 알맞은 be동사의 현재형을 사용하여 문장을 완성하시오.

01 (this book / interesting / very) ______________________________

02 (my father / busy / all the time) ______________________________

03 (Gina and Jack / tall and thin) ______________________________

04 (the man / a / actor / popular) ______________________________

05 (my friends / from / Seoul) ______________________________

06 (that pretty girl / my daughter) ______________________________

07 (the boxes / big and heavy) ______________________________

08 (you and James / baseball players / good) ______________________________

UNIT 03 be동사의 현재형 축약

〈인칭대명사+be동사의 현재형〉만 줄여 쓸 수 있다는 점에 유의하세요.

주어		be동사의 현재형	축약형
1인칭 단수	I	am	I'm
2인칭 단수	You	are	You're
모든 복수	We, You, They		We're, You're, They're
	You and I, My parents		축약 ×
3인칭 단수	He, She, It	is	He's, She's, It's
	The man, My teacher		축약 ×

다음 밑줄 친 부분을 축약해서 쓰시오. (단, 축약할 수 없는 경우에는 X 표시할 것)

01 Your books are on the desk. ________

02 It is my new bag. ________

03 They are in the park. ________

04 A rose is a flower. ________

05 She is beautiful and kind. ________

06 The boy is a soccer player. ________

07 You are smart and brave. ________

08 I am a good student. ________

09 We are in the same class. ________

UNIT 04 be동사의 과거형

be동사의 과거형은 주어에 따라 was, were 둘 중 하나를 선택하세요.

주어		be동사의 현재형	be동사의 과거형
1인칭 단수	I	am	was
3인칭 단수	He, She, It	is	
2인칭 단수	You	are	were
모든 복수	We, You, They		

다음 우리말과 같도록 괄호 안의 말과 be동사를 사용하여 바르게 영작하시오.

01 그 영화는 너무 슬펐다. (the movie / so sad) ________

02 Sally와 Sam은 친한 친구였다. (close friends) ________

03 내 가방은 탁자 위에 있었다. (on the table) ________

04 그 그림들은 벽에 있었다. (the pictures / on the wall) ________

05 그 가게는 문을 닫았다. (the store / closed) ________

06 그와 나는 동갑이었다. (the same age) ________

07 Kate와 Jack은 극장에 있었다. (in the theater) ________

08 날씨는 시원했다. (the weather / cool) ________

09 그 고양이들은 작았다. (the cats / small) ________

UNIT 05 be동사의 부정문

be동사의 부정은 be동사 뒤에 not을 써야 해요.

be동사의 현재형 부정		축약	be동사의 과거형 부정		축약
am	+not	×	was	+not	wasn't
is		isn't			
are		aren't	were		weren't

참고 am not은 축약하지 않아요. 또한, 〈인칭대명사+be동사의 과거형(was, were)〉도 축약하지 않아요.

다음 문장을 부정문으로 바꾸어 쓰시오.

01 Bill and I are happy. ______

02 It is a new bicycle. ______

03 My sisters are beautiful. ______

04 He and I were police officers. ______

05 My mom was busy last night. ______

06 An apple is on the table. ______

07 The students were late for school. ______

08 The cat was on the sofa this morning. ______

UNIT 06 be동사의 의문문

be동사로 질문할 때는 be동사를 주어 앞에 쓰는 어순이 된다는 것을 기억하세요.

be동사의 의문문	긍정의 대답	부정의 대답
Be동사+주어 ~?	Yes, 인칭대명사+be동사.	No, 인칭대명사+be동사+not.
Are you ~?	Yes, I am.	No, I am not.
Was Jinho ~?	Yes, he was.	No, he was not[wasn't].

다음 문장을 의문문으로 바꾸어 쓰시오.

01 His job is interesting. ______

02 The shop was open yesterday. ______

03 Your father was a good doctor. ______

04 You were at home last night. ______

05 Mr. Kim is his math teacher. ______

06 Jessica and her sister are happy. ______

07 My brothers were here yesterday. ______

08 The dirty shoes are in the basket. ______

09 This was your favorite book. ______

UNIT 07 be동사 종합

문장이 평서문, 부정문 또는 의문문인지를 판단하여 알맞은 be동사를 사용하세요.

평서문	주어에 따라 현재형은 am, are, is, 과거형은 was, were	She was tired.
부정문	be동사 뒤에 not을 쓴다. 부정형은 축약 가능	She wasn't tired.
의문문	be동사를 주어 앞으로 이동	Was she tired?

다음 문장을 괄호 안의 문장으로 바꾸어 쓰시오.

01 Mina and Junsu are my cousins. (부정문)

→ ______

02 Was Mr. Johnson your teacher? (평서문)

→ ______

03 The story was short and interesting. (의문문)

→ ______

04 Minsu and I are in the same class. (과거형)

→ ______

05 Are they in the kitchen now? (평서문)

→ ______

06 This apple pie is very delicious. (부정문)

→ ______

07 James is your close friend. (의문문)

→ ______

08 Her watch was in her bag. (부정문)

→ ______

09 Bill and his sister were at the zoo on Sunday. (의문문)

→ ______

중간고사·기말고사 실전문제

객관식 (01~15) / 주관식 (16~30)

학년과 반 이름 객관식 / 15문항 주관식 / 15문항

[01~03] 다음 대화의 빈칸에 알맞은 것을 고르시오.

01

A: __________ your sister a singer?
B: Yes, she is.

① Am ② Are
③ Is ④ Was
⑤ Were

02

A: Are Jane and Tom elementary school students?
B: Yes, __________ are.

① you ② we
③ she ④ he
⑤ they

03

A: Were you at home last Sunday?
B: No, __________.

① I was ② she isn't
③ I'm not ④ I wasn't
⑤ we were

[04~05] 다음 빈칸에 알맞지 않은 것을 고르시오.

04

__________ is very strong.

① He ② Her uncle
③ They ④ She
⑤ Jimmy

05

__________ are at the airport now.

① He
② They
③ His parents
④ Sienna and Mira
⑤ Kate and her brother

06 다음 밑줄 친 부분의 뜻이 나머지 넷과 다른 하나는?

① Your bag is on the chair.
② He was at home last night.
③ She is in Busan now.
④ Weren't you with Zoe last Saturday?
⑤ Ryan is my brother.

07 다음 빈칸에 들어갈 말이 나머지 넷과 다른 하나는?

① They ________ in Japan last week.
② You ________ at school last Monday.
③ Her parents ________ busy this morning.
④ My room ________ dirty yesterday.
⑤ My neighbors ________ loud last night.

08 다음 밑줄 친 부분 중 어법상 어색한 것은?

① The TV program was funny.
② Brad and Mark are the same age.
③ Sarah and I was in the hospital last night.
④ The musical was amazing.
⑤ Those shoes were comfortable.

09 다음 우리말을 영어로 바르게 옮긴 것은?

> 그 식당은 어제 문을 열지 않았다.

① The restaurant is open yesterday.
② The restaurant are open yesterday.
③ The restaurant aren't open yesterday.
④ The restaurant wasn't open yesterday.
⑤ The restaurant weren't open yesterday.

10 다음 괄호 안의 ①~⑤ 중 not이 들어갈 알맞은 곳은?

> (①) You (②) were (③) afraid (④) of (⑤) dogs.

11 다음 밑줄 친 부분을 인칭대명사로 잘못 바꾼 것은?

① Brian and Stella are happy at the news. → They
② James is a police officer. → He
③ Jisu and I are best friends. → They
④ You and Sangho play tennis every day. → You
⑤ The lamb is so cute. → It

12 다음 짝지어진 대화 중 어법상 어색한 것을 모두 고르면?

① A: Was it hot in Busan?
B: Yes, it was.
② A: Were the students nervous for the test?
B: No, they wasn't.
③ A: Is your father still angry?
B: No, he is.
④ A: Is Sandy in the library now?
B: Yes, she is.
⑤ A: Is that your bag?
B: Yes, it is.

13 다음 중 밑줄 친 부분을 줄여 쓸 수 없는 것은?

① I am not a student.
② Your dog was not here.
③ The dishes are not dirty.
④ Her friends were not happy.
⑤ The calendar is not on the desk.

14 다음 ⓐ~ⓔ 중 어법상 옳은 것끼리 짝지어진 것은?

ⓐ He were a famous actor. ⓑ Were you in the room then? ⓒ Amy and her brother is on a boat. ⓓ The eraser is in my pencil case. ⓔ Cherries is good for health.

① ⓐ, ⓑ ② ⓐ, ⓔ ③ ⓑ, ⓒ
④ ⓑ, ⓓ ⑤ ⓒ, ⓓ

15 다음 중 어법상 어색한 것은?

① My dog is very fat.
② Tony was a golf player before.
③ The swimming pool wasn't clean.
④ Sujin's aunt was in Paris three years ago.
⑤ Is Jimmy and Tom on the soccer team?

[16~18] 다음 문장에서 어법상 어색한 부분을 찾아 바르게 고쳐 쓰시오.

16 This chocolate cake are not delicious.

_______________ → _______________

17 Jessica and Semin are at home an hour ago.

_______________ → _______________

18 Was you and Andy at the party last night?

_______________ → _______________

[19~20] 다음 우리말과 같도록 괄호 안의 단어를 바르게 배열하시오.

19

네 전화기는 여기 없었다. (here / not / your / phone / was)

→ _______________________________

20

우리는 수업에 늦지 않았다.
(were / late / we / not / for / class)

→ ______________________________

21 다음 문장에서 I를 Mr. Brown으로 바꿔 완전한 문장으로 쓰시오.

I am a firefighter.

→ ______________________________

22 다음 표를 보고, 빈칸에 알맞은 말을 |보기|에서 골라 쓰시오.

	Sharon	Ryan
hairdresser	○	○
in Hong Kong	X	○

|보기|
is isn't are aren't

(1) Sharon and Ryan __________ hairdressers.

(2) Ryan __________ in Hong Kong, but Sharon __________ there.

23 다음 빈칸에 공통으로 들어갈 알맞은 말을 쓰시오.

• __________ Kate free this morning?
• I __________ in the school band last year.

24 다음 빈칸에 알맞은 인칭대명사를 쓰시오.

I have a little brother. __________ is four years old. __________ is so cute. Every day __________ play together in our garden.

25 다음 빈칸에 알맞은 말을 넣어 대화를 완성하시오.

A: __________ you at home yesterday?
B: No, I __________. I was at the movie theater.

[26~28] 다음 표를 보고, be동사 또는 인칭대명사 등을 사용하여 빈칸에 알맞은 말을 쓰시오.

Name	Age	Nationality	Personality
Grace	12	Italy	shy
Irene	10	Canada	friendly
Jisu	12	Korea	funny

26 Jisu ________ 12 years old. She ________ funny.

27 Grace and Jisu ________ the same age. ________ are 12 years old.

28 Grace: ________ you from Italy?
Irene: No, ________ ________.
________ from ________.

29 다음 우리말과 같도록 괄호 안의 단어를 사용하여 영작하시오.

> 네 생일 선물은 내 가방 안에 있다.
> (birthday / present / bag)

→ ________________________________

30 다음 글을 읽고, 물음에 답하시오.

> Yesterday was Minho's birthday. Jane was at his birthday party. Semin was there, too.

(1) 다음 빈칸에 알맞은 말을 넣어 질문에 대한 대답을 완성하시오.

> A: Were Jane and Semin at Mike's birthday party yesterday?
> B: ________, ________ ________. They were at Minho's birthday party.

(2) 윗글의 밑줄 친 부분을 부정문으로 바꿔 쓰시오.

→ ________________________________

CHAPTER

02

일반동사

UNIT 01 일반동사의 현재형 1

일반동사의 현재형은 동사원형을 쓰지만, 주어가 3인칭 단수일 때는 동사원형에 -s를 붙이는 것에 유의하세요.

일반동사 현재형			
일반적인 주어	동사원형	3인칭 단수 주어	동사원형+-s
I like English.		She likes English.	

다음 빈칸에 괄호 안의 동사를 현재형으로 쓰시오.

01 We ___________ bicycles every morning. (ride)

02 The sun ___________ in the east. (rise)

03 I ___________ my grandparents every weekend. (visit)

04 He ___________ a cake in the kitchen. (make)

05 Sally ___________ lunch at twelve o'clock. (eat)

06 You ___________ history at school. (learn)

07 Mr. Brown ___________ up early every morning. (get)

08 They ___________ together on Sundays. (clean)

09 My uncle ___________ from Canada. (come)

UNIT 02 일반동사의 현재형 2

3인칭 단수 주어의 일반동사 현재형을 만들 때 주의해야 할 점을 알아 두세요.

대부분의 동사	-s	drink – drinks (마시다), sing – sings (노래하다)
-o, -s, -x, -sh, -ch	-es	do – does (하다), finish – finishes (마치다), mix – mixes (섞다)
자음+y	y 삭제, -ies	cry – cries (울다), try – tries (해 보다), study – studies (공부하다)
모음+y	-s	play – plays (놀다), buy – buys (사다), enjoy – enjoys (즐기다)
불규칙	have	have – has (가지다, 먹다)

다음 빈칸에 괄호 안의 동사를 현재형으로 쓰시오.

01 Children ___________ in the playground. (play)

02 She ___________ her time in Bangkok. (enjoy)

03 Ms. White ___________ a book in her bag. (carry)

04 The baby ___________ every night. (cry)

05 He ___________ his teeth after every meal. (brush)

06 Lisa and I ___________ to the library after school. (go)

07 Minsu ___________ good friends. (have)

08 The kite ___________ high in the sky. (fly)

09 Mr. Kim is a teacher. He ___________ math to his students. (teach)

UNIT 03 일반동사의 과거형 규칙 변화 1

일반동사의 과거형은 동사원형 뒤에 -ed를 붙이세요.

일반동사의 현재형 규칙 변화		일반동사의 과거형 규칙 변화	
일반적인 주어	동사원형	모든 주어	동사원형+-ed
3인칭 단수 주어	동사원형+-s		

다음 빈칸에 괄호 안의 동사를 과거형으로 쓰시오.

01 I __________ a big family. (want)

02 They __________ up late last night. (stay)

03 Mina __________ dinner for her family. (cook)

04 Junho __________ his mother early in the morning. (call)

05 We __________ on the phone for an hour. (talk)

06 The accident __________ last Saturday. (happen)

07 Tim and Jane __________ the school bus this morning. (miss)

08 It was hot in the room. I __________ the window. (open)

UNIT 04 일반동사의 과거형 규칙 변화 2

일반동사의 과거형을 만들 때 주의해야 할 점을 알아 두세요.

대부분의 동사	-(e)d	자음+y	y 삭제, -ied
단모음+단자음	마지막 자음 추가, -ed	모음+y	-ed

다음 동사의 과거형을 빈칸에 쓰시오.

01 accept – __________

02 add – __________

03 agree – __________

04 beg – __________

05 believe – __________

06 borrow – __________

07 collect – __________

08 copy – __________

09 cover – __________

10 cry – __________

11 decide – __________

12 depend – __________

13 drop – __________

14 enjoy – __________

15 fail – __________

16 finish – __________

17 hope – __________

18 hurry – __________

19 laugh – __________

20 learn – __________

21 marry – __________

22 plan – __________

23 play – __________

24 raise – __________

25 remember – __________

26 save – __________

27 smile – __________

28 stop – __________

29 study – __________

30 thank – __________

31 touch – __________

32 try – __________

33 use – __________

34 visit – __________

35 wait – __________

36 walk – __________

37 watch – __________

38 worry – __________

UNIT 05 일반동사의 과거형 불규칙 변화

다음 동사의 과거형을 빈칸에 쓰시오.

01 become – ________
02 begin – ________
03 bet – ________
04 bind – ________
05 bite – ________
06 bleed – ________
07 blow – ________
08 break – ________
09 bring – ________
10 build – ________
11 buy – ________
12 catch – ________
13 choose – ________
14 come – ________
15 cut – ________
16 do – ________
17 draw – ________
18 drink – ________
19 drive – ________
20 eat – ________
21 fall – ________
22 feed – ________
23 feel – ________
24 fight – ________
25 find – ________
26 fly – ________
27 forget – ________
28 forgive – ________
29 get – ________
30 give – ________
31 go – ________
32 grow – ________
33 have – ________
34 hear – ________
35 hit – ________
36 hold – ________
37 hurt – ________
38 keep – ________
39 know – ________
40 lead – ________
41 leave – ________
42 lend – ________
43 let – ________
44 lose – ________
45 make – ________
46 mean – ________
47 meet – ________
48 pay – ________
49 put – ________
50 read – ________
51 ride – ________
52 ring – ________
53 rise – ________
54 run – ________
55 say – ________
56 see – ________
57 sell – ________
58 send – ________
59 set – ________
60 shoot – ________
61 shut – ________
62 sing – ________
63 sit – ________
64 sleep – ________
65 speak – ________
66 spend – ________
67 spread – ________
68 stand – ________
69 steal – ________
70 swim – ________
71 take – ________
72 teach – ________
73 tell – ________
74 think – ________
75 throw – ________
76 understand – ________
77 wake – ________
78 wear – ________
79 win – ________
80 write – ________

UNIT 06 일반동사의 부정문

일반동사의 부정문은 〈조동사 do/does/did+not〉을 동사원형 앞에 써야 해요.

일반동사의 현재 부정문			일반동사의 과거 부정문	
일반적인 주어	do not[don't]	+동사원형	모든 주어	did not[didn't]+동사원형
3인칭 단수 주어	does not[doesn't]			

다음 문장을 부정문으로 바꾸어 쓰시오.

01 My father watched TV after dinner. ______

02 We need a new computer. ______

03 He called me last night. ______

04 The teacher plays the guitar. ______

05 They go there every day. ______

06 My brother has a new camera. ______

07 I did my homework yesterday. ______

UNIT 07 일반동사의 의문문

일반동사의 의문문은 조동사 Do/Does/Did를 주어 앞에 쓰세요.

일반동사의 현재 의문문			일반동사의 과거 의문문	
Do	+일반적인 주어	+동사원형 ~?	Did	+모든 주어+동사원형 ~?
Does	+3인칭 단수 주어			

참고 대답할 때도 조동사를 이용해서 대답해요.

다음 우리말과 같도록 괄호 안의 말을 사용하여 의문문을 만들고 대답을 완성하시오. (단, 부정의 대답은 축약형으로 쓸 것)

01 그는 어제 컴퓨터 게임을 했니? (computer games / yesterday / play)

→ ______ – Yes, ______.

02 그 여자는 이 아파트에 사니? (live / in this apartment)

→ ______ – No, ______.

03 너는 그때 라디오를 들었니? (listen / then / to the radio)

→ ______ – No, ______.

04 Tom과 Jenny는 자신들의 일을 좋아하니? (like / their jobs)

→ ______ – No, ______.

05 그녀는 지난주에 이 잡지를 샀니? (last week / buy / this magazine)

→ ______ – Yes, ______.

06 Jason은 주말에 늦잠을 자니? (late / on weekends / sleep)

→ ______ – Yes, ______.

UNIT 08 일반동사 종합

문장이 평서문, 부정문 또는 의문문인지를 판단하여 알맞은 일반동사를 사용하세요.

평서문	현재형은 동사원형으로 쓰거나 동사원형 뒤에 -s를 붙이세요.	She likes movies.
	과거형은 동사원형 뒤에 -ed를 붙이세요.	She liked movies.
부정문	주어+do/does/did+not+동사원형의 어순으로 쓰세요.	She didn't like movies.
의문문	Do/Does/Did+주어+동사원형 ~?의 어순으로 쓰세요.	Did she like movies?

다음 문장을 괄호 안의 문장으로 바꾸어 쓰시오.

01 Did Kevin move here five years ago? (평서문)

→ ______________________________

02 She did her homework after dinner. (현재형)

→ ______________________________

03 I talked with my teacher after class. (부정문)

→ ______________________________

04 He rides a bike on weekends. (의문문)

→ ______________________________

05 The class begins at nine o'clock. (과거형)

→ ______________________________

06 The students ask questions in class. (의문문)

→ ______________________________

07 They arrived in Seoul at noon. (부정문)

→ ______________________________

08 The girl lost her bag at school. (의문문)

→ ______________________________

09 He washes his face before breakfast. (부정문)

→ ______________________________

중간고사·기말고사 실전문제

객관식 (01~15) / 주관식 (16~30)

정답과 해설 • 62쪽

학년과 반 이름 객관식 / 15문항 주관식 / 15문항

[01~03] 다음 빈칸에 알맞은 것을 고르시오.

01

___________ eats garlic.

① He ② I
③ You ④ Grace and I
⑤ They

02

___________ don't like cats.

① Mike ② I
③ She ④ My aunt
⑤ Your father

03

___________ they study French?

① Is ② Do
③ Does ④ Were
⑤ Are

[04~05] 다음 빈칸에 알맞지 않은 것을 고르시오.

04

___________ take a test every month.

① I
② We
③ They
④ Her uncle
⑤ Jimmy and his brother

05

Do ___________ know the facts?

① you
② his parents
③ your mom
④ the children
⑤ you and your friends

[06~07] 다음 대화의 빈칸에 알맞은 것을 고르시오.

06

A: Does Nina take a bus to school? B: ___________

① Yes, she is.
② No, she isn't.
③ Yes, she does.
④ No, she didn't.
⑤ Yes, she did.

07

A: Do you believe in Santa Claus? B: ___________

① Yes, I am.
② No, I didn't.
③ Yes, I was.
④ Yes, I did.
⑤ No, I don't.

[08~10] 다음 중 어법상 어색한 것을 고르시오.

08 ① They didn't know his address.
② Mina has three sisters.
③ You live in Seoul.
④ They doesn't have cars.
⑤ Julia passed the exam.

09 ① Jimin told me about the rumor.
② They didn't understood the questions.
③ Jake wanted a tablet PC for a gift.
④ Your dog looks healthy.
⑤ He doesn't spend much money on clothes.

10 ① Susan plays the piano as a hobby.
② The bus stoped at Seoul Tower.
③ She drank some orange juice.
④ Daniel enjoys extreme sports.
⑤ I bought a new T-shirt yesterday.

11 다음 빈칸에 공통으로 들어갈 말로 알맞은 것은? (대·소문자 무시)

- ________ Sangmin know about the concert?
- My friend ________ not eat any meat.

① do ② is
③ be ④ are
⑤ does

12 다음 대답에 대한 질문으로 알맞은 것은?

A: ________________________
B: Yes, they did. They had great fun.

① Do they have fun at the beach?
② Was they have fun at the beach?
③ Does they have fun at the beach?
④ Did they have fun at the beach?
⑤ Did they had fun at the beach?

13 다음 중 어법상 옳은 것끼리 짝지어진 것은?

ⓐ She droped her basket on the ground.
ⓑ He worried about his grade.
ⓒ Minsu finishd his presentation.
ⓓ They sold delicious cupcakes.
ⓔ Jian helpped me with my homework.

① ⓐ, ⓑ ② ⓐ, ⓔ
③ ⓑ, ⓒ ④ ⓑ, ⓓ
⑤ ⓒ, ⓓ

14 다음 우리말을 영어로 바르게 옮긴 것은?

Kate와 Jenny는 그를 잘 알지 못한다.

① Kate and Jenny don't know him very well.
② Kate and Jenny weren't know him very well.
③ Kate and Jenny wasn't know him very well.
④ Kate and Jenny didn't know him very well.
⑤ Kate and Jenny doesn't know him very well.

15 다음 문장을 괄호 안의 문장으로 바르게 바꾸지 못한 것은?

① They take a walk outside. (과거형)
→ They taked a walk outside.
② Alex loves Indian food. (의문문)
→ Does Alex love Indian food?
③ She cuts the orange in half. (과거형)
→ She cut the orange in half.
④ You lost your wallet last week. (의문문)
→ Did you lose your wallet last week?
⑤ Sumi reads many books this summer. (과거형)
→ Sumi read many books this summer.

[16~17] 다음 우리말과 같도록 괄호 안의 동사를 사용하여 문장을 완성하시오.

16

그 막대 사탕은 이상한 맛이 난다. (taste)

→ The lollipop ______________ funny.

17

그 버스 운전사는 조심스럽게 운전하지 않았다. (drive)

→ The bus driver ______________ carefully.

[18~19] 다음 문장을 괄호 안의 문장으로 바꿔 쓰시오.

18 My coach drinks coffee every day. (부정문)

→ ________________________________

19 Jimmy went to bed before 9 last night. (의문문)

→ ________________________________

20 다음 글의 밑줄 친 부분을 어법에 맞게 고쳐 쓰시오.

Minho and his brother (1) <u>get</u> up early this morning. They were hungry. So, they (2) <u>make</u> something to eat. They made pancakes. They tasted good.

(1) get → ____________

(2) make → ____________

21 다음 질문에 대한 긍정의 대답을 쓰시오.

Did she enjoy her trip last weekend?

→ ________, ________ ________.

22 다음 질문에 대한 부정의 대답을 쓰시오.

Did your classmates come here?

→ ________, ________ ________.

23 다음 동사의 과거형을 쓰시오.

(1) grow – ____________

(2) fight – ____________

(3) forget – ____________

(4) spread – ____________

24 다음 괄호 안의 단어를 사용하여 대화를 완성하시오.

A: ________ ________ ________ sledding yesterday? (go)
B: No, they didn't. They were busy yesterday.

[25～26] 다음 우리말과 같도록 괄호 안의 말을 사용하여 영작하시오. (단, 필요시 동사 변형 가능)

25

그는 작년에 안동으로 이사를 갔다. (move to / Andong / last year)

→ ____________________

26

Grace는 끈적한 것을 밟았다. (step on / something sticky)

→ ____________________

27 다음 문장을 |보기|와 같이 바꿔 쓰시오.

|보기|
I read the newspaper in the morning.
→ He reads the newspaper in the morning.

They watch TV after lunch.
→ Jinsu ____________________.

28 다음은 어제 민수와 Jane이 한 일과 하지 않은 일을 나타낸 표이다. 표를 잘 보고, 질문에 답하시오.

	go to the library	play tennis	do homework
Minsu	○	○	○
Jane	X	○	X

(1) A: Did Minsu go to the library yesterday?
B: ________, ________ ________.

(2) A: Did Jane do her homework yesterday?
B: ________, ________ ________.

(3) A: Did Minsu and Jane play tennis yesterday?
B: ________, ________ ________.

29 다음 문장에서 어법상 어색한 부분을 두 군데 찾아 바르게 고쳐 쓰시오.

She usually eat breakfast, but this morning she skiped it.

(1) ________ → ________

(2) ________ → ________

30 다음 글의 밑줄 친 ⓐ~ⓔ 중 어법상 어색한 것을 두 개 찾아 기호를 쓰고, 바르게 고쳐 쓰시오.

Sam ⓐ found a bug in his lap. The bug ⓑ runned. It ⓒ hid under the chair. Sam ⓓ found it. He ⓔ puted it in a jar.

(1) ________ → ________

(2) ________ → ________

내가 가장 취약한 부분에 대해
요점 정리를 해 보세요.

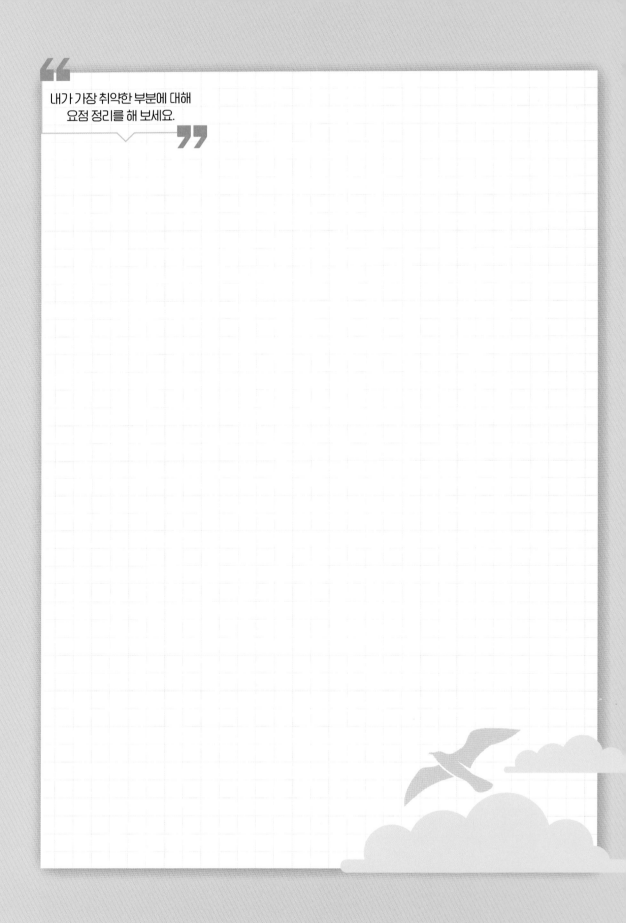

CHAPTER

03

시제

UNIT 01 현재시제

어떤 상황에서 현재시제를 써야 하는지 파악하세요.

현재시제를 써야 할 때	현재의 상태	반복적 행동, 습관	속담, 격언	과학적인 사실, 진리

다음 괄호 안의 말을 바르게 배열하여 현재시제 문장을 완성하시오. (단, 필요시 동사 변형 가능)

01 (my mother / coffee / in the morning / drink) ______________________

02 (they / for class / be / every time / late) ______________________

03 (Kate / go / bed / late / to / at night) ______________________

04 (study / my brother / every day / math) ______________________

05 (Mike / in his pocket / a pen / have) ______________________

06 (my sister and I / English / speak / every day) ______________________

07 (8 hours / we / a day / sleep) ______________________

08 (exercise / she / in the park / every night) ______________________

09 (spend / with / the weekends / he / his family) ______________________

UNIT 02 과거시제

다음의 과거 시간 부사(구)와 함께 이미 끝난 일이나 역사적 사실을 말할 때는 과거시제를 써야 해요.

last ~	지난 ~에	~ ago	~ 전에	then	그때
yesterday	어제	the other day	얼마 전	in+과거 연도	~년에

다음 우리말과 같도록 괄호 안의 말을 바르게 배열하시오. (단, 필요시 동사 변형 가능)

01 그는 아침에 샤워를 했다. (take a shower / he / in the morning)

→ ______________________

02 나는 지난밤에 컴퓨터 게임을 하지 않았다. (don't play / computer games / I / last night)

→ ______________________

03 나의 고모는 지난달에 뉴욕에 도착했다. (arrive / last month / my aunt / in New York)

→ ______________________

04 콜럼버스는 1492년에 아메리카 대륙을 발견했다. (America / in 1492 / discover / Columbus)

→ ______________________

05 그 학생들이 오늘 아침에 창문을 깨뜨렸니? (break / the students / do / the window / this morning)

→ ______________________

06 그녀는 지난 주말에 친구들과 캠핑을 갔었다. (go camping / last weekend / she / with her friends)

→ ______________________

UNIT 03 미래시제 1: will의 긍정문과 축약형

조동사 will은 미래의 계획이나 주어의 의지를 나타내며, 〈조동사 will+동사원형〉의 형태로 써야 해요.

구분	현재	과거	미래
be동사	am, are, is	was, were	will+동사원형
일반동사	동사원형(+-s) / 불규칙 변화	동사원형+-ed / 불규칙 변화	
의미	~이다, ~(에) 있다, ~하다	~였다, ~(에) 있었다, ~했다	~일 것이다, ~할 것이다

다음 괄호 안의 말과 will을 사용하여 미래시제 문장을 완성하시오. (단, 축약이 가능할 경우 축약형으로 쓸 것)

01 (get / by subway / they / there) ______

02 (my sister / to the party / tonight / come) ______

03 (send / tomorrow / I / an e-mail / to you) ______

04 (my parents / at a hotel / stay / in Toronto) ______

05 (he / music / listen to / after dinner) ______

06 (play / soccer / we / after school) ______

07 (they / to London / fly / tomorrow morning) ______

08 (the woman / at the coffee shop / meet / her friends) ______

UNIT 04 미래시제 2: will의 부정문과 의문문

부정문과 의문문은 동사원형은 그대로 두고 조동사 will을 사용해야 해요.

구분	긍정문	부정문	의문문
어순	will+동사원형	will not+동사원형	Will+주어+동사원형 ~?
예문	He will be home.	He will not be home.	Will he be home?
축약	He'll be home.	He'll not be home. / He won't be home.	—

참고 의문문에 대한 대답은 Yes, 주어+will. / No, 주어+won't.와 같이 해야 해요.

다음 문장을 괄호 안의 문장으로 바꾸어 쓸 때 빈칸에 알맞은 말을 쓰시오.

01 Ms. Kim will buy a new car next year.

→ (부정문) Ms. Kim ______ a new car next year.

→ (의문문) ______ a new car next year? – No, ______.

02 My father will wash the dishes after dinner.

→ (부정문) My father ______ the dishes after dinner.

→ (의문문) ______ the dishes after dinner? – Yes, ______.

03 Mina and Jinho will go shopping this weekend.

→ (부정문) Mina and Jinho ______ shopping this weekend.

→ (의문문) ______ shopping this weekend? – Yes, ______.

UNIT 05 미래시제 3: be going to

'~할 예정이다'와 같이 계획된 미래의 일은 〈be going to+동사원형〉으로 쓰세요.

구분	긍정문	부정문	의문문
어순	be going to+동사원형	be동사+not+going to+동사원형	Be동사+주어+going to+동사원형 ~?

다음 문장을 괄호 안의 문장으로 바꾸어 쓸 때 빈칸에 알맞은 말을 쓰시오. (단, 부정의 대답은 be동사와 not을 축약할 것)

01 They are going to have lunch at 12:30.
→ (부정문) They ______________________ at 12:30.
→ (의문문) ______________________ at 12:30? – Yes, ________.

02 Jason is going to visit his grandmother next Sunday.
→ (부정문) Jason ______________________ next Sunday.
→ (의문문) ______________________ next Sunday? – No, ________.

03 My sister is going to buy a new cell phone next month.
→ (부정문) My sister ______________________ next month.
→ (의문문) ______________________ next month? – Yes, ________.

04 We are going to go there next year.
→ (부정문) We ______________________ next year.
→ (의문문) ______________________ next year? – No, ________.

UNIT 06 시제 판단

동사의 형태는 문맥과 시간 부사(구)로 시제를 판단하여 결정하세요.

현재시제	과거시제	미래시제
내용과 문맥으로 판단	과거 시간 부사(구) last ~, ~ ago, yesterday, the other day, then, in+과거 연도 등	미래 시간 부사(구) tomorrow, next ~, ~ later, in+미래 연도 등

참고 만약 현재시제라면 주어에 따라 동사의 형태를 다시 결정해야 해요.

다음 문장을 괄호 안의 문장으로 바꾸어 쓰시오.

01 My mother went to church. (현재 긍정문) ______________________

02 Will you get a haircut? (과거 의문문) ______________________

03 Mina will read the magazine. (과거 부정문) ______________________

04 We didn't make cupcakes. (미래 긍정문) ______________________

05 He worked at the store. (현재 의문문) ______________________

06 Chris joins the soccer club. (미래 부정문) ______________________

07 My family won't go to the museum. (과거 긍정문) ______________________

UNIT 07 진행형 만드는 법

동사원형에 -ing를 붙이는 규칙을 알아 두세요.

대부분의 동사	동사원형+-ing	-ie로 끝나는 동사	ie를 y로 바꾸고+-ing
-e로 끝나는 동사	e를 빼고+-ing	1음절에 단모음+단자음	마지막 자음 추가+-ing
2음절에 단모음+단자음으로 끝나고, 강세가 뒤에 있는 동사			마지막 자음 추가+-ing

다음 동사의 -ing형을 빈칸에 쓰시오.

01 arrive – ________
02 bake – ________
03 begin – ________
04 believe – ________
05 climb – ________
06 close – ________
07 come – ________
08 control – ________
09 dance – ________
10 die – ________
11 fly – ________
12 get – ________
13 give – ________
14 have – ________
15 lie – ________
16 love – ________
17 make – ________
18 open – ________
19 put – ________
20 run – ________
21 save – ________
22 shop – ________
23 sit – ________
24 smile – ________
25 stop – ________
26 study – ________
27 swim – ________
28 take – ________
29 win – ________
30 write – ________

UNIT 08 현재진행형의 긍정문

현재 진행 중인 일을 나타내는 현재진행형은 〈be동사의 현재형+동사-ing〉의 형태로 be동사는 주어의 인칭과 수에 맞춰 쓰세요.

현재형	I have breakfast.	She goes to school.
현재진행형	I am[I'm] having breakfast now.	She is[She's] going to school now.

다음 괄호 안의 말을 사용하여 현재진행형 문장을 완성하시오.

01 (you / a blue shirt / wear) ________
02 (cut / the cake / I / with my family) ________
03 (an e-mail / to James / she / send) ________
04 (Bill and Seho / the street / cross / now) ________
05 (my father / the windows / clean) ________
06 (now / we / study / English) ________
07 (the girl / in the park / walk / her dog) ________
08 (wait / the students / at the bus stop) ________
09 (soccer / the children / over there / play) ________

UNIT 09 현재진행형의 부정문

'~하고 있지 않다'를 의미하는 현재진행형의 부정문은 be동사 뒤에 not을 붙이세요.

현재진행형의 긍정문	They're having breakfast now.	She's going to school now.
현재진행형의 부정문	They're not[They aren't] having breakfast now.	She's not[She isn't] going to school now.

다음 우리말과 같도록 괄호 안의 말을 사용하여 문장을 완성하시오. (단, 필요시 동사 변형 가능)

01 내 남동생과 나는 라디오를 듣고 있지 않다. (listen to / the radio)

→ My brother and I ______________________.

02 그녀의 아들은 과일을 먹고 있지 않다. (eat / fruit)

→ Her son ______________________.

03 너는 장난감 자동차를 만들고 있지 않다. (make / a toy car)

→ You ______________________.

04 Jones 씨는 그의 친구에게 편지를 쓰고 있지 않다. (write / a letter / to his friend)

→ Mr. Jones ______________________.

05 내 친구들은 영화를 보고 있지 않다. (watch / a movie)

→ My friends ______________________.

06 나는 지금 신문을 읽고 있지 않다. (read / a newspaper)

→ I'm ______________________ now.

UNIT 10 현재진행형의 의문문

'~하는 중이니?'라는 현재진행형의 의문문은 be동사만 주어 앞에 쓰세요.

현재진행형의 의문문	Are they having breakfast now?	Is she going to school now?

다음 문장을 의문문으로 바꾸고, 알맞은 대답을 쓰시오. (단, 부정의 대답은 축약형으로 쓸 것)

01 He is washing his hands. ______________ – Yes, __________.

02 Tom and Bill are playing games. ______________ – Yes, __________.

03 She is reading an interesting book. ______________ – No, __________.

04 Your father is watching TV. ______________ – No, __________.

05 Jenny is studying at the library. ______________ – Yes, __________.

06 The boys are having pizza together. ______________ – Yes, __________.

07 The girl is running to the bus. ______________ – No, __________.

08 You are cleaning your room. ______________ – Yes, __________.

09 The students are solving the problem. ______________ – No, __________.

UNIT 11 과거진행형의 긍정문

과거의 특정 시점에 진행되고 있던 동작은 be동사만 과거형으로 써서 과거진행형으로 만드세요.

현재진행형	She is having breakfast now.	They are going to school now.
과거진행형	She was having breakfast at that time.	They were going to school that day.

다음 우리말과 같도록 괄호 안의 동사를 활용하여 빈칸에 알맞은 말을 쓰시오.

01 그녀는 어제 산책하고 있었다. (take) → She ______________ a walk yesterday.

02 나는 그것에 관해 얘기하고 있었다. (talk) → I ______________ about it.

03 우리는 버스를 기다리고 있었다. (wait) → We ______________ for a bus.

04 Jason은 수영장에서 수영하고 있었다. (swim) → Jason ______________ in the pool.

05 그는 작년에 대만에서 살고 있었다. (live) → He ______________ in Taiwan last year.

06 그들은 책을 읽고 있었다. (read) → They ______________ a book.

UNIT 12 과거진행형의 부정문과 의문문

과거진행형의 부정문과 의문문도 모두 be동사의 과거형을 사용하는 것을 기억하세요.

구분	긍정문	부정문	의문문
어순	be동사의 과거형+동사-ing	be동사의 과거형+not+동사-ing	Be동사의 과거형+주어+동사-ing ~?

참고 Was he eating?
긍정 대답: Yes, he was. / 부정 대답: No, he wasn't.

다음 문장을 괄호 안의 문장으로 바꾸어 쓸 때 빈칸에 알맞은 말을 쓰시오. (단, 부정의 대답은 축약형으로 쓸 것)

01 Sarah was making a sandwich for lunch.
→ (부정문) Sarah ______________ a sandwich for lunch.
→ (의문문) ______________ a sandwich for lunch? – Yes, ______________.

02 They were having a meeting last Monday.
→ (부정문) They ______________ a meeting last Monday.
→ (의문문) ______________ a meeting last Monday? – Yes, ______________.

03 He was cleaning his house this morning.
→ (부정문) He ______________ his house this morning.
→ (의문문) ______________ his house this morning? – No, ______________.

04 My sister was playing the piano on the stage.
→ (부정문) My sister ______________ the piano on the stage.
→ (의문문) ______________ the piano on the stage? – No, ______________.

중간고사·기말고사 실전문제

객관식 (01~15) / 주관식 (16~30)

학년과 반　　　이름　　　객관식　　/ 15문항　　주관식　　/ 15문항

[01~04] 다음 빈칸에 알맞은 것을 고르시오.

01

Tony and Sam ___________ badminton every Saturday.

① play　② plays
③ to play　④ is playing
⑤ was playing

02

They ___________ a new car last year.

① buy
② will buy
③ bought
④ was buying
⑤ are buying

03

Heejin will have a party ___________.

① last Friday
② yesterday
③ at that time
④ tomorrow
⑤ an hour ago

04

My dog was sick ___________.

① someday　② now
③ last night　④ tomorrow
⑤ next Sunday

05 다음 빈칸에 공통으로 들어갈 말로 알맞은 것은?

• It ___________ cold tomorrow.
• Susan ___________ 16 years old next year.

① is　② is going to
③ was　④ will be
⑤ be

06 다음 대화의 빈칸에 공통으로 들어갈 cook의 형태로 알맞은 것은?

A: What are you ___________?
B: I am ___________ a roast.
A: It looks delicious.

① cook　② cooked
③ to cook　④ will cook
⑤ cooking

07 다음 대화의 빈칸에 알맞은 것은?

> A: Is the gardener watering the flowers?
> B: ________________

① Yes, he is.
② Yes, they was.
③ No, he wasn't.
④ Yes, he does.
⑤ No, they aren't.

08 다음 |보기|와 같이 동사의 형태를 바꾼 것 중 어색한 것은?

> |보기|
> look – looking

① tie – tieing
② give – giving
③ see – seeing
④ run – running
⑤ buy – buying

09 다음 빈칸에 들어갈 말이 순서대로 짝지어진 것은?

> • The woman is ____________ a novel.
> • ____________ the old man entering the Italian restaurant?

① read – Does ② read – Did
③ reading – Is ④ reads – Was
⑤ reading – Are

10 다음 밑줄 친 부분 중 어법상 어색한 것은?

① Peter is not packing his bag now.
② The kitten is lieing on my blanket.
③ My brother is eating some salad.
④ His friends are sitting on a bench.
⑤ Is Mina taking a walk now?

11 다음 문장을 괄호 안의 문장으로 바르게 바꾸지 못한 것은?

> Grace and Tommy have dinner together.

① Grace and Tommy had dinner together. (과거시제)
② Do Grace and Tommy having dinner together? (현재 의문문)
③ Grace and Tommy will have dinner together. (미래시제)
④ Grace and Tommy were having dinner together. (과거진행형)
⑤ Grace and Tommy are having dinner together. (현재진행형)

[12~13] 다음 중 어법상 어색한 것을 고르시오.

12 ① Her little sister usually sleeps at 9 p.m.
② My cousin is having a motorbike.
③ Sujin is listening to pop songs.
④ He moved to Seoul two years ago.
⑤ The teacher looks tired today.

13 ① Paris was the capital of France.
② It didn't rain much last summer.
③ The Second World War ended in 1945.
④ The sky was clear yesterday.
⑤ Sandy will go to the mall tomorrow.

14 다음 대답에 대한 질문으로 알맞은 것은?

A: ______________________
B: He will hike the mountain.

① What was Jeremy doing 6 hours ago?
② Did Jeremy hike the mountain?
③ What will Jeremy do tomorrow?
④ What is Jeremy doing now?
⑤ Does Jeremy hike the mountain?

15 다음 |보기|의 밑줄 친 부분과 쓰임이 같은 것은?

|보기|
He is going to the library now.

① You and I are going to travel to Jeju Island.
② My parents are going to eat out tonight.
③ Tony is going to leave Busan tomorrow.
④ Sora is going to the mall to buy clothes.
⑤ He is going to buy a new bicycle.

[16~17] 다음 괄호 안의 단어를 알맞은 형태로 바꿔 빈칸에 쓰시오.

16 Mr. Lee always __________ books when he stays at home. (read)

17 Yujin __________ a diary in English last Sunday. (write)

18 다음 문장을 be going to를 사용하여 바꿔 쓰시오.

Clara will play the piano with Minho.

→ Clara ______________________.

19 다음 괄호 안의 말을 사용하여 주어진 질문에 대한 알맞은 대답을 쓰시오.

A: What are you going to do today?
B: ______________________
(study / at the library)

20 다음 문장을 의문문으로 바꿔 쓰시오.

It is going to rain this afternoon.

→ ____________________

21 다음 질문에 대한 알맞은 대답을 쓰시오.

A: Jenny, did you drink lemonade at the cafe?
B: ________, ________ ________.
I ________ watermelon juice.

[22~24] 다음 우리말과 같도록 괄호 안의 말을 바르게 배열하시오.

22 그는 오늘 밤 Kate와 데이트를 하려고 한다.
(he / Kate / tonight / with / have a date / is going to)

→ ____________________

23 그녀는 멋진 주말을 보내고 있니?
(she / weekend / a / having / is / great)

→ ____________________

24 미나의 아버지는 30분 전에 거실을 청소하고 계셨다.
(Mina's father / 30 minutes ago / cleaning / was / the living room)

→ ____________________

25 다음 괄호 안의 동사를 사용하여 빈칸에 알맞은 말을 쓰시오.

Emily ________ (go) to the gym an hour ago. She ________ (meet) Sam there. Now they are ________ (go) to a Korean restaurant. They are going ________ (have) *bibimbap* for lunch.

[26~27] 다음 그림을 보고, 대화를 완성하시오.

26

A: What is Minho doing?
B: He ______________________.

27

A: Is Grace running now?
B: ________, ________ ________.
She is ________ on the bench and reading a book.

[28~30] 다음 글을 읽고, 질문에 답하시오.

Amy is ten years old. She has a little brother. He is five years old. Amy was watering flowers in the garden an hour ago. Her brother was playing with his toy truck at that time. Now, they are washing their hands.

28 What was Amy doing an hour ago?

→ ______________________ an hour ago.

29 How old will Amy's brother be next year?

→ ______________________ next year.

30 Are Amy and her brother playing hide and seek now?

→ No, ____________. They are ________ ______________________.

CHAPTER

04

조동사

UNIT 01 can

조동사 can은 '~할 수 있다'라는 의미 말고도 다양한 의미를 나타낼 수 있음을 기억하세요.

능력	I can swim.	요청	Can you wait?
가능	I can help you.	추측	He can be busy.
허가	You can stay here.	금지	You cannot stay here.

다음 괄호 안의 동사와 can 또는 can't를 사용하여 문장을 완성하시오.

01 Jinsu is strong. He ____________ the heavy table. (move)

02 A: ____________ I ____________ in this pool? B: No, ____________. (swim)

03 Sally is a good singer. She ____________ very well. (sing)

04 I can't find my pen. ____________ I ____________ your pen? (borrow)

05 My brother is sick. He ____________ to the concert. (go)

06 He is the best runner. He ____________ very fast. (run)

07 I can play the guitar, but my sister ____________ the guitar. (play)

08 She didn't finish her homework. She ____________ shopping with me. (go)

09 A: ____________ you ____________ me your car? B: No, ____________. (lend)

UNIT 02 be able to

능력이나 가능을 나타내는 〈be able to+동사원형〉은 조동사 can과 바꾸어 쓸 수 있어야 해요.

긍정문	현재	I am able to swim.	→ I can swim.
	과거	I was able to swim.	→ I could swim.
	미래	I will be able to swim.	–
부정문		I am not able to swim.	→ I cannot[can't] swim.
의문문		Are you able to swim?	→ Can you swim?

다음 문장을 괄호 안의 문장으로 바꾸어 쓰시오.

01 I'm able to sing the song. (부정문) ____________ the song.

02 You are able to read the book. (의문문) ____________ the book?

03 He is able to get up early. (미래시제) ____________ early.

04 He was able to find his key. (can 사용) ____________ his key.

05 They can get some money. (able 사용) ____________ some money.

06 We were able to visit him. (부정문) ____________ him.

07 Tony is able to carry the boxes. (의문문) ____________ the boxes?

08 The birds can fly so well. (able 사용) ____________ so well.

09 She is able to draw a picture.(과거시제) ____________ a picture.

UNIT 03 may

조동사 may의 3가지 의미를 기억해 두세요.

추측	허가	금지
~일지도 모른다	~해도 된다, ~해도 될까요?	~하면 안 된다

주의 may의 부정형은 may not으로 쓰고, 축약하지 않아요.

다음 우리말과 같도록 괄호 안의 말과 may를 사용하여 바르게 영작하시오.

01 그녀는 회의에 올지도 모른다. (come / to the meeting) ______

02 제가 당신의 딸과 얘기를 나눠도 될까요? (talk to / daughter) ______

03 그는 직장에 있을지도 모른다. (be at work) ______

04 밤에 비 올지도 모른다. (rain) ______

05 너는 이 빵을 먹어도 된다. (eat) ______

06 내가 네 자전거를 빌려도 될까요? (borrow / bicycle) ______

07 너는 여기서 담배를 피워서는 안 된다. (smoke) ______

08 너는 이 영화를 좋아하지 않을지도 모른다. (like / this movie) ______

09 제가 친구들이랑 외출해도 될까요? (go out / with my friends) ______

UNIT 04 can과 바꿔 쓸 수 있는 조동사

조동사 can은 조동사 may 또는 be able to와 바꾸어 쓸 수 있어야 해요.

추측	~일 수 있다	can = may	금지	~할 수 없다	cannot = may not
	~일지도 모른다			~하면 안 된다	
허가	~할 수 있다	can = may	능력/가능	~할 수 있다	can = be able to
	~해도 된다				

다음 문장에서 어법상 어색한 부분을 찾아 바르게 고쳐 쓰시오.

01 It may being fine tomorrow morning. ______ → ______

02 Can she plays the violin? ______ → ______

03 We may are not here tomorrow. ______ → ______

04 Jisu cannot taking off her coat. ______ → ______

05 I don't able to sing it in English. ______ → ______

06 May I do take a message for you? ______ → ______

07 The boy can't reads the sign. ______ → ______

08 You don't may watch TV after dinner. ______ → ______

09 The man may is tired. ______ → ______

UNIT 05 must

'~해야 한다'라는 의무나 '~임에 틀림없다'라는 강한 추측을 표현할 때 조동사 must를 쓰세요.

의무	~해야 한다	We must follow the rules.
금지	~하면 안 된다	You must not tell lies.
강한 추측	~임에 틀림없다	She must be rich.

주의 부정의 강한 추측은 can't[cannot](~일 리가 없다)로 써요. The story can't be true.

다음 괄호 안의 단어와 must 또는 must not을 사용하여 문장을 완성하시오.

01 I'm very thirsty. I ______________ something. (drink)

02 You look very pale. You ______________. (sick)

03 I'll be late for work. I ______________. (hurry)

04 The classrooms are very dirty. The students ______________ them. (clean)

05 We ______________ pictures in the museum. (take)

06 This is an interesting book. You ______________ it. (read)

07 There are no buses. We ______________ home. (walk)

08 My hands are dirty. I ______________ them. (wash)

UNIT 06 have to

have/has to는 의미상 must와 바꾸어 쓰지만, 부정문은 서로 다른 의미인 것에 주의해야 해요.

긍정문	의무	We have to pay.	~해야 한다
부정문	불필요	We don't have to pay.	~해야 하는 건 아니다
의문문	의무	Do we have to pay?	~해야 할까?

주의 주어가 3인칭 단수면 has to로 써야 하며, 과거형(~했어야 했다)은 had to로 써요.

다음 문장에서 어법상 어색한 부분을 찾아 바르게 고쳐 쓰시오.

01 You has to keep a diary. ______________ → ______________

02 I have to washing my dad's car. ______________ → ______________

03 Jason have to come back home by 6 o'clock. ______________ → ______________

04 You doesn't have to clean your room. ______________ → ______________

05 She has to wears a helmet. ______________ → ______________

06 We have to win the game yesterday. ______________ → ______________

07 She has not to study tonight. ______________ → ______________

08 Do he have to sing a song here now? ______________ → ______________

09 I have to walked home last night. ______________ → ______________

UNIT 07 should

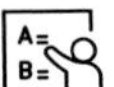
조동사 should는 '~해야 한다'라는 뜻으로 충고나 제안을 할 때 써요.

긍정문	~해야 한다, ~하는 게 좋겠다	You should wash your hands.
부정문	~하면 안 된다, ~하지 않는 게 좋겠다	You should not[shouldn't] play games too much.
의문문	~해야 하나?, ~하는 게 좋을까?	Should I take the bus? – Yes, you should. / No, you shouldn't.

다음 우리말과 같도록 괄호 안의 말과 should를 사용하여 문장을 완성하시오.

01 내 신발은 더럽다. 나는 그것을 빨아야 한다. (wash)

→ My shoes are dirty. I ______________________ them.

02 지금 눈이 오고 있다. 너는 오늘 운전을 하지 않는 게 좋겠다. (drive)

→ It's snowing now. You ______________________ today.

03 그것은 좋은 영화이다. 우리는 가서 그것을 봐야 한다. (go and see)

→ It's a great movie. We ______________________ it.

04 그는 엄청 피곤해 보인다. 그는 쉬어야 한다. (rest)

→ He looks so tired. He ______________________.

05 그녀는 하루 종일 TV를 본다. 그녀는 그렇게 많이 TV를 봐서는 안 된다. (watch)

→ She watches TV all day. She ______________________ TV so much.

06 A: 내가 저 기차를 타야 하니? (take)

B: 응, 타야 해.

→ A: ______________________ that train?

B: Yes, ______________________.

중간고사·기말고사 실전문제

객관식 (01~15) / 주관식 (16~30)

학년과 반 | 이름 | 객관식 / 15문항 | 주관식 / 15문항

[01~02] 다음 빈칸에 알맞은 것을 고르시오.

01 The girl can __________ very well.

① dance ② dancing
③ dances ④ danced
⑤ to dance

02 The students must __________ sad.

① is ② was
③ were ④ be
⑤ are

[03~06] 다음 우리말과 같도록 빈칸에 알맞은 것을 고르시오.

03 I __________ play the piano like a musician.
(나는 음악가처럼 피아노를 칠 수 있다.)

① am ② will
③ must ④ may
⑤ can

04 You __________ go home now.
(너는 지금 집에 가도 된다.)

① will ② may
③ should ④ must
⑤ have to

05 He __________ do the dishes this evening.
(그는 오늘 저녁에 설거지를 해야 한다.)

① may ② will
③ can ④ must
⑤ have to

06 You __________ go to bed early for tomorrow.
(너는 내일을 위해 일찍 잠자리에 드는 게 좋겠다.)

① will ② may
③ can ④ must
⑤ should

[07~08] 다음 중 밑줄 친 부분의 의미가 나머지 넷과 다른 하나를 고르시오.

07 ① Can he jump high?
② Can she run fast?
③ Can you do everything?
④ Can I open the window?
⑤ Can the boy fix the computer?

08 ① Jim didn't go to school. He may be sick.
② You may use this computer for 30 minutes.
③ I can't believe the rumor. It may be false.
④ She may come to the party. She looks free.
⑤ He may be angry. You should say sorry to him.

[09~11] 다음 우리말을 영어로 바르게 옮긴 것을 고르시오.

09

너는 여기에 주차해서는 안 된다.

① You must park here.
② You must not park here.
③ You don't have to park here.
④ You not must park here.
⑤ You have to park here.

10

그녀는 오늘 피곤할지도 모른다.

① She may is tired today.
② She may be tire today.
③ She may tired today.
④ She may be tired today.
⑤ She may being tired today.

11

그는 금메달을 딸 수 있을 것이다.

① He was able to win the gold medal.
② He must win the gold medal.
③ He will can win the gold medal.
④ He will is able to win the gold medal.
⑤ He will be able to win the gold medal.

[12~13] 다음 중 어법상 어색한 것을 고르시오.

12 ① I can speak Spanish very well.
② We must following the rules.
③ My sister may not come to the party.
④ The boy can answer the question.
⑤ You should see a doctor.

13 ① Can you sing well?
② May I come in?
③ Do she have to leave home early?
④ Can I have some more?
⑤ Should I go there by bus?

[14~15] 다음 대화의 빈칸에 알맞은 것을 고르시오.

14

A: May I take a picture?
B: ________________ You can't take photos here.

① Sure.
② Of course.
③ No, you don't.
④ You don't have to.
⑤ I'm afraid you may not.

15

A: Must I find your lost wallet?
B: ________________ I already found it.

① Yes, you do.
② No, you won't.
③ Yes, you must.
④ No, you shouldn't.
⑤ No, you don't have to.

[16~18] 다음 우리말과 같도록 조동사와 주어진 단어를 사용하여 문장을 완성하시오.

16

너는 이 문제를 풀 수 있니? (solve)

→ ________________ this problem?

17

그는 그녀에게 전화 걸 필요가 없었다. (call)

→ He ________________ her.

18

그들은 그 상자를 열어서는 안 된다. (open)

→ They ________________ the box.

[19~20] 다음 두 문장이 같은 의미가 되도록 주어진 단어를 활용하여 빈칸에 알맞게 쓰시오.

19 Minsu must finish his homework today. (have)

→ Minsu ________ ________ finish his homework today.

20 My uncle can drive a truck. (able)

→ My uncle ________ ________ ________ drive a truck.

[21~24] 다음 문장에서 어법상 어색한 부분을 찾아 바르게 고쳐 쓰시오.

21 You can stays here for a few weeks.

________ → ________

22 She have to take the medicine.

________ → ________

23 My neighbor not may be ready to learn the truth.

________ → ________

24 He must visited his grandparents next week.

________ → ________

[25~26] 다음 우리말과 같도록 괄호 안의 말을 바르게 배열하시오.

25 너희들은 다른 사람들에게 친절하게 해야 한다. (others / to / you / should / be / nice)

→ ________________

26 저에게 물을 좀 가져다주시겠어요? (you / me / bring / some water / can)

→ ________________

[27～28] 다음 우리말과 같도록 괄호 안의 말을 사용하여 문장을 완성하시오.

27

우리는 제시간에 그곳에 도착할 수 있었다.
(in time / able / there / arrive)

→ ______________________________

28

그 학생들은 교실을 청소해야 하나요?
(the classroom / clean / the students / have)

→ ______________________________

[29～30] 다음 주어진 |조건|을 이용하여 우리말을 영어로 옮겨 쓰시오.

29

|조건|
1. 충고를 나타내는 조동사를 사용할 것
2. 단어 watch, much, too를 사용할 것
3. 6 단어로 쓸 것

너는 TV를 너무 많이 보지 않는 게 좋겠다.

→ ______________________________

30

|조건|
1. 강한 추측을 나타내는 조동사를 사용할 것
2. 단어 useful, for, machine을 사용할 것
3. 7 단어로 쓸 것

그 기계는 우리에게 유용한 것임에 틀림없다.

→ ______________________________

CHAPTER

05

명사와 관사

UNIT 01 셀 수 있는 명사와 부정관사 a(n)

셀 수 있는 명사가 하나(단수 명사)면 명사 앞에 부정관사 a(n)를 붙여야 해요.

	a+첫 발음이 자음인 명사	an+첫 발음이 모음인 명사
부정관사+명사	a house	an eraser
부정관사+형용사+명사	a white eraser	an honest boy

다음 우리말과 같도록 괄호 안의 단어와 a 또는 an 중 알맞은 것을 사용하여 문장을 완성하시오.

01 그는 비싼 자동차를 가지고 있다. (expensive / car)
→ He has ______________________.

02 그녀는 모자 한 개와 우산 한 개를 살 것이다. (hat / umbrella)
→ She is going to buy ______________ and ______________.

03 Tony는 하루에 세 번 이를 닦는다. (day)
→ Tony brushes his teeth three times ______________.

04 나는 펜 한 개와 지우개 한 개를 가지고 있다. (pen / eraser)
→ I have ______________ and ______________.

05 나는 삼촌이 한 명 있다. 그는 기술자이다. (uncle / engineer)
→ I have ______________. He is ______________.

06 너는 사과를 원하니 아니면 오렌지를 원하니? (apple / orange)
→ Do you want ______________ or ______________?

UNIT 02 셀 수 있는 명사의 규칙 복수형 1

셀 수 있는 명사가 둘 이상(복수 명사)이면 부정관사 a(n)를 빼고 명사 뒤에 -s를 써서 복수형으로 만드세요.

단수 명사		복수 명사	
a chair	an artist	chairs	artists

다음 괄호 안의 단어를 알맞은 형태로 바꾸어 빈칸에 쓰시오.

01 I have a dog. My friend has two ______________. (dog)

02 Do you have many ______________? (book)

03 There is one ______________ on the plate. (cookie)

04 ______________ are playing guitar in the classroom. (student)

05 Two ______________ are playing computer games. (boy)

06 Three ______________ are around the table. (chair)

07 My cat has big black ______________ and a long ______________. (eye / tail)

08 My sister has a lot of ______________ and ______________. (doll / toy)

09 Ann put five ______________ and five ______________ on the table. (fork / spoon)

UNIT 03 셀 수 있는 명사의 규칙 복수형 2

-s 이외의 명사의 복수형을 만드는 다음의 규칙을 알아 두세요.

-s, -x, -ch, -sh	-es	자음+y	y 삭제, -ies
자음+o	-es (예외) piano–pianos, photo–photos	-f, -fe	f(e) 삭제, -ves (예외) roof–roofs, chef–chefs

다음 명사의 복수형을 빈칸에 쓰시오.

01 피아노 piano – ________
02 이야기 story – ________
03 버스 bus – ________
04 교회 church – ________
05 지붕 roof – ________
06 요리사, 주방장 chef – ________
07 벤치 bench – ________
08 접시 dish – ________
09 토마토 tomato – ________
10 상자 box – ________
11 나뭇잎 leaf – ________
12 라디오 radio – ________
13 붓 brush – ________
14 책꽂이 shelf – ________
15 여우 fox – ________
16 열쇠 key – ________
17 칼 knife – ________
18 수업 class – ________
19 도시 city – ________
20 손목시계 watch – ________
21 감자 potato – ________
22 드레스 dress – ________
23 늑대 wolf – ________
24 사진 photo – ________
25 영웅 hero – ________
26 손가락 finger – ________
27 아기 baby – ________
28 파리 fly – ________

UNIT 04 셀 수 있는 명사의 불규칙 복수형

명사의 복수형이 불규칙인 경우에는 무조건 외워야 해요.

단 · 복수 형태가 다른 명사	man – men woman – women person – people tooth – teeth foot – feet goose – geese child – children mouse – mice ox – oxen
단 · 복수 형태가 같은 명사	sheep – sheep deer – deer salmon – salmon

다음 명사의 복수형을 빈칸에 쓰시오.

01 양 sheep – ________
02 여자 woman – ________
03 거위 goose – ________
04 어린이 child – ________
05 황소 ox – ________
06 발 foot – ________
07 사슴 deer – ________
08 쥐 mouse – ________
09 이, 치아 tooth – ________
10 남자 man – ________
11 연어 salmon – ________
12 사람 person – ________

UNIT 05 셀 수 없는 명사

셀 수 없는 명사는 부정관사 a(n)를 붙이지 않고, 항상 단수형으로 쓴다는 데에 유의하세요.

추상명사	고유명사	물질명사
형체 없이 추상적인 개념 또는 감정	사람, 지명, 월, 요일 등 고유의 이름	나누어 셀 수 없는 물질

주의 고유명사의 첫 글자는 항상 대문자로 써야 해요.

다음 문장에서 어법상 어색한 부분을 찾아 바르게 고쳐 쓰시오.

01 He doesn't like to have breads in the morning. ________ → ________

02 She comes from a Canada. ________ → ________

03 An English is my favorite subject. ________ → ________

04 My sister spends a lot of moneys on phones. ________ → ________

05 Mina gave some juices to her teacher. ________ → ________

06 I want to go to new york this vacation. ________ → ________

07 She gave some cheeses to me. ________ → ________

08 Do you want some butters on your toast? ________ → ________

09 A spring is over and summer is here. ________ → ________

UNIT 06 셀 수 없는 명사의 수량 표현

셀 수 없는 명사는 용기나 단위를 이용하여 셀 수 있다는 점을 알아 두세요.

a piece of	~ 한 조각	a slice of	~ (얇게 썬) 한 조각
a glass of	~ 한 잔	a bottle of	~ 한 병
a cup of	~ 한 컵	a bowl of	~ 한 그릇

주의 2개 이상일 경우, 용기나 단위를 나타내는 명사를 복수형으로 만들어야 해요.

참고 항상 복수로 쓰는 두 개가 한 쌍을 이루는 명사는 pair로 셀 수 있어요.

다음 우리말과 같도록 괄호 안의 단어를 사용하여 문장을 완성하시오.

01 나는 매일 우유 한 잔을 마신다. (milk) → I drink ________ every day.

02 그는 피자 세 조각을 먹었다. (pizza) → He ate ________.

03 그녀는 신발 한 켤레를 샀다. (shoes) → She bought ________.

04 나는 하루에 커피 한 컵을 마신다. (coffee) → I drink ________ a day.

05 그는 매일 10잔의 물을 마신다. (water) → He drinks ________ every day.

06 내게 종이 다섯 장을 갖다 줘. (paper) → Bring me ________.

UNIT 07 정관사 the

특정한 것을 가리킬 때는 명사 앞에 '그'라는 의미의 정관사 the를 쓰세요.

앞에 나왔던 명사를 가리킬 때	I have a pen. The pen is red.
서로 무엇을 말하는지 알고 있을 때	Could you open the door?
수식을 받아 무엇인지 분명할 때	The flowers on the table are roses.
관용적으로 the를 붙이는 경우	the sun, the moon, the earth, the sky, the Internet

다음 문장의 밑줄 친 The[the]와 쓰임이 같은 것을 |보기|에서 골라 기호를 쓰시오.

|보기|
ⓐ I have a dog. The dog is black and white.
ⓑ The sun rises in the east.
ⓒ The vase on the desk is from China.
ⓓ Will you close the door?

01 I can play the violin very well. ________

02 The book on the desk is very interesting. ________

03 There is a clock on the wall. The clock is big. ________

04 The children in the room like apples. ________

05 There is a tree in my garden. My cat likes to sleep under the tree. ________

06 The sky is blue and the sun is shining. ________

07 Can you pass me the newspaper, please? ________

08 The flowers in this garden are beautiful. ________

09 My brother has a computer. The computer is new. ________

UNIT 08 관사의 생략

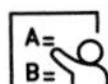

다음의 경우에는 명사 앞에 아무 관사도 쓰지 않아야 해요.

식사, 운동 종목, 과목	교통수단	본래의 용도대로 이용
lunch / soccer / math	by car, on foot	go to bed 잠자리에 들다

다음 문장에서 어법상 어색한 부분을 찾아 바르게 고쳐 쓰시오.

01 I always go to school by the subway. ________ → ________

02 Tom goes to the work at 8 o'clock. ________ → ________

03 My favorite sport is the basketball. ________ → ________

04 Mr. Kim teaches a math at school. ________ → ________

05 My friend was having the breakfast. ________ → ________

06 My father goes to work by a car. ________ → ________

07 We often have a lunch at 12 o'clock. ________ → ________

08 We played a soccer together after school. ________ → ________

UNIT 09 There is / are

There is/are ~는 '~가/들이 있다'라는 표현으로 뒤에 쓰는 명사의 수에 맞춰 is 또는 are를 선택하세요.

There is	+단수 명사	There is a computer in my room.	현재(~가 있다)
There was		There was water in the bottle.	과거(~가 있었다)
There are	+복수 명사	There are some books on your desk.	현재(~들이 있다)
There were		There were many trees in the garden.	과거(~들이 있었다)

주의 셀 수 없는 명사는 항상 단수 취급하므로 There is/was ~로 써야 해요.

다음 우리말과 같도록 괄호 안의 단어를 사용하여 문장을 완성하시오. (단, 필요시 단어 변형 가능)

01 차고에 자동차가 한 대 있다. (car) → ______________ in the garage.

02 병 안에 약간의 우유가 있었다. (some / milk) → ______________ in the bottle.

03 벽에 그림 한 점이 있다. (picture) → ______________ on the wall.

04 밖에 많은 학생들이 있다. (many / student) → ______________ outside.

05 접시 위에 음식이 좀 있었다. (some / food) → ______________ on the dish.

06 내 가방에 많은 책들이 있었다. (many / book) → ______________ in my bag.

UNIT 10 There is / are의 부정문과 의문문

There is/are ~의 부정문과 의문문은 모두 be동사만 이용하세요.

긍정문	There+be동사+명사	There was water in the bottle.	
부정문	There+be동사+not+명사	There were not many trees here.	be동사 뒤에 not 추가
의문문	Be동사+there+명사?	Was there a plan B? – Yes, there was. No, there wasn't.	be동사를 문두에 씀

다음 문장을 괄호 안의 문장으로 바꾸어 쓰시오.

01 There is a house around here. (부정문)

→ ______________ around here.

02 There are 7 days in a week. (의문문)

→ ______________ in a week? – Yes, ______________.

03 There was much water in the glass. (의문문)

→ ______________ in the glass? – No, ______________.

04 There are two baseballs on the sofa. (과거시제 부정문)

→ ______________ on the sofa.

05 Are there a book and two pencils on the desk? (평서문)

→ ______________ on the desk.

중간고사·기말고사 실전문제

객관식 (01~15) / 주관식 (16~30)

정답과 해설 • 70쪽

학년과 반　　　이름　　　객관식　　/ 15문항　주관식　　/ 15문항

01 다음 중 명사의 단수형과 복수형이 <u>잘못</u> 짝지어진 것은?

① bus – buses
② city – cities
③ wolf – wolves
④ clock – clocks
⑤ fox – foxies

02 다음 중 셀 수 없는 명사끼리 짝지어진 것은?

① apple, snow, watch
② coffee, advice, eraser
③ air, brush, meat
④ snow, love, Monday
⑤ sugar, book, milk

[03~05] 다음 빈칸에 들어갈 수 <u>없는</u> 것을 고르시오.

03

I will buy a ___________ in that store.

① dish　② egg
③ tomato　④ potato
⑤ basket

04

There are ___________ on the table.

① an orange　② two forks
③ some apples　④ five dishes
⑤ three potatoes

05

Many ___________ are in the living room.

① people　② chairs
③ children　④ woman
⑤ plants

06 다음 중 수량을 표현하는 방식이 나머지 넷과 <u>다른</u> 하나는?

① cake　② rice
③ paper　④ bread
⑤ furniture

07 다음 중 밑줄 친 부분의 의미가 나머지 넷과 <u>다른</u> 하나는?

① Can you bring me <u>a</u> fork?
② We go to church once <u>a</u> week.
③ There is <u>a</u> watermelon in the basket.
④ I need <u>a</u> lemon and two onions.
⑤ He keeps <u>a</u> cow and three chickens.

[08~09] 다음 빈칸에 알맞은 것을 고르시오.

08

Tom gave me a __________ yesterday.

① boxes ② toys
③ pens ④ rulers
⑤ notebook

09

I have a __________ of milk every morning.

① slice ② piece
③ glass ④ pair
⑤ cups

[10~11] 다음 밑줄 친 ①~⑤ 중 어법상 어색한 것을 고르시오.

10

She bought(①) me(②) two pairs(③) of(④) pant(⑤) last week.

11

Students usually go(①) to the school(②) five(③) times(④) a week(⑤).

[12~13] 다음 우리말을 영어로 바르게 옮긴 것을 고르시오.

12

그들은 도둑의 두 발을 밧줄로 묶었다.

① They tied the thief's foot together with rope.
② They tied the thief's foots together with rope.
③ They tied the thief's a feet together with rope.
④ They tied the thief's feet together with rope.
⑤ They tied the thief's feets together with rope.

13

나는 점심으로 피자 두 조각과 주스 한 병을 먹었다.

① I had two pizza and a juice for lunch.
② I had two pizzas and a juice for lunch.
③ I had two piece of pizza and a bottle of juice for lunch.
④ I had two pieces of pizza and a bottle of juice for lunch.
⑤ I had two pieces of pizzas and a bottle of juice for lunch.

[14~15] 다음 중 어법상 어색한 것을 고르시오.

14 ① The man could carry five boxes.
② There is a house in the woods.
③ You don't have to bring an umbrella.
④ There was no time to think.
⑤ A lion is looking at deers.

15 ① He bought three notebooks for his son.
② I read a interesting story yesterday.
③ Please give me a cup of water.
④ The earth goes round the sun.
⑤ Look at the yellow and red leaves.

[16~18] 다음 괄호 안의 단어를 어법상 알맞은 형태로 고쳐 쓰시오.

16

We need five forks and (knife) for the dinner table.

→ ____________

17

There were a lot of (mouse) and rats in the countryside.

→ ____________

18

We can see many (piano) at the shop.

→ ____________

[19~21] 다음 괄호 안에서 알맞은 말을 고르시오.

19 The boys are from (England / an England).

20 Could you give me some (information / informations) about it?

21 The stars were shining in (sky / the sky).

[22~23] 다음 문장에서 어법상 어색한 부분을 찾아 바르게 고쳐 쓰시오.

22 The white dove is the symbol of a peace.

____________ → ____________

23 The dolls on the desk is so cute.

____________ → ____________

[24~26] 다음 우리말과 같도록 괄호 안의 단어를 바르게 배열하시오. (단, 필요시 단어 변형 가능)

24

우리는 저녁으로 빵 두 덩어리와 치즈 한 조각이 필요하다.
(and / piece / of / cheese / a / bread / loaf / of)

→ We need two ________________
________________ for dinner.

25

그 마을의 집들은 뾰족한 지붕들을 가지고 있다.
(roof / house / have / steep)

→ The ________________
in the town.

26

신발장에 신발 두 켤레가 있니?
(shoe / be / there / pair / of / two)

→ ________________
on the shoe shelf?

[27~29] 다음 글에서 어법상 어색한 부분을 세 군데 찾아 바르게 고쳐 쓰시오.

I am at a restaurant with my family for the lunch. I'd like to have a sandwich and a bottle of water. My brother wants a piece of pizza and a glass of orange juice. My mom wants a piece of pizza and a glass of orange juice. My dad wants a piece of pizza and a bottle of water. We need to order a sandwich, three piece of pizza, two bottles of waters and two glasses of orange juice.

27 ________________ → ________________

28 ________________ → ________________

29 ________________ → ________________

30 다음 주어진 |조건|을 이용하여 우리말을 영어로 옮겨 쓰시오.

|조건|
1. There is/are 구문을 사용할 것
2. 단어 in, goose, the yard를 사용하되 필요시 단어 변형 가능
3. 7 단어로 쓸 것

거위 세 마리가 마당에 있다.

→ ________________

CHAPTER

06

대명사

UNIT 01 인칭대명사의 격변화

격에 따른 인칭대명사의 변화를 확인하세요.

	주격	소유격	목적격	소유대명사	주격	소유격	목적격	소유대명사
1인칭	I	my	me	mine	we	our	us	ours
2인칭	you	your	you	yours	you	your	you	yours
3인칭	he	his	him	his	they	their	them	theirs
	she	her	her	hers				
	it	its	it	×				

다음 문장에서 어법상 어색한 부분을 찾아 바르게 고쳐 쓰시오.

01 My father gave me a dog. Its cute. ________ → ________

02 I found your keys. I put it on your desk. ________ → ________

03 Mr. Kim is a teacher. He is we English teacher. ________ → ________

04 There is a bag on the table. That is me bag. ________ → ________

05 This notebook is her. Can I borrow it? ________ → ________

06 Mike and I play soccer every day. They are best friends. ________ → ________

07 My shoes are black, but your are white. ________ → ________

08 Who is the boy? Why are you looking at he? ________ → ________

UNIT 02 재귀대명사

재귀대명사를 어떤 경우에 사용하는지 파악하세요.

재귀	주어와 같은 목적어일 때	I love myself. (○) I love me. (×)	목적어이므로 생략 불가
강조	'직접'이라는 의미를 강조할 때	We made the cake (ourselves). We (ourselves) made the cake.	강조 역할로 생략 가능

다음 문장의 밑줄 친 부분과 쓰임이 같은 것을 |보기|에서 골라 기호를 쓰시오.

|보기|
ⓐ She herself went there. ⓑ He likes himself a lot.

01 I myself did the work. ________

02 Semin made the doll herself. ________

03 He praised himself. ________

04 I saw myself in the mirror. ________

05 The cat will look after itself. ________

06 We made this house ourselves. ________

07 They hid themselves under the table. ________

UNIT 03 지시대명사

'이것', '저 사람들'과 같이 사람이나 사물을 가리킬 때는 지시대명사를 쓰세요.

가까이 있는 사물이나 사람		멀리 있는 사물이나 사람	
this	these	that	those
이것, 이쪽, 이분	이것들, 이 사람들, 이분들	저것, 저쪽, 저분	저것들, 저 사람들, 저분들

다음 우리말과 같도록 지시대명사와 괄호 안의 단어를 사용하여 바르게 영작하시오. (단, 필요시 단어 변형 가능)

01 이것들은 너의 가방들이다. (bag) ______________________

02 저것은 그의 앨범이니? (album) ______________________

03 이것은 정말 큰 집이다. (really) ______________________

04 저것은 Jessica의 고양이가 아니다. (cat) ______________________

05 이것은 Mike의 책이다. (book) ______________________

06 저것들은 내 남동생의 장난감들이 아니다. (toy) ______________________

07 이것들이 네 안경이니? (glasses) ______________________

08 저것은 민수의 축구공이다. (Minsu) ______________________

09 이것들은 Judy의 새 모자들이다. (hat) ______________________

UNIT 04 지시형용사

지시대명사는 명사를 수식하는 지시형용사로도 쓸 수 있다는 점을 알아 두세요.

가까이 있는 사물이나 사람을 수식		멀리 있는 사물이나 사람을 수식	
this	these	that	those
이 ~	이 ~(들)	저 ~	저 ~(들)

다음 우리말과 같도록 지시형용사와 괄호 안의 단어를 사용하여 빈칸에 쓰시오. (단, 필요시 단어 변형 가능)

01 너는 은행에서 저 여자를 봤니? (woman) → Did you see ______________ in the bank?

02 이 접시들을 부엌으로 가져다주세요. (dish) → Take ______________ to the kitchen, please.

03 실례합니다, 이 가방이 당신 건가요? (bag) → Excuse me, is ______________ yours?

04 너는 저 그림이 마음에 드니? (picture) → Do you like ______________?

05 저 사과들은 맛있어 보인다. (apple) → ______________ look delicious.

06 너는 이 곰 인형을 원하니? (teddy bear) → Do you want ______________?

07 저기 있는 저 남자는 인기 가수이다. (man) → ______________ over there is a popular singer.

08 이 자동차는 비싸지만 아주 좋다. (car) → ______________ is expensive, but it's very nice.

09 이쪽으로 와서 이 학생들과 만나라. (student) → Come and meet ______________ over here.

UNIT 05 비인칭대명사 it

계절, 날짜, 요일 등에 사용하는 it은 가리키는 대상이 없고 해석하지 않는 점에 주의하세요.

인칭대명사 it (그것)		This pencil is red. It is mine.
비인칭대명사 it (의미 ×)	계절, 날짜, 요일, 시간, 날씨, 거리, 명암	It is summer. It is hot today.

다음 문장의 밑줄 친 It[it]과 쓰임이 같은 것을 |보기|에서 골라 기호를 쓰시오.

|보기|
ⓐ It is a sunny day.　　ⓑ It is a new computer.

01 It is five kilometers to the bus stop. ____________

02 Look at the dog. It looks so cute. ____________

03 It is rainy and windy. ____________

04 It is August 15th. ____________

05 How far is it to your school? ____________

06 I took a stone and threw it. ____________

07 It is almost spring. ____________

08 It gets dark so early in the winter. ____________

UNIT 06 부정대명사 1

정해지지 않은 불특정한 사람이나 물건 또는 앞에 언급된 명사와 같은 종류를 언급할 때는 부정대명사 one을 써요.

부정대명사	정해지지 않은 것, 앞에 언급한 명사	one 단수	ones 복수
인칭대명사	정해진 것	it 단수	they, them 복수

다음 빈칸에 알맞은 말을 |보기|에서 골라 쓰시오.

|보기|
it　one　ones　they　them

01 Is that your newspaper? Can I see ____________?

02 This shirt is too small. Can I try a bigger ____________?

03 My chair is too old. I need a new ____________.

04 She doesn't like white pants. She likes blue ____________.

05 He borrowed books from the library. ____________ are so funny.

06 That is my dad's car. He always parks ____________ there.

07 My sister has pretty dolls. She likes ____________ very much.

08 A: Do you have a red dress?　B: Yes, I have ____________.

09 A: What is this?　B: ____________ is my cat's house.

UNIT 07 부정대명사 2

정해진 범위 안에서 하나씩 가리킬 때 one, another, the other를 차례대로 써요.

2개 중	one	하나	3개 중	one	하나
	the other	나머지 하나		another	또 다른 하나
				the other	나머지 하나

다음 우리말과 같도록 빈칸에 알맞은 말을 쓰시오.

01 상자 안에 공이 두 개 있다. 한 개는 나의 것이고, 나머지 한 개는 너의 것이다.
→ There are two balls in the box. ____________ is mine, and ____________ is yours.

02 이 복사기는 작동하지 않아요. 다른 것을 사용해도 되나요?
→ This copy machine doesn't work. Can I use ____________ one?

03 당신이 원하시면 나머지 하나도 가져가실 수 있어요. → You can take ____________ if you want.

04 그는 딸이 두 명 있다. 한 명은 12살이고, 나머지 한 명은 14살이다.
→ He has two daughters. ____________ is twelve years old, and ____________ is fourteen.

05 그녀는 펜이 세 개 있다. 한 개는 녹색, 또 다른 하나는 검은색, 그리고 나머지 하나는 빨간색이다.
→ She has three pens. ____________ is green, ____________ is black, and ____________ is red.

UNIT 08 부정대명사 3

여러 개의 대상이 있는 상황에서 쓸 수 있는 대명사를 알아 두세요.

some	others	the others
몇몇	다른 몇몇	나머지 모두

다음 우리말과 같도록 괄호 안의 말을 바르게 배열하시오.

01 어떤 학생들은 버스를 타고 갔고, 어떤 학생들은 기차를 타고 갔다.
(went / by bus / students / some / and / by train / went / others)
→ ____

02 일부는 배드민턴을 하고, 나머지는 모두 책을 읽고 있다.
(playing / are / reading / are / books / badminton / and / some / the others)
→ ____

03 일부는 야구공들이고, 일부는 축구공들이다.
(others / are / are / and / baseballs / soccer balls / some)
→ ____

04 그 소년들 몇몇은 여기 있는데, 나머지 소년들은 모두 어디 있니?
(some / the others / are / where / here / of / the boys / are / but)
→ ____

중간고사·기말고사 실전문제

객관식 (01~15) / 주관식 (16~30)

학년과 반 이름 객관식 / 15문항 주관식 / 15문항

01 다음 중 단어의 성격이 나머지 넷과 <u>다른</u> 하나는?

① his ② your
③ its ④ me
⑤ their

[02~03] 다음 빈칸에 알맞은 것을 고르시오.

02

__________ laptop is thin and light.

① He ② She
③ Us ④ My
⑤ It

03

We are going to meet __________.

① they ② their
③ theirs ④ its
⑤ them

[04~05] 다음 빈칸에 공통으로 들어갈 말을 고르시오.

04

• __________ is already 9 o'clock.
• __________ is September 13th.

① This ② That
③ These ④ One
⑤ It

05

• She lost her umbrella. She has to buy __________.
• I have two skirts. __________ is black, and the other is pink.

① it ② one
③ ones ④ them
⑤ some

06 다음 밑줄 친 부분의 쓰임이 나머지 넷과 <u>다른</u> 하나는?

① <u>It</u> is his pencil.
② I love <u>it</u> very much.
③ What day is <u>it</u>?
④ <u>It</u> is under the desk.
⑤ <u>It</u> is my favorite subject.

[07~08] 다음 대화의 빈칸에 알맞은 것을 고르시오.

07

A: Is this Jane's bag?
B: No, it's __________.

① he ② mine
③ him ④ your
⑤ me

08

> A: I like Brian and James.
> B: Me, too. ___________ are very kind.

① He　② She
③ We　④ They
⑤ It

09 다음 대화의 빈칸에 들어갈 말이 순서대로 짝지어진 것은?

> A: Who are the two girls in this picture?
> B: ___________ is my sister, and ___________ is my cousin.

① One – another
② One – others
③ One – the other
④ Another – the others
⑤ Another – another

[10~11] 다음 우리말을 영어로 바르게 옮긴 것을 고르시오.

10

> 그녀의 오빠는 중학생이다.

① She brother is a middle school student.
② Hers brother is a middle school student.
③ Her brother is a middle school student.
④ She's brother is a middle school student.
⑤ His brother is a middle school student.

11

> 몇몇은 피자를 주문했고, 나머지 사람들은 모두 스파게티를 주문했다.

① One ordered pizza, and others ordered spaghetti.
② One ordered pizza, and the others ordered spaghetti.
③ Some ordered pizza, and others ordered spaghetti.
④ Some ordered pizza, and another ordered spaghetti.
⑤ Some ordered pizza, and the others ordered spaghetti.

12 다음 밑줄 친 부분을 생략할 수 있는 것은?

① I saw him myself.
② I'm proud of myself.
③ My uncle taught himself.
④ We should love ourselves.
⑤ The girl introduced herself.

[13~14] 다음 중 어법상 어색한 것을 고르시오.

13 ① This is my brother's pen.
② I don't like this sunglasses.
③ Can I borrow those books?
④ I want to buy these sneakers.
⑤ These are comfortable chairs.

14 ① The red car is yours.
② We are looking at the pictures.
③ That is her backpack.
④ It's tail is very short.
⑤ The park is near our house.

15 다음 밑줄 친 부분의 쓰임이 같은 것끼리 짝지어진 것은?

ⓐ <u>This</u> book is a best seller. ⓑ <u>This</u> house has a yellow door. ⓒ <u>This</u> is my family's car. ⓓ What is <u>this</u> box? ⓔ <u>This</u> is a toy robot.

① ⓐ, ⓒ ② ⓐ, ⓔ
③ ⓐ, ⓑ, ⓓ ④ ⓑ, ⓒ
⑤ ⓒ, ⓓ, ⓔ

[16~18] 다음 괄호 안에서 알맞은 말을 골라 쓰시오.

16 (She / Her) drank a cup of juice.

→ ____________________

17 (That / Those) people built this building.

→ ____________________

18 I don't like the color of this T-shirt. Do you have a blue (one / it)?

→ ____________________

[19~21] 다음 밑줄 친 부분을 대신할 수 있는 대명사를 <u>한 단어로</u> 쓰시오.

19 The blue one is <u>my pen</u>.

→ ____________________

20 Those are <u>their cameras</u>.

→ ____________________

21 Did you see <u>her hat</u>?

→ ____________________

[22~24] 다음 문장에서 어법상 어색한 부분을 찾아 바르게 고쳐 쓰시오.

22 That is cloudy today.

_______________ → _______________

23 My mom baked the bread itself.

_______________ → _______________

24 Susan is Paul sister.

_______________ → _______________

[25~26] 다음 우리말과 같도록 괄호 안의 단어를 바르게 배열하시오. (단, 필요시 단어 변형 가능)

25

저 차들은 정말 멋지고 비싸다. (nice / car / that / really / be)

→ _______________ and expensive.

26

그 어린이들은 그들 자신을 보호할 수 있다. (protect / can / them)

→ The children _______________.

[27~29] 다음 글에서 어법상 어색한 부분을 세 군데 찾아 바르게 고쳐 쓰시오.

> Some people have hobbies, and others don't. I have two hobbies. One is reading books, and other is swimming. My brother has three hobbies. One is playing computer games, anothers is mountain climbing, and others is taking a walk. My sister has no special hobbies.

27 _______________ → _______________

28 _______________ → _______________

29 _______________ → _______________

30 다음 주어진 |조건|을 이용하여 우리말을 영어로 옮겨 쓰시오.

|조건|
1. 의문사 how를 사용할 것
2. 단어 is, from, house, school, to, far를 사용할 것
3. 9 단어로 쓸 것

너의 집에서 학교까지 거리가 얼마나 되니?

→ _______________

내가 가장 취약한 부분에 대해
요점 정리를 해 보세요.

CHAPTER

07

형용사와 부사의 비교 표현

UNIT 01 형용사

서로 반대되는 의미를 가진 형용사끼리 묶어서 암기하세요.

다음 형용사의 반대말을 빈칸에 쓰시오.

01 능력 있는 able ↔ 능력 없는 ________

02 밝은 ________ ↔ 어두운 dark

03 바쁜 ________ ↔ 한가한 free

04 깨끗한 clean ↔ 더러운 ________

05 위험한 ________ ↔ 안전한 safe

06 깊은 deep ↔ 얕은 ________

07 부지런한 ________ ↔ 게으른 lazy

08 마른 dry ↔ 젖은 ________

09 쉬운 easy ↔ 어려운 ________

10 비어 있는 ________ ↔ 가득 찬 full

11 비싼 ________ ↔ 싼 cheap

12 뚱뚱한 ________ ↔ 마른 skinny

13 좋은 ________ ↔ 나쁜 bad

14 행복한 happy ↔ 불행한 ________

15 건강한 ________ ↔ 아픈 sick

16 무거운 ________ ↔ 가벼운 light

17 높은 high ↔ 낮은 ________

18 배고픈 ________ ↔ 배가 찬 full

19 친절한 kind ↔ 불친절한 ________

20 긴 ________ ↔ 짧은 short

21 늙은 old ↔ 젊은, 어린 ________

22 열린 open ↔ 닫힌 ________

23 예의 바른 ________ ↔ 무례한 rude

24 예쁜 pretty ↔ 못생긴 ________

25 부유한 rich ↔ 가난한 ________

26 똑똑한 smart ↔ 어리석은 ________

27 강한 ________ ↔ 약한 weak

28 키 큰 tall ↔ 키 작은 ________

29 두꺼운 ________ ↔ 얇은 thin

30 현명한 wise ↔ 현명하지 못한 ________

UNIT 02 형용사의 역할

형용사는 명사를 수식하거나 보어 역할을 한다는 것을 알아 두세요.

명사 수식	주격보어	목적격보어
They built the strong bridge.	This question is difficult.	She makes her mother happy.

다음 문장의 밑줄 친 부분과 쓰임이 같은 것을 |보기|에서 골라 기호를 쓰시오.

|보기|
ⓐ She is smart.
ⓑ She is a smart student.

01 Your new bag is nice. ________

02 He is a good baseball player. ________

03 Mary and I ate sweet ice cream. ________

04 Tony is angry now. ________

05 I keep my room clean. ________

06 A tall boy is coming here. ________

07 This computer game is interesting. ________

UNIT 03 수량형용사 1: some, any

'약간, 얼마간의, 어떤'을 표현하고자 할 때는 some이나 any를 쓰세요.

some	주로 긍정문	There are some books.	약간의 책들 〈복수 명사 앞〉
		She has some time.	약간의 시간 〈셀 수 없는 명사 앞〉
any	주로 부정문과 의문문	Are there any books?	책이 (어떤 것이라도) 있니?
		She doesn't have any time.	그녀는 약간의 시간도 없다.

다음 빈칸에 some 또는 any 중 알맞은 것을 쓰시오.

01 There are ___________ oranges.

02 Tom doesn't have ___________ books.

03 My sister bought ___________ new shoes.

04 Do you have ___________ questions?

05 Give me ___________ advice, please.

06 They don't have ___________ children.

07 There are ___________ flowers.

08 Is there ___________ milk in the house?

UNIT 04 수량형용사 2: many, much, a lot of

'많은'이라는 뜻의 many, much, a lot of, lots of가 어떤 명사와 함께 쓰이는지 익히세요.

(수가) 많은	many	+ 복수 명사	There are many animals.
(양이) 많은	much	+ 셀 수 없는 명사	There is not much time.
많은	a lot[lots] of	+ 복수 명사 / 셀 수 없는 명사	There are a lot of animals.

다음 우리말과 같도록 괄호 안의 단어와 |보기|에서 알맞은 것을 골라 문장을 완성하시오. (단, 중복 가능)

|보기|

many　　much　　a lot of　　lots of

01 도로에 차들이 많았나요? (cars)

→ Were there ______________________ on the road?

02 그는 그녀에게 많은 꽃을 주었다. (flowers)

→ He gave ______________________ to her.

03 너는 돈을 얼마나 가지고 있니? (money)

→ How ______________________ do you have?

04 너는 일주일에 몇 시간이나 일하니? (hours)

→ How ______________________ do you work in a week?

05 Jessica는 그녀의 반에 친구들이 많지 않다. (friends)

→ Jessica doesn't have ______________________ in her class.

06 Tony는 스포츠에 많은 관심이 없다. (interest)

→ Tony doesn't have ______________________ in sports.

UNIT 05 수량형용사 3: (a) few, (a) little

비슷해 보이지만 틀리기 쉬운 (a) few와 (a) little의 쓰임을 잘 구별해야 해요.

조금/약간 있는	a few	+ 복수 명사	I have a few books.	긍정의 의미를 포함
	a little	+ 셀 수 없는 명사	I have a little time.	
거의 없는	few	+ 복수 명사	I have few books.	부정의 의미를 포함
	little	+ 셀 수 없는 명사	I have little time.	

주의 a를 뺀 few와 little은 부정의 뜻으로 '거의 없는'이라는 의미라는 데 주의하세요.

다음 우리말과 같도록 괄호 안의 단어와 |보기|에서 알맞은 것을 골라 문장을 완성하시오. (단, 필요시 단어 변형 가능)

|보기|
a few a little few little

01 여기에는 학생들이 거의 없다. (student) → There are ______________ here.

02 그는 오늘 약간의 우유를 마셨다. (milk) → He drank ______________ today.

03 먹을 음식이 거의 없다. (food) → There is ______________ to eat.

04 저기에 몇 개의 사탕들이 있다. (candy) → There are ______________ there.

05 나는 게임 할 약간의 시간이 있다. (time) → I have ______________ for games.

06 몇몇 아이들이 저기서 놀고 있다. (child) → ______________ are playing there.

UNIT 06 부사의 역할

수식하는 말에 따라 달라지는 부사의 위치를 파악하세요.

형용사 수식	형용사 바로 앞	동사(구) 수식	주로 문장의 맨 뒤
다른 부사 수식	수식하는 부사 바로 앞	문장 전체 수식	문장의 맨 앞

다음 우리말과 같도록 괄호 안의 말을 바르게 배열하시오.

01 이 게임은 너무 흥미진진하다. (this game / exciting / very / is)

→ ______________________________

02 그녀는 오늘 아침 일찍 도착했다. (arrived / early / she / this morning)

→ ______________________________

03 Mike는 농구를 매우 잘한다. (plays / well / basketball / very / Mike)

→ ______________________________

04 커피를 너무 많이 마시지 마라. (coffee / much / drink / don't / too)

→ ______________________________

05 그 의사는 모든 사람들에게 매우 친절했다. (very / kind / was / the doctor / everyone / to)

→ ______________________________

UNIT 07 부사의 형태 1

부사는 very처럼 자체가 부사인 것도 있지만, 대부분 형용사에 -ly를 붙여 만들 수 있어요.

대부분의 경우	자음+-y로 끝나는 경우	-le로 끝나는 경우
+-ly	y를 i로 바꾸고+-ly	e를 없애고+-y

주의 〈명사+-ly〉는 형용사예요. → lovely 사랑스러운 / friendly 상냥한 / daily 매일의 / timely 시기적절한

다음 우리말과 같도록 괄호 안에서 알맞은 것을 고르시오.

01 그것을 조심해서 옮겨 주세요! → Move it (careful / carefully), please!

02 Sally는 안전하게 한국에 도착했다. → Sally arrived back in Korea (safe / safely).

03 우리는 지난밤 파티를 정말로 즐겼다. → We (real / really) enjoyed the party last night.

04 우리는 보통 8시에 아침을 먹는다. → We (usual / usually) eat breakfast at eight.

05 그녀는 나를 슬프게 쳐다봤다. → She looked at me (sad / sadly).

06 그 아이들은 행복하게 놀고 있다. → The children are playing (happy / happily).

UNIT 08 부사의 형태 2

형용사와 부사의 형태가 같은 단어에 유의하세요.

early	이른 / 일찍	high	높은 / 높이	long	긴 / 길게
late	늦은 / 늦게	hard	어려운, 딱딱한 / 열심히	pretty	예쁜 / 꽤
fast	빠른 / 빠르게	near	가까운 / 가까이		

주의 -ly가 붙어 다른 뜻이 되는 단어에 유의하세요.
lately 최근에 / hardly 거의 ~않다 / highly 매우, 대단히 / nearly 거의 / closely 면밀히, 꼼꼼히

다음 우리말과 같도록 괄호 안에서 알맞은 것을 골라 빈칸에 쓰시오.

01 Mike는 오늘 아침 학교에 지각했다. (late / lately)
→ Mike was ____________ for school this morning.

02 당신은 여기에서 가까운 곳에 사세요? (near / nearly)
→ Do you live ____________ here?

03 나의 꿈은 가까운 미래에 이루어질 것이다. (near / nearly)
→ My dream will come true in the ____________ future.

04 그 담장은 너무 높다. (high / highly)
→ The fence is too ____________.

05 오늘 비가 심하게 내리고 있다. (hard / hardly)
→ It is raining ____________ today.

06 James와 나는 늦은 저녁에 만났다. (late / lately)
→ James and I met in the ____________ evening.

UNIT 09 빈도부사

어떤 일이 얼마나 자주 일어나는지에 따라서 부사를 알맞게 선택해야 해요.

always	usually	often	sometimes	hardly/seldom	never
항상	보통, 대개	종종, 자주	가끔, 때때로	거의 ~않다	절대 ~않다

주의 빈도부사를 쓰는 위치에 주의하세요. ① be동사 뒤 ② 일반동사 앞 ③ 조동사 뒤

다음 우리말과 같도록 괄호 안의 말과 빈도부사를 써서 문장을 완성하시오. (단, 필요시 동사 변형 가능)

01 나는 보통 농구를 한다. (basketball / play) → I ______________________.

02 그녀는 가끔 일찍 일어난다. (early / get up) → She ______________________.

03 그는 절대 제시간에 오지 않는다. (come) → He ______________________ on time.

04 엄마와 나는 자주 수영하러 간다. (swimming / go) → Mom and I ______________________.

05 Jenny의 방은 항상 깨끗하다. (clean / is) → Jenny's room ______________________.

06 나는 거기에 절대 안 갈 거다. (will / go) → I ______________________ there.

UNIT 10 too, either

'또한, 역시'를 의미하며 동의나 공감을 나타낼 때, 긍정문에서는 too를, 부정문에서는 either를 사용해야 해요.

긍정의 동의 · 공감	A: I know him.	B: I know him, too.	= Me, too.
부정의 동의 · 공감	A: I'm not old.	B: I'm not old, either.	= Me, neither.

다음 우리말과 같도록 too 또는 either를 사용하여 문장을 완성하시오.

01 Sam은 수학 시험에 통과하지 못했다. 나 또한 수학 시험에 통과하지 못했다.
→ Sam didn't pass the math test. I ______________________.

02 이 셔츠는 너무 비싸다. 저 가방 역시 너무 비싸다.
→ This shirt is too expensive. That bag ______________________.

03 준수는 영어를 말할 수 없다. 소라 또한 영어를 말할 수 없다.
→ Junsu can't speak English. Sora ______________________.

04 나는 사과를 좋아하지 않는다. 내 여동생 또한 사과를 좋아하지 않는다.
→ I don't like apples. My sister ______________________.

05 나는 오늘 숙제를 끝내야 한다. James 또한 오늘 숙제를 끝내야 한다.
→ I must finish my homework today. James ______________________.

06 나의 엄마는 TV 보는 걸 좋아하시지 않는다. 나 또한 TV 보는 걸 좋아하지 않는다.
→ My mom doesn't like watching TV. I ______________________.

UNIT 11 비교급과 최상급 만드는 방법

다음 단어의 비교급과 최상급을 빈칸에 쓰시오.

01	화난	angry	– ________	– ________
02	나쁜/나쁘게	bad/badly	– ________	– ________
03	아름다운	beautiful	– ________	– ________
04	큰	big	– ________	– ________
05	조심하는	careful	– ________	– ________
06	조심하여	carefully	– ________	– ________
07	편안한	comfortable	– ________	– ________
08	위험한	dangerous	– ________	– ________
09	맛있는	delicious	– ________	– ________
10	어려운	difficult	– ________	– ________
11	부지런한	diligent	– ________	– ________
12	더러운	dirty	– ________	– ________
13	쉬운	easy	– ________	– ________
14	쉽게	easily	– ________	– ________
15	비싼	expensive	– ________	– ________
16	뚱뚱한	fat	– ________	– ________
17	상냥한	friendly	– ________	– ________
18	좋은	good	– ________	– ________
19	무거운	heavy	– ________	– ________
20	뜨거운	hot	– ________	– ________
21	아픈	ill	– ________	– ________
22	중요한	important	– ________	– ________
23	게으른	lazy	– ________	– ________
24	양이 적은	little	– ________	– ________
25	사랑스러운	lovely	– ________	– ________
26	많은	many/much	– ________	– ________
27	인기 있는	popular	– ________	– ________
28	예쁜	pretty	– ________	– ________
29	조용한	quiet	– ________	– ________
30	슬픈	sad	– ________	– ________
31	심각한, 진지한	serious	– ________	– ________
32	끔찍한	terrible	– ________	– ________
33	얇은	thin	– ________	– ________
34	못생긴	ugly	– ________	– ________
35	잘	well	– ________	– ________

UNIT 12 원급 비교

'~만큼 …한/하게'는 〈as+형용사/부사의 원급+as〉로 표현하세요.

형용사	She is	as	kind	as	him[he is].
부사	She can swim	as	well	as	him[he can].

주의 부정문(~만큼 …하지 않다)에서는 〈not+as[so]+형용사/부사의 원급+as〉로 쓸 수 있어요.

다음 우리말과 같도록 괄호 안의 단어를 사용하여 빈칸에 쓰시오.

01 민호는 준수만큼 영어를 잘 말할 수 있다. (well)

→ Minho can speak English ______________________ Junsu.

02 수영은 스키만큼 흥미진진하다. (exciting)

→ Swimming is ______________________ skiing.

03 나의 강아지는 너의 고양이만큼 영리하다. (smart)

→ My dog is ______________________ your cat.

04 Jane은 내 여동생만큼 예쁘지 않다. (not / pretty)

→ Jane ______________________ my sister.

05 이 컴퓨터는 저 컴퓨터만큼 비싸지 않다. (not / expensive)

→ This computer ______________________ that one.

UNIT 13 비교급

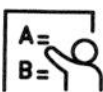

비교 표현 '~보다 더 …한/하게'는 〈비교급+than ~〉의 형태로 써야 해요.

형용사 비교급+than	부사 비교급+than
She is taller than her mom.	She can run faster than her dad.

다음 그림을 보고, 괄호 안의 단어를 사용하여 문장을 완성하시오.

01

02

03

04

01 ⓐ Minsu is ______________ Junho. (fast) ⓑ Junho is ______________ Minsu. (slow)

02 ⓐ Mary's hair is ______________ Jane's. (long) ⓑ Jane's hair is ______________ Mary's. (short)

03 ⓐ Bill is ______________ Jenny. (tall) ⓑ Jenny is ______________ Bill. (short)

04 ⓐ The blue pencil is ______________ the red one. (long)

ⓑ The red pencil is ______________ the blue one. (short)

UNIT 14 최상급

다음 최상급 표현의 쓰임을 알아 두세요.

the+최상급	one of the+최상급+복수 명사
가장 ~한/하게	가장 ~한 것들 중 하나

참고 최상급 뒤에 〈in+단수 명사(장소나 집단)〉가 오면 '~에서 가장 …한'을 의미하고, 〈of+복수 명사〉가 오면 '~들 중에서 가장 …한'을 뜻해요.

다음 우리말과 같도록 괄호 안의 단어를 활용하여 문장을 완성하시오.

01 John은 반에서 가장 키가 작은 학생이다. (short / student)
→ John is ______________________ in his class.

02 서울은 한국에서 가장 큰 도시이다. (big / city)
→ Seoul is ______________________ in Korea.

03 김 선생님은 우리 학교에서 가장 친절한 선생님이시다. (kind / teacher)
→ Mr. Kim is ______________________ in my school.

04 에베레스트 산은 세계에서 가장 높은 산이다. (high / mountain)
→ Mt. Everest is ______________________ in the world.

05 지수는 시험에서 가장 최악의 점수를 받았다. (bad / scores)
→ Jisu got ______________________ in the exam.

06 그 교회는 이 마을에서 가장 오래된 건물들 중 하나이다. (old / buildings)
→ The church is one of ______________________ in the town.

UNIT 15 비교 표현 종합

원급, 비교급, 최상급에 관한 기본 사항을 표에서 다시 확인한 후 종합해서 연습하세요.

원급	as ~ as ...	…만큼 ~한/하게	as ~ as 사이에 원급을 써요.
비교급	-er[more ~] than ...	…보다 더 ~한/하게	전치사 than과 함께 써요.
최상급	the -est[most ~] in/of ...	…에서/중에서 가장 ~한/하게	최상급 앞에 the를 붙여요.

다음 우리말과 같도록 괄호 안의 단어를 사용하여 문장을 완성하시오.

01 영어는 수학만큼 재미있다. (interesting) → English is ______________________ math.

02 이 집이 저 집보다 더 넓다. (large) → This house is ______________________ that one.

03 Jen은 학교에서 가장 인기 있는 학생이다. (popular) → Jen is ______________________ student in school.

04 Bill은 그의 학교에서 가장 빠르다. (fast) → Bill is ______________________ in his school.

05 이 사과가 저것보다 더 달다. (sweet) → This apple is ______________________ that one.

06 소라는 Tom만큼 뚱뚱하지 않다. (not / fat) → Sora is ______________________ Tom.

중간고사·기말고사 실전문제

객관식 (01~15) / 주관식 (16~30)

학년과 반 이름 객관식 / 15문항 주관식 / 15문항

01 다음 중 짝지어진 두 단어의 관계가 나머지 넷과 다른 하나는?

① real – really
② safe – safely
③ careful – carefully
④ friend – friendly
⑤ angry – angrily

[02~03] 다음 빈칸에 들어갈 수 없는 것을 고르시오.

02

She is a __________ girl.

① diligent ② pretty
③ gently ④ lovely
⑤ smart

03

There are __________ people in the square.

① some ② much
③ many ④ a lot of
⑤ lots of

04 다음 중 단어의 성격이 나머지 넷과 다른 하나는?

① timely ② never
③ often ④ hardly
⑤ usually

05 다음 중 비교급과 최상급 형태 변화를 나타내는 빈칸에 들어갈 수 있는 것은?

________ – ________er – ________est

① hot ② deep
③ lucky ④ serious
⑤ large

06 다음 밑줄 친 부분을 바르게 고친 것은?

<u>Little</u> books are available for visitors in this library.

① Much ② Few
③ A little ④ Very
⑤ Hardly

07 다음 괄호 안의 ①~⑤ 중 always가 들어갈 위치로 알맞은 곳은?

> My father (①) cooks (②) delicious (③) food (④) for (⑤) us.

[08~10] 다음 빈칸에 알맞은 것을 고르시오.

08

> ___________, the train didn't leave yet.

① Luck
② Lucky
③ Luckily
④ Luckier
⑤ Luckiest

09

> How ___________ sisters does Brian have?

① much
② a little
③ little
④ a lot
⑤ many

10

> Tom is as ___________ as Jenny.

① politer
② taller
③ biggest
④ smart
⑤ badly

[11~12] 다음 밑줄 친 ①~⑤ 중 어법상 어색한 것을 고르시오.

11

> The boys(①) can(②) swim(③) very(④) fastly(⑤).

12

> This(①) book is(②) interestinger(③) than(④) that one(⑤).

[13~14] 다음 우리말을 영어로 바르게 옮긴 것을 고르시오.

13

> 내 가방은 내 남동생 것만큼 크지 않다.

① My bag is as big as my brother's.
② My bag isn't as big as my brother's.
③ My bag isn't as big so my brother's.
④ My bag isn't so bigger as my brother's.
⑤ My bag is not as so big as my brother's.

14

> 나는 내 컴퓨터에 많은 사진을 저장했다.

① I stored some pictures in my computer.
② I stored many picture in my computer.
③ I stored lots of pictures in my computer.
④ I stored a lot of picture in my computer.
⑤ I stored a few pictures in my computer.

15 다음 중 어법상 어색한 것은?

① I don't have any plans.
② She eats too much junk food.
③ We have little information about it.
④ I saved a few money to buy a new smartphone.
⑤ There are few children in the playground.

[16~18] 다음 빈칸에 괄호 안의 말을 어법상 알맞은 형태로 쓰시오.

16

The children are playing ________ (happy) on the beach.

17

He is ________(young) than my brother.

18

Out of the three ways to help him, it was the ________(good) way.

[19~21] 다음 빈칸에 알맞은 말을 |보기|에서 골라 쓰시오.

|보기|

danger	many	late
dangerous	much	lately

19 They are in a ________ situation.

20 We don't have ________ time. Hurry up!

21 My brother always gets up ________.

[22~23] 다음 문장에서 어법상 어색한 부분을 찾아 바르게 고쳐 쓰시오.

22

A: I failed the exam. B: I couldn't pass the exam, too.

________ → ________

23

About 100 years ago, the terriblest war happened.

_______________ → _______________

[24~26] 다음 우리말과 같도록 괄호 안의 단어를 바르게 배열하시오. (단, 필요시 단어 추가나 변형 가능)

24

그는 너무 빨리 먹는 것 같다. (too / he / eat / quick)

→ I think _______________________.

25

나의 아들은 요즘 좀처럼 TV를 보지 않는다. (seldom / son / watch / TV / my)

→ _______________________
these days.

26

정직은 인생에서 가장 중요한 것들 중 하나이다. (one / the / honesty / important / of / thing / is)

→ _______________________
_______________________ in life.

[27~29] 다음 표를 보고, 괄호 안의 단어를 사용하여 비교 문장을 완성하시오.

	Eddy	Peter	Sam	John
Height	156	159	176	168
Weight	54	63	69	72
Age	14	14	16	15

27 __________ is __________ than Sam.
(heavy)

28 __________ __________ the __________
of the four. (tall)

29 __________ is __________ __________
as Peter. (old)

30 다음 주어진 |조건|을 이용하여 우리말을 영어로 옮겨 쓰시오.

|조건|
1. 비교급 표현을 사용할 것
2. 단어 spaghetti, pizza, delicious, much를 사용하되 필요시 단어 변형 가능
3. 7 단어로 쓸 것

스파게티가 피자보다 훨씬 더 맛있었다.

→ _______________________
____

내가 가장 취약한 부분에 대해
요점 정리를 해 보세요.

CHAPTER

08

의문사 의문문

UNIT 01 의문사 & who(m) 의문문

의문사 who가 문장에서 어떻게 쓰이는지 확인하세요.

누구 (보어)	누가 (주어)	누구를 (목적어)
Who is she?	Who knows you?	Who(m) do you like?

다음 우리말과 같도록 who(m)과 괄호 안의 말을 사용하여 바르게 영작하시오. (단, 필요시 동사 변형 가능)

01 누가 노래를 부르니? (sing / the song) ____________________

02 누가 James를 봤니? (see) ____________________

03 그가 누구를 초대했나요? (invite) ____________________

04 누가 케이크를 만들고 있니? (make / the cake) ____________________

05 네가 가장 좋아하는 가수는 누구니? (your favorite singer) ____________________

06 누가 지금 공원에서 놀고 있니? (play / in the park / now) ____________________

07 누가 이 휴대폰을 사용하니? (use / this cell phone) ____________________

08 누가 이 음식을 요리했나요? (cook / this food) ____________________

09 그녀는 누구와 이야기하고 있는 중이니? (talk to) ____________________

UNIT 02 what 의문문

의문사 what이 의문문에서 어떻게 쓰이는지 확인하세요.

무엇 (보어)	무엇이 (주어)	무엇을 (목적어)
What is this?	What makes you mad?	What do you like?

다음 주어진 대답에 알맞은 질문을 괄호 안의 말을 바르게 배열하여 완성하시오.

01 (what / want / you / do)?

→ A: ____________________ B: I want some butter.

02 (do / did / she / what / yesterday)?

→ A: ____________________ B: She went shopping with her friends.

03 (in / is / this box / what)?

→ A: ____________________ B: There are some books in it.

04 (Jason / interested / is / in / what)?

→ A: ____________________ B: He is interested in music.

05 (what / favorite / your / subject / is)?

→ A: ____________________ B: My favorite subject is English.

06 (looking for / what / is / he)?

→ A: ____________________ B: He is looking for his cell phone.

UNIT 03 when/where 의문문

'언제'를 물을 때는 when, '어디'를 물을 때는 where를 써야 해요.

when	where
언제	어디에, 어디서

참고 시간을 묻는 when은 what time으로 바꾸어 쓸 수 있어요. When did she go to bed? = What time ~?

다음 우리말과 같도록 괄호 안의 말과 알맞은 의문사를 사용하여 바르게 영작하시오.

01 너는 언제 그녀를 만났니? (meet) ____________________

02 너희는 언제 소풍을 가니? (go on a picnic) ____________________

03 너는 언제 숙제를 하니? (do / your homework) ____________________

04 그는 오늘 아침에 어디에 있었니? (was / this morning) ____________________

05 그들은 일요일마다 어디에 가니? (go / on Sundays) ____________________

06 너는 몇 시에 자니? (time / go to bed) ____________________

07 그녀는 그 상자를 어디에 두었니? (put / the box) ____________________

08 너는 그 드레스를 어디서 샀니? (buy / the dress) ____________________

09 그들은 어디서 축구를 하니? (play soccer) ____________________

UNIT 04 why/how 의문문

'왜'를 물을 때는 why, '어떤, 어떻게'를 물을 때는 how를 써야 해요.

why	how
왜	어떤, 어떻게

다음 질문에 알맞은 대답을 |보기|에서 골라 기호를 쓰시오.

[01~05]

|보기|
ⓐ I came by taxi.
ⓑ Because I got up late.
ⓒ Because he is sick.
ⓓ She walks to school.
ⓔ Because he will go abroad to study.

01 A: How did you come? B: ________

02 A: Why is Minho in bed? B: ________

03 A: How does she go to school? B: ________

04 A: Why were you late for school yesterday? B: ________

05 A: Why did John quit his job? B: ________

[06~09]

|보기|
ⓐ We're taking the train.
ⓑ Because she wanted to talk to him.
ⓒ Because I want to study English.
ⓓ I met her at the party yesterday.

06 A: How will you travel? B: ________

07 A: Why did she call him? B: ________

08 A: How do you know her? B: ________

09 A: Why are you going to America? B: ________

UNIT 05 <how+형용사/부사> 의문문

'얼마나 ~한/하게'라고 물을 때는 〈how+형용사/부사〉로 만들어 하나의 의문사처럼 쓰세요.

얼마나 자주	How often	(수가) 얼마나 많이	How many
몇 살 (얼마나 오래된)	How old	(가격/양이) 얼마(나 많이)	How much
얼마나 긴(길게)	How long	얼마나 먼	How far
얼마나 키가 큰	How tall		

주의 How many/much 뒤에 명사를 쓸 수 있고, 〈How many/much+명사〉를 하나의 의문사로 취급해요.

다음 대답을 보고, 빈칸에 알맞은 말을 |보기|에서 골라 쓰시오. (단, 중복 가능)

|보기|

How old	How tall	How much	How many
How big	How often	How far	How long

01 A: ________________ does he play tennis?
B: He plays tennis every day.

02 A: ________________ did you stay there last summer?
B: I stayed for a week.

03 A: ________________ is it from here to the airport?
B: About four miles.

04 A: ________________ brothers do you have?
B: I have one brother.

05 A: ________________ is your brother?
B: He's 150cm tall.

06 A: ________________ did you wait?
B: I waited for two hours.

07 A: ________________ does your father drive to work?
B: Twice in one week.

08 A: ________________ tables are there in this room?
B: There are two tables in this room.

09 A: ________________ are those earrings?
B: They are five thousand won.

UNIT 06 <what/which/whose+명사> 의문문

의문사 what, which, whose 뒤에 명사를 써서 하나의 의문사처럼 쓰는 법을 알아 두세요.

의미	의문사	+ 명사	+ 의문문	해석
무슨 ~	What	time	is it?	몇 시니?
		day	is it?	무슨 요일이니?
		color	do you like?	너는 무슨 색을 좋아하니?
어느 ~	Which	one	do you like better?	너는 어느 것을 더 좋아하니?
		subject	is more difficult?	어느 과목이 더 어렵니?
누구의 ~	Whose	bag	is this?	이것은 누구의 가방이니?
		shoes	are these?	이것은 누구의 신발이니?

참고 what은 정해지지 않은 대상 중에서 선택을 필요로 할 때 쓰는 반면, which는 정해진 대상 중에서 선택할 때 쓴다는 점에 유의하세요.

다음 대답에 알맞은 질문을 〈의문사+명사〉의 형태로 괄호 안의 단어를 바르게 배열하시오.

01 (gloves / these / are / whose)?
→ A: ______________________ B: They are Mina's.

02 (movie / he / see / which / want / does / to)?
→ A: ______________________ B: He wants to see the horror movie.

03 (time / is / your / birthday / what / party)?
→ A: ______________________ B: At seven in the evening.

04 (cell phone / you / did / whose / borrow)?
→ A: ______________________ B: I borrowed my sister's.

05 (which / do / you / pet / a cat / a dog / or / want)?
→ A: ______________________ B: I want a cat.

06 (subject / studying / now / what / they / are)?
→ A: ______________________ B: They are studying history.

중간고사·기말고사 실전문제

객관식 (01~15) / 주관식 (16~30)

학년과 반 　　　　 이름 　　　　 객관식 　　 / 15문항 　 주관식 　　 / 15문항

[01~03] 다음 빈칸에 알맞은 것을 고르시오.

01

_________ is your new teacher?

① Who ② What
③ When ④ Why
⑤ Whose

02

_________ did you do at home yesterday?

① Who ② What
③ Which ④ Where
⑤ Whose

03

_________ subject do you like better, science or math?

① Who ② When
③ Where ④ Whose
⑤ Which

[04~05] 다음 빈칸에 공통으로 들어갈 말을 고르시오.

04

• _________ do you play the guitar?
• _________ did he return from the trip?

① Who ② What
③ Which ④ When
⑤ Whose

05

• _________ often do you eat out?
• _________ many bags does she have?

① What ② When
③ How ④ Why
⑤ Which

[06~07] 다음 대화의 빈칸에 알맞은 것을 고르시오.

06

A: _________ is Kevin absent from school?
B: Because he is sick.

① Who ② Why
③ How ④ What
⑤ When

07

A: __________ was the interview with the company?
B: It was very good.

① How　② Why
③ When　④ Whose
⑤ Which

[08~09] 다음 대화의 밑줄 친 ①~⑤ 중 어법상 어색한 것을 고르시오.

08

A: ① What ② did you ③ saw in the garden?
B: I ④ saw a squirrel ⑤ in the garden.

09

A: ① What time ② does you usually ③ go ④ to work?
B: Between 8 ⑤ and 9.

10 다음 우리말을 영어로 바르게 옮긴 것은?

너는 반지를 어디서 찾았니?

① Whose ring is this?
② How do you like this ring?
③ Why did you find the ring?
④ When did you find the ring?
⑤ Where did you find the ring?

[11~12] 다음 중 어법상 어색한 것을 고르시오.

11
① Whose socks are these?
② What subject does Jane teach?
③ How long will you stay in Los Angeles?
④ How much books did you read this week?
⑤ Which bus do you take, number 10 or 11?

12
① Where does this bus go?
② Who ate my bulgogi burger?
③ What your brother did study at college?
④ Why is your sister so busy today?
⑤ When do you plan to do your English homework?

13 다음 빈칸에 들어갈 말이 순서대로 짝지어진 것은?

- ______ is the closest bank?
- ______ did you buy your laptop computer?
- ______ one do you want to watch, *Harry Potter* or *Frozen*?

① Who – What – Why
② Whose – Who – Why
③ When – How – Which
④ Where – Whom – How
⑤ Where – When – Which

14 다음 빈칸에 들어갈 말이 나머지 넷과 다른 하나는?

① ______ did Alex fix the printer?
② ______ much money do you have?
③ ______ far is it from here to the library?
④ ______ does Somin go to school every day?
⑤ ______ kind of decoration do you want on the table?

15 다음 ⓐ~ⓔ 중 어법상 옳은 것끼리 짝지어진 것은?

ⓐ Who gave you the bicycle?
ⓑ What color are Jane's umbrella?
ⓒ When will the English test start?
ⓓ What vegetable do you hate, onions or carrots?
ⓔ How many times do you go to the theater in a month?

① ⓐ, ⓑ　② ⓐ, ⓓ
③ ⓐ, ⓒ, ⓔ　④ ⓑ, ⓒ, ⓓ
⑤ ⓒ, ⓓ, ⓔ

[16~18] 다음 빈칸에 알맞은 말을 |보기|에서 골라 쓰시오.

|보기|

Who	What	Where
How old	How long	How far

16 ______ did you see a mouse?

17 ______ are you planning to stay here?

18 ______ restaurant did Jack and his family eat dinner at yesterday?

[19~20] 다음 문장에서 어법상 어색한 부분을 찾아 바르게 고쳐 쓰시오.

19

What do Julia enjoy doing in her spare time?

______ → ______

20 When time do you usually get up on Sundays?

_______________ → _______________

[21~23] 다음 대화의 빈칸에 알맞은 의문사를 쓰시오.

21
A: __________ did he open the window?
B: Because it was hot.

22
A: __________ do you take a shower?
B: I take a shower three or four times a week.

23
A: __________ will attend the seminar this evening?
B: A woman in the Sales Department.

[24~26] 다음 우리말과 같도록 괄호 안의 단어를 바르게 배열하시오.

24 너는 보라색과 주황색 중에서 어떤 색깔을 좋아하니?

→ ______________________________, purple or orange?
(do / which / like / color / you)

25 당신의 비행기는 몇 시에 출발합니까?

→ What ______________________________?
(does / time / your / leave / plane)

26 제가 공항까지 어떻게 갈 수 있나요?

→ ______________________________?
(how / get / I / can / to / airport / the)

[27~28] 다음 중 어법상 어색한 문장을 두 개 찾아 바르게 고쳐 쓰시오.

ⓐ Who brother is that boy?
ⓑ When is your mom's birthday?
ⓒ Where did you leaving your wallet?
ⓓ How was your trip to London during the vacation?
ⓔ Which sport is your favorite, tennis or basketball?

27 ________________ → ________________

28 ________________ → ________________

[29~30] 다음 대화의 밑줄 친 우리말을 주어진 단어를 사용하여 영작하시오.

29

A: Jake, 너는 언제 나에게 이메일을 보냈니?
(when / send / to / the e-mail)
B: Two days ago.
A: Really? I'll check again.

→ ________________________________

30

A: Excuse me. 여기에서 시청까지 얼마나 걸리나요?
(how / take / here / City Hall)
B: It takes 15 minutes by subway.
A: Thank you.

→ ________________________________

CHAPTER

09

문장의 종류

UNIT 01 명령문

'~해라, ~하세요'와 같은 명령문은 주어 You를 없애고, 동사원형으로 문장을 시작해야 해요.

	긍정 명령문		부정 명령문	
be동사	Be	quiet.	Don't be	quiet.
일반동사	Close	the door.	Don't close	the door.

다음 문장을 |보기|와 같이 명령문으로 바꾸어 쓰시오.

|보기|

You should do your best. → Do your best.

You shouldn't take a picture here. → Don't take a picture here.

01 You shouldn't sit on the desk. → ______________________

02 You shouldn't eat too much. → ______________________

03 You should open the box. → ______________________

04 You should sing a song together. → ______________________

05 You shouldn't swim in this river. (never 사용) → ______________________

06 You should carry this bag for me. → ______________________

07 You shouldn't watch TV after dinner. → ______________________

08 You shouldn't use this computer. → ______________________

UNIT 02 청유문

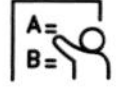

'~하자'처럼 같이 하자고 제안을 할 때 〈Let's+동사원형〉으로 쓰세요.

	긍정 청유문		부정 청유문	
be동사	Let's be	quiet.	Let's not be	quiet.
일반동사	Let's close	the door.	Let's not close	the door.

다음 우리말과 같도록 어법상 어색한 부분을 찾아 바르게 고쳐 쓰시오.

01 Let's goes swimming on Sunday. (일요일에 수영하러 가자.) __________ → __________

02 Let's eating something there. (거기서 뭔가 좀 먹자.) __________ → __________

03 Let's don't stop there. (거기서 멈추지 말자.) __________ → __________

04 Lets get some exercise. (운동을 좀 하자.) __________ → __________

05 Let's to go to his birthday party. (그의 생일 파티에 가자.) __________ → __________

06 Let's not to leave too late. (너무 늦게 떠나지 말자.) __________ → __________

07 Let's has a pet at home. (집에서 애완동물을 키우자.) __________ → __________

08 Let's will go skiing tomorrow. (내일 스키 타러 가자.) __________ → __________

09 Let's do not that again. (다시는 그러지 말자.) __________ → __________

UNIT 03 부가의문문 1

평서문 뒤에 '그렇지?, 그렇지 않니?'라고 확인을 구하는 부가의문문의 사용법을 알아 두세요.

	평서문,	+부가의문문		평서문,	+부가의문문
be동사	긍정	be동사의 부정형+주격 인칭대명사?	일반동사	긍정	do동사의 부정형+주격 인칭대명사?
	부정	be동사의 긍정형+주격 인칭대명사?		부정	do동사의 긍정형+주격 인칭대명사?

주의 대답은 긍정이면 무조건 Yes, 부정이면 무조건 No로 해야 해요.

주의 부가의문문에서 am의 부정은 aren't로 한다는 것에 주의하세요. I am too late, aren't I?

다음 빈칸에 알맞은 부가의문문과 대답을 쓰시오.

01 She is kind. ________________? – Yes, ________________.

02 Sam is a writer. ________________? – No, ________________.

03 You like swimming. ________________? – Yes, ________________.

04 He didn't clean his room. ________________? – Yes, ________________.

05 You were tired yesterday. ________________? – No, ________________.

06 You don't like pop music. ________________? – No, ________________.

07 The girl runs fast. ________________? – Yes, ________________.

08 This suitcase is not yours. ________________? – No, ________________.

09 Mina and Minji are sisters. ________________? – No, ________________.

UNIT 04 부가의문문 2

조동사가 있는 문장이나 명령문, 청유문의 부가의문문을 만드는 방법에 유의하세요.

	평서문,	+부가의문문		평서문,	+부가의문문
조동사	긍정	조동사의 부정형+주격 인칭대명사?	명령문	긍정/부정	will you?
	부정	조동사의 긍정형+주격 인칭대명사?	청유문		shall we?

다음 빈칸에 알맞은 부가의문문을 쓰시오.

01 Turn on the light. ________________?

02 You won't be late. ________________?

03 They will come to Korea. ________________?

04 Mary can't dance well. ________________?

05 Let's have lunch here. ________________?

06 My brother can ride a bicycle. ________________?

07 It won't rain tomorrow. ________________?

08 Let's not waste time. ________________?

UNIT 05 부정의문문

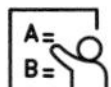

'~이지 않니?'와 같이 부정으로 질문할 때는 부정의문문을 쓰세요.

	긍정의문문	부정의문문
be동사	Were you angry?	Weren't you angry?
일반동사	Do you like music?	Don't you like music?
조동사	Can you speak English?	Can't you speak English?

주의 대답은 부가의문문처럼 긍정이면 무조건 Yes, 부정이면 무조건 No로 해야 해요.

다음 우리말과 같도록 괄호 안의 단어를 사용하여 질문을 완성하시오.

01 그녀는 책을 읽고 있지 않지? (read) → ____________________ a book?

02 너는 나와 낚시하러 가지 않을래? (go) → ____________________ fishing with me?

03 그는 패션에 관심 있지 않니? (interested) → ____________________ in fashion?

04 너는 내 휴대폰을 사용하지 않았지? (use) → ____________________ my cell phone?

UNIT 06 선택의문문

둘 중 하나를 고르도록 묻고자 할 때는 or를 넣어 선택의문문으로 만드세요.

일반의문문	선택의문문
Is this cap yours?	Is this cap yours or your brother's?
Who ate my pizza?	Who ate my pizza, Tom or Jerry?
What do you want?	Which do you want, tea or juice?

다음 우리말과 같도록 괄호 안의 말을 사용하여 바르게 영작하시오.

01 너는 돌아가고 싶니 아니면 여기 있고 싶니? (want / return / stay)

→ ____________________

02 너와 Jason 중에서 누가 더 빨리 달리니? (runs / faster)

→ ____________________

03 너는 축구와 야구 중 어느 스포츠를 좋아하니? (sports / prefer / soccer / baseball)

→ ____________________

04 그는 사무실에 오늘 올까요 아니면 내일 올까요? (come / the office / today / tomorrow)

→ ____________________

05 너는 점심으로 샌드위치가 좋니 아니면 햄버거가 좋니? (like / for / would / a sandwich / a hamburger)

→ ____________________

06 이것과 저것 중 어느 책상이 더 크니? (desk / bigger / this one / that one)

→ ____________________

UNIT 07 what으로 시작하는 감탄문

'정말[참] ~한 …이구나!'와 같이 명사에 대한 감탄을 나타낼 때는 what으로 시작하는 감탄문으로 표현하세요.

What	–	(형용사)	셀 수 없는 명사	(주어+동사)!	What big bread (it is)!
	a(n)	(형용사)	셀 수 있는 단수 명사		What a wonderful world (it is)!
	–	(형용사)	셀 수 있는 복수 명사		What fast boys (they are)!

다음 우리말과 같도록 괄호 안의 단어를 바르게 배열하시오.

01 그녀는 정말 똑똑한 소녀구나! (smart / what / she / is / girl / a)

→ ____________________

02 야구는 정말 흥미진진한 게임이구나! (what / is / exciting / an / game / baseball)

→ ____________________

03 그들은 정말 좋은 사람들이구나! (nice / are / people / they / what)

→ ____________________

04 이것들은 정말 맛있는 사과들이구나! (apples / what / these / delicious / are)

→ ____________________

05 그것은 정말 오래된 미술관이구나! (museum / it / an / what / is / old)

→ ____________________

06 당신은 정말 아름다운 집을 가지고 있군요! (you / a / what / lovely / have / house)

→ ____________________

UNIT 08 how로 시작하는 감탄문

'정말[참] ~하구나!'와 같이 형용사나 부사에 대한 감탄은 how로 시작하는 감탄문으로 표현하세요.

How	형용사	(주어+동사)!	How big (the apple is)!
	부사		How fast (the boys can run)!

다음 우리말과 같도록 괄호 안의 단어를 사용하여 바르게 영작하시오.

01 이 케이크는 정말 맛있구나! (delicious) ____________________

02 그녀는 정말 행복해 보이는구나! (looks) ____________________

03 그 남자는 정말 공손하구나! (polite) ____________________

04 그녀는 정말 느리게 걷는구나! (slowly) ____________________

05 그 이야기는 정말 재미있군요! (interesting) ____________________

06 그 영화는 정말 지루했구나! (boring) ____________________

중간고사·기말고사 실전문제

객관식 (01~15) / 주관식 (16~30)

학년과 반 　 이름 　 객관식 　 / 15문항 　 주관식 　 / 15문항

[01~02] 다음 빈칸에 알맞은 것을 고르시오.

01

Julia is in the kitchen, ___________ she?

① is 　 ② are
③ does 　 ④ isn't
⑤ doesn't

02

___________ a fantastic trip!

① How 　 ② Why
③ What 　 ④ Whose
⑤ Which

[03~04] 다음 빈칸에 공통으로 들어갈 말을 고르시오.

03

• Do you go to school by bus ___________ on foot? • Which do you like better, beef ___________ pork?

① or 　 ② in
③ to 　 ④ but
⑤ and

04

• ___________ play tennis, shall we? • ___________ not forget their names.

① Do 　 ② Be
③ Don't 　 ④ Never
⑤ Let's

05 다음 빈칸에 들어갈 말이 나머지 넷과 다른 하나는?

① Dogs are the best pets, ___________ they?
② Your husband cooks well, ___________ he?
③ ___________ they drinking too much coffee?
④ ___________ you a member of the golf club?
⑤ Mina and Alex are studying in the library, ___________ they?

[06~07] 다음 중 어법상 어색한 것을 고르시오.

06 ① What a cute doll this is!
② Let's start our first music class!
③ How the ice cream delicious is!
④ Don't be afraid of making mistakes.
⑤ Spend time with your family in the new year.

07 ① Don't eat the cookies, will you?
② Minsu is wearing a blue shirt, isn't he?
③ You will go to bed early tonight, can't you?
④ Most of the students like to dance, don't they?
⑤ Sarah went to the Busan International Film Festival yesterday, didn't she?

08 다음 밑줄 친 부분을 바르게 고친 것은?

> There are two colors. Whose color do you want, pink or navy?

① Which ② Who
③ Where ④ How
⑤ When

09 다음 대화의 빈칸에 알맞은 것은?

> A: Mina invited you to her birthday party, ____________?
> B: Yes, she did.

① is she ② isn't she
③ did she ④ doesn't she
⑤ didn't she

10 다음 우리말을 영어로 바르게 옮긴 것은?

> 네 아버지는 차를 운전할 수 없니?

① Does your father drive?
② Can't your father drive?
③ Isn't your father a good driver?
④ Your father can drive, can't he?
⑤ Your father won't drive, will he?

11 다음 대화의 빈칸에 알맞은 것을 모두 고르면?

> A: Mike and Jessica usually go to concerts together, don't they?
> B: ____________

① Yes, they do.
② Yes, they are.
③ Yes, they were.
④ No, they don't.
⑤ No, they didn't.

12 다음 문장을 감탄문으로 바르게 바꾼 것은?

> She is a very famous lawyer.

① What a famous lawyer is she!
② What she is a famous lawyer!
③ What a famous lawyer she is!
④ What is a famous lawyer she!
⑤ What she a famous lawyer is!

13 다음 빈칸에 들어갈 말이 순서대로 짝지어진 것은?

> • ____________ a beautiful flower this is!
> • Who is the winner of the card game, Jisu ____________ Alex?
> • Thomas worked for the sick and poor. ____________ nice!

① How – or – What
② What – or – How
③ Who – but – How
④ What – and – How
⑤ How – and – Which

14 다음 밑줄 친 부분을 바르게 고치지 못한 것은?

① Driving carefully! The road is slippery.
→ Drive
② We can't meet her often, will we?
→ can
③ Is your sister a student and a professor?
→ or
④ What amazing the pyramids are!
→ How
⑤ Let's have a cup of coffee, will you?
→ do you

15 다음 중 어법상 어색한 문장의 개수는?

> • Let's make not any decisions now.
> • How fluently she speaks Korean!
> • Looks at the board and choose your favorite book.
> • Jina wasn't late for school this morning, were she?
> • Which do you prefer, Chinese food or Japanese food?

① 1개 ② 2개
③ 3개 ④ 4개
⑤ 5개

[16~18] 다음 괄호 안에서 알맞은 말을 골라 쓰시오.

16 (Whose / Which / Who) movies do you like better, comedies (and / so / or) animations?

→ ____________________

17

> A: Mr. Jones is a great film director, (isn't he / is he / does he)?
> B: No, he isn't. His movies are boring.

→ ____________________

18

A: Didn't you and your sister have a good time at the beach?
B: Yes, (they did / I did / we did). There were a lot of stars in the sky.

→ ________________

[19~21] 다음 문장에서 어법상 <u>어색한</u> 부분을 찾아 바르게 고쳐 쓰시오.

19 What an interesting story they are!

________________ → ________________

20 My brother won't get the job, should we?

________________ → ________________

21 Everyone, please sit on your chair and not move.

________________ → ________________

[22~23] 다음 대화의 빈칸에 알맞은 대답을 쓰시오.

22

A: It is a great place for swimming and fishing, isn't it?
B: ________, ________ ________.
Let's bet who catches the most fish.

23

A: Doesn't Bill like watching sports?
B: ________, ________ ________.
He likes watching dramas.

[24~26] 다음 우리말과 같도록 괄호 안의 단어를 바르게 배열하시오.

24

그녀는 "정말 멋진 세상이야!"라고 생각했다.
(world / what / wonderful / a)

→ "________________!" she thought.

25

수미가 수영 대회에서 1등을 했다. 그녀는 정말 빨리 수영하는구나!
(she / how / swims / fast)

→ Sumi won first place in the swimming contest. ________________!

26

문을 열지 맙시다, 그럴까요?
(the / shall / not / let's / open / we / door)

→ ________________________________?

[27~28] 다음 글에서 어법상 어색한 부분을 두 군데 찾아 바르게 고쳐 쓰시오.

It's a sunny day. Today, my family is going to go camping. Everyone is happy. How a wonderful day! My mom says "It is lovely weather, doesn't it?"

27 ______________ → ______________

28 ______________ → ______________

[29~30] 다음 대화의 밑줄 친 우리말을 괄호 안의 말을 사용하여 영작하시오.

29

A: You don't have any brothers or sisters, do you?
B: 아니, 없어. 난 외동이야. (I / only / child)
A: Aren't you lonely?
B: Hmm. Sometimes I feel lonely.

→ ________________________________

30

A: What should we eat for dinner?
B: How about fish?
A: 저녁으로 생선 먹지 말자. (let's / have)
Let's have chicken.
B: Sounds good.

→ ________________________________

CHAPTER

10

문장의 형식

UNIT 01 문장의 요소

문장을 구성하는 5대 요소인 주어, 동사(서술어), 목적어, 보어, 수식어를 외워 두세요.

주어	문장의 주체 (~은/는/이/가)	보어	주어나 목적어 보충 설명
동사	주어의 상태, 동작 서술 (~이다, ~하다)	수식어	명사, 동사, 문장 수식
목적어	동작의 대상 (~을/를, ~에게)		

다음 |보기|와 같이 문장 요소에 밑줄을 긋고, 문장 요소에 약자를 쓰시오.

|보기|

Sally helps her mother every evening. (S: 주어, V: 동사, C: 보어, O: 목적어, M: 수식어)
S V O M

01 Today is Sunday.

02 Mr. Smith bought his son a new car.

03 I met my friends in the park.

04 My brother is very smart.

05 You get up early every morning.

06 She studies English every day.

07 They called their baby Star.

08 They are swimming in the sea.

UNIT 02 1형식 / 2형식 문장

〈주어+동사〉 뒤에 보어가 있는지 없는지에 따라 문장의 1형식 또는 2형식으로 구분하세요.

1형식	주어+동사	The train/arrived (on time).	주어와 동사만으로 완전한 문장
2형식	주어+동사+보어	She/became/a nurse (in 2020).	보어가 없으면 불완전한 문장

참고 부사, 전치사구와 같은 부사적 수식어는 구성 요소에서 제외해요.

다음 문장의 문장 요소에 밑줄을 긋고, 문장 요소에 약자를 쓴 후 빈칸에 문장 형식을 쓰시오.

01 Mike runs very fast. ______

02 She looks young. ______

03 Sally's backpack is blue. ______

04 Judy dances very well. ______

05 The teacher is tall and handsome. ______

06 She walks to school every morning. ______

07 My father is a famous cook. ______

08 We went to the library every day. ______

09 The leaves turn red in autumn. ______

10 Our family lived in America for two years. ______

UNIT 03 감각동사+형용사

2형식 문장에는 be동사와 감각동사가 주로 사용돼요. be동사와 감각동사가 취하는 보어의 종류와 그 의미를 파악하세요.

보어를 취하는 동사		보어	의미
be동사	be, am, are, is, was, were	명사, 형용사	~이다, ~하다
감각동사	feel, look, sound, smell, taste	형용사	~하게 느끼다, ~해 보이다, ~한 소리가 나다, ~한 냄새가 나다, ~한 맛이 나다

참고 감각동사 뒤에 명사를 쓰려면 〈감각동사+like+(a/an)+명사〉로 쓰면 돼요.

다음 우리말과 같도록 괄호 안의 단어를 사용하여 바르게 영작하시오. (단, 필요시 동사 변형 가능)

01 그것은 나쁜 냄새가 난다. (smell / bad) ______

02 이 파이는 맛이 좋다. (good / taste) ______

03 그는 매우 친절해 보인다. (kind / look / so) ______

04 이 비누는 냄새가 좋다. (soap / good / smell) ______

05 그것은 촉감이 매우 부드럽다. (soft / very / feel) ______

06 그녀는 소년처럼 보인다. (like / look) ______

UNIT 04 3형식 문장

〈주어+동사〉 뒤에 보어(~이다)가 오면 2형식, 목적어(~을, ~를)가 오면 3형식 문장이라는 점을 꼭 알아 두세요.

3형식	주어+동사+목적어	The train/takes/us (to Busan).	목적어(~을, ~를)가 없으면 불완전

다음 우리말과 같도록 괄호 안의 말을 바르게 배열하시오.

01 그녀는 바이올린을 매우 잘 연주한다. (she / the violin / well / plays / very)

→ ______

02 그는 파란 셔츠를 입고 있다. (he / a blue shirt / wearing / is)

→ ______

03 나는 어젯밤에 파티에서 Tom을 만났다. (met / last night / at the party / Tom / I)

→ ______

04 내 여동생과 나는 매일 아침 산책을 한다. (I / take / every morning / a walk / my sister / and)

→ ______

05 그녀는 보통 아침으로 샐러드를 먹는다. (she / a salad / eats / for breakfast / usually)

→ ______

06 그들은 주말에 함께 영어를 공부한다. (English / they / on weekends / together / study)

→ ______

UNIT 05 4형식 문장

목적어 두 개 '~에게'와 '~을'을 취하는 4형식 동사들을 알아 두세요.

4형식 어순	수여동사(~에게 …을 ~해주다)	간접목적어	직접목적어
	give, make, show, send, ask, tell, lend, get, bring, teach, buy, cook, bake 등	~에게	~을

다음 우리말과 같도록 괄호 안의 말을 사용하여 4형식 문장으로 완성하시오. (단, 필요시 동사 변형 가능)

01 그는 그의 딸에게 의자를 만들어 줄 것이다. (a chair / make / his daughter)

→ He ______________________________.

02 James는 주말마다 우리에게 수영을 가르쳐 준다. (us / on weekends / teach / swimming)

→ James ______________________________.

03 나는 내 여동생에게 새 드레스를 사 주었다. (my sister / buy / a new dress)

→ I ______________________________.

04 나의 삼촌은 그의 아들에게 장난감 상자를 만들어 주었다. (a toy box / make / his son)

→ My uncle ______________________________.

05 나는 내 친구에게 생일 카드를 보낼 것이다. (send / a birthday card / my friend)

→ I ______________________________.

06 Lisa는 그녀의 부모님께 그 소식을 말씀 드렸다. (the news / her parents / tell)

→ Lisa ______________________________.

UNIT 06 3형식 ↔ 4형식 문장 전환

4형식 문장을 3형식으로 바꿀 때, 동사에 따라 사용하는 전치사에 유의하세요.

3형식 어순	수여동사	직접목적어		간접목적어
		직접목적어 (~을)	to	간접목적어 (~에게)
	get, make, buy, cook, bake, build, find		for	
	ask, inquire	a question, a favor	of	

다음 문장을 4형식 문장은 3형식으로, 3형식 문장은 4형식으로 바꾸어 쓰시오.

01 My parents bought me a new bicycle. → My parents bought ______________________________.

02 He gave her a lot of presents. → He gave ______________________________.

03 She bought us some cookies. → She bought ______________________________.

04 He gave some money to his son. → He gave ______________________________.

05 I'll make a pretty bag for my mother. → I'll make ______________________________.

06 Sam sent me a message. → Sam sent ______________________________.

UNIT 07 5형식 문장의 목적격보어 1

목적어 뒤에 목적어를 설명하는 명사나 형용사 보어가 있는 5형식 문장을 알아 두세요.

5형식 어순	명사/형용사를 목적격보어로 쓰는 5형식 동사	목적어	목적격보어
	make, call, name, find, keep, elect, think, believe, consider 등	~을, ~이/가	명사, 형용사

다음 우리말과 같도록 괄호 안의 말을 바르게 배열하시오.

01 그들은 그 아기를 Lisa라고 이름 지었다. (they / Lisa / named / the baby)

→ ______________________________

02 내 남동생은 그의 방을 깨끗하게 유지했다. (my brother / his room / clean / kept)

→ ______________________________

03 그 이야기는 우리를 기쁘게 만들었다. (the story / happy / us / made)

→ ______________________________

04 우리는 그 컴퓨터 게임이 재미있다는 것을 알았다. (the computer game / we / found / interesting)

→ ______________________________

05 그 남자를 화나게 하지 마라. (make / angry / don't / the man)

→ ______________________________

06 그 뉴스는 그녀를 유명하게 만들었다. (famous / her / made / the news)

→ ______________________________

UNIT 08 5형식 문장의 목적격보어 2

목적격보어로 to부정사를 쓰는 동사들을 알아 두세요.

5형식 어순	to부정사를 목적격보어로 쓰는 5형식 동사	목적어	목적격보어
	want, ask, tell, expect, enable, encourage, allow, advise, order, get, permit, force 등	~에게, ~가	to부정사 (~하기를/~하라고)

참고 to부정사의 부정은 to 앞에 not을 쓰면 돼요.

다음 우리말과 같도록 괄호 안의 동사를 사용하여 빈칸에 알맞은 형태로 쓰시오. (단, 필요시 동사 변형 가능)

01 그는 내가 의사가 되기를 바란다. (be / want) → He ______________ a doctor.

02 그녀는 그에게 그것을 가져오라고 부탁했다. (ask / bring) → She ______________ it.

03 그는 그녀에게 휴식을 취하라고 말했다. (tell / take) → He ______________ a rest.

04 나는 그녀가 피아노 치는 것을 허락했다. (allow / play) → I ______________ the piano.

05 그녀는 나에게 가라고 충고했다. (advise / go) → She ______________.

06 나는 그에게 그 문제를 풀도록 용기를 북돋았다. (solve / encourage) → I ______________ the problem.

UNIT 09 5형식 문장의 목적격보어 3

사역동사(~에게 …하도록 시키다)는 목적격보어를 원형부정사로 쓰세요.

	원형부정사를 목적격보어로 쓰는 사역동사	목적어	목적격보어	의미
5형식 어순	make, have	~이/가	원형부정사	~가 …하게 만들다, 시키다
	let			~가 …하게 두다

참고 원형부정사란 to부정사에서 to가 없는 동사원형으로 쓰는 부정사를 말해요.

주의 help는 목적격보어로 to부정사와 원형부정사 모두를 쓰지만, get은 오직 to부정사만 써야 해요.

다음 우리말과 같도록 괄호 안의 말을 바르게 배열하시오.

01 그는 나에게 이 가방들을 옮기도록 시켰다. (had / carry / these bags / me / he)

→ ______________________________

02 제가 도와드리겠습니다. (let / you / help / me)

→ ______________________________

03 나는 그에게 그것을 하도록 시키겠다. (do / have / him / I'll / it)

→ ______________________________

04 그녀는 내게 숙제를 하도록 시켰다. (me / made / my homework / she / do)

→ ______________________________

05 제가 당신에게 제 친구를 소개하겠습니다. (let / introduce / my friend / me / you / to)

→ ______________________________

06 그는 그의 여동생이 영어 공부하는 것을 도와준다. (study / helps / he / his sister / English)

→ ______________________________

중간고사·기말고사 실전문제

객관식 (01~15) / 주관식 (16~30)

정답과 해설 • 81쪽

학년과 반　　이름　　객관식　　/ 15문항　　주관식　　/ 15문항

[01~02] 다음 빈칸에 알맞은 것을 고르시오.

01

Black coffee ______ bitter.

① gives　② makes
③ tastes　④ watches
⑤ sounds

02

Regular exercise can help you ______ weight.

① lose　② lost
③ losing　④ to losing
⑤ to be lost

[03~04] 다음 밑줄 친 부분을 어법에 맞게 고친 것을 고르시오.

03

My father won't let me <u>going</u> surfing every weekend.

① go　② goes
③ to go　④ gone
⑤ to going

04

This blanket is made from wool. So it feels very <u>softly</u>.

① soften　② soft
③ softness　④ to soften
⑤ softing

05 다음 빈칸에 들어갈 말이 순서대로 짝지어진 것은?

• Sora bought a new coat ______ me.
• Jessica asked me ______ lend her some money.

① to – to　② of – for
③ from – into　④ for – like
⑤ for – to

[06~07] 다음 중 어법상 <u>어색한</u> 것을 고르시오.

06 ① The leaves turned yellow.
② The sun is shining brightly.
③ His attitude made them angrily.
④ Most of us eat too much meat.
⑤ Jimin lent her friend her new bag.

07 ① I want you do your homework now.
② Ms. Han made her son-in-law a lawyer.
③ Mary helped him to finish painting the wall.
④ I don't think a lot of money makes me happy.
⑤ This house keeps them safe from wild animals.

08 다음 밑줄 친 부분의 쓰임이 나머지 넷과 <u>다른</u> 하나는?

① The movie <u>made</u> him a big star.
② This black shirt <u>makes</u> you look slim.
③ My mom <u>makes</u> me water the flowers.
④ The machine <u>made</u> our work go quickly.
⑤ Peter <u>made</u> some new friends during the festival.

[09~10] 다음 우리말을 영어로 바르게 옮긴 것을 고르시오.

09

하늘에 있는 구름은 용처럼 보인다.

① The cloud in the sky sees a dragon.
② The cloud in the sky looks a dragon.
③ The cloud in the sky saw like a dragon.
④ The cloud in the sky looks like a dragon.
⑤ The cloud in the sky looked like a dragon.

10

그는 나에게 아침에 일찍 일어나라고 말했다.

① He told me get up early in the morning.
② He tells me to get up early in the morning.
③ He told me getting up early in the morning.
④ He told me to get up early in the morning.
⑤ He tells to get me up early in the morning.

11 다음 주어진 문장과 의미가 같은 것은?

She asked a hard question of me.

① She asked a hard question me.
② She asked me a hard question.
③ She asked me of a hard question.
④ She asked a hard question to me.
⑤ She asked for me a hard question.

12 다음 빈칸 ⓐ~ⓔ에 알맞지 <u>않은</u> 것은?

- He ____ⓐ____ for a large company.
- The TV show sounds ____ⓑ____.
- She bought a necklace ____ⓒ____ her mom.
- Ms. Oliver made him ____ⓓ____ her car.
- My father doesn't allow me ____ⓔ____ too much junk food.

① ⓐ works　　② ⓑ interesting
③ ⓒ for　　④ ⓓ to fix
⑤ ⓔ to eat

13 다음 |보기|의 밑줄 친 look과 쓰임이 같은 것은?

|보기|
This ring looks really expensive.

① Please take a look at the map.
② This bread looks delicious. Can I try it?
③ Can you help me look for my passport?
④ I'm really looking forward to meeting him.
⑤ Look both ways carefully before crossing the street.

14 다음 중 어법상 어색한 부분을 바르게 고친 것을 모두 고르면?

- You must kept your hands cleanly.
- My mother wanted me eating more fruits and vegetables.
- Tony has his sister to return the books to the library yesterday.

① kept → keep
② cleanly → cleaned
③ eating → to eat
④ has → will have
⑤ to return → returning

15 다음 ⓐ~ⓔ 중 어법상 옳은 것끼리 짝지어진 것은?

ⓐ This story sounds strangely.
ⓑ My grandmother made a doll for me.
ⓒ I gave a letter my dad on his last birthday.
ⓓ I will tell him to follow the instructions below.
ⓔ Jiho got a new cell phone. It made him happy.

① ⓐ, ⓑ ② ⓐ, ⓒ
③ ⓑ, ⓓ, ⓔ ④ ⓒ, ⓓ
⑤ ⓒ, ⓓ, ⓔ

[16~17] 다음 빈칸에 알맞은 말을 쓰시오.

16 My friend Alex sent some snacks and books __________ me.

17 Jessica is making furniture __________ Yujin as a wedding present.

[18~20] 다음 문장에서 어법상 어색한 부분을 찾아 바르게 고쳐 쓰시오.

18 Look at the old couple. They look happily.

__________ → __________

19 She helped Tommy choosing some new clothes.

__________ → __________

20 Please don't ask me explain the problem. You wouldn't understand.

__________ → __________

[21~23] 다음 괄호 안의 단어를 사용하여 우리말과 같도록 빈칸에 알맞은 말을 쓰시오.

21

이 운동복은 편안해 보여요. 제가 한 번 입어 볼게요. (comfortable)

→ This sportswear __________ __________. I want to try it on.

22

소미와 민호는 그들의 정원을 아름답게 유지하기 위해 최선을 다했다. (keep / beautiful)

→ Somi and Minho did their best to __________ __________ __________ __________.

23

부탁 하나만 들어줄래요? 제게 물 한 컵을 가져다 주세요. (bring / to)

→ Can you do me a favor? Please __________ __________ __________ __________ __________ __________ __________.

[24~25] 다음 대화의 밑줄 친 우리말을 3형식과 4형식 문장으로 영작하시오.

24

A: What does Mr. Jacob teach? B: Jacob 씨는 우리에게 영어를 가르치셔.

→ ____________________ (3형식)

→ ____________________ (4형식)

25

A: What did she buy at the shop? B: 그녀는 그녀의 남동생에게 장갑 한 켤레를 사 주었어.

→ ____________________ (3형식)

→ ____________________ (4형식)

[26~28] 다음 대화의 상황에 맞게 빈칸에 알맞은 말을 쓰시오.

26

Alex: Can I borrow your textbook?
Jane: No!

→ Jane wouldn't let ______________________
______________________________.

27

Jian's brother: Jian, you can wear my sunglasses.
Jian: Thank you.

→ Jian's brother allowed ________________
______________________________.

28

Dad: Did you wash your hands? I told you to wash your hands when you get home.
Boy: Okay, I'll do that.

→ My dad makes ______________________
____________________ when I get home.

[29~30] 다음 대화에서 어법상 어색한 부분을 두 군데 찾아 바르게 고쳐 쓰시오.

A: How about going to the concert this weekend?
B: I'm sorry, but I can't. My mom won't let going me there. The math contest is just around the corner. My mom will make me to study for the contest this weekend.
A: Well, then let's go to a concert next time.
B: Thank you.

29 __________________ → __________________

30 __________________ → __________________

내가 가장 취약한 부분에 대해
요점 정리를 해 보세요.

CHAPTER

11

to부정사와 동명사

UNIT 01 to부정사의 명사적 용법 1

동사를 명사(~하기, ~하는 것)처럼 사용하려면 〈to부정사+동사원형〉의 형태로 만들어야 해요.

명사 역할 – 주어	주의
To become a scientist takes years. 과학자가 되는 것은 수년이 걸린다.	① to부정사는 뒤에 목적어나 부사구를 취할 수 있다. ② to부정사 주어는 3인칭 단수 취급한다. ③ to부정사의 부정은 to 앞에 not을 쓴다.

참고 to부정사(구) 주어(진주어)는 문장 뒤로 옮길 수 있는데, 이때 가(짜)주어 It을 주어 자리에 넣어야 해요.
It takes years to become a scientist.

다음 문장을 |보기|와 같이 가주어 It으로 시작하는 문장으로 바꾸어 쓰시오.

|보기|
To study English is fun. → It is fun to study English.

01 To get a job is very hard. → ______

02 To eat a lot is bad. → ______

03 To learn swimming is very exciting. → ______

04 To solve this problem is not easy. → ______

05 To read books is very useful. → ______

UNIT 02 to부정사의 명사적 용법 2

to부정사를 명사처럼 be동사 뒤에서 주격보어로 쓸 때는 '~하는 것(이다)'라고 해석해요.

명사 역할 – 주격보어	주의
My dream is to become a scientist. 나의 꿈은 과학자가 되는 것이다.	① to부정사는 뒤에 목적어나 부사구를 취할 수 있다. ② to부정사의 부정은 to 앞에 not을 쓴다.

다음 우리말과 같도록 괄호 안의 말을 바르게 배열하시오.

01 나의 취미는 영어책을 읽는 것이다. (read / my hobby / to / is / English books)
→ ______

02 나의 아버지의 계획은 새 차를 사는 것이다. (my father's plan / to / a new car / is / buy)
→ ______

03 Sally의 일은 옷을 디자인하는 것이다. (to / clothes / is / design / Sally's job)
→ ______

04 Mike의 취미는 그림을 그리는 것이다. (to / pictures / draw / is / Mike's hobby)
→ ______

05 나의 숙제는 일기를 쓰는 것이다. (keep / to / my homework / a diary / is)
→ ______

UNIT 03 to부정사의 명사적 용법 3

to부정사는 '~하는 것을'이라는 뜻으로 목적어 역할을 할 수 있어요. to부정사를 목적어로 쓰는 동사들을 파악하세요.

want, would like 원하다	hope 바라다	plan 계획하다	refuse 거절하다
wish 소망하다	promise 약속하다	choose 선택하다	fail 실패하다
expect 예상하다	agree 동의하다	decide 결정하다	need 필요가 있다

다음 우리말과 같도록 괄호 안의 단어를 사용하여 문장을 완성하시오. (단, 필요시 동사 변형 가능)

01 그는 해외로 갈 계획이다. (plan / go) → He ______________ abroad.

02 나는 그것을 안 하기로 결심했다. (decide / not / do) → I ______________ it.

03 그들은 지금 수영하기를 원한다. (want / swim) → They ______________ now.

04 그는 어떤 것도 말하지 않기로 약속했다. (promise / say) → He ______________ anything.

05 나는 그 가수를 만나기를 바란다. (hope / meet) → I ______________ the singer.

06 그녀는 산책하기로 동의했다. (agree / take) → She ______________ a walk.

UNIT 04 to부정사의 형용사적 용법

to부정사는 '~(해야) 할, ~하는'의 의미로 형용사처럼 명사를 꾸밀 수 있는데, 이때 어순에 주의하세요.

어순	형용사	명사	형용사	형용사 역할 to부정사
일반적인 명사의 경우	many	books		to read (읽어야 할, 읽을)
-thing/-one/-body의 경우		something	interesting	

다음 우리말과 같도록 괄호 안의 말을 바르게 배열하시오.

01 Tony는 만날 친구들이 많다. (friends / meet / a lot of / to)
→ Tony has ______________.

02 그녀는 먹을 과일이 약간 있다. (fruit / eat / to / some)
→ She has ______________.

03 추워요. 저에게 뜨거운 마실 것 좀 주세요. (hot / drink / something / to)
→ I feel cold. Give me ______________.

04 우리는 함께 얘기할 기회가 없다. (no / to / chance / talk)
→ We have ______________ together.

05 우리는 해야 할 숙제가 많다. (a lot of / do / to / homework)
→ We have ______________.

06 그는 먹을 것을 찾았다. (eat / something / to)
→ He looked for ______________.

UNIT 05 to부정사의 부사적 용법 1

to부정사가 주어, 목적어, 보어가 아니라면 부사의 역할을 하는 것으로 판단하세요.

~하기 위해서 (목적)	I exercise to lose weight.	몸무게를 줄이기 위해 운동한다.
~하게 되어, ~해서 (감정의 원인)	I'm happy to see you again.	너를 다시 만나서 행복하다.

다음 문장의 밑줄 친 부분과 쓰임이 같은 것을 |보기|에서 골라 기호를 쓰시오.

|보기|
ⓐ Sally went out to meet him. ⓑ I'm pleased to hear the news.

01 We went shopping to buy a bag. ______

02 I'm very happy to meet you again. ______

03 He studies very hard to pass the exam. ______

04 I turned on the TV to watch the soccer game. ______

05 He was pleased to hear from you. ______

06 My family went to a restaurant to have dinner. ______

07 I'm sorry to call you so late. ______

UNIT 06 to부정사의 부사적 용법 2

to부정사는 목적, 감정의 원인 이외에도 여러 의미로 쓰이므로 문맥에 맞게 해석해야 해요.

~하기에 …한 (형용사 수식)	This sentence is hard to understand.	이해하기에 어려운
~하다니 …한 (판단의 근거)	She must be clever to think of such an idea.	생각하다니 영리한
~해서 (결국) …하다 (결과)	The poor girl grew up to be a famous star.	자라서 스타가 됐다

다음 우리말과 같도록 괄호 안의 말을 바르게 배열하시오.

01 그녀는 커서 유명한 무용가가 되었다. (she / be / a famous dancer / to / grew up)

→ ______

02 그것을 믿다니 Sam은 바보임에 틀림없다. (Sam / believe / must / a fool / to / it / be)

→ ______

03 그 질문은 대답하기 어려웠다. (was / the question / answer / hard / to)

→ ______

04 그녀가 그렇게 말하다니 화난 것이 틀림없다. (she / so / say / be / angry / to / must)

→ ______

05 너의 전화번호는 기억하기 쉽다. (to / easy / your phone number / remember / is)

→ ______

06 영어는 배우기에 어렵지 않다. (not / English / to / difficult / is / learn)

→ ______

UNIT 07 동명사의 역할 1

동사를 명사처럼 쓸 때는 동사를 to부정사나 동명사(동사원형+-ing)로 만드세요.

명사 역할 – 주어	명사 역할 – 보어
Becoming a scientist takes years. 과학자가 되는 것은 수년이 걸린다.	My dream is becoming a scientist. 나의 꿈은 과학자가 되는 것이다.

다음 우리말과 같도록 괄호 안의 말을 바르게 배열하시오.

01 영어를 가르치는 것은 재미있다. (interesting / English / is / teaching)

→ ______________________________

02 내가 가장 좋아하는 취미는 산에 오르는 것이다. (mountains / is / my favorite hobby / climbing)

→ ______________________________

03 그녀의 좋은 습관은 아침에 일찍 일어나는 것이다. (getting up / is / in the morning / her good habit / early)

→ ______________________________

04 컴퓨터 게임을 하는 것은 아이들을 신나게 만든다. (computer games / excited / makes / playing / children)

→ ______________________________

05 나의 계획은 오늘 밤에 영화를 보는 것이다. (a movie / my plan / watching / tonight / is)

→ ______________________________

UNIT 08 동명사의 역할 2

to부정사만 목적어로 쓸 수 있는 동사가 있듯이, 동명사만 목적어로 쓰는 동사를 파악하세요.

enjoy 즐기다	keep 계속 ~하다	imagine 상상하다	practice 연습하다
avoid 피하다	quit 그만 두다	deny 부정하다	give up 포기하다
finish 마치다	mind 신경 쓰다	suggest 제안하다	consider 고려하다

참고 동명사는 to부정사와 달리, 전치사의 목적어로도 쓸 수 있어요.

다음 문장에서 어법상 어색한 부분을 찾아 바르게 고쳐 쓰시오.

01 He enjoyed made new friends. ____________ → ____________

02 I finished to write letters in English. ____________ → ____________

03 Thank you for listen to me. ____________ → ____________

04 Why does the boy keep shout? ____________ → ____________

05 Jessica can't give up to write music. ____________ → ____________

06 Did you finish do your homework? ____________ → ____________

07 Do you mind close the window? ____________ → ____________

08 She doesn't enjoy to eat fast food. ____________ → ____________

09 My father quit to smoking a year ago. ____________ → ____________

UNIT 09 동명사 목적어 vs. to부정사 목적어

동사별로 목적어를 to부정사로 쓸지, 동명사로 쓸지, 아니면 둘 다 쓸 수 있는지를 파악하세요.

to부정사만 목적어로 취하는 동사	want, would like, wish, expect, hope, promise, agree, plan, choose, decide, refuse, fail, need
동명사만 목적어로 취하는 동사	enjoy, keep, imagine, practice, avoid, quit, deny, give up, finish, mind, suggest, consider
둘 다 목적어로 취하는 동사	like, love, hate, prefer, begin, start, continue

다음 우리말과 같도록 괄호 안의 동사를 알맞은 형태로 빈칸에 쓰시오.

01 그녀는 그녀의 차를 팔기로 결심했다. (decide / sell)

→ She ______________________ her car.

02 시간을 낭비하는 것을 피하라. (avoid / waste)

→ ______________________ time.

03 그는 대학에 들어가기를 바란다. (hope / enter)

→ He ______________________ college.

04 우리는 거실 청소를 마쳤다. (finish / clean)

→ We ______________________ the living room.

05 소라는 그 동아리에 가입하기로 약속했다. (promise / join)

→ Sora ______________________ the club.

06 나는 그를 보리라 기대한다. (expect / see)

→ I ______________________ him.

07 나는 그녀의 옷을 훔친 것을 부인했다. (deny / steal)

→ I ______________________ her clothes.

08 부모님은 콘서트 보는 것을 즐기셨다. (enjoy / watch)

→ My parents ______________________ the concert.

09 그녀의 아들은 해외에서 공부하기로 동의했다. (agree / study)

→ Her son ______________________ abroad.

10 내 여동생은 갤러리에서 일하는 것을 관뒀다. (quit / work)

→ My sister ______________________ at the gallery.

11 그 범죄자는 어떤 질문에도 대답하기를 거부했다. (refuse / answer)

→ The criminal ______________________ any questions.

12 창문 좀 열어주시겠어요? (mind / open)

→ Would you ______________________ the window?

UNIT 10 동명사의 관용 표현

동명사와 자주 쓰이는 관용 표현은 외워야 쓸 수 있어요.

go -ing	~하러 가다	be busy -ing	~하느라 바쁘다
How/What about -ing?	~하는 게 어때?	spend+시간/돈+-ing	시간/돈을 ~하는 데 쓰다

다음 우리말과 같도록 괄호 안의 말을 사용하여 문장을 완성하시오. (단, 필요시 동사 변형 가능)

01 나는 하루 종일 숙제를 하느라 바빴다. (busy / do)

→ I ______________________________ my homework all day.

02 그는 그 일을 끝마치는 데 1주일이 걸렸다. (spend / finish / a week)

→ He ______________________________ the work.

03 점심 식사 같이 하는 게 어때? (how / have)

→ ______________________________ lunch together?

04 나는 이번 토요일에 엄마와 쇼핑을 갈 것이다. (go / shop)

→ I will ______________________________ with my mom this Saturday.

05 너의 부모님께 편지를 쓰는 게 어때? (what / write)

→ ______________________________ a letter to your parents?

06 아빠와 나는 매주 일요일을 테니스를 치면서 보낸다. (spend / play / every Sunday)

→ My father and I ______________________________ tennis.

07 미나는 리포트를 끝내느라 엄청 바쁘다. (busy / so / finish)

→ Mina ______________________________ her report.

중간고사·기말고사 실전문제

객관식 (01~15) / 주관식 (16~30)

학년과 반 | 이름 | 객관식 / 15문항 | 주관식 / 15문항

[01~03] 다음 빈칸에 알맞은 것을 고르시오.

01

Somi loves ________ to classical music.

① listen ② listens
③ listened ④ to listen
⑤ to listening

02

________ badminton is one of my mom's hobbies.

① Play ② Plays
③ Playing ④ Played
⑤ To playing

03

________ is important to finish the work on time.

① It ② There
③ Be ④ Do
⑤ That

[04~05] 다음 빈칸에 알맞지 않은 것을 고르시오.

04

We ________ to visit there.

① hope ② want
③ enjoy ④ plan
⑤ promise

05

Mr. Kim ________ talking with her.

① stopped ② avoided
③ finished ④ enjoyed
⑤ decided

06 다음 밑줄 친 부분을 어법에 맞게 고친 것은?

Get more information, visit our office.

① Gets ② Got
③ To be got ④ To get
⑤ To getting

07 다음 밑줄 친 ①~⑤ 중 어법상 어색한 것은?

> ① My father ② made sandwiches ③ and *gimbap* ④ eat ⑤ for lunch.

08 다음 밑줄 친 부분 중 어법상 어색한 것은?

① How about having some milk?
② What about going out for a walk?
③ Ms. Han was busy to answer the phone calls.
④ When young, I used to go fishing every weekend.
⑤ Minsu spends a lot of time watching soccer games.

[09~10] 다음 중 어법상 어색한 것을 고르시오.

09 ① I got a chance to be an actress.
② Do you need warm anything to drink?
③ Judy went to the bakery to buy a cake.
④ Are you expecting to win the gold medal?
⑤ I hope to move to a new house next year.

10 ① Her first job was selling cosmetics.
② Peter is interested in riding horses.
③ Don't give up learning something new.
④ Do you want to go camping with me?
⑤ Skipping breakfast are not good for your health.

[11~12] 다음 빈칸에 들어갈 말이 순서대로 짝지어진 것을 고르시오.

11

> • She was busy ________ for the exam.
> • His hobby is ________ furniture by himself.

① studies – makes
② studied – made
③ studying – making
④ to study – making
⑤ studying – to making

12

> • They are looking for a hotel ________.
> • It is bad manners ________ such a question.

① stay in – ask
② stayed in – asked
③ staying in – asking
④ to stay in – to ask
⑤ to stay in – to asking

[13~14] 다음 밑줄 친 부분과 쓰임이 같은 것을 고르시오.

13

She has many interesting books to read.

① To tell lies is wrong.
② I want to play the violin.
③ Jina grew up to be a fashion designer.
④ Maria saved money to go to Spain.
⑤ We don't have time to take a trip.

14

The players were so excited to win the game.

① My hobby is to collect antiques.
② Jisu was surprised to see him again.
③ Josh promised to be back before midnight.
④ He must be crazy to go out in this weather.
⑤ There are lots of interesting movies to watch.

15 다음 중 어법상 어색한 문장의 개수는?

- John finished reading the letter.
- Thank you for listen to my problems.
- I went to the library to return the books.
- I turned on my computer in order to check my e-mail.
- It is very difficult living without a smartphone these days.

① 1개 ② 2개 ③ 3개
④ 4개 ⑤ 5개

[16~18] 다음 문장에서 어법상 어색한 부분을 찾아 바르게 고쳐 쓰시오.

16 Would you mind close the door?

__________ → __________

17 Sophia went to the station to seen her uncle off.

__________ → __________

18 By recycle paper and cans, we can preserve the earth.

__________ → __________

[19~20] 다음 빈칸에 괄호 안의 말을 어법상 알맞은 형태로 쓰시오.

19

Mr. Smith stopped ____________ (smoke) because his doctor advised him to do so.

20

Nancy was happy ____________ (hear) the news.

[21~22] 다음 |보기|에서 단어를 고른 후 어법에 맞게 바꿔 대화를 완성하시오.

|보기|

eat turn go take see

21

A: Why did you go to the teacher's office yesterday?
B: I went there ________ ________ in my homework.

22

A: Why did you go to the top of the mountain?
B: I went there ________ ________ the sunrise.

[23~24] 다음 우리말과 같도록 괄호 안의 단어를 바르게 배열하시오.

23

밖이 더워. 마실 차가운 거 있니?
(cold / to / anything / drink)

→ It's hot outside. Do you have ____________ ____________________?

24

그녀는 좋은 자리를 잡기 위해서 일찍 도착했다.
(order / good / in / to / a / get / seat)

→ She arrived early ____________________ ____________________.

[25~26] 다음 대화에서 어법상 어색한 부분을 두 군데 찾아 바르게 고쳐 쓰시오.

A: What do you want to do this Saturday?
B: Well, I want to going hike with my dad. How about you?
A: I plan visiting my grandmother.
B: That sounds great.

25 ____________ → ____________

26 ____________ → ____________

[27～28] 다음 두 문장을 to부정사를 사용하여 의미가 같은 한 문장으로 바꿔 쓰시오.

27

- Mike wants to buy a house.
- He'll live in the house.

→ ______________________________

____

28

- Suji has a lot of homework.
- She has to finish it by tomorrow.

→ ______________________________

____

[29～30] 다음 우리말과 같도록 괄호 안의 단어를 사용하여 문장을 완성하시오. (단, 필요시 동사 변형 가능)

29

Julia는 책 읽는 것을 끝냈고, 친구들과 사진 찍는 것을 즐겼다.
(finish / enjoy / a book / pictures)

→ Julia ______________________________
and she ______________________________
with her friends.

30

세호는 축구하는 것을 즐기고, 장래에 축구 선수가 되기를 원한다.
(enjoy / play / be / future)

→ Seho ____________________ and he wants ______________________________.

CHAPTER

12

전치사

UNIT 01 시간 전치사 1

'(언제) ~에'라는 표현은 시간을 나타내는 명사에 따라 전치사 in, on, at 중 하나를 쓰세요.

in	기간이 있는 시간 (월, 오전, 오후, 연도)	on	날짜, 요일 (며칠, 무슨 요일, ~날)	at	정확한 시각 (몇 시, 몇 시 몇 분)

다음 괄호 안의 말과 알맞은 전치사를 사용하여 빈칸에 쓰시오.

01 우리는 보통 정오에 점심을 먹는다. (noon) → We usually have lunch ______________.

02 겨울 방학은 12월에 시작한다. (December) → Winter vacation starts ______________.

03 그 수업은 매일 8시에 시작한다. (8) → The class begins ______________ every day.

04 너는 저녁에 집에 있을 거니? (the evening) → Will you be home ______________?

05 나는 일요일에 그를 만날 것이다. (Sunday) → I'm going to meet him ______________.

06 나의 선생님은 2012년에 한국에 오셨다. (2012) → My teacher came to Korea ______________.

UNIT 02 시간 전치사 2

전치사 in, on, at 이외의 시간을 나타내는 전치사를 알아 두세요.

before	~ 전에	for	~ 동안 (구체적인 시간 동안)	from ~ to ...	~부터 …까지
after	~ 후에	during	~ 동안 (특정 행사, 기간 동안)		

다음 괄호 안의 말과 |보기|에서 알맞은 말을 골라 우리말과 같도록 문장을 완성하시오.

|보기|

for during before after from ~ to ...

01 나의 아버지는 월요일부터 금요일까지 일하신다. (Monday / Friday)
→ My father works ______________.

02 그는 지난밤에 3시간 동안 책을 읽었다. (hours)
→ He read a book ______________ last night.

03 그녀는 퇴근 후에 매일 수영하러 간다. (work)
→ She goes swimming every day ______________.

04 우리는 해가 뜨기 전에 공항으로 떠났다. (sunrise)
→ We left for the airport ______________.

05 나는 보통 낮 동안 TV를 보지 않는다. (the day)
→ I don't usually watch TV ______________.

06 그는 일주일 동안 우리와 함께 머물렀다. (a week)
→ He stayed with us ______________.

UNIT 03 장소 전치사

'(어디) ~에'라는 표현은 장소를 나타내는 명사에 따라 전치사 in, on, at 중 하나를 쓰세요.

in	어떤 공간이나 넓은 장소 안에 (방, 건물, 도시, 나라)	on	면에 붙어 위에 (바닥, 벽, 도로)	at	공간이 없는 장소나 하나의 지점에 (정류장, 공항)

다음 빈칸에 in, on, at 중에서 알맞은 전치사를 쓰시오.

01 I'm waiting for her __________ the school gate.
02 This is the most famous restaurant __________ Seoul.
03 Three girls are sitting __________ the bench.
04 There are a lot of people __________ the bus stop.
05 *The Mona Lisa* is the most famous painting __________ the world.
06 Baseball players are practicing __________ the field.
07 There is no one __________ the building.
08 Will you be __________ home tomorrow evening?

UNIT 04 위치 전치사

위치를 나타내는 다양한 전치사와 그 의미를 암기하세요.

near	~ 가까이	under	~ 아래	behind	~ 뒤에	next to	~ 옆에
over	~ 위로	between	~ 사이에	in front of	~ 앞에	across from	~ 맞은편에

다음 그림을 보고, 빈칸에 알맞은 말을 |보기|에서 골라 쓰시오.

|보기|
over under between behind in front of next to

01 Mina is sitting ______________ Sue and Junho.
02 Judy is standing ______________ Mina.
03 Sue is sitting ______________ Kevin.
04 Sejin is standing ______________ Judy.

05 Birds are flying ______________ the tree.
06 There are two cats ______________ the table.
07 The swing is ______________ the table.
08 The balls are ______________ the table and the swing.

UNIT 05 방향 전치사

방향을 나타내는 주요 전치사와 그 의미를 암기하세요.

to	~로, ~까지	into	~ 안으로	up	~ 위로
from	~에서부터	out of	~ 밖으로	down	~ 아래로

다음 우리말과 같도록 빈칸에 알맞은 전치사를 쓰시오.

01 계단 아래로 떨어지지 않도록 조심해라.

→ Be careful not to fall ___________ the stairs.

02 그녀는 문을 열고 방 안으로 들어갔다.

→ She opened the door and went ___________ the room.

03 그는 자전거에서 내려 언덕을 걸어 올라갔다.

→ He got off his bike and walked ___________ the hill.

04 우체국에 어떻게 가나요?

→ How can I get ___________ the post office?

05 밖에서 기다리지 마라! 집 안으로 들어와라.

→ Don't wait outside! Come ___________ the house.

06 서울에서 부산까지 기차로 4시간 정도 걸린다.

→ It takes about 4 hours ___________ Seoul ___________ Busan by train.

07 너는 왜 창문 밖으로 네 가방을 던졌니?

→ Why did you throw your bag ___________ the window?

08 거미 한 마리가 벽을 기어오르고 있다.

→ A spider is climbing ___________ the wall.

09 그녀는 다음 주 금요일에 인도네시아로 여행을 갈 것이다.

→ She is traveling ___________ Indonesia next Friday.

10 날이 어두워지고 있다. 산을 내려갑시다.

→ It's getting dark. Let's walk ___________ the mountain.

11 곰 두 마리가 동굴 밖으로 나왔다.

→ Two bears came ___________ the cave.

12 나는 버스정류장에서 집으로 걸어갔다.

→ I walked home ___________ the bus stop.

UNIT 06 주요 전치사

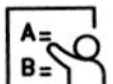 시간 · 장소 · 위치 · 방향 전치사 외에 자주 쓰는 전치사의 쓰임과 의미를 알아 두세요.

about	~에 대해	for	~을 위해	with	~와, ~을 가지고
of	~의	like	~처럼, ~ 같은	because of	~ 때문에

다음 빈칸에 알맞은 말을 |보기|에서 골라 쓰시오.

|보기|
of　for　about　like　with　because of

01 She eats enough vegetables ________________ good health.

02 I'd like to have a house ________________ a big garden.

03 It was a small animal ________________ a rat.

04 What is the title ________________ this song?

05 I came home ________________ my sister after school.

06 My brother is studying hard ________________ the exam.

07 Lisa was sorry ________________ the mistake.

08 The garden looked ________________ a jungle.

09 The old woman walked slowly ________________ her bad leg.

10 Do you know the capital ________________ Egypt?

11 I want to know ________________ your hobby.

12 A lot of shops closed ________________ the storm.

중간고사·기말고사 실전문제

객관식 (01~15) / 주관식 (16~30)

학년과 반 이름 객관식 / 15문항 주관식 / 15문항

[01~03] 다음 빈칸에 알맞은 것을 고르시오.

01

I worked at the store ________ 3 months.

① for ② in ③ from
④ with ⑤ during

02

There is a bus stop ________ the building.

① after ② out of
③ about ④ because of
⑤ in front of

03

They all enjoyed themselves ________ the garden party.

① in ② on ③ at
④ over ⑤ next to

[04~05] 다음 우리말과 같도록 빈칸에 알맞은 것을 고르시오.

04

Sir, what can I do ________ you?
(손님, 무엇을 도와 드릴까요?)

① of ② to ③ with
④ for ⑤ about

05

A rabbit is running ________ the hill.
(토끼가 언덕 위로 뛰어 가고 있다.)

① from ② up ③ down
④ near ⑤ under

[06~07] 다음 빈칸에 들어갈 말이 순서대로 짝지어진 것을 고르시오.

06

- Her plane arrives ________ eight thirty.
- Mr. Kim traveled around the world ________ 2018.

① at – in ② in – on
③ at – to ④ from – to
⑤ into – on

07

- She shares a room ________ her sister.
- Do you want to know more ________ the artist, Frida Kahlo?

① from – of
② with – about
③ with – like
④ over – about
⑤ between – because

08 다음 괄호 안의 ①~⑤ 중 because of가 들어갈 알맞은 곳은?

(①) Last weekend, (②) we couldn't (③) go camping (④) the heavy rain (⑤).

09 다음 빈칸에 들어갈 말이 나머지 넷과 다른 하나는?

① There is a hospital ________ my office.
② The handle ________ this pot is broken.
③ One ________ my goals is to be an actor.
④ They came out ________ the forest at night.
⑤ He made a speech in front ________ many people.

10 다음 밑줄 친 부분 중 어법상 어색한 것은?

① The laptop is on the table.
② Turn right at the second corner.
③ Jisu went to see her uncle in October.
④ Alex will meet his friend during 7 o'clock.
⑤ I'm going to watch the movie on Saturday.

[11~12] 다음 중 어법상 어색한 것을 고르시오.

11 ① I phoned my brother before going out.
② You can pick only one between the two.
③ The moon is over the roof of my house.
④ My aunt lived in Mexico from 1990 in 2010.
⑤ Julia has to finish the homework during the vacation.

12 ① What do you have at the box?
② Did you brush your teeth after dinner?
③ The church is located next to the river.
④ Three girls were under the parasol in the garden.
⑤ My boss will have a big announcement at 2 o'clock on Friday.

13 다음 우리말을 영어로 바르게 옮긴 것은?

나는 초대장을 봉투 안에 넣었다.

① I put the invitation card to the envelope.
② I put the invitation card for the envelope.
③ I put the invitation card into the envelope.
④ I put the invitation card because of the envelope.
⑤ I put the invitation card across from the envelope.

14 다음 밑줄 친 부분을 바르게 고치지 못한 것은?

① Yesterday I stayed home because a high fever. → because of
② My puppy is sleeping over the sofa in the living room. → on
③ Teddy put the gift for his wife from the table. → like
④ Mina walked with the street to go to the library. → up
⑤ When the alarm went off, people ran about the building. → out of

15 다음 중 어법상 어색한 문장의 개수는?

- The pencil fell between the books.
- The squirrel is climbing down the tree.
- They are looking for someone like you.
- She is going away during two weeks in December.
- Mr. Green met a lot of people at the concert hall.

① 1개　② 2개　③ 3개
④ 4개　⑤ 5개

[16~18] 다음 문장에서 어법상 어색한 부분을 찾아 바르게 고쳐 쓰시오.

16 We're going to visit Jeju in March 30th to April 3rd. I can't wait!

________ → ________

17 What time do you usually wake up at the morning?

________ → ________

18 The train will be delayed because an unexpected accident.

________ → ________

[19~20] 다음 빈칸에 알맞은 말을 |보기|에서 골라 쓰시오.

|보기|
like over about behind

19 There is a parking lot __________ the post office.

20 What a beautiful house! It's __________ a palace.

[21~22] 다음 |보기|에서 알맞은 말을 골라 대화를 완성하시오.

|보기|
in on at for during

21
A: How long did you sleep?
B: I slept __________ an hour and half.

22
A: Mom, I can't find my cell phone. I think I lost it.
B: I saw it __________ the bed __________ the evening.

[23~24] 다음 빈칸에 공통으로 알맞은 전치사를 쓰시오.

23
- Some apples fell __________ the tree.
- The shop is across __________ the police station.

→ __________

24
- This rock looks __________ a mushroom.
- When I was young, I was short __________ you.

→ __________

[25~26] 다음 우리말과 같도록 괄호 안의 단어를 바르게 배열하시오.

25
많은 사람들이 12월 31일에 ABC 타워에 모일 것이다.

→ Many people will gather __________
__________.
(at / Tower / ABC / 31st / on / December)

26
우리 이 화초를 창문 앞에 둘까?

→ Shall we put __________
__________?
(plant / in / this / front / window / of / the)

[27~28] 다음 대화에서 어법상 어색한 부분을 두 군데 찾아 바르게 고쳐 쓰시오.

A: Hello.
B: Hello, Yujin. This is Alex. Can you tell me how to get to your house?
A: Where are you?
B: I'm front the bookstore.
A: Go straight two blocks and turn left in the bakery. My house is across from the cafe.
B: Okay. Thank you.

27 ________________ → ________________

28 ________________ → ________________

[29~30] 다음 우리말과 같도록 괄호 안의 말을 사용하여 문장을 완성하시오.

29

김 선생님은 공항에 오늘 아침 9시에 도착했다.
(at / o'clock / the airport)

→ Mr. Kim arrived ________________ ________________ this morning.

30

사다리 아래를 걷는 것은 불운을 가져온다고 믿어진다.
(walking / brings / luck / a ladder / bad)

→ It is believed that ________________ ________________.

CHAPTER

13

접속사

UNIT 01 등위접속사 1: and, but

앞뒤 말을 파악하여 and(그리고) 또는 but(그러나)으로 연결하세요.

and	~와, 그리고	but	~이지만, 하지만

다음 두 문장을 접속사 and 또는 but을 사용하여 한 문장으로 쓰시오.

01 She likes cats. + She doesn't pet them.

→ ______________________________

02 I stayed at home. + I played computer games.

→ ______________________________

03 He can play the guitar. + He can't play the piano.

→ ______________________________

04 She went to the window. + She looked out.

→ ______________________________

05 Jake wants to drink some milk. + He doesn't have any money.

→ ______________________________

UNIT 02 등위접속사 2: or, so

앞뒤 말을 파악하여 or(또는) 또는 so(그래서)로 연결하세요.

or	또는, ~이거나	so	그래서, ~이므로

다음 우리말과 같도록 괄호 안의 말을 접속사 or 또는 so를 사용하여 바르게 배열하시오.

01 그는 너무 친절해서 모든 사람이 그를 좋아한다. (him / everyone / likes)

→ He is very kind ______________________________.

02 너는 열쇠를 책상 위에 두었니 아니면 서랍 속에 두었니? (on the desk / in the drawer)

→ Did you put the key ______________________________?

03 너는 집에 있어도 되고 나와 쇼핑을 가도 된다. (shopping / with / me / go)

→ You can stay at home ______________________________.

04 나는 돈이 없어서 그 책을 살 수 없다. (I / the book / buy / can't)

→ I have no money ______________________________.

05 Judy는 저녁 식사 후에 설거지를 하거나 방을 청소한다. (the dishes / her room / cleans / washes)

→ Judy ______________________________ after dinner.

06 너무 시끄러워서 너의 말을 잘 들을 수 없다. (hear / I / can't / well / you)

→ It is very noisy. ______________________________.

UNIT 03 종속접속사 1: when, before, after

앞뒤 문맥에 맞게 시간을 나타내는 접속사를 사용하세요.

when	~할 때, ~하면	before	~하기 전에	after	~한 후에

다음 우리말과 같도록 괄호 안의 말과 알맞은 접속사를 사용하여 문장을 완성하시오. (단, 필요시 동사 변형 가능)

01 너의 엄마는 네가 나가기 전에 너와 얘기하고 싶어 하신다. (go out)

→ Your mom wants to talk to you ______________________.

02 내가 버스를 기다리고 있을 때 비가 내리기 시작했다. (wait for / the bus)

→ It began to rain ______________________.

03 너는 여기로 이사 오기 전에 어디에서 살았었니? (move)

→ Where did you live ______________________?

04 너는 자전거를 탈 때에는 헬멧을 써야 한다. (ride / a bicycle)

→ You have to wear a helmet ______________________.

05 Sally는 잠자리에 들기 전에 보통 책을 읽는다. (go to bed)

→ Sally usually reads a book ______________________.

06 Mike는 그의 남동생이 집에 온 후에 나갈 수 있다. (come home)

→ Mike can go out ______________________.

UNIT 04 종속접속사 2: because, if

앞뒤 문맥에 맞게 조건이나 이유를 나타내는 접속사를 사용하세요.

because	~하기 때문에	if	~한다면

주의 시간이나 조건을 나타내는 부사절에서는 현재시제가 미래시제를 대신해요.

다음 두 문장을 괄호 안의 접속사를 사용하여 한 문장으로 쓰시오.

01 They didn't swim in the river. + The water was cold. (because)

→ ______________________, they didn't swim in the river.

02 You meet her. + Give her this letter. (if)

→ Give her this letter ______________________.

03 She took an umbrella. + It was going to rain. (because)

→ She took an umbrella ______________________.

04 My uncle can't buy the car. + It is too expensive. (because)

→ ______________________, my uncle can't buy it.

05 It is nice outside. + I will go swimming. (if)

→ I will go swimming ______________________.

UNIT 05 종속접속사 3: that

하나의 절 앞에 접속사 that(~하다는 것)을 붙여서 하나의 명사처럼 사용하세요.

that절	의미: 그가 늦게 일어난다는 것	주의
주어	That he gets up late is unbelievable.	that절은 단수 취급
목적어	No one knows (that) he gets up late.	목적어 that절의 that은 생략 가능
보어	The truth is that he gets up late.	

참고 that절이 주어 역할을 할 때에는 보통 가주어 It을 주어 자리에 쓰고, 진짜 주어인 that절은 문장 뒤로 옮길 수 있어요.
→ It is unbelievable that he gets up late.

다음 우리말과 같도록 괄호 안의 말과 접속사 that을 사용하여 문장을 완성하시오. (단, 필요시 동사 변형 가능)

01 Judy는 유명한 영화배우가 되기를 바란다. (be / a famous movie star / will)
→ Judy hopes ______________________________.

02 문제는 그녀의 아버지가 아파서 누워 계시다는 것이다. (be ill / in bed)
→ The problem is ______________________________.

03 그는 네가 곧 돌아오기를 바란다. (come back / soon / will)
→ He hopes ______________________________.

04 Jason은 네가 그를 기다리고 있다는 것을 알고 있다. (are / wait for)
→ Jason knows ______________________________.

05 그녀가 내일 떠난다는 것은 사실이다. (leave / will)
→ It is true ______________________________.

06 좋은 소식은 여름 방학이 오고 있다는 것이다. (come / the summer vacation)
→ The good news is ______________________________.

중간고사·기말고사 실전문제

객관식 (01~15) / 주관식 (16~30)

정답과 해설 • 87쪽

학년과 반 　　 이름 　　 객관식 　　 / 15문항 　　 주관식 　　 / 15문항

[01~03] 다음 빈칸에 알맞은 것을 고르시오.

01

You ________ I are close friends.

① or 　　 ② so
③ and 　　 ④ but
⑤ that

02

She didn't notice ________ she left her cell phone in the taxi.

① that 　　 ② when
③ before 　　 ④ after
⑤ because

03

________ you finish your homework, you can play the computer game.

① So 　　 ② And
③ But 　　 ④ After
⑤ That

[04~05] 다음 우리말과 같도록 빈칸에 알맞은 것을 고르시오.

04

The puppy is very small ________ very brave.
(그 강아지는 매우 작지만 매우 용감하다.)

① and 　　 ② but
③ or 　　 ④ before
⑤ because

05

________ it snows tomorrow, we will build a snowman.
(내일 눈이 온다면, 우리는 눈사람을 만들 것이다.)

① If 　　 ② So
③ When 　　 ④ That
⑤ After

06 다음 괄호 안의 ①~⑤ 중 because가 들어갈 알맞은 곳은?

Chris (①) went (②) to (③) the dentist (④) he had (⑤) a toothache.

07 다음 빈칸에 공통으로 들어갈 알맞은 것은?

> • Which would you like, tea ________ coffee?
> • I take a walk ________ watch a movie in my free time.

① so ② or
③ if ④ but
⑤ and

08 다음 우리말을 영어로 옮길 때, 빈칸 (A), (B)에 알맞은 것은?

> 네가 택시를 탄다면, 10분밖에 걸리지 않을 것이다.
> → If you ___(A)___ a taxi, it ___(B)___ only 10 minutes.

	(A)		(B)
①	take	–	takes
②	took	–	is taken
③	takes	–	took
④	take	–	will take
⑤	will take	–	will take

[09~10] 다음 밑줄 친 부분의 쓰임이 나머지 넷과 다른 하나를 고르시오.

09 ① I wear an apron when I cook.
② When do you play the violin?
③ When you feel sleepy, don't drive.
④ Emily was 32 when she got married.
⑤ What do you want to be when you grow up?

10 ① I think that Sujin is smart.
② That he missed his flight is true.
③ Teddy said that the movie was boring.
④ The problem is that we have no money.
⑤ You'll stay in that house with your sister.

11 다음 중 어법상 어색한 것은?

① I studied hard, so I got a good grade.
② That he became a scientist surprises us.
③ Will you go to the party if he invites you?
④ It was Saturday when I saw your parents.
⑤ Julia is waving her arms and shouted at me.

12 다음 빈칸에 들어갈 말이 나머지 넷과 다른 하나는?

① You can stay here ________ you want.
② Please call me ________ you have time.
③ ________ I get up early, I can catch the bus.
④ The flight was canceled ________ there was a storm.
⑤ ________ you take the subway, you will arrive on time.

13 다음 빈칸 (A)~(C)에 들어갈 알맞은 것은?

- It's my day off ___(A)___ I can go hiking.
- ___(B)___ he goes out, he takes his two dogs with him.
- Always look both ways ___(C)___ you cross the street.

	(A)		(B)		(C)
①	or	–	After	–	that
②	so	–	Before	–	but
③	so	–	When	–	before
④	and	–	When	–	after
⑤	but	–	Because	–	so

14 다음 빈칸 ⓐ~ⓔ에 알맞지 <u>않은</u> 것은?

- Alex is kind ___ⓐ___ his friends like him.
- The fact is ___ⓑ___ you are not diligent.
- My mom will take a rest ___ⓒ___ go shopping.
- The museum closed ___ⓓ___ they arrived.
- Mina left Seoul ___ⓔ___ arrived in Daejeon 2 hours later.

① ⓐ so ② ⓑ when
③ ⓒ or ④ ⓓ before
⑤ ⓔ and

15 다음 두 문장을 접속사를 사용하여 한 문장으로 바르게 연결한 것은?

- Mike is hungry.
- Mike didn't eat anything this morning.

① Mike is hungry and he didn't eat anything this morning.
② Mike is hungry so he didn't eat anything this morning.
③ When Mike is hungry, he didn't eat anything this morning.
④ After Mike is hungry, he didn't eat anything this morning.
⑤ Mike is hungry because he didn't eat anything this morning.

[16~18] 다음 빈칸에 알맞은 말을 |보기|에서 골라 쓰시오.

|보기|
and but that before if

16 Somin likes beef, ___________ she doesn't like pork.

17 Please turn off the lights ___________ you go out.

18 It is true ___________ the company will close the business next month.

[19~20] 다음 문장에서 어법상 어색한 부분을 찾아 바르게 고쳐 쓰시오.

19 You'll get healthier if you will exercise regularly.

_______________ → _______________

20 Minsu enjoys watching TV and to play basketball.

_______________ → _______________

[21~22] 다음 우리말과 같도록 빈칸에 알맞은 말을 쓰시오.

21

나는 그가 그 일을 맡을 거라고 생각한다.

→ I __________ __________ he will accept the job.

22

그의 목표는 대회에서 우승하고 가수가 되는 것이다.

→ His goal is to win the contest __________ __________ a singer.

[23~24] 다음 문장 중 어법상 어색한 문장을 두 개 찾아 바르게 고쳐 쓰시오.

ⓐ Today is Sunday, but I have to work.
ⓑ Come to my office before you leave.
ⓒ I watch a sad movie after I want to cry.
ⓓ It is not true that she will run for president.
ⓔ My friend was in the hospital, or I visited my friend after school.

23 _______________ → _______________

24 _______________ → _______________

[25~26] 다음 대화의 빈칸에 괄호 안의 단어를 바르게 배열하시오.

25

A: How old were you _______________ _______________?
(you / when / won / award / in / the / 2018)
B: I was 10 years old.

26

A: How do you know so much about Rome?
B: _______________ _______________, I know the city well.
(I / for / because / years / lived / in / Rome / 7)

[27~28] 다음 우리말과 같도록 괄호 안의 말을 사용하여 문장을 완성하시오.

27

네가 이 약을 먹으면 너는 더 괜찮아질 거야.
(take / medicine / get better)

→ If ______________________________
______________________________.

28

내 삼촌이 오늘 밤 우리 집에 올 거라는 것은 확실하다.
(certain / come / tonight)

→ It ______________________________
______________________________.

[29~30] 다음 괄호 안의 접속사를 사용하여 두 문장을 한 문장으로 바꿔 쓰시오.

29

• We couldn't play tennis.
• It was raining. (because)

→ ______________________________
____

→ ______________________________
____

30

• Raise your right hand.
• You have a question. (when)

→ ______________________________
____

→ ______________________________
____

내가 가장 취약한 부분에 대해
요점 정리를 해 보세요.

EBS

MY GRAMMAR COACH

내신기출 N제 중1

Philosophy
EBS 30일 인문학
처음 하는 철학 공부
윤주연 지음
EBS BOOKS

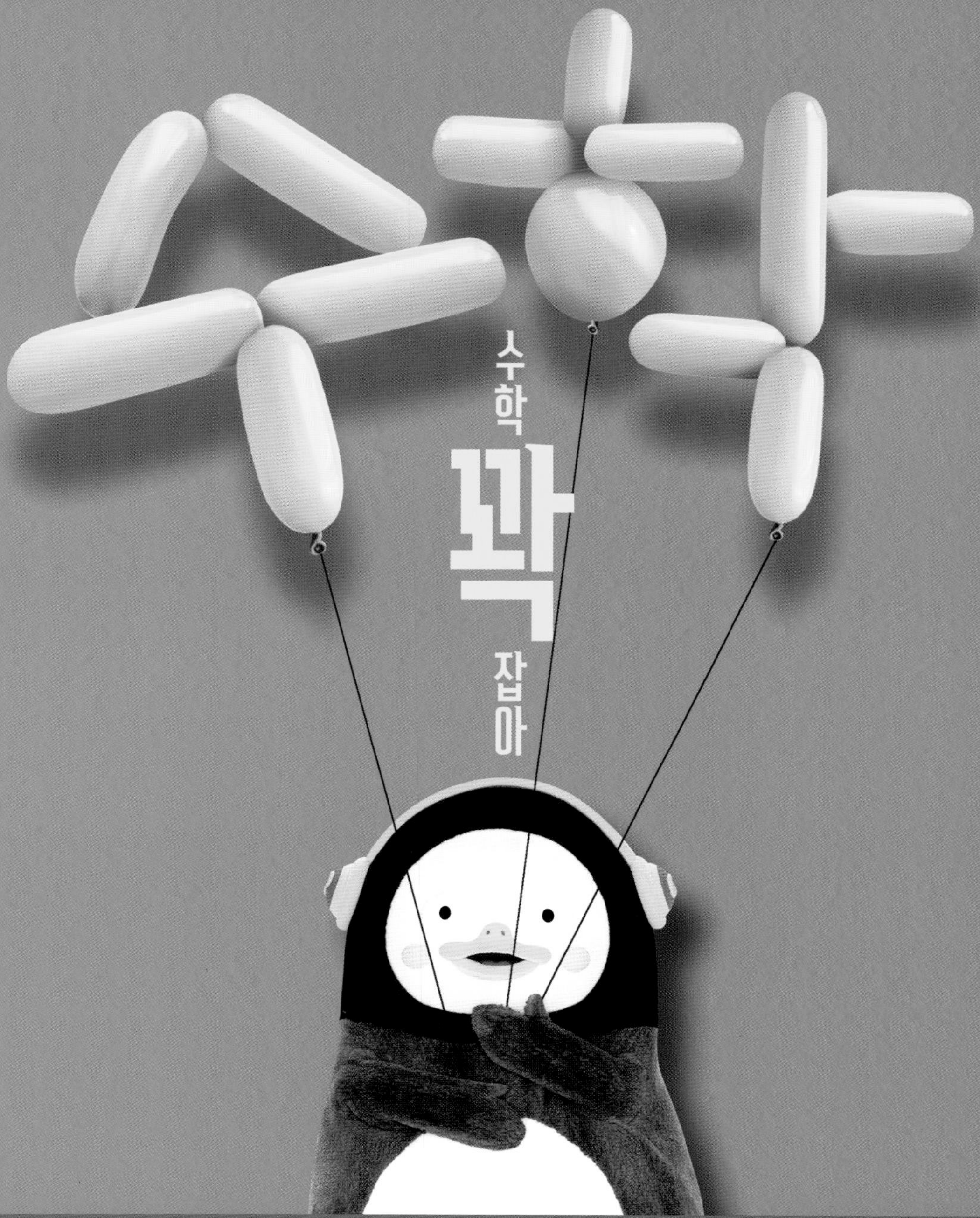

사회를 한 권으로
가뿐하게!

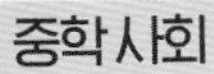

중학사회

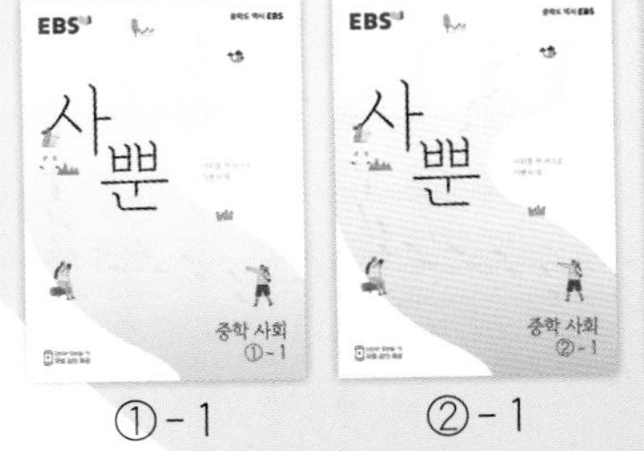

①-1 ②-1 ①-2 ②-2

중학역사

①-1 ②-1 ①-2 ②-2

EBS

중 | 학 | 도 | 역 | 시 EBS

중학 내신 영문법의 결정판

MY GRAMMAR COACH

내신기출 N제

don't worry be happy

DON'T WORRY BE HAPPY

DONT WORRY BE HAPPY

정답과 해설

MY GRAMMAR COACH

내신기출 N제 중 1

정답과 해설

CHAPTER 01 인칭대명사와 be동사

Unit 01 p. 14

A

01 She
02 He
03 It
04 We
05 He
06 They
07 It
08 She
09 You
10 They
11 We
12 She
13 They
14 It
15 He
16 You

B

01 She
02 He
03 They
04 They
05 We
06 They
07 He
08 She
09 they

Unit 02 p. 15

A

01 am
02 is
03 are
04 are
05 is
06 is
07 is
08 is
09 are
10 are
11 are
12 are

B

01 I am very thirsty.
02 You are a pianist.
03 He is a great cook.
04 My friends and I are in the house.
05 My dad is very angry.
06 They are my best friends.
07 Your keys are on the table.

내신기출 ④

Unit 03 p. 16

A

01 You're
02 I'm
03 It's
04 They're
05 He's
06 She's
07 We're
08 You're

B

01 It's a black cat.
02 I'm very hungry.
03 We're brothers.
04 X
05 He's in the bedroom.
06 X
07 You're my students.
08 She's from New York.
09 They're fourteen years old.

Unit 04 p. 17

A

01 were
02 was
03 were
04 were
05 was
06 were
07 was
08 was
09 were
10 were
11 were
12 was
13 were
14 were

B

01 I was happy.
02 She was a nurse.
03 We were a little tired.
04 He was fat then.
05 You were short last year.
06 It was on the sofa.

07 My parents were busy.
08 The shirt was dirty.
09 They were healthy.

내신 기출 ③

Unit 05 p. 18

A

01 I'm not
02 you aren't[you're not]
03 he isn't[he's not]
04 she isn't[she's not]
05 they aren't[they're not]
06 we aren't[we're not]
07 the boy isn't
08 Jessie isn't
09 you weren't
10 he wasn't
11 she wasn't
12 it wasn't
13 they weren't
14 we weren't
15 the woman wasn't
16 Tom and I weren't

B

01 I am[I'm] not hungry.
02 You are not[You aren't, You're not] hardworking.
03 She was not[wasn't] a ballerina.
04 He is not[He isn't, He's not] my teacher.
05 This bag is not[isn't] heavy.
06 You were not[weren't] six years old.
07 It is not[It isn't, It's not] my cell phone.
08 They were not[weren't] in the classroom.
09 I was not[wasn't] sick yesterday.

Unit 06 p. 19

A

01 Are, I
02 Is, isn't
03 Is, she
04 Are, they
05 Was, it
06 Were, weren't
07 Were, they
08 Was, wasn't

B

01 Are you fourteen years old?
02 Is he a famous dancer?
03 Are they in the library?
04 Was Kathy a good swimmer?
05 Were the dishes clean?
06 Is the movie boring?
07 Are Mina and I free now?
08 Were Lisa and Kevin your classmates?
09 Were they very close last year?

Unit 07 p. 20

A

01 They → We
02 was nurses → were nurses
03 isn't → am not
04 wasn't → weren't
05 Was → Is
06 Is it → Are they
07 you → they
08 she wasn't → they weren't

B

01 I am[I'm] not good at swimming.
02 My daughter was in hospital.
03 Are you thirsty and hungry?
04 They are not[They're not/They aren't] best friends.
05 Was Peter a basketball player?
06 The new car is not[isn't] very expensive.
07 We were not[weren't] busy yesterday.
08 Are the games very interesting?
09 Is she a good dentist?

내신 기출 ②

중간고사 • 기말고사 실전문제 pp. 21~27

객관식 정답 [01~25]

01 ⑤	**02** ④	**03** ①	**04** ③	**05** ③
06 ②	**07** ①	**08** ⑤	**09** ⑤	**10** ④
11 ③	**12** ③	**13** ③	**14** ③	**15** ⑤
16 ⑤	**17** ④	**18** ③	**19** ②	**20** ③
21 ②	**22** ③	**23** ⑤	**24** ⑤	**25** ④

주관식 정답 [26~50]

26 it isn't
27 we aren't
28 he was
29 Brian wasn't in China in 2020.
30 Peter and I weren't late for school.
31 ⓑ
32 ⓒ
33 Are the dishes
34 Is your father
35 (1) Yes, they are. (2) No, they aren't.
36 The bride was beautiful
37 Tom and his brother were at the beach
38 This bag was on sale
39 너와 John은 나의 반 친구이다.
40 우리는 테니스 팀의 팀원이었다.
41 No, it isn't
42 are → is
43 is → are
44 This computer game is not[isn't] interesting.
45 Were Roy and Tom at the shop?
46 are, are, teacher, is, actor
47 No, she isn't
48 Yes, she is
49 His birthday was last Sunday.
50 Daisy and Zoe weren't nurses five years ago.

해설

01 ①은 It – is, ②는 Mr. Park – is ③은 I – am ④는 Your pencils – are로 바꿔 줘야 한다.

02 주어인 Jason은 3인칭 단수이며, last week는 과거시제와 함께 사용하므로 be동사의 과거형 중 was를 사용해야 한다.

03 now는 현재시제와 함께 사용해야 하며 주어인 Hawaii는 3인칭 단수이므로 be동사 is를 사용해야 한다.

04 A의 질문에서 주어가 복수이고, 보어인 doctors를 수반하므로 빈칸에는 Are가 알맞다. 또한 B의 대답이 긍정이므로 aren't가 아닌 are를 사용해야 한다.

05 be동사의 부정문은 be동사 다음에 not을 붙여 표현한다.

06 They는 3인칭 복수이므로 wasn't가 아닌 weren't를 사용해야 한다.

07 주어인 your father는 3인칭 단수이고, 대답은 부정이므로, 빈칸에는 he isn't가 알맞다.

08 A 질문의 주어가 you and your brother이므로 B의 대답에서 주어는 1인칭 복수 인칭대명사인 we를 사용해야 하며, 시점이 yesterday이므로 be동사의 과거시제를 사용해야 한다.

09 A 질문의 주어가 3인칭 단수 he이므로 B의 대답의 주어도 he가 되어야 한다. 또한, 대답이 Yes로 시작하는 긍정문이므로 he was로 대답한다.

10 ①②③⑤의 be동사는 '~이다'의 의미로 사용되었고 ④의 be동사는 '~에 있다'의 의미로 사용되었다.

11 질문의 주어가 Linda and her husband이므로, 대답할 때 주어 역시 3인칭 복수형인 they를 사용해야 한다.
→ Yes, they were.

12 ③의 주어가 His son이므로 be동사는 단수형인 was를 사용한다.

13 The sandwiches가 복수이므로 be동사는 was가 아닌 were를 사용해야 한다.

14 ①의 주어는 Laura and I로 1인칭 복수이기 때문에 be동사는 are를 사용한다. ②의 주어는 your sister로 3인칭 단수이기 때문에 be동사 is를 사용해야 한다. ④의 주어는 They로 3인칭 복수이므로 be동사 weren't로 표현해야 한다. ⑤의 주어는 That으로 3인칭 단수이기 때문에 be동사 is를 사용해야 한다.

15 ①②③④는 be동사 was가 들어가고, ⑤는 주어가 Jisu and Laura로 3인칭 복수이기 때문에 be동사 were를 사용한다.

16 주어가 My sister and I로 1인칭 복수이기 때문에 동사는 are를 사용해야 하고, 우리말과 일치하도록 are 다음에 not을 붙여 부정문으로 써야 한다.

17 내가 가장 좋아하는 과목이 English와 science이므로 주어도 복수형으로 My favorite subjects로 쓰고, be동사도 복수형인 are를 사용한다.

18 (a)의 문장의 주어는 Jiho로 3인칭 단수이므로 is를 사용해야 한다. (b)에서 not은 be동사의 뒤에 위치한다. (c)의 주어 Sujin and I는 복수이므로 be동사 are를 사용해야 한다.

19 (a)의 주어 Brian은 3인칭 단수이기 때문에 be동사는 Are가 아닌 Is를 사용해야 한다. (b)의 주어는 He로 3인칭 단수이기 때문에 be동사는 was를 사용해야 한다. (d)에서 not am은 am not으로 고쳐 쓰는 것이 맞다.

20 Minsu는 3인칭 단수이므로 be동사 is나 was를 사용할 수 있다.

21 질문의 주어가 Sophia로 3인칭 단수이므로, 대답할 때에도 주어 she를 사용해야 한다. 부정으로 답할 경우에는 No, she isn't.로, 긍정으로 답할 때에는 Yes, she is.로 표현한다.

22 그림에서 회색 고양이는 집 안에 있지 않고, 밖에 있다. 따라서 The gray cat isn't inside the house.로 표현해야 한다. 두 번째 문장에서 주어는 앞 문장의 The gray cat을 가리키는 대명사가 되어야 하므로 It을 사용한다.

23 그림에서 아이들은 화창한 날씨가 아닌, 비가 오는 날씨지만 웅덩이에서 즐겁게 놀고 있다. 따라서, 이와 일치하는 표현은 The weather isn't sunny, but the children aren't sad.이다.

24 표를 보면, Jason이 가장 좋아하는 음식은 스파게티이므로 Jason의 대답은 부정문 No, it isn't.가 되어야 한다. 또, Grace의 질문의 주어가 *kimchi*이므로 Jason의 대답의 주어는 *kimchi*를 대신할 수 있는 인칭대명사인 it을 사용해야 한다.

25 ① Grace의 나이는 30세이다. ② Jason은 축구선수가 맞다. ③ Grace의 나이는 30세, Jason의 나이는 32세로 두 사람의 나이는 같지 않다. ⑤ Jason의 나이는 32세다.

26 her room은 3인칭 단수이며 사물이므로, 인칭대명사 it으로 대신할 수 있다. 또한, B의 대답이 No로 시작하고 있으므로 부정문의 형태로 써야 한다.

27 you and your brother는 2인칭 복수 주어이기 때문에, 인칭대명사 we로 대신한다. 또한, B의 대답이 No로 시작하고 있으므로, 부정문의 형태로 쓴다.

28 Sam은 3인칭 단수 주어이므로, 인칭대명사 he로 대신할 수 있으며, B의 대답이 긍정이므로, 빈칸에는 he was가 적당하다.

29 was not의 축약형은 wasn't이다.

30 were not의 축약형은 weren't이다.

[31~32] ⓐ He is hungry.에서 be동사 is는 '~하다'라는 뜻으로 쓰이고 있다. ⓑ Kelly is a lawyer.에서 be동사 is는 '~이다'라는 뜻으로 쓰이고 있다. ⓒ My hairpins are in my bag.에서 be동사 are는 '~(에) 있다'라는 뜻으로 쓰이고 있다.

31 내 여동생과 나는 고등학생이다.

32 그의 개는 나무 아래에 있다.

33 be동사의 의문문의 어순은 〈be동사+주어 ~?〉이다. 주어 the dishes가 복수이므로, be동사는 are를 사용한다.

34 B의 대답에 있는 be동사 is를 의문문의 맨 앞에 쓴다.

35 주어 Amy and Grace는 3인칭 복수형을 가리키는 인칭대명사 they로 대신할 수 있다.

36 The bride를 주어로 하는 문장이다.

37 Tom and his brother가 한 덩어리로서 주어 역할을 한다.

38 on sale: 할인 판매 중인

41 공은 회색이 아니라 노란색이다. 또한, A의 질문의 주어가 the ball이므로, 이와 어울리는 인칭대명사는 it이다.

42 주어인 The new jacket은 3인칭 단수이므로 be동사 is를 써야 한다.

43 주어인 Stella and her sister는 3인칭 복수이므로 be동사는 are를 사용해야 한다.

44 be동사의 부정은 〈be동사+not〉의 어순으로 표현한다.

45 주어가 3인칭 복수이므로 be동사 Were를 써야 한다.

46 첫 번째 칸에는 주어가 Kate and Daniel이므로 be동사 are를 써야 한다. 두 번째 칸에는 주어가 They이므로 are를 쓴다. 상단의 표에 Kate의 직업이 teacher임을

알 수 있다. 따라서 세 번째 칸에는 teacher를 써야 한다. 네 번째 칸에는 주어인 She에 어울리는 be동사인 is를 써야 한다. 표를 통해, Daniel의 직업이 actor임을 알 수 있다. 따라서 마지막 칸에는 actor를 써야 한다.

[**47~48**] [해석] Sarah는 중학교 학생이다. 그녀는 14살이다. 그녀는 영국 출신이다. 그녀는 훌륭한 배드민턴 선수이다.

47 Sarah는 축구 선수가 아니라, 배드민턴 선수이다. 따라서 부정문으로 대답한다.

48 Sarah가 영국 출신인 것은 사실이므로 긍정문의 형태로 대답한다.

49 3인칭 단수인 his birthday에 어울리는 과거형 be동사는 was이다.

50 5년 전은 과거이므로 be동사의 과거형인 were를 사용하며, 부정의 의미를 담기 위해서 not을 붙인다.

[CHAPTER 02 일반동사]

Unit 01

p. 30

A

01 reads
02 tells
03 read
04 sing
05 runs
06 gives
07 write
08 eat
09 gets
10 begin
11 meet
12 knows
13 walks
14 listens
15 like
16 make

B

01 enjoy
02 lives
03 works
04 read
05 wants
06 love
07 walk
08 listen
09 know

Unit 02

pp. 31~32

A

01 does
02 buys
03 cries
04 has
05 mixes
06 goes
07 watches
08 studies
09 says
10 finishes
11 passes
12 flies
13 fixes
14 plays
15 worries
16 teaches
17 enjoys
18 pushes
19 touches
20 tries

B

01 play
02 goes
03 studies
04 washes
05 has
06 does
07 enjoys
08 watches
09 do

C

01 crys → cries
02 enjoys → enjoy
03 go → goes
04 has → have
05 washs → washes
06 plays → play
07 have → has
08 carrys → carries

D

01 has
02 plays
03 study
04 goes
05 catches
06 worries
07 does
08 washes

내신기출 ③

Unit 03

p. 33

A

01 called
02 played
03 watched
04 cooked
05 talked
06 opened
07 worked
08 enjoyed
09 cleaned
10 listened
11 visited
12 helped
13 looked
14 started
15 wanted
16 finished

B

01 brushed
02 watched
03 worked
04 visited
05 enjoyed
06 played
07 finished
08 walked
09 started

Unit 04

p. 34

01 accepted
02 added
03 agreed
04 begged
05 believed
06 borrowed
07 collected
08 copied
09 covered
10 cried
11 decided
12 depended
13 died
14 dropped
15 enjoyed
16 entered
17 failed
18 finished
19 happened
20 hurried
21 laughed
22 learned
23 married
24 needed
25 passed
26 planned
27 pulled
28 pushed
29 raised
30 remembered
31 saved
32 smelled
33 sounded
34 stayed
35 stopped
36 studied
37 touched
38 tried
39 watched
40 worried

Unit 05

p. 36

01 stole
02 swam
03 sat
04 slept
05 spoke
06 spent
07 drank
08 left
09 lent
10 lost
11 made
12 meant
13 thought
14 read[red]
15 spread
16 threw
17 brought
18 built
19 bought
20 caught
21 chose
22 came
23 did
24 drew
35 went
26 grew
27 had
28 heard
29 kept
30 knew
31 led
32 took
33 taught
34 met
35 paid
36 rode
37 rang
38 rose
39 ran
40 got
41 gave
42 let
43 put
44 said
45 saw
46 sold
47 sent
48 sang
49 drove
50 ate
51 fell
52 fed
53 felt
54 fought

55 understood
56 woke
57 became
58 began
59 broke
60 wore
61 won
62 wrote
63 cost
64 cut
65 hit
66 hurt
67 found
68 flew
69 forgot
70 forgave

Unit 06 p. 37

A

01 don't have
02 doesn't play
03 didn't watch
04 don't go
05 didn't come
06 don't stay
07 didn't see
08 doesn't drink

B

01 I do not[don't] like this car.
02 She does not[doesn't] cook well.
03 We did not[didn't] have a good time.
04 They did not[didn't] work today.
05 My sister does not[doesn't] ride a bike.
06 Jenny did not[didn't] finish her homework.
07 He does not[doesn't] know my number.
08 I did not[didn't] go to the restaurant.
09 You did not[didn't] win the game.

Unit 07 p. 38

A

01 Do you like chocolate?
02 Does she live near here?
03 Did your mother call you?
04 Does Kevin have two brothers?
05 Does she clean her room?
06 Did he study math?
07 Do they have breakfast at seven?
08 Did Sam stay at home?

B

01 Do you like horror movies? – Yes
02 Does your dad work at a bank? – he doesn't
03 Did she finish her homework? – Yes
04 Did Jen and Sam go to the party? – they did
05 Do you help your mom? – No
06 Do you and your brother enjoy jogging? – we don't

Unit 08 p. 39

A

01 Does
02 bought
03 have
04 didn't go
05 slept
06 doesn't like
07 takes
08 got

B

01 Does she know the song?
02 We don't go to school together.
03 Do they help each other?
04 She made this cake.
05 The teacher taught music.
06 Did they go to the park?
07 She didn't read the book yesterday.

내신기출 ③

중간고사 • 기말고사 실전문제 pp. 40~46

객관식 정답 [01~25]

01 ④	02 ③	03 ④	04 ⑤	05 ②
06 ③	07 ③	08 ⑤	09 ③	10 ①
11 ④	12 ④	13 ⑤	14 ③	15 ③
16 ②	17 ②	18 ③	19 ③	20 ③
21 ②	22 ④	23 ③	24 ②	25 ③

주관식 정답 [26~50]

26 (1) eats (2) catches (3) flies (4) practices
27 has
28 play
29 brushes

30 (1) dropped (2) obeyed (3) left (4) drew
31 Lucas does not[doesn't] play soccer twice a week.
32 A: Does Lucas play soccer twice a week?
B: No, he doesn't.
33 Does your grandmother get up
34 planned
35 dropped
36 (1) raised (2) won
37 didn't stay
38 caught
39 ⓔ → didn't find
40 ⓓ → didn't take
41 No, she didn't.
42 Yes, she did.
43 like, doesn't like, likes, doesn't like
44 A bird fell from its nest.
45 I bought a new bag.
46 우리 부모님은 한 달에 두 번 등산을 하신다.
47 Susan은 어젯밤에 배가 아팠다.
48 My brother sleeps late every Saturday.
49 (1) runs → ran (2) rises → rose
50 (1) came → comes (2) turns → turn

해설

01 -x로 끝나는 일반동사의 3인칭 단수 현재형은 동사원형에 -es를 붙인다.

02 -o로 끝나는 일반동사의 3인칭 단수 현재형은 동사원형에 -s를 붙인다.

03 일반동사의 의문문에서는 조동사 do 혹은 does를 사용한다. 이 문장에서는 3인칭 복수인 주어 they가 쓰였으므로, 빈칸에는 Do를 쓴다.

04 keep의 3인칭 단수 현재형인 keeps가 쓰였으므로 빈칸에는 3인칭 단수 주어가 와야 한다.

05 일반동사의 3인칭 단수 현재형의 의문문은 〈Does+주어+동사원형 ~?〉의 어순으로 쓴다. 그러므로, ⓑ looks는 look으로 고쳐야 한다.

06 visit처럼 강세가 앞에 오는 2음절 동사는 과거형으로 바꿀 때, 동사원형에 -ed만 붙여 사용한다. (visit – visited)

07 mean의 과거형은 meant이다.

08 일반동사의 3인칭 단수 현재형의 부정문은 〈주어+doesn't+동사원형〉의 어순으로 쓴다.

09 does는 3인칭 단수 주어와 함께 쓴다. your sisters는 3인칭 복수이므로 Do를 써야 한다.

10 일반동사의 과거형 의문문에는 〈Yes, 주어+did.〉 혹은 〈No, 주어+didn't.〉로 답한다. 2인칭 주어를 사용한 의문문에는 1인칭 주어로 답한다.

11 주어가 3인칭 단수일 때 일반동사 현재형의 의문문은 〈Yes, 주어+does.〉 혹은 〈No, 주어 doesn't.〉로 답한다.

12 일반동사의 의문문은 〈Do/Does/Did+주어+동사원형 ~?〉의 순서로 쓴다.

13 주어인 Jason이 3인칭 단수이며, 일반동사 의문문이므로 〈Does+주어+동사원형 ~?〉의 어순으로 쓴다.

14 주어가 Timothy and Paul로 3인칭 복수이므로 부정문을 쓸 때는 〈주어+don't+동사원형〉의 순서로 쓴다.

15 동사 build의 과거형은 built이다.

16 동사 spend의 과거형은 spent이다. 현재시제로 쓰려면 spends로 고쳐야 한다.

17 동사 find의 과거형은 found이다.

18 B의 대답이 No, I didn't.이므로 A의 질문은 일반동사의 과거 의문문의 형태가 되어야 한다. 따라서 〈Did+주어+동사원형 ~?〉의 순서로 써야 한다.

19 B의 대답이 Yes, they do.이므로 A의 질문은 〈Do+주어+동사원형 ~?〉의 형태로 써야 한다.

20 stop은 〈단모음+단자음〉으로 끝나는 일반동사이므로, 과거형은 마지막 자음을 한 번 더 쓰고, -ed를 붙여 stopped로 쓴다.

21 (a) 주어가 3인칭 단수이므로 do not이 아닌 does not을 써야 한다.
(c) keep의 과거형은 kept이다.

22 (a) three years ago는 과거 시점이므로 live의 과거형인 lived를 쓴다.
(b) yesterday는 과거 시점이므로, lose의 과거형인 lost를 쓴다.
(c) every day는 현재시제와 함께 쓸 수 있으므로 go의 3인칭 현재 단수형인 goes를 쓴다.

23 '풀 위에 누웠다'의 뜻으로 쓰기 위해서는 동사 lie의 과거형인 lay를 써야 한다.

24 글 전체가 과거이므로, (B)의 동사 puts는 과거형 put으로 고쳐야 한다.
[해석] 농부가 나가서 씨앗을 심었다. 그는 씨앗을 땅 속에 뿌렸다. 씨앗들은 건강하고 강하게 자랐다. 수확의 때가 되어 농부는 많은 수확물을 갖게 되었다. 그는 행복했다.

25 swim의 과거형은 swam으로 써야 한다.
[해석] Daisy에게 – 어떻게 지내니? 우리 가족은 주말에 해변에서 시간을 보냈어. 날씨가 화창하고 매우 더웠어. 우리는 바다에서 수영을 했단다. 우리 오빠와 나는 모래성을 만들었어. 내 여동생은 아버지와 연 날리기를 했단다. 우리는 멋진 시간을 보냈어. 곧 만나. – 너의 친구 Clara가

26 일반동사의 3인칭 단수형은 동사원형에 -s 혹은 -es를 붙여 쓴다. fly와 같이 〈자음+y〉로 끝나는 동사는 y를 없애고 -ies로 바꿔 쓴다.

27 주어 Tim이 3인칭 단수이기 때문에 동사 have는 3인칭 단수 현재형인 has로 고친다.

28 주어가 Carrie and her father로 3인칭 복수이므로 일반동사의 원형을 쓴다.

29 주어가 3인칭 단수이므로 brush의 3인칭 단수 현재형인 brushes를 쓴다.

31 주어인 Lucas는 3인칭 단수이므로 부정문을 쓸 때 does not 혹은 doesn't 다음에 동사원형 play를 쓴다.

32 3인칭 단수 주어인 Lucas와 일반동사의 현재형이 함께 쓰였으므로 의문문으로 바꿀 때 〈Does+주어+동사원형 ~?〉의 순서로 쓴다.

33 B의 대답이 Yes, she does.로 3인칭 단수 현재형으로 쓰고 있으므로 A의 의문문은 〈Does+주어+동사원형 ~?〉의 어순을 따른다.

34 plan은 〈단모음+단자음〉으로 끝나는 동사이므로 과거형을 쓸 때 마지막 자음을 한 번 더 쓰고 -ed를 붙인다.

35 drop은 〈단모음+단자음〉으로 끝나는 동사이므로 과거형을 쓸 때 마지막 자음을 한 번 더 쓰고 -ed를 붙인다.

36 (1) raise와 같이 -e로 끝나는 동사는 과거형으로 고칠 때 동사 뒤에 -d만 붙인다.
(2) last week로 보아 빈칸에는 win의 과거형인 won이 오는 게 맞다.

37 일반동사의 과거 부정문은 〈didn't+동사원형〉의 형태로 쓴다.

38 catch의 과거형은 caught이다.

39 '찾을 수 없었다'는 didn't 뒤에 동사원형 find를 붙여야 한다. find의 과거형은 found인데, 동사 found(설립하다)와 잘 구분해야 한다.
[해석] 잎들이 떨어졌다. 겨울이 오고 있었다. 다람쥐 한 마리가 겨울에 먹을 음식을 찾아 다녔다. 다람쥐는 나무 위와 덤불 아래를 찾아보았다. 그러나 다람쥐는 어떤 먹이도 구하지 못했다.

40 일반동사 과거의 부정은 didn't[did not]을 사용하고, 그 뒤에 동사원형을 쓴다.
[해석] 어제는 Jake의 생일이었다. 그는 친구들을 초대했다. 그는 많은 선물을 받았다. 점심을 먹고, 그는 친구들과 해변에 갔다. 거기까지 가는 데에 시간이 많이 걸리지 않았다. 그들은 해변에서 멋진 시간을 보냈다.

41 Mandy가 하이킹을 한 날은 토요일이다.

42 표를 보면, Mandy는 지난 토요일과 일요일 모두 테니스를 쳤다.

43 Stella와 Aiden은 각각 3인칭 단수 주어이므로 일반동사를 쓸 때 3인칭 단수 현재형을 쓴다. 하지만 Stella and Aiden은 복수 주어이다.

44 fall의 과거형은 fell이다.

45 buy의 과거형은 bought이다.

48 My brother는 3인칭 단수 주어이기 때문에 동사원형 sleep의 뒤에 -s를 붙여 sleeps로 바꿔 쓴다.

49 yesterday morning으로 보아, 동사 runs는 과거형 ran으로 고치는 게 맞다. 또한, 동사 rises 역시 과거형 rose가 되어야 한다.
[해석] Amy는 어제 아침에 산꼭대기까지 뛰어 갔다. 그녀는 하늘을 보았다. 그때 태양이 동쪽에서 떠올랐다. 그것은 놀라웠다.

50 (1) 문단 전체의 시제가 현재이며 여름 다음에 가을이 오는 것은 불변의 진리이므로 현재 시제로 써야 한다. 따라서 came을 3인칭 단수 현재형인 comes로 바꿔 쓴다.
(2) 주어가 3인칭 복수 Leaves이므로 동사 turns는 turn으로 고쳐야 한다.
[해석] 나는 가을을 좋아한다. 가을은 여름 다음에 온다. 공기가 차가워진다. 나뭇잎은 빨간색, 노란색, 주황색으로 바뀐다. 동물들은 겨울을 준비한다.

CHAPTER 03 시제

Unit 01 p. 48

A

01 am
02 makes
03 keeps
04 looks
05 live
06 has
07 sets
08 reads
09 equals
10 get
11 is
12 exercises
13 run
14 goes
15 comes
16 freezes

B

01 is in his twenties
02 get up at seven in the morning
03 have ears
04 rises in the morning
05 calls her parents every day
06 closes at six
07 listen to music after dinner
08 go to work by subway

내신기출 ②

Unit 02 p. 49

A

01 I was very tired
02 The boys were in the yard
03 Did you sleep well
04 He drank milk
05 They built the Eiffel Tower
06 I met my friends
07 Mom made cookies
08 They visited their grandpa

B

01 Jenny and I went on a picnic yesterday.
02 Did he buy this house a year ago?
03 Was the weather good last week?
04 James didn't come back last night.
05 Alexander Graham Bell invented the telephone in 1876.

Unit 03 p. 50

A

01 will meet
02 will walk
03 will be
04 will take
05 will buy
06 will visit
07 will play

B

01 I'll go to the library.
02 He'll be at home today.
03 The store will open next month.
04 Tom will be with us soon.
05 The train will arrive in five minutes.
06 They'll come back tomorrow.
07 We'll take a trip next week.
08 She'll wash her car this Sunday.

내신기출 ①

Unit 04 p. 51

A

01 visits → visit
02 will leave not → will not[won't] leave
03 Will do → Will
04 watches → watch
05 washs → washes
06 not will → will not[won't]
07 do → will
08 willn't → won't

B

01 will not[won't] be, Will she be, she will
02 will not[won't] read, Will Jack read, he won't
03 will not[won't] make, Will he make, he won't
04 will not[won't] work, Will your idea work, it will

Unit 05
pp. 52~53

A

01 I am going to be a singer.

02 We are not[We aren't, We're not] going to clean the kitchen.

03 Are you going to have a math exam?

04 He is going to visit Europe.

05 We are not[We aren't, We're not] going to be late for the concert.

06 I am going to finish my homework.

07 She is going to arrive here at nine.

08 My dad is going to watch TV.

09 We are going to meet him at the mall.

10 Are they going to play soccer?

B

01 is not[isn't] going to be sunny, Is it going to be sunny, it isn't

02 are not[aren't] going to arrive early, Are we going to arrive early, we are

03 are not[aren't] going to learn English, Are we going to learn English, we aren't

04 is not[isn't] going to sing for us, Is she going to sing for us, she isn't

C

01 I'm going to leave for Europe

02 She's going to be back

03 He isn't[He's not] going to go out

04 We're going to paint the desk

05 Are you going to visit me

06 Is she going to be home

07 He's going to see Mr. Kim

D

01 am going to take

02 is going to visit

03 am going to eat

04 are going to buy

05 are going to close

06 is going to stay

07 are going to send

내신기출 ④ → rain

Unit 06
p. 54

A

01 goes

02 ended

03 will not[won't] come

04 was not[wasn't] tall

05 will take

06 Did, look – she did

07 Do, write – I don't

08 Is, going to buy – he isn't

B

01 It cost a lot of money.

02 He has breakfast at eight.

03 The meeting will[is going to] end at five.

04 Did they eat Italian food?

05 He doesn't[does not] like the game.

06 I didn't read the book all night.

07 Will he[Is he going to] be in the library?

내신기출 ③

Unit 07
p. 56

01 arriving
02 baking
03 beginning
04 believing
05 bringing
06 calling
07 camping
08 climbing
09 closing
10 coming
11 controlling
12 dancing
13 dying
14 drinking
15 driving
16 entering
17 flying
18 getting
19 giving
20 going
21 having
22 lying
23 listening
24 loving
25 making
26 opening
27 playing
28 putting
29 reading
30 riding
31 running
32 saving
33 saying
34 shopping
35 singing
36 sitting

37 smiling
38 starting
39 stopping
40 studying
41 swimming
42 taking
43 teaching
44 visiting
45 winning
46 writing

내신 기출 ③

Unit 08

p. 57

A

01 I am[I'm] listening to music.
02 He is[He's] writing a letter.
03 She is[She's] talking on the phone.
04 You are[You're] washing the dishes.
05 I am[I'm] doing my homework.
06 They are[They're] having lunch.
07 The girls are sitting on the sofa.
08 We are[We're] swimming in the pool.

B

01 I'm reading a book.
02 He's drawing a picture.
03 They're playing on the grass.
04 A bird is flying high.
05 She's lying on the bed.
06 My brother is having breakfast.
07 The man is looking at the map.
08 Mina and I are singing a song.

내신 기출 ②

Unit 09

p. 58

A

01 I am[I'm] not studying math.
02 He is not[He isn't, He's not] taking a shower.
03 Mike is not[isn't] watching TV.
04 She is not[She isn't, She's not] playing the piano.
05 They are not[They aren't, They're not] taking a walk.
06 You are not[You aren't, You're not] exercising.
07 My father is not[isn't] washing his car.
08 The mouse is not[isn't] eating cheese.

B

01 aren't discussing the problem
02 isn't riding a bicycle
03 isn't fixing the car
04 aren't having dinner
05 isn't brushing her teeth

Unit 10

p. 59

A

01 Are, doing, am
02 Are, helping, are
03 Am, speaking, are not[aren't]
04 Are, eating, are
05 Is, wearing, is

B

01 Is he running to school
– he is
02 Is she making a sandwich
– she isn't[she's not]
03 Are you looking at the pictures
– I am
04 Is Sam waiting for the train – he isn't[he's not]
05 Is your mom talking on the phone
– she isn't[she's not]
06 Are they using the computer
– they aren't[they're not]

내신 기출 ①

Unit 11

p. 60

A

01 She was running at the park.
02 I was going to the library.
03 He was putting on his jacket.
04 You were walking to school.
05 They were playing the violins.
06 Kate was drinking some juice.
07 We were traveling to Paris.
08 John was taking pictures of his family.

B

01 was reading

02 was wearing

03 was writing

04 were having

05 were watching

06 was shining, were singing

Unit 12

p. 61

A

01 was not[wasn't] having

02 was not[wasn't] washing

03 Were your parents eating

04 was not[wasn't] sending

05 Was your mother making

06 were not[weren't] studying

07 was not[wasn't] working

08 Were you sleeping

B

01 were not[weren't] making, Were you making, I was

02 was not[wasn't] crossing, Was she crossing, she was

03 was not[wasn't] watching, Was he watching, he was not[wasn't]

04 were not[weren't] taking, Were the children taking, they were not[weren't]

중간고사 • 기말고사 실전문제

pp. 62~68

객관식 정답 [01~25]

01 ⑤	**02** ③	**03** ④	**04** ②	**05** ③
06 ④	**07** ③	**08** ③	**09** ⑤	**10** ②
11 ①	**12** ⑤	**13** ④	**14** ④	**15** ⑤
16 ④	**17** ③	**18** ④	**19** ②	**20** ③
21 ④	**22** ③	**23** ⑤	**24** ④	**25** ⑤

주관식 정답 [26~50]

26 Kate and Ben are going to sell their toys.

27 Tom is not[isn't] going to walk to school tomorrow.

28 are sitting

29 is baking

30 Is she going to leave for London soon?

31 making

32 will[is going to] open

33 arrived

34 They are making a sandcastle.

35 No, she isn't

36 Cathy's cat is jumping on the bench.

37 Was your father cleaning the bathroom an hour ago?

38 Lauren will be a middle school student next year.

39 will be

40 played

41 (1) was (2) goes

42 He is going to have lunch with Sam.

43 will play basketball

44 went, was drinking, was flying a kite, stopped

45 was, took, is, will[is going to] take

46 Peter is not going to buy a new car.

47 Jane goes to the beach every summer.

48 Is Tom going to his dad's office now?

49 (1) ⓒ → ate (2) ⓔ → bake

50 She is making hot chocolate (with her sister now).

해설

01 next Saturday가 있으므로 미래시제로 표현한다.

02 불변의 진리는 현재시제로 표현한다.

03 미래시제와 함께 쓸 수 있는 부사구로 적당한 것은 next Monday이다.

04 현재시제와 함께 쓸 수 있는 부사구로 적당한 것은 every day이다. 반복되는 습관은 현재시제로 표현한다.

05 enter와 같이 2음절 동사이면서 강세가 1음절에 오는 동사는 진행형을 만들 때, 동사원형에 -ing를 붙여서 쓴다. enterring → entering

06 역사적 사실은 과거시제로 쓴다. next year는 미래시제와 함께 쓰는 부사구이다.

07 친구들과 점심을 먹고 있다는 B의 대답을 통해 빈칸에는 부정문이 와야 함을 알 수 있다. A의 질문이 현재진행형 시제이므로, 대답은 be동사의 현재형을 써야 한다.

08 B가 피시 앤 칩스를 요리하는 중이라고 대답하는 것으로 볼 때, B의 대답은 긍정문이 되어야 한다. A의 질문이 과거진행형이므로, B의 대답은 be동사의 과거형을 써야 한다.

09 know는 진행형 시제로 쓸 수 없다.

10 want는 진행형 시제로 쓸 수 없다.

11 B의 대답이 과거진행형이므로 질문도 과거진행형으로 써야 한다.

12 B의 대답이 be going to를 사용한 미래시제이므로 질문도 미래시제로 써야 한다.

13 첫 문장은 진행형 시제로 be동사 is나 was를 쓸 수 있다. 두 번째 문장은 yesterday를 볼 때, 과거진행형으로 써야 한다. 따라서 공통으로 들어갈 말은 was[Was]이다.

14 Lynn will not go camping this weekend.

15 내년에 일어날 일이므로 미래시제로 표현해야 한다. 미래시제의 부정문은 will not[won't] 혹은 〈be동사의 현재형+not+going to〉를 활용하여 표현한다.

16 해석상 과거진행형으로 써야 한다.

17 첫 번째 문장은 부사구 at that time과 flying이 있으므로 과거진행형으로 써야 한다. 따라서 빈칸에는 be동사의 과거형을 써야 한다. 두 번째 문장은 now가 있으므로 현재진행형으로 써야 한다. 따라서 빈칸에는 be동사의 현재형을 써야 하며 주어가 the children으로 3인칭 복수이기 때문에 Are를 쓰는 것이 맞다.

18 과거진행형은 〈be동사의 과거형+동사-ing〉 어순으로 써야 한다. 따라서 The baby was taking a nap.으로 바꿔 써야 한다.

19 ① 역사적 사실은 과거시제로 표현해야 한다. (ends → ended) ③ 과학적 · 일반적 사실은 현재시제로 표현한다. (freeze → freezes) ④ now가 있으므로 현재시제로 표현해야 한다. (was → is) ⑤ yesterday가 있으므로 과거시제로 써야 한다. (Are → Were)

20 ① 부사 tomorrow가 문장 끝에 있으므로 이 문장은 미래시제로 써야 한다. (opened → will open) ② 과학적 사실은 현재시제로 쓴다. (were → are) ④ last night이 있으므로 과거시제로 써야 한다. (is → was) ⑤ next year가 있으므로 미래시제로 써야 한다. (visited → will visit)

21 ① yesterday가 있으므로 과거시제로 써야 한다. (is not going to → did not) ② have가 소유의 의미로 쓰일 때에는 진행형 시제를 쓸 수 없다. (is having → has) ③ 미래시제를 쓸 때에는 be going to 다음에 동사원형을 써야 한다. (practicing → practice) ⑤ always가 있으므로 3인칭 단수를 주어로 하는 현재시제로 써야 한다.(drink → drinks)

22 A의 질문이 과거진행형이므로 B의 대답도 과거진행형으로 써야 한다.

23 미래시제를 쓸 때에는 be going to 다음에 동사원형을 써야 한다. (is going take → is going to take)
[해석] Rose는 유럽으로 여행을 떠났다. 그녀는 어제 파리에 도착했다. 그녀는 어젯밤에 에펠탑에 갔다. 그녀는 오늘 오후에 루브르 박물관을 방문할 것이다. 그녀는 내일 센강에서 크루즈를 탈 것이다.

24 (A) Jenny and Amy는 3인칭 복수이므로 be동사를 is가 아닌 are를 써야 한다. (B) soon이 있으므로 미래시제로 써야 한다. was going to를 is going to로 바꿔 써야 한다. (C) not will → will not (E) will not 다음에는 동사원형을 써야 한다. (will not goes → will not go)

25 첫 번째 문장에서 a few days ago가 있으므로 과거시제로 써야 한다. (→ made) 두 번째 문장은 this weekend가 있으므로 미래시제로 쓴다. (→ will go) 세 번째 문장은 then이 있으므로 과거시제로 써야 하며 주어가 3인칭 복수이므로 be동사 were를 써야 한다.

26 미래시제를 쓸 때, will 대신 be going to를 쓸 수 있다.

27 won't[will not]은 〈be동사+not+going to+동사원형〉으로 쓸 수 있다.

28 현재진행형은 〈be동사+동사-ing〉로 표현한다. 주어가 Young mothers and their children으로 복수이므로 be동사 are를 쓴다. 〈단모음+단자음〉으로 끝나는 동사의 진행형은 마지막 자음을 한 번 더 쓰고 -ing를 붙여 쓴다.

29 주어 Catherine은 3인칭 단수이므로 동사는 is가 알맞다. e로 끝나는 동사의 진행형은 e를 빼고 뒤에 -ing를 붙여 쓴다.

30 be going to를 사용하여 미래시제를 쓸 때, 의문문은 〈Be동사+주어+going to+동사원형 ~?〉 어순으로 쓴다.

31 현재진행형은 〈be동사의 현재형+동사원형-ing〉로 표현한다.

32 문장 끝에 tomorrow가 있으므로 미래를 나타내는 〈will [is going to]+동사원형〉으로 표현해야 한다.

33 yesterday가 있으므로 동사를 과거시제로 써야 한다.

34 질문의 시제가 현재진행형이므로 대답도 현재진행형으로 써야 한다.

35 어머니는 수영을 하지 않고, 책을 읽고 있기 때문에 부정문으로 답해야 한다.

36 해석상 현재진행형으로 표현해야 한다.

37 해석상 과거진행형으로 표현해야 한다.

38 해석상 미래시제로 써야 한다. will 다음에는 동사원형을 써야 한다.

39 someday는 미래시제와 함께 쓰는 부사이다.

40 last Sunday는 과거를 나타내는 부사구이므로 과거시제로 써야 한다.

41 (1) two years ago는 과거시제와 함께 써야 한다.
(2) every morning은 반복되는 습관을 나타내는 부사구로 현재시제에서 쓰인다.
[해석] Jenny는 2년 전에 아팠다. 그녀는 그 당시 병원에 있었다. 하지만, 지금 그녀는 건강하다. 그녀는 요즘 매일 아침 조깅을 한다.

42 질문이 be going to를 써서 미래시제로 표현되어 있으므로 대답도 동일하게 be going to를 활용한 미래시제로 쓰여야 한다.

43 일정표에 따르면 Ted는 3시에 쇼핑몰에 가지 않고, 농구를 할 예정이다.

44 첫 번째 문장은 yesterday가 있으므로 동사를 과거형 went로 쓴다. 캠핑을 간 것은 과거의 일이므로, 모든 문장은 과거시제 혹은 과거진행형으로 쓴다.
[해석] Emily와 그녀의 가족은 어제 캠핑을 갔다. 그녀의 아버지는 정오에 점심을 만들고 계셨다. 그녀의 어머니는 커피를 마시고 계셨다. 그녀의 남동생은 연을 날리고 있었다. Emily는 자전거를 세우고, 내렸다. 그녀는 아름다운 경치를 즐겼다.

45 첫 번째 문장은 last year가 있으므로 과거시제로 쓴다. 두 번째 문장도 작년에 일어난 일이므로 과거시제로 쓴다. 네 번째 문장은 now가 있으므로 현재시제로 쓴다. 다섯 번째 문장은 next year에 일어날 일이므로 미래시제로 쓴다.
[해석] Jake는 작년에 하와이에 있었다. 그는 거기에서 서핑 수업을 받았다. 그는 서핑을 매우 열심히 연습했다. 그는 지금은 서핑을 능숙하게 잘한다. 그는 내년에 서핑 대회에 참가할 것이다.

46 be going to를 활용하여 미래시제를 쓸 때, 부정문에서는 be동사 다음에 not을 붙여 표현한다.

47 매해 여름 반복되는 일을 나타내는 문장이므로 현재시제로 표현한다. 또한, 3인칭 단수 주어 Jane에 맞춰 goes를 써야 한다.

48 해석상 현재진행형으로 써야 한다. 현재진행형은 〈be동사의 현재형+V-ing〉로 표현한다.

[49~50] [해석] Emma는 7살이다. 그녀는 초콜릿을 매우 좋아한다. 그녀는 어제 초콜릿 칩 쿠키를 먹었다. 지금은 언니와 함께 핫 초콜릿을 만들고 있다. 그녀는 내일은 초콜릿 머핀을 구울 것이다.

49 (1) yesterday는 과거시제와 함께 쓰는 부사이다.
(2) be going to 다음에는 동사원형을 써야 한다.

50 질문이 현재진행형이므로 대답도 현재진행형으로 쓴다.

CHAPTER 04 조동사

Unit 01
p. 70

A

01 ⓐ
02 ⓑ
03 ⓒ
04 ⓓ
05 ⓐ
06 ⓒ
07 ⓐ
08 ⓕ
09 ⓓ
10 ⓕ
11 ⓔ
12 ⓓ
13 ⓔ
14 ⓑ

B

01 can't sleep
02 can speak
03 can't move
04 can't come
05 Can, open
06 Can, see
07 can be

내신 기출 ①

Unit 02
p. 71

A

01 am able to dance
02 is able to play
03 is not[isn't] able to drive
04 Are you able to speak
05 is able to read
06 Are you able to come
07 are not[aren't] able to win
08 Is she able to solve

B

01 Will we be able to catch the bus?
02 She will be able to finish it.
03 The baby is not[isn't] able to walk.
04 Can he fix it?
05 I will not[won't] be able to do it.
06 Were you able to get it?

Unit 03
p. 72

A

01 허가
02 추측
03 허가
04 추측
05 금지
06 추측
07 금지
08 허가
09 추측
10 허가
11 추측
12 허가
13 금지
14 추측
15 허가
16 추측

B

01 You may go home early.
02 May I use your pen?
03 It may be cold tomorrow.
04 He may not come today.
05 This cat may be hungry.
06 May I go out tonight?
07 She may be in her room.
08 You may not use my phone.
09 May I open the window?

Unit 04
p. 73

A

01 ⓒ
02 ⓐ
03 ⓒ
04 ⓐ
05 ⓓ
06 ⓒ
07 ⓓ
08 ⓓ
09 ⓐ
10 ⓑ

B

01 She is able to sing really well.
02 You may ride my bike.
03 They may not eat here.
04 It may rain this afternoon.
05 You are not[aren't] able to lift it alone.
06 May I use your computer?
07 It may be a real story.

내신 기출 ③

Unit 05 p. 74

A

01 의무
02 강한 추측
03 의무
04 의무
05 강한 추측
06 금지
07 의무
08 강한 추측
09 강한 추측
10 의무
11 금지
12 의무
13 강한 추측
14 강한 추측
15 금지
16 의무

B

01 must take
02 must not cross
03 must return
04 must lock
05 must be
06 must not turn on
07 must not sound
08 must be hardworking
09 must carry

Unit 06 pp. 75~76

A

01 I have to finish
02 You don't have to go
03 Do I have to read
04 You don't have to wear
05 She had to take off
06 He doesn't have to be
07 Tom has to learn

B

01 Do I must → Do I have to[Must I]
02 has to arrived → had to arrive
03 will has to → will have to
04 must to → has to[must]
05 don't has to → doesn't have to
06 will must → will have to

C

01 have to catch the train
02 don't have to go there
03 had to call the doctor
04 has to buy some books
05 doesn't have to attend the meeting
06 will have to take the test

D

01 have to work
02 don't have to buy
03 doesn't have to go
04 has to change
05 have to take
06 don't have to make
07 have to study
08 has to finish

내신 기출 ③

Unit 07 p. 77

A

01 should pass
02 should not[shouldn't] speak
03 should read
04 Should the girl wear
05 shouldn't[should not] go
06 Should we get
07 should not[shouldn't] be late
08 Should I do

B

01 should be kind
02 should not[shouldn't] make a noise
03 should go
04 should wear
05 should not[shouldn't] waste
06 Should she look for, she shouldn't

중간고사 • 기말고사 실전문제 pp. 78~84

객관식 정답 [01~25]

01 ⑤	**02** ③	**03** ①	**04** ⑤	**05** ②
06 ④	**07** ⑤	**08** ②	**09** ④	**10** ⑤
11 ③	**12** ①	**13** ②	**14** ④	**15** ②
16 ④	**17** ③	**18** ⑤	**19** ②	**20** ③
21 ②	**22** ④	**23** ⑤	**24** ③	**25** ⑤

주관식 정답 [26~50]

26 does → do
27 has → have
28 mays → may
29 May I call you
30 Can dogs see
31 must[should] not forget
32 don't have to prepare
33 able to run
34 don't have to go
35 must not tell
36 has to be
37 were able to play
38 Can I introduce myself
39 You must not park in front of
40 may have the wrong number
41 can play the flute and the guitar
42 No, can't
43 Tony and Becky can play
44 Children may not come into
45 Do we have to go
46 checking → check
47 not must → must not
48 to use → use
49 Customers will be able to buy the new smartphone
50 We didn't have to visit the store.

해설

01 '~할 수 있다'라는 능력을 나타낼 때는 조동사 can을 사용한다.

02 '~하지 않는 게 좋겠다'라는 의미로, 충고를 나타내는 should의 부정은 should not[shouldn't]으로 나타낼 수 있다.

03 상대방에게 요청을 할 때는 조동사 can을 사용하여 〈Can+주어+동사원형 ~?〉으로 나타낼 수 있다.

04 조동사 뒤에는 항상 동사원형을 써야 하므로 3인칭 단수형인 exercises는 들어갈 수 없다.

05 주어가 3인칭 단수이므로 have to는 has to의 형태로 들어가야 한다.

06 can이 능력이나 가능을 나타낼 때는 be able to로 바꾸어 쓸 수 있으며, could는 can의 과거형이고 주어가 복수이므로 be동사는 were를 써야 한다.

07 must가 의무를 나타낼 때는 have to로 바꾸어 쓸 수 있는데, 주어가 3인칭 단수이므로 has to로 써야 한다.

08 '~해야 할까?'라는 의미는 should의 의문문으로 나타낼 수 있다.

09 '~가 아닐지도 모른다'는 조동사 may의 부정형인 may not으로 나타낼 수 있다.

10 '~할 수 있을 것이다'는 will be able to로 쓴다.

11 '비가 올 것 같다'는 말에 '너는 우산을 가져가는 게 좋겠어.'라고 충고해야 하므로 조동사 should가 들어가야 한다.

12 '가장 친한 친구가 중국으로 이사 갔어.'라고 말했으므로, '너는 틀림없이 그녀가 무척 보고 싶겠다.'라고 대답해야 한다. 따라서 강한 추측을 나타내는 조동사 must가 들어가야 한다.

13 첫 번째 빈칸에는 '~일지도 모른다'라는 의미의 추측을 나타내는 may가, 두 번째 빈칸에는 '~해도 좋다'라는 의미의 허가를 나타내는 may가 들어가야 한다.

14 첫 번째 빈칸에는 '~임에 틀림없다'라는 의미의 강한 추측을 나타내는 must가, 두 번째 빈칸에는 '~해야 한다'라는 의미의 의무를 나타내는 must가 들어가야 한다.

15 상대방에게 요청할 때는 May가 아닌 Can[Could]을 써야 한다.

16 can의 미래시제는 will be able to로 써야 한다.

17 must의 부정은 must not으로 써야 한다.

18 조동사 뒤에는 반드시 동사원형을 써야 하므로 cleans를

clean으로 고쳐야 한다.

19 조동사 뒤에는 항상 동사원형이 온다.

20 ③은 '~할 수 있다'라는 능력을 나타내고, 나머지는 모두 '~해도 된다'라는 의미의 허가를 나타낸다.

21 ②는 '~임에 틀림없다'라는 강한 추측을 나타내고, 나머지는 모두 '~해야 한다'라는 의미의 의무를 나타낸다.

22 조동사 can이 능력, 가능을 나타낼 때만 be able to로 바꿔 쓸 수 있다.

23 조동사 must가 의무를 나타낼 때만 have to로 바꿔 쓸 수 있다.

24 첫 번째 문장: be able to 다음에는 동사원형을 써야 하므로 speaks를 speak로 고쳐야 한다.
네 번째 문장: 주어가 복수이므로 has를 have로 고쳐야 한다.

25 (b): 조동사 뒤에는 동사원형을 써야 하므로 dances를 dance로 고쳐야 한다.
(d): 전화기를 사용해도 되냐고 묻는 말에 I'm sorry.라고 말했으므로 부정의 대답인 may not이 되어야 한다.

26 조동사 뒤에는 동사원형을 써야 한다.

27 앞에 Does가 있으므로 has는 동사원형인 have가 되어야 한다.

28 조동사는 주어의 인칭과 수에 상관없이 동일한 형태로 써야 한다.

29 Yes, you may.라고 대답하고 있으므로, '내가 전화해도 될까?'라고 묻는 May I call you?를 써야 한다.

30 '아니, 그럴 수 없어. 개들은 노란색과 파란색만 볼 수 있어.'라고 답하고 있으므로, can을 써서 '개들이 빨간색을 볼 수 있니?'라고 질문해야 한다.

31 '~해서는 안 된다'는 must not 또는 should not으로 쓴다.

32 '~할 필요가 없다'는 don't have to로 쓴다.

33 능력, 가능은 can 또는 be able to로 쓸 수 있는데 문장 앞에 Is가 있으므로 able to를 이용하여 써야 한다.

34 오늘은 휴일이라고 했으므로 학교에 갈 필요가 없다는 말이 되어야 한다.

35 깜짝 파티라고 했으므로 '너는 그녀에게 말하면 안 된다'라는 말이 되어야 한다.

36 의무를 나타내는 must는 have to로 바꿔 쓸 수 있다. 주어가 3인칭 단수이므로 has to로 쓴다.

37 능력, 가능을 나타내는 can은 be able to로 바꿔 쓸 수 있는데 주어가 복수이고 문장의 시제가 과거이므로 be동사는 were로 쓴다.

38 '내가 ~해도 될까요?'라고 요청할 때는 Can I ~?나 May I ~?로 쓴다.

39 '~해서는 안 된다'는 must의 부정인 must not으로 쓴다.

40 '~일지도 모른다'는 조동사 may로 쓴다.

41 Tony는 플루트와 기타를 연주할 수 있다.

42 Becky는 플루트를 연주할 수 없다.

43 기타는 Tony와 Becky 둘 다 연주할 수 있다.

44 '~하면 안 된다'는 조동사 may의 부정형인 may not으로 쓴다.

45 '~해야 하니?'라는 의미가 되어야 하고 주어진 단어에 to가 있으므로 have to의 의문문으로 쓴다.

46 조동사 뒤에는 동사원형을 써야 한다.

47 조동사의 부정문은 조동사 뒤에 not을 써서 만든다.

48 조동사 뒤에는 동사원형을 써야 한다.

49 능력, 가능을 나타내는 can의 미래시제는 will be able to로 나타낼 수 있다.

50 '~할 필요가 없었다'는 have to의 과거 부정인 didn't have to로 쓴다.

CHAPTER

05 명사와 관사

Unit 01

p. 86

A

01 a
02 an
03 an
04 a
05 an
06 a
07 an
08 an
09 a
10 an
11 an
12 a

B

01 a week
02 a woman, a bus
03 An elephant, a big animal
04 a month
05 a small bed, an old desk
06 a cat, a young cat

Unit 02

p. 87

A

01 eggs
02 a tree
03 books
04 stars
05 a chair
06 pencils
07 a car
08 students
09 ants
10 a house
11 an hour
12 pictures
13 desks
14 birds
15 girls
16 an animal

B

01 pictures
02 cars
03 teacher
04 cookies
05 roses
06 girls
07 a student
08 hours
09 sons, daughter
10 nose, ears
11 hamburger, apples
12 eraser, pencils

Unit 03

p. 88

01 pianos
02 stories
03 buses
04 clocks
05 roofs
06 guitars
07 baskets
08 dishes
09 tomatoes
10 boxes
11 leaves
12 fingers
13 brushes
14 shelves
15 watches
16 keys
17 knives
18 classes
19 stores
20 foxes
21 zoos
22 dresses
23 wolves
24 photos
25 heroes
26 knives
27 babies
28 chickens
29 flies
30 potatoes
31 cities
32 radios
33 horses
34 benches
35 chefs
36 churches

Unit 04

p. 89

A

01 sheep
02 women
03 geese
04 children
05 oxen
06 feet
07 deer
08 mice
09 teeth
10 men
11 salmon
12 people

B

01 story → stories
02 box → boxes
03 boy → boys
04 sheeps → sheep
05 potato → potatoes
06 family → families

내신 기출 ①

Unit 05

p. 90

A

01 love, Korea, help, water
02 Jack, peace, honesty
03 Seoul, advice, truth

04 Emily, sugar, coffee, America
05 snow, paper, beauty
06 April, rain, joy
07 Paris, air, money, time
08 bread, hair, information

B
01 an information → information
02 coffees → coffee
03 flours → flour
04 a Seoul → Seoul
05 sugars → sugar
06 waters → water
07 a cheese → cheese
08 a Jessica → Jessica
09 a true love → true love

Unit 06 p. 91

A
01 a glass of
02 a pair of
03 a bottle of
04 a bowl of
05 four cups of
06 three pieces of
07 a slice of
08 two bowls of

B
01 a cup of tea
02 five pairs of socks
03 two pieces of cheese cake
04 three bottles of orange juice
05 a piece of toast

Unit 07 p. 92

A
01 the
02 the
03 the
04 a, an
05 The

B
01 ⓒ
02 ⓓ
03 ⓐ
04 ⓑ
05 ⓐ
06 ⓑ

내신기출 ②

Unit 08 p. 93

A
01 ×
02 the
03 ×
04 a
05 ×
06 ×
07 ×
08 ×
09 a
10 The
11 ×
12 the

B
01 sugar → the sugar
02 the work → work
03 the feet → foot
04 a piano → the piano
05 a dinner → dinner
06 MP3 player → an MP3 player
07 the tennis → tennis
08 the music → music
09 a university → university

내신기출 ③

Unit 09 p. 94

A
01 is
02 are
03 salt
04 were
05 was
06 are
07 were
08 water
09 were
10 was

B
01 There is much milk
02 There are many cars
03 There was a lot of snow
04 There are many rooms
05 There are four seasons

내신기출 ②

Unit 10 p. 95

A
01 apples
02 isn't

03 weren't
04 wasn't
05 a park, there is
06 Are, there aren't
07 Was, there was
08 Were, there weren't

B
01 There were not[weren't] many eggs
02 Was there a soccer game
03 There was a post office
04 There was not[wasn't] a lot of snow
05 Is there an elephant
06 Were there many people

중간고사 • 기말고사 실전문제 pp. 96~102

객관식 정답 [01~25]

01 ③	02 ③	03 ⑤	04 ④	05 ④
06 ⑤	07 ①	08 ②	09 ②	10 ⑤
11 ④	12 ⑤	13 ⑤	14 ③	15 ⑤
16 ③	17 ②	18 ②	19 ①	20 ④
21 ⑤	22 ②	23 ③	24 ③	25 ②

주관식 정답 [26~50]

26 The
27 a
28 The
29 hair
30 The
31 is
32 stories
33 oxen
34 radios
35 an → a
36 by a subway → by subway
37 a → an
38 two pieces of cake
39 a new pair of glasses
40 Salmon swim up the river
41 pair
42 piece
43 the
44 a
45 ×
46 a school bus → school bus
47 I love a scarf → I love the scarf
48 color → colors
49 We can see many people and deer at the park.
50 There are five bottles of water in the box.

해설

01 photo는 o로 끝나는 명사이지만 복수형은 끝에 -s만 붙인다.
① boys ② benches ④ wolves ⑤ chefs

02 앞에 an이 있으므로 빈칸에는 첫 발음이 모음인 단수 명사 eraser만 들어갈 수 있다.

03 There are 뒤에는 복수 명사를 써야 하는데, sheep은 단수형과 복수형이 동일한 명사이므로 빈칸에 들어갈 수 있다.

04 gloves는 두 개가 쌍을 이루어 하나가 되는 명사이므로 항상 복수로 쓰고 pair를 이용하여 개수를 센다.

05 baby의 복수형은 y를 없애고 -ies를 붙인다.

06 빈칸 앞에 two가 있으므로 빈칸에는 셀 수 있는 명사의 복수형이 들어가야 하는데 cheese는 셀 수 없는 명사이므로 들어갈 수 없다. salmon은 단수형과 복수형이 동일하다.

07 빈칸 앞에 the가 있으므로 관사를 쓰지 않는 운동 이름은 빈칸에 들어갈 수 없다.

08 추상명사인 love는 셀 수 없으므로 부정관사 a를 붙이지 않는다.

09 ②에는 하나를 가리키는 의미의 a가 들어갈 수 있고, ①, ④는 관용적으로, the[The]를 써야 하고, ③은 관사를 쓰지 않으며, ⑤는 수식을 받는 대상이므로 The를 써야 한다.

10 첫 번째 빈칸 앞에 Three가 있으므로 man의 복수형인

men이 들어가야 하고, 두 번째 빈칸 뒤에 are가 있으므로 child의 복수형인 children이 들어가야 한다.

11 첫 번째 빈칸 앞에 There are가 있으므로 fly의 복수형인 flies가 들어가야 하고, 두 번째 빈칸에는 의미상 tooth의 복수형인 teeth가 들어가야 한다.

12 추상명사는 셀 수 없는 명사이므로 복수형으로 쓰지 않는다.

13 교통수단 앞에는 관사를 쓰지 않는다.

14 earth 앞에는 관용적으로 the를 써야 한다.

15 deer는 단수형과 복수형이 같은 명사이고, 이 문장에서는 복수형으로 쓰였으므로 be동사는 are가 되어야 한다.

16 sheep은 단수형과 복수형이 같은 명사이고, mouse의 복수형은 mice이다.

17 woman의 복수형은 women이고 coffee는 셀 수 없는 명사이므로 복수형으로 쓸 수 없으며 용기나 단위를 이용하여 셀 수 있다.

18 foot의 복수형은 feet이다.

19 honest는 첫 발음이 모음이기 때문에 a가 아닌 an을 써야 하고 나머지는 모두 a를 써야 한다.

20 악기 이름(①)과, 서로 무엇을 말하는지 아는 명사를 말할 때(②, ⑤), 수식을 받아 무엇인지 분명할 때(③)는 앞에 the를 쓴다. ④는 막연한 소풍을 말하고 있으므로 a를 써야 한다.

21 meat는 셀 수 없는 명사이므로 복수형으로 쓸 수 없고, '얇은 고기 두 덩어리'는 two slices of meat로 써야 한다.

22 월 이름 March는 고유명사로, 셀 수 없는 명사이므로 a를 붙일 수 없다.

23 hour는 첫 발음이 모음으로 시작하기 때문에 a가 아닌 an을 써야 한다.

24 두 번째 문장: advice는 추상명사로 셀 수 없기 때문에 복수형으로 쓸 수 없다.
네 번째 문장: chef는 f로 끝나는 명사이지만 복수형은 예외로 끝에 -s만 붙인다.

25 (a) 과목명 앞에는 관사를 쓰지 않는다.
(d) salt는 셀 수 없는 물질명사이므로 앞에 a를 쓰지 않는다. '그' 소금을 건네달라는 의미이므로 the로 쓴다.
(e) pants는 두 개가 쌍을 이루어 하나가 되는 명사로 항상 복수형으로 써야 한다.

26 명사가 수식을 받아 무엇인지 분명할 때는 앞에 the를 쓴다.

27 '~마다'라는 의미는 a로 쓸 수 있다.

28 sun은 관용적으로 the를 붙이는 명사이다.

29 hair는 물질명사로 셀 수 없는 명사이다. 단, 머리카락 한 가닥은 a hair로 표현할 수 있다.

30 앞에 나왔던 명사를 가리킬 때는 the를 쓴다.

31 뒤에 셀 수 없는 명사가 나왔으므로 are가 아닌 is를 써야 한다.

32 story는 y를 없애고 -ies를 붙여 복수형을 만든다.

33 ox의 복수형은 oxen이다.

34 radio는 o로 끝나는 명사이지만 복수형은 예외로 끝에 -s만 붙인다.

35 university는 u로 시작하지만 첫 발음이 자음이므로 an을 a로 고쳐야 한다.

36 교통수단 앞에는 관사를 쓰지 않는다.

37 X-ray는 첫 발음이 모음이기 때문에 a가 아닌 an을 써야 한다.

38 셀 수 없는 명사인 cake는 piece로 개수를 센다.

39 안경은 두 개가 쌍을 이루어 하나가 되는 명사이므로 glass에 -es를 붙여 사용한다.

40 salmon은 단수형과 복수형이 동일한 명사이다.

41 pants와 shoes는 두 개가 쌍을 이루어 하나가 되는 명사로 개수를 셀 때는 pair로 센다.

42 셀 수 없는 명사인 furniture와 information을 셀 때는 piece로 센다.

43 서로 무엇인지 알고 있는 것을 말할 때는 명사 앞에 the를 쓴다.

44 특정 게임이 아닌 막연히 다른 하나의 게임을 의미하므로 명사 앞에 a를 써야 한다.

45 교통수단 앞에는 관사를 쓰지 않는다.

46 〈by+교통수단〉일 때, 명사 앞에 a를 쓰지 않는다.

47 앞에 나왔던 명사를 언급할 때는 명사 앞에 the를 쓴다.

48 명사 앞에 many가 있으므로 복수형으로 써야 한다.

49 deer는 단수형과 복수형이 같은 명사이다.

50 물 다섯 병은 five bottles of water로 쓰고, five bottles는 복수이므로 There are로 쓴다.

CHAPTER 06 대명사

Unit 01 p. 104

A

01 his
02 us
03 Her
04 them
05 hers
06 Its
07 They

B

01 cats → cat's
02 her → hers
03 Bills → Bill's
04 me → mine
05 They → We
06 It's → Its
07 mine → me
08 She → her

Unit 02 p. 105

A

01 myself
02 yourself
03 himself
04 myself

B

01 ⓐ
02 ⓑ
03 ⓐ
04 ⓐ
05 ⓑ

내신 기출 ①

Unit 03 p. 106

A

01 This
02 That
03 These
04 Those
05 That
06 This
07 Those
08 this

B

01 That is not[isn't] my suitcase.
02 Are these your family photos?
03 This is a very delicious apple.
04 Are those my (little) sister's gloves?
05 Is that his old jacket?
06 That is my favorite singer.
07 Are those your classmates?
08 These are letters from my parents.
09 This is my best friend.

Unit 04 p. 107

A

01 대
02 형
03 형
04 대
05 대
06 형
07 형
08 대
09 대
10 형

B

01 This man
02 That box
03 These books
04 these beautiful flowers
05 that movie
06 those shoes
07 This coat
08 those people
09 These flowers

내신 기출 ①

Unit 05 p. 108

A

01 ⓑ
02 ⓐ
03 ⓔ
04 ⓒ
05 ⓕ
06 ⓓ

B

01 ⓐ
02 ⓐ
03 ⓑ
04 ⓐ
05 ⓐ
06 ⓐ
07 ⓑ
08 ⓐ
09 ⓐ

Unit 06

p. 109

A

01 one
02 one
03 ones
04 one
05 it
06 ones
07 it
08 one

B

01 one
02 it
03 ones
04 it
05 they
06 ones
07 it, one
08 it
09 them

Unit 07

p. 110

A

01 another
02 the other
03 the other
04 another
05 another
06 the other

B

01 another
02 the other
03 one
04 One, the other
05 One, another, the other

Unit 08

p. 111

A

01 others
02 others
03 the others
04 others
05 others

B

01 Some people are hardworking but others are lazy.
02 Some are apples but the others are oranges.
03 Some of these people use English but the others use Korean.
04 Some are black, others are white, but the others are gray.

내신기출 ②

중간고사 • 기말고사 실전문제

pp. 112~118

객관식 정답 [01~25]

01 ①	**02** ④	**03** ③	**04** ②	**05** ⑤
06 ①	**07** ⑤	**08** ④	**09** ④	**10** ①
11 ④	**12** ④	**13** ④	**14** ①	**15** ②
16 ⑤	**17** ⑤	**18** ③	**19** ②	**20** ④
21 ④	**22** ②	**23** ③	**24** ②	**25** ⑤

주관식 정답 [26~50]

26 hers
27 ourselves
28 one
29 It
30 one
31 It
32 Her
33 Her
34 They
35 them
36 that → it
37 it → them
38 yourself → yourselves
39 Mike's brother is a high school student.
40 One is long, and the other is short.
41 These books are mine.
42 It
43 one[One]
44 your dress
45 (a), (d), (e)
46 One students → Some students
47 other is a Jindo → another is a Jindo
48 I love it → I love them
49 I myself sent her an email
50 It will rain this evening.

해설

01 문장의 주어로 '~은/는/이/가'의 의미를 나타내므로 인칭대명사의 주격을 써야 한다.

02 명사 앞에 쓰여 '~의'라는 의미를 나타내므로 인칭대명사의 소유격을 써야 한다.

03 전치사의 목적어로 쓰였으므로 인칭대명사의 목적격을 써야 한다.

04 〈소유격+명사〉는 소유대명사로 나타낼 수 있으며, '그녀의 인형'이므로 '그녀의 것'이라는 의미의 hers로 바꿔 쓸 수 있다.

05 복수인 we의 재귀대명사는 ourselves이다.

06 '그 스마트패드는 그녀의 것이다'라는 문장은 '그것은 그녀의 스마트패드이다'라는 의미이므로 빈칸에는 인칭대명사의 소유격 her가 들어가야 한다.

07 동사의 목적어로 쓰여 '~을/를'이라는 의미의 인칭대명사의 목적격이 쓰여야 하므로 소유격인 their는 쓸 수 없다.

08 '이 ~'라는 의미로 단수 명사를 수식하는 지시형용사 This가 쓰였으므로 복수 명사는 빈칸에 들어갈 수 없다.

09 목적어에 '그들 자신'이라는 의미의 재귀대명사가 쓰였으므로 I가 포함된 주어는 올 수 없다.

10 ①은 '그것'이라는 의미의 인칭대명사이고, 나머지는 모두 비인칭주어이다. (② 날짜 ③ 날씨 ④시간 ⑤ 거리)

11 ④는 '이것들'이라는 의미의 지시대명사이고, 나머지는 모두 '이 ~들'이라는 의미의 지시형용사이다.

12 정해진 그것을 나타내는 것이 아니라 같은 종류의 불특정한 것을 가리키고 있으므로 it을 부정대명사 one으로 고쳐야 한다.

13 주어 she 자신이 동작의 대상이 되고 있으므로 재귀대명사인 herself를 써야 한다.

14 명암을 나타내는 비인칭주어 It으로 고쳐야 한다.

15 첫 번째 빈칸에는 뒤에 복수 명사가 나오므로 '저 ~들'이라는 의미의 지시형용사 Those가 들어가야 하고, 두 번째 빈칸에는 단수 명사가 나오므로 지시대명사 This가 들어가야 한다.

16 첫 번째 빈칸에는 '나를'을 뜻하는 목적격인 me가 들어가야 하고, 두 번째 빈칸에는 '나 자신'이라는 의미로 재귀대명사 myself가 들어가야 한다.

17 '저 ~'이라는 의미로 단수 명사를 수식하므로 지시형용사 That을 써야 하고, '그의 것'이라는 소유대명사는 his로 쓴다.

18 '직접'이라는 의미로 주어 He의 동작이나 행위를 강조하고 있으므로 주어 다음에 재귀대명사 himself를 써서 표현할 수 있다.

19 '몇몇은 ~, 나머지 다른 것들은 …'은 Some ~, the others ...로 나타낸다.

20 ⓐ에는 '~의'라는 의미를 나타내는 소유격 Her가 들어가야 하고, ⓑ에는 '~을/를'이라는 의미로 동사의 목적어가 되는 목적격 her가 들어가야 한다.

21 ④에는 '그것의'라는 의미의 소유격 Its가 들어가야 하고, ①, ⑤에는 인칭대명사의 주격 It이, ②, ③에는 비인칭주어 It[it]이 들어가야 한다.

22 ②는 앞에서 언급되었던 정해진 그것을 말하므로 It이 들어가야 하고, 나머지는 모두 정해지지 않은 물건을 가리키므로 one이 들어가야 한다.

23 ③번은 재귀대명사가 재귀용법으로 쓰였으므로 생략할 수 없고, 나머지는 모두 강조용법으로 쓰였으므로 생략이 가능하다.

24 날씨를 나타내는 문장이므로 That을 비인칭주어 It으로 고쳐야 한다.

25 '나의'라는 의미가 되어야 하므로 me를 인칭대명사의 소유격 my로 고쳐야 한다.

26 '그녀의 것'이라는 의미가 되어야 하므로 소유대명사 hers를 써야 한다.

27 주어 We의 동작이 스스로 영향을 미치고 있으므로 재귀대명사를 써야 한다.

28 정해지지 않은 불특정한 물건을 가리키므로 부정대명사 one을 써야 한다.

29 앞에서 언급된 정해진 대상을 나타내므로 인칭대명사 It을 써야 한다.

30 앞에서 언급한 것과 같은 종류의 것을 가리키므로 부정대명사 one을 써야 한다.

31 날짜를 나타내는 비인칭주어 It을 쓸 수 있다.

32 '그녀는 귀여운 인형을 가지고 있다.'는 '그녀의 인형은 귀엽다.'로 바꿔 쓸 수 있다.

33 명사 앞에 쓰여 '~의'라는 의미를 나타내므로 인칭대명사의 소유격으로 써야 한다.

34 '은/는/이/가'라는 의미로 문장의 복수 주어이므로 인칭대명사의 주격 They로 써야 한다.

35 '~을/를'이라는 의미로 문장의 복수 목적어이므로 they의 목적격 them으로 써야 한다.

36 거리를 나타낼 때는 비인칭주어 it을 써야 한다.

37 '~을/를'이라는 의미로 앞에 나온 복수 목적어 these tickets를 받으므로 인칭대명사의 목적격 them으로 써야 한다.

38 James and you이므로 복수 재귀대명사인 yourselves로 써야 한다.

39 명사의 소유격은 's로 나타낼 수 있다.

40 둘 중 하나는 one, 나머지 하나는 the other로 쓴다.

41 '이 ~들'이라는 의미로 복수 명사를 수식하는 지시형용사이므로 These로 써야 하고, '나의 것'은 소유대명사 mine으로 써야 한다.

42 첫 번째 빈칸에는 날씨를 나타내는 비인칭주어 It이 들어가야 하고, 두 번째 빈칸에는 시간을 나타내는 비인칭주어 It이 들어가야 한다.

43 첫 번째 빈칸에는 정해지지 않은 불특정한 물건을 가리키는 부정대명사 one이 들어가야 하고, 두 번째 빈칸에는 둘 중 하나를 말할 때 쓰는 부정대명사 One이 들어가야 한다.

44 소유대명사는 〈소유격+명사〉로 나타낼 수 있다.

45 (b): to 다음에 나온 he를 전치사의 목적어 역할을 하는 목적격 인칭대명사 him으로 고쳐야 한다.
(c) '너의 여동생'이라는 의미가 되어야 하므로 yours를 인칭대명사의 소유격 your로 고쳐야 한다.

46 동사가 have의 형태이므로, 주어는 복수여야 한다.

47 대상이 3개일 때, 두 번째로 가리키는 단수의 명사는 another로 표현한다.

48 three dogs는 복수이므로 them으로 대신할 수 있다.

49 '직접'이라는 의미로 주어의 동작이나 행위를 강조할 때 재귀대명사를 쓸 수 있다.

50 비인칭주어 It을 써서 날씨를 나타낼 수 있다.

CHAPTER 07 형용사와 부사의 비교 표현

Unit 01 p. 120

01 unable
02 dark
03 dirty
04 safe
05 shallow
06 closed
07 wet
08 difficult[hard]
09 full
10 cheap
11 unhappy
12 sick
13 light
14 low
15 young
16 rude
17 poor
18 foolish
19 weak
20 short
21 thin
22 unwise

Unit 02 p. 121

A

01 a shirt
02 The girl
03 My brother
04 a rose
05 a book
06 She
07 The house
08 a boy
09 the car
10 a table
11 a cat
12 The movie
13 These boxes
14 The woman

B

01 ⓐ
02 ⓑ
03 ⓑ
04 ⓐ
05 ⓐ
06 ⓑ
07 ⓐ
08 ⓑ

내신기출 ①

Unit 03 p. 122

A

01 some
02 any
03 some
04 any
05 some
06 some
07 any
08 some

B

01 any
02 some
03 any
04 some
05 any
06 some, any
07 some
08 some, any
09 any, some

Unit 04 p. 123

A

01 many
02 many
03 much
04 Many
05 much
06 much
07 many
08 much

B

01 much water
02 Many[A lot of, Lots of] people
03 much[a lot of, lots of] money
04 many sisters
05 many[a lot of, lots of] books
06 much[a lot of, lots of] information

Unit 05 p. 124

A

01 a few
02 a little
03 a little
04 A few
05 little
06 few
07 little
08 a few

B

01 little rain
02 a few people
03 a little cheese
04 few words
05 little time

Unit 06 p. 125

A

01 good
02 well
03 start
04 difficult
05 her daughter passed the exam
06 plays (the piano)
07 high
08 Tim got better after three days

B

01 ⓓ
02 ⓐ
03 ⓒ
04 ⓑ
05 ⓒ
06 ⓐ

내신기출 ②

Unit 07 p. 126

A

01 quickly
02 slowly
03 easily
04 happily
05 strangely
06 usually
07 kindly
08 simply
09 sadly
10 really
11 angrily
12 gently
13 carefully
14 luckily
15 safely
16 heavily

B

01 carefully
02 quietly
03 slowly
04 Suddenly
05 easy, easily
06 safely, safe

Unit 08 p. 127

A

01 늦은
02 늦게(까지)
03 최근에
04 일찍
05 이른
06 어려운
07 열심히
08 거의 ~하지 않다
09 높이
10 높은
11 매우
12 꽤
13 예쁜
14 가까이
15 가까운
16 거의

B

01 nearly
02 recently
03 highly
04 hard
05 closely
06 hardly

Unit 09

p. 128

A

01 My brother and I always eat breakfast.
02 He usually goes to school by bus.
03 Sally is sometimes late for school.
04 We often ride our bicycles on weekends.
05 We will never forget you.
06 She seldom goes swimming in the sea.

B

01 is never late
02 hardly/seldom read books
03 is sometimes absent
04 usually go to school
05 will always remember

Unit 10

p. 129

A

01 too
02 either
03 too
04 too
05 either

B

01 likes it, too
02 don't drink it, either
03 enjoy it, too
04 didn't feed it, either
05 can swim, too

내신기출 ②

Unit 11

pp. 130~132

A

01 abler[more able] – ablest[most able]
02 angrier – angriest
03 worse – worst
04 more beautiful – most beautiful
05 bigger – biggest
06 more boring – most boring
07 braver – bravest
08 brighter – brightest
09 busier – busiest
10 more careless – most careless
11 more carefully – most carefully
12 cheaper – cheapest
13 cleaner – cleanest
14 colder – coldest
15 more comfortable – most comfortable
16 more dangerous – most dangerous
17 darker – darkest
18 deeper – deepest
19 more delicious – most delicious
20 more difficult – most difficult
21 more hardworking – most hardworking
22 dirtier – dirtiest
23 more easily – most easily
24 more exciting – most exciting
25 more expensive – most expensive
26 more famous – most famous
27 faster – fastest
28 fatter – fattest
29 more foolish – most foolish
30 fresher – freshest
31 friendlier – friendliest
32 better – best
33 greater – greatest
34 more handsome[handsomer] – most handsome[handsomest]
35 happier – happiest
36 harder – hardest
37 healthier – healthiest
38 heavier – heaviest
39 more helpful – most helpful
40 higher – highest
41 hotter – hottest
42 more important – most important
43 more interesting – most interesting
44 kinder – kindest
45 larger – largest

46 lazier – laziest
47 lighter – lightest
48 less – least
49 longer – longest
50 lovelier – loveliest
51 lower – lowest
52 luckier – luckiest
53 more – most
54 nicer – nicest
55 noisier – noisiest
56 older – oldest
57 politer[more polite] – politest[most polite]
58 more popular – most popular
59 prettier – prettiest
60 more quickly – most quickly
61 quieter – quietest
62 richer – richest
63 ruder – rudest
64 sadder – saddest
65 safer – safest
66 more serious – most serious
67 shallower – shallowest
68 shorter – shortest
69 more slowly – most slowly
70 smaller – smallest
71 smarter – smartest
72 stronger – strongest
73 sunnier – sunniest
74 sweeter – sweetest
75 taller – tallest
76 tastier – tastiest
77 more terrible – most terrible
78 thicker – thickest
79 thinner – thinnest
80 more useful – most useful
81 weaker – weakest
82 wider – widest
83 wiser – wisest
84 younger – youngest

Unit 12

p. 133

A

01 너의 남동생[형]만큼 나이가 많은
02 James만큼 강한
03 너만큼 키가 크지는 않은
04 Judy의 신발만큼 비싼
05 네 여동생[언니]의 머리카락만큼 긴
06 소라가 할 수 있는 만큼 빠르게
07 Mary가 하는 것만큼 잘
08 탁자만큼 무겁지는 않은

B

01 as beautiful as
02 as good as
03 not as[so] polite as
04 as high as
05 as brave as
06 not as[so] large as

Unit 13

p. 134

A

01 stronger
02 bigger
03 hotter
04 better
05 early
06 much
07 more
08 difficult

B

01 ⓐ higher than ⓑ lower than
02 ⓐ heavier than ⓑ lighter than
03 ⓐ bigger than ⓑ smaller than
04 ⓐ more expensive than ⓑ cheaper than

Unit 14

p. 135

A

01 the tallest
02 the largest
03 the fastest
04 the smartest
05 the biggest
06 the youngest
07 the oldest
08 men

B

01 the most

02 The most comfortable seats

03 the busiest cities

04 the longest river

05 the hottest month

06 the most famous singers

Unit 15

p. 136

A

01 as well as

02 not as[so] dirty

03 the youngest

04 more important

05 the best student

06 the most expensive

B

01 the most beautiful

02 more difficult than

03 as cheap as

04 the greatest soccer player

05 not as[so] heavy as

06 much faster than

내신기출 ②

중간고사 • 기말고사 실전문제

pp. 137~143

객관식 정답 [01~25]

01 ③	**02** ⑤	**03** ②	**04** ④	**05** ②
06 ③	**07** ④	**08** ③, ⑤	**09** ⑤	**10** ⑤
11 ①	**12** ④	**13** ①	**14** ③	**15** ②
16 ④	**17** ③	**18** ①	**19** ①	**20** ①
21 ④	**22** ②	**23** ⑤	**24** ②	**25** ②

주관식 정답 [26~50]

26 is always

27 hot

28 high

29 much

30 much

31 many

32 most boring

33 skinnier

34 beautiful

35 go sometimes → sometimes go

36 angrily → angry

37 little → few

38 Does James often visit

39 one of the widest rooms

40 as famous as her

41 most

42 much

43 thicker

44 as cheap as

45 the most interesting

46 make usually → usually make

47 any → some

48 a little onions → a few onions

49 Mike, the tallest

50 Fortune will never smile upon him.

해설

01 hard는 형용사와 부사의 형태가 같은 단어이며, hardly는 '거의 ~하지 않다'라는 의미이다.

02 rain은 셀 수 없는 명사이므로 수량형용사 little이 들어가야 한다.

03 문장 전체를 수식하여 그 뜻을 분명하게 하는 역할을 하는 것은 부사이다.

04 '~보다'라는 의미의 than이 있으므로 비교급으로 써야 하며, good의 비교급은 better이다.

05 빈도부사는 be동사나 조동사 뒤에, 일반동사 앞에 쓴다.

06 well – better – best

07 첫 번째 빈칸에는 형용사 sorry를 수식하는 부사 형태가

들어가야 하고, 두 번째 빈칸에는 부정문에서 '또한, 역시' 라는 동의를 나타내므로 either가 들어가야 한다.

08 '~만큼 …하지 못하는'이라는 말은 〈not as[so]+형용사/부사+as〉를 이용해서 표현할 수 있다.

09 salt는 셀 수 없는 명사이므로 수량형용사 a few는 쓸 수 없다.

10 most가 있으므로 끝에 -st를 붙여 최상급을 만드는 large는 빈칸에 들어갈 수 없다.

11 '훨씬 더'라는 의미로 비교급을 강조할 때는 비교급 앞에 much, even, far, still, a lot 등을 쓴다.

12 수량형용사 much는 셀 수 없는 명사 앞에 써야 한다.

13 첫 번째 빈칸에는 비교급이 쓰였으므로 '~보다'라는 의미의 than이 들어가야 하고, 두 번째 빈칸에는 '~에서'를 뜻하는 in이 들어가야 한다.

14 첫 번째 빈칸에는 water가 셀 수 없는 명사이므로 수량형용사 much를 써야 하고, 두 번째 빈칸에는 횟수를 나타내는 times가 셀 수 있는 명사이므로, many를 써야 한다.

15 bad의 최상급은 worst이다.

16 '절대 ~하지 않다'는 빈도부사 never로 표현할 수 있다. never는 이미 부정의 의미가 있으므로, 따로 not을 쓰지 않는다는 것에 유의해야 한다.

17 '가장 ~한[하게]'는 〈the+최상급〉으로 써야 하며, tall의 최상급은 tallest이다.

18 '가끔'은 빈도부사 sometimes로 표현하며, 빈도부사는 일반동사 앞에 써야 한다.

19 ①은 최상급이므로 most가 들어가야 하고, 나머지는 모두 비교급이므로 more가 들어가야 한다.

20 a little, little은 셀 수 없는 명사 앞에 쓰는 수량형용사이므로 students 앞에 쓸 수 없다. A few가 되어야 한다.

21 '가장 ~한 것들 중 하나'라는 표현은 〈one of the+최상급+복수 명사〉로 쓰므로 city를 복수형인 cities로 써야 한다.

22 보어로 쓰여 주어를 보충 설명하는 것은 형용사이므로 easily를 easy로 고쳐야 한다.

23 셀 수 있는 명사의 복수형인 cars가 나왔으므로 a little을 a few로 고쳐야 한다.

24 '훨씬 더'라는 의미로 비교급을 강조할 때는 비교급 앞에 much, even, far, still, a lot 등을 쓰며, very는 비교급을 수식할 수 없다.

25 (a) '또한, 역시'라는 동의를 나타낼 때, 긍정문에서는 either가 아닌 too를 써야 한다.
(c) 문장 전체를 수식하여 그 뜻을 분명하게 하는 역할을 하는 것은 부사이므로 Fortunate를 Fortunately로 고쳐야 한다.
(e) 명사 앞에서 명사를 꾸며 주는 역할을 하는 것은 형용사이므로 strongly를 strong으로 고쳐야 한다.

26 빈도부사는 be동사 뒤에 써야 한다.

27 '~만큼 …하지 못하는'이라는 말은 〈not as[so]+형용사/부사+as〉로 쓸 수 있다.

28 high는 형용사와 부사가 같은 형태의 단어이고, highly는 '매우, 대단히'라는 의미의 부사이다.

29 money는 셀 수 없는 명사이므로 수량형용사 much를 써야 한다.

30 salt는 셀 수 없는 명사이므로 수량형용사 much를 써야 한다.

31 things는 셀 수 있는 명사의 복수형이므로 수량형용사 many를 써야 한다.

32 앞에 the가 있고, '세상에서 가장 지루한'이라는 의미가 되어야 하므로 최상급으로 써야 한다.

33 '~보다'라는 의미의 than이 있으므로 비교급으로 써야 한다.

34 보어로 쓰여, 주어를 보충 설명하는 역할을 하므로 형용사의 형태로 써야 한다.

35 빈도부사는 일반동사 앞에 써야 한다.

36 보어로 쓰여 목적어를 보충 설명하는 역할을 하는 것은 부사가 아닌 형용사이다.

37 days는 셀 수 있는 명사이므로 수량형용사 a few를 써야 한다.

38 빈도부사는 일반동사 앞에 쓰므로 visit 앞에 써야 한다.

39 '가장 ~한 것들 중 하나'라는 표현은 〈one of the+최상급+복수 명사〉로 쓰며, wide의 최상급은 widest이다.

40 '~만큼 …한[하게]'이라는 의미는 〈as+형용사/부사+as〉 형태의 원급 비교로 나타낼 수 있다.

41 첫 번째 빈칸에는 '많이'라는 의미의 부사 much의 최상

급인 most가 들어가야 하고, 두 번째 빈칸에는 expensive의 최상급인 most expensive의 most가 들어가야 한다.

42 첫 번째 빈칸에는 '많은'을 의미하며, 셀 수 없는 명사 time 앞에 쓸 수 있는 수량형용사 much가 들어가야 하고, 두 번째 빈칸에는 '훨씬'이라는 의미로 비교급을 강조할 수 있는 부사 much가 들어가야 한다.

43 책 B는 책 A보다 더 두껍다.

44 책 A는 책 C만큼 가격이 싸다.

45 책 C는 셋 중 가장 흥미로운 책이다.

46 빈도부사는 일반동사 앞에 써야 한다.

47 긍정문에서는 any가 아닌 some을 쓴다.

48 셀 수 있는 명사의 복수형 앞에는 a few를 쓴다.

49 Tom과 Brian은 키가 같고 이들보다 Mike가 더 크다. Bob은 Mike보다 작으므로 가장 키가 큰 소년은 Mike이다.

50 '절대 ~하지 않다'는 빈도부사 never로 나타낼 수 있고, 빈도부사는 조동사 뒤, 일반동사 앞에 쓴다. never에는 이미 부정의 의미가 있으므로, 따로 not을 쓰지 않는다는 것에 유의해야 한다.

CHAPTER 08 의문사 의문문

Unit 01 p. 146

A

01 Who
02 What
03 When
04 Where
05 Why
06 How
07 Who(m)
08 When

B

01 Who is your teacher?
02 Who closed the door?
03 Who(m) does she teach?
04 Who was with Tom yesterday?
05 Who lives in this house?
06 Who(m) does Jessica like?
07 Who helps your parents?

Unit 02 p. 147

A

01 ⓐ
02 ⓓ
03 ⓒ
04 ⓔ
05 ⓑ

B

01 What does she have
02 What do you do on Sundays
03 What is that over there
04 What did John talk about
05 What are you doing now

내신기출 ②

Unit 03 p. 148

A

01 When
02 Where
03 Where
04 When
05 Where
06 What
07 When
08 Where

B

01 Where is your bag?
02 When does the movie begin?
03 Where does Judy live?
04 When do you go to school?
05 Where is the bookstore?
06 When will Sam and Tom go there?
07 When does his father come home?
08 Where did you go yesterday?
09 What time does the hospital open?

Unit 04 p. 149

A

01 Why
02 How
03 Why
04 How
05 How
06 Why
07 How
08 Why

B

01 ⓒ
02 ⓔ
03 ⓐ
04 ⓑ
05 ⓓ
06 ⓕ
07 ⓘ
08 ⓖ
09 ⓗ

Unit 05 pp. 150～151

A

01 old
02 tall
03 big[large]
04 often
05 far
06 long
07 many

B

01 How old
02 How tall
03 How often
04 How many
05 How far
06 How long
07 How much

C

01 ⓕ
02 ⓓ
03 ⓒ
04 ⓐ
05 ⓗ
06 ⓑ
07 ⓔ
08 ⓖ

D

01 How big is your new apartment?
02 How long should you wait here?
03 How tall is the 63 Building?
04 How often do you brush your teeth?
05 How far is it from his house to the office?
06 How many people were there at the concert?

내신 기출 ③

Unit 06 p. 152

A

01 Which
02 Whose
03 What
04 Whose
05 Which

B

01 What time does the movie begin
02 Which bag do you prefer
03 Whose umbrella is this
04 What color is your mother's car
05 What day is it today
06 Which bike is faster

중간고사 • 기말고사 실전문제 pp. 153～158

객관식 정답 [01～25]

01 ①	**02** ②	**03** ④	**04** ②	**05** ④
06 ①	**07** ⑤	**08** ③	**09** ①	**10** ①, ⑤
11 ③	**12** ④	**13** ⑤	**14** ①	**15** ③
16 ②	**17** ②	**18** ⑤	**19** ③	**20** ③
21 ②	**22** ④	**23** ⑤	**24** ③	**25** ④

주관식 정답 [26～50]

26 How old
27 When
28 Why

29 are → do
30 you did → did you
31 How → Why
32 How old
33 How often
34 How much
35 What song
36 Which (one)
37 Why
38 What
39 Why were you late for
40 What are you going to watch
41 How often does she take pictures
42 (d) want → wants
43 (e) go → going
44 Where can I try on
45 How many suits do you have
46 What time do you want to check out
47 When → Where
48 How we → How do we
49 Whose → Which
50 When did Mary and Tom know the result of the test?

해설

01 '어떻게'라는 의미의 의문사는 How이다.

02 '언제'라는 의미의 의문사는 When이다.

03 '얼마나 자주'라는 의미는 How often으로 표현한다.

04 '누가'라는 의미의 의문사는 Who이다.

05 '무슨'이라는 의미의 의문사는 What이다.

06 Which size do you need이므로 세 번째로 오는 단어는 do이다.

07 How many people came to your이므로 세 번째로 오는 단어는 people이다.

08 '어디, 어디서'라는 의미의 의문사는 Where이다.

09 '왜'라는 의미의 의문사는 Why이다.

10 ② got → get, ③ many → much, ④ Whose → Which가 되어야 한다.

11 '얼마나 오래'라는 의미의 How long이 알맞다.

12 '무엇을'이라는 의미의 What이, '누구를'이라는 의미의 Who(m)이 알맞다.

13 '누구의'라는 의미의 Whose가, '어느'라는 의미의 Which가 알맞다.

14 '왜'라는 의미의 Why가 알맞다. 또한, people이 셀 수 있는 명사이므로 '얼마나 많은'이라는 의미의 How many가 알맞다.

15 ③에는 What이, 나머지에는 When/Where가 들어간다.

16 의문사 다음에 do동사가 와야 하므로 Minho does가 아니라 does Minho가 되어야 한다.

17 주어가 you이므로 does가 아니라 do가 되어야 한다.

18 주어가 3인칭 단수이므로 do가 아니라 does가 되어야 한다.

19 do동사 다음에 나오는 일반동사는 동사원형이 되어야 하므로 uses가 아니라 use가 되어야 한다.

20 '얼마나 큰'이라는 의미의 의문사는 How big이다.

21 〈의문사+do동사+주어+동사원형 ~?〉의 형태로 써야 한다. 주어가 she이므로 does가 되어야 하고, look 다음에는 형용사 tired가 와야 한다.

22 순서대로 Who, What, How, Which가 들어간다.

23 이유를 말하고 있으므로 Why does he drink water?로 물어야 한다.

24 첫 번째 문장은 likes가 아니라 like, 세 번째 문장은 does가 아니라 did, 네 번째 문장은 heard가 아니라 hear가 되어야 한다.

25 왜 컵케이크를 만드냐는 질문에 만드는 방법을 말하는 대답은 자연스럽지 않다.

26 '얼마나 오래된'이라는 의미의 표현은 How old이다.

27 '언제'라는 의미의 의문사는 When이다.

28 '왜'라는 의미의 의문사는 Why이다.

29 일반동사 think가 있으므로 do가 알맞다.

30 〈의문사+do동사+주어+동사원형 ~?〉의 형태이므로 did you가 알맞다.

31 Because로 대답하고 있으므로, 질문은 Why ~?로 해야 한다.

32 '몇 살'이라는 의미는 How old로 표현한다.

33 '얼마나 자주'는 How often으로 쓴다.

34 sugar는 셀 수 없는 명사이므로 '얼마나 많이'라는 의미의 의문사로 How much가 와야 한다.

35 '무슨'이라는 의미의 의문사는 What이다.

36 '어느 것'이라는 의미의 의문사는 Which (one)이다.

37 '왜'라는 의미의 의문사는 Why이다.

38 '몇 시'라는 의미의 의문사는 What time이다.

39 〈의문사+be동사+주어 ~?〉의 형태로 써야 한다.
be late for ~에 늦다

40 〈의문사+be동사+주어 ~?〉의 형태로 써야 한다.
be going to ~할 것이다

41 〈How often+do동사+주어+동사원형 ~?〉의 형태로 써야 한다.

42 who가 주어로 쓰일 경우 3인칭 단수 취급하므로 wants가 되어야 한다.

43 be going to 의문문이므로 When are we going to ~?가 되어야 한다.

44 〈Where+조동사+주어+동사원형 ~?〉의 형태로 써야 한다.
try on ~을 입어보다

45 suits는 셀 수 있는 명사이므로 How many를 써서 나타낸다.

46 〈What time+do동사+주어+동사원형 ~?〉의 형태로 써야 한다.
check out (호텔에서) 나가다

47 장소로 대답하고 있으므로 '어디에서'라는 의미의 Where가 알맞다.

48 〈의문사+do동사+주어+동사원형 ~?〉의 형태이므로 How 뒤에 do가 와야 한다.

49 '어느 것'이라는 의미의 표현은 Which one이다.

50 '언제 Mary와 Tom은 시험 결과를 알았니?'라는 의미가 되도록 '언제'라는 의미의 의문사 When으로 시작하고, 과거 시제이므로 did를 쓴 후 주어 다음에 동사원형 know를 써야 한다.

CHAPTER 09 문장의 종류

Unit 01 p. 160

A

01 Be kind
02 write
03 Don't waste
04 Be quiet
05 Don't be late
06 Study
07 Don't run
08 Never break

B

01 Be honest all the time.
02 Don't play soccer in the garden.
03 Read a lot of books.
04 Never lie.
05 Don't make any noise in the library.
06 Be a good student.
07 Come back home by six.
08 Turn off your phone during the show.

Unit 02 p. 161

A

01 Let's go
02 Let's sing
03 Let's not take
04 Let's go on
05 Let's walk
06 Let's not talk about
07 Let's join

B

01 does wash → wash
02 Let → Let's
03 are → be
04 to tell → tell
05 be not → not be
06 has → have
07 crossing → cross
08 inviting → invite
09 to buy → buy

내신기출 ①

Unit 03 p. 162

A

01 isn't she
02 is she
03 didn't he
04 wasn't it
05 doesn't he
06 don't you
07 did they

B

01 isn't this, it is

02 doesn't she, she does

03 don't they, they don't

04 weren't they, they were

05 does she, she doesn't

06 are they, they are

07 weren't you, I wasn't

08 doesn't she, she does

09 did he, he didn't

Unit 04

p. 163

A

01 can't she

02 shall we

03 will you

04 will you

05 shall we

06 won't it

B

01 can't he

02 will you

03 shall we

04 will you

05 won't you

06 will you

07 shall we

08 will you

09 shouldn't she

내신기출 ③

Unit 05

p. 164

A

01 Aren't you

02 Isn't he

03 Don't they

04 Doesn't she

05 Didn't you

06 Aren't they

07 Can't you

08 Shouldn't she

B

01 Aren't you cold – I'm not

02 Doesn't he know – he doesn't

03 Can't you finish – No, I can't.

04 Didn't she call – Yes, she did.

Unit 06

p. 165

A

01 Is, or

02 Do, or

03 Who, or

04 Which, or

05 Are, or

06 Which, or

07 Does, or

08 Which, or

B

01 Is that man your brother or your uncle?

02 Do you want a window seat or an aisle seat?

03 Who cleaned the room, Jessica or Sally?

04 Is she reading a book or a magazine?

05 Which color do you like better, black or white?

06 When are you free, on Friday or on Saturday?

Unit 07

p. 166

A

01 What a nice dress (it is)!

02 What old paintings (they have)!

03 What a kind girl (she is)!

04 What smart students (they are)!

05 What a generous boy (he is)!

06 What an interesting game (it is)!

07 What a wonderful day (it was)!

08 What good basketball players (they are)!

B

01 What a tall building it is!

02 What a big house this is!

03 What a beautiful garden it is!

04 What nice weather it is!

05 What an expensive car he has!

06 What a fantastic trip they had!

Unit 08

p. 167

A

01 How large (this room is)!

02 How fast (the man walks)!

03 How easy (the test was)!

04 How delicious (this dish is)!

05 How expensive (the ring is)!

06 How early (she gets up)!

07 How cute (the cat is)!

B

01 How brave the boy was!

02 How heavy this backpack is!

03 How beautiful these flowers are!

04 How brightly the stars shine!

05 How fast time goes by!

내신기출 How sad (the movie was)! / What a sad movie (it was)!

중간고사 • 기말고사 실전문제

pp. 168～174

객관식 정답 [01～25]

01 ②	**02** ①	**03** ③	**04** ⑤	**05** ④
06 ③	**07** ①	**08** ④	**09** ①	**10** ①
11 ②	**12** ③	**13** ②	**14** ②	**15** ⑤
16 ③	**17** ⑤	**18** ②	**19** ③, ④	**20** ④
21 ①	**22** ④	**23** ②	**24** ⑤	**25** ②

주관식 정답 [26～50]

26 How

27 What

28 How pretty your blue dress is!

29 What a wonderful lady she is!

30 How bravely he did it!

31 Yes, he can

32 No, I didn't

33 Yes, they will

34 go

35 aren't

36 weren't there

37 (a) buy not → not buy

38 (e) doesn't → didn't

39 What a nice garden you have

40 Don't forget to wash your hands

41 doesn't exercise every day, does she

42 Which subject do you like better, music or art

43 Wears → Wear

44 Not do → Do not[Don't]

45 Avoided → Avoid

46 didn't he, No, he isn't

47 don't you, isn't it

48 isn't it, won't you, aren't they

49 What a fast ball Tina throws!

50 Which sport do you like better, swimming or tennis?

해설

01 부정 명령문은 〈Don't+동사원형 ~〉 형태로 쓴다.

02 a funny book이 단수형이므로 it is가 알맞다.

03 명령문 뒤에 오는 부가의문문은 항상 will you?를 쓴다.

04 감탄문에서 뒤에 명사가 오면 What이, 뒤에 형용사가 오면 How가 와야 한다.

05 영국 출신이 아니라 미국 출신이므로 부정의 표현이 와야 한다. Jerry and Julia를 가리키는 대명사는 they이다.

06 선택의문문에서 '누가'를 의미하는 의문사는 Who이다.

07 긍정 명령문은 동사원형으로 시작한다.

08 '~하지 말자'는 〈Let's not+동사원형 ~〉으로 나타낸다.

09 "How clean and beautiful[beautiful and clean] this city is!" he said.가 되어야 하므로 여섯 번째로 오는 단어는 city이다.

10 과거를 나타내므로 Did로 시작해야 한다.

11 부정 명령문은 〈Don't+동사원형 ~.〉으로 나타내고, 일반동사 현재형(긍정)의 부가의문문은 〈don't+주어?〉로 나타낸다.

12 looks가 일반동사 현재형이므로 부가의문문은 doesn't로 시작하고, 부정의문문의 주어가 she이므로 Doesn't가 와야 한다.

13 ②에는 How가 들어가고, 나머지에는 What이 들어간다.

14 made가 일반동사 과거형이므로 didn't가, Tom and I는 we로 나타내므로 didn't we가 되어야 한다.

15 Let's, do, What, should 순으로 들어가야 한다.

16 Not let's는 Let's not이 되어야 한다.

17 명령문이므로, visits는 동사원형 visit이 되어야 한다.

18 부가의문문은 명령문 뒤에서 항상 will you?로 쓴다.

19 ① are → don't, ② will → can't, ⑤ does → won't 가 되어야 한다.

20 앞 문장에 won't가 있으므로 첫 번째 빈칸에는 will이 들어가야 하고, 일반동사 현재형 loves가 있으므로 두 번째 빈칸에는 doesn't가 들어가야 한다.

21 둘 다 부정의문문으로, 첫 번째는 주어가 your father이므로 Isn't가, 두 번째는 '~할 수 없다'라는 의미의 조동사 Can't가 알맞다.

22 둘 다 명령문으로, 첫 번째 빈칸에는 '먹어 보다'라는 의미의 동사 Try가, 두 번째는 부정을 나타내는 〈Don't+동사원형〉의 형태가 와야 한다.

23 will you → shall we, didn't → was가 되어야 한다.

24 shoes가 복수이므로 What expensive shoes these are!가 되어야 한다.

25 앞 문장에서 과거형 didn't가 쓰였으므로 부가의문문 do you?는 did you?가 되어야 한다.

26 빈칸 뒤에 형용사가 나왔으므로 How가 알맞다.

27 빈칸 뒤에 명사가 나왔으므로 What이 알맞다.

28 〈How+형용사+주어+동사!〉 어순이 되어야 한다.

29 〈What+a(n)+형용사+단수 명사+주어+동사!〉 어순이 되어야 한다.

30 〈How+부사+주어+동사+목적어!〉 어순이 되어야 한다.

31 그는 문제를 풀 수 있다는 긍정의 의미이므로 Yes, he can.으로 써야 한다.

32 내가 방 청소를 하지 않았다는 부정의 의미이므로 No, I didn't.로 써야 한다.

33 그들은 결혼식에 갈 거라는 긍정의 의미이므로 Yes, they will.로 써야 한다.

34 Let's 다음에는 동사원형이 와야 한다.

35 앞 문장에 I'm[I am]이 쓰인 경우에 부가의문문은 aren't I?가 되어야 한다.

36 앞 문장에 There were가 있으므로 weren't there?가 되어야 한다.

37 '~하지 말자'는 〈Let's not+동사원형 ~〉으로 나타낸다.

38 동사 put은 과거형으로 쓰였으므로 didn't가 되어야 한다. 참고로 현재형이라면 주어가 She이므로 puts가 되어야 한다.

39 〈What+a(n)+형용사+단수 명사+주어+동사!〉 어순이 되어야 한다.

40 부정 명령문은 〈Don't+동사원형 ~〉 형태로 쓴다.

41 일반동사 현재형 doesn't exercise가 쓰였으므로 부가의문문은 does she?가 되어야 한다.

42 선택의문문에서는 Which 다음에 바로 명사가 오고, 골라야 하는 두 단어 사이에 접속사 or를 써 준다.

43 명령문은 동사원형으로 써야 한다.

44 부정 명령문은 Do not 또는 Don't로 써야 한다.

45 명령문은 동사원형으로 시작해야 한다.

46 일반동사 과거형 had가 쓰였으므로 didn't 뒤에 Your father를 가리키는 대명사 he를 써 준다. 또한, 별로 다치지 않아서 집에 계시다는 내용이 있으므로 부정의 대답이 와야 한다.

47 일반동사 현재형 like가 쓰였으므로 부가의문문은 don't you?로 써 준다. 또한, Today는 it으로 써 준다.

48 앞 문장에 It is가 있을 때 부가의문문은 isn't it?으로, you will은 won't you?로, They are는 aren't they?로 써 준다.

49 〈What+a(n)+형용사+단수 명사+주어+동사!〉 어순에 맞게 쓴다. Tina가 3인칭 단수이므로 throws가 되어야 한다.

50 〈Which+명사 ~, A or B?〉 어순에 맞게 쓴다.

CHAPTER 10 문장의 형식

Unit 01 p. 176

A

01 S
02 V
03 O
04 C
05 M
06 C
07 V
08 S
09 M
10 O
11 C
12 V
13 S
14 V
15 O
16 C

B

01 He is an English teacher.
S V C

02 She will go to Canada.
S V M

03 You look tired today.
S V C M

04 The game made us excited.
S V O C

05 She visited her parents yesterday.
S V O M

06 Bill likes Jessica very much.
S V O M

07 My father made me a kite.
S V O O

08 Junsu is playing basketball.
S V O

Unit 02 p. 177

A

01 1
02 2
03 2
04 2
05 1
06 1
07 2
08 1
09 1
10 2
11 2
12 1

B

01 The sun rises in the east. 1
S V M

02 The earth moves around the sun. 1
S V M

03 This sandwich tastes good. 2
S V C

04 The singer became popular. 2
S V C

05 The game was exciting. 2
S V C

06 My sister and I felt cold. 2
S V C

07 He is waiting at the bus stop. 1
S V M

08 The boys are playing now. 1
S V M

내신기출 ③

Unit 03 p. 178

A

01 happily → happy
02 greatly → great
03 sweetly → sweet
04 looks → looks like
05 sounds like → sounds
06 badly → bad
07 looks → looks like
08 look like → look

B

01 Amy's voice sounded strange on the phone.
02 This bread tastes great.
03 This cloth feels soft and smooth.
04 James looks Korean.
05 This flower looks pretty and smells good.

Unit 04 p. 179

A

01 My sister has a guitar.
S V O

02 The woman sells flowers in the shop.
S V O M

03 The boys look so funny.
S V C

04 Kites are flying in the sky.
S V M

05 Jason plays basketball well.
S V O M

06 My father reads the news online.
S V O M

B

01 All the students like her.

02 Jessica will wear a long dress.

03 My mother likes trees and flowers.

04 I want some bread and milk.

05 We usually have dinner at seven.

내신기출 ③

Unit 05

p. 180

A

01 her

02 a new computer

03 teaches

04 Mary and I

05 her son

06 his bicycle

07 yesterday

08 some books

B

01 bought his wife a coat

02 made her father a sweater

03 sent me an e-mail

04 showed him my new watch

05 bring me some apples

06 lent me his cell phone

Unit 06

pp. 181~182

A

01 to

02 to

03 for

04 to

05 of

06 for

07 for

B

01 I asked a favor of the librarian.

02 Mr. Kim taught us tennis.

03 Minho wrote a birthday card to her.

04 His mom made a pizza for us.

05 Mina brought me a glass of water.

06 She told an interesting story to her daughter.

C

01 to → for

02 for → to

03 them → to them

04 for → to

05 to a gift → a gift

06 for → of

07 I → me

08 his daughter → for his daughter

D

01 bought a ring for her

02 made a special pizza for us

03 taught guitar to me

04 brought an umbrella to me

05 sends an e-mail to him

06 give a tennis racket to you

내신기출 ①

Unit 07

p. 183

A

01 The news made me surprised.
S V O OC

02 They called him John.
S V O OC

03 She named her dog Happy.
S V O OC

04 Tony bought his friend a pretty hat.
S V O O

05 He found the bank easily.
S V O M

06 She keeps her room clean.
S V O OC

07 She made her son a pilot.
S V O OC

08 My brother made me angry.
S V O OC

B

01 He made his son an engineer.
02 I found the box empty.
03 Our family calls our cat Sally.
04 The sun keeps us warm.
05 Fresh food makes us healthy.
06 They elected Aiden president.

Unit 08

p. 184

A

01 asked me to clean
02 wants her son to be
03 told me to wash
04 wants you to do
05 wanted me to study
06 advised me to take
07 asked him to return
08 told me not to wait

B

01 asked me to come
02 wants me to meet
03 told his son to stop
04 wants me to go shopping
05 advised me not to go
06 told us not to be late

Unit 09

p. 185

A

01 to go → go
02 brushed → brush
03 went → go
04 to wait → wait
05 carrying → carry
06 to sing → sing
07 wrote → (to) write
08 doing → do

B

01 Her mother made her stay at home.
02 James made her leave at once.
03 His father made him get up early.
04 I'll have him send a letter to you.
05 They got me to buy a new bag.
06 Mary helped her mother clean the house.

중간고사 • 기말고사 실전문제

pp. 186~192

객관식 정답 [01~25]

01 ④	**02** ②	**03** ④	**04** ③	**05** ②
06 ②	**07** ③	**08** ④	**09** ⑤	**10** ①
11 ③	**12** ⑤	**13** ④	**14** ②	**15** ②
16 ⑤	**17** ①	**18** ④, ⑤	**19** ③	**20** ①
21 ⑤	**22** ④	**23** ②	**24** ②	**25** ③, ④

주관식 정답 [26~50]

26 young
27 sleep
28 expected
29 soft
30 feel
31 drinking → to drink
32 stay → to stay
33 I waited → me wait
34 looks like an elephant
35 give you a foot massage
36 I want you to drive
37 a question of you
38 some food for her friends
39 me finish my homework
40 Jenny (to) open the window
41 My dad bought me a new pair of shoes.
또는 My dad bought a new pair of shoes for me.
42 The last scene made all of us cry.
43 to laugh → laugh
44 staying → stay
45 He had me wash his car, he gave me some pocket money
46 • Suji gave some flowers to her parents.
• Suji gave her parents some flowers.
47 • Minsu baked some cupcakes for his parents.
• Minsu baked his parents some cupcakes.
48 • Jina wrote a thank-you letter to her parents.
• Jina wrote her parents a thank-you letter.

49 My teacher had me share my book with Jennie.

50 Kate asked Aiden to help her after school.

해설

01 〈help+목적어+(to) 동사원형〉 형태이므로 play 또는 to play가 알맞다.

02 감각동사 look 다음에는 형용사가 와야 한다. 더 예뻐 보인다는 말이 있으므로 good이 알맞다.

03 ask는 목적격보어로 to부정사를 취한다.

04 let은 목적격보어로 동사원형을 취한다.

05 ②는 1형식 문장이고, 나머지는 모두 5형식 문장이다.

06 감각동사 feel 다음에는 형용사가 와야 하므로 felt so tiredly는 felt so tired가 되어야 한다.

07 직접목적어가 대명사일 경우 4형식은 쓸 수 없고, 3형식만 가능하다. 따라서 cooked to me it은 cooked it for me가 되어야 한다.

08 〈allow+목적어+to부정사〉 형태이므로 swim 앞에 to가 들어가야 한다.

09 look like는 '~처럼 보이다'라는 의미로 뒤에 명사가 나온다.

10 〈make+목적어+동사원형〉 형태로 동사원형 feel이 오고, 감각동사 feel 다음에는 형용사가 와야 한다.

11 수여동사 show는 간접목적어 앞에 to를 쓰고, ask는 간접목적어 앞에 of를 쓴다.

12 〈feel+형용사〉, 〈keep+목적어+형용사〉 형태이므로 둘 다 형용사가 온다.

13 목적격보어로 둘 다 동사원형이 왔으므로 help와 make 동사가 들어가야 한다.

14 look 다음에는 형용사가 와야 하므로 look health는 look healthy가 되어야 한다.

15 수여동사 make는 간접목적어 앞에 for를 쓰므로 to me는 for me가 되어야 한다.

16 to make me study harder가 되어야 하므로 네 번째로 오는 단어는 study이다.

17 expect Tom to win the car race가 되어야 하므로 네 번째로 오는 단어는 win이다.

18 ① I → me, ② reasonably → reasonable, ③ remembering → remember가 되어야 한다.

19 ③에는 for가 들어가고, 나머지에는 to가 들어간다.

20 〈give+직접목적어(my bike)+to+간접목적어(my neighbor)〉 형태가 되어야 한다.

21 〈ask+목적어+to부정사〉 형태가 되어야 한다.

22 ⓓ에는 직접목적어 happiness가 들어가야 한다.

23 ⓐ에는 〈make+목적어+동사원형〉 형태로 laugh가, ⓑ에는 〈let+목적어+동사원형〉 형태로 go가, ⓒ에는 〈expect+목적어+to부정사〉 형태로 to pass가 알맞다.

24 (d) feeling healthily는 feel healthy로, (e) the visitors to the painting은 to를 삭제하거나 the painting to the visitors가 되어야 한다.

25 ① looks → looks like, ② for → to, ⑤ to look → look이 되어야 한다.

26 look 다음에는 형용사가 와야 하는데 아빠가 20살 정도로 보인다는 내용이므로 young이 알맞다.

27 〈let+목적어+동사원형〉 형태이므로 sleep이 알맞다.

28 목적격보어로 to부정사가 왔으므로 expected가 알맞다.

29 feel 다음에는 형용사가 와야 한다.

30 〈make+목적어+동사원형〉 형태이므로 feel이 알맞다.

31 〈advise+목적어+to부정사〉 형태이므로 to drink가 알맞다.

32 〈allow+목적어+to부정사〉 형태이므로 to stay가 알맞다.

33 〈make+목적어+동사원형〉 형태이므로 me wait가 알맞다.

34 look like는 '~처럼 보이다'라는 의미로 뒤에 명사가 나온다.

35 〈give+간접목적어(you)+직접목적어(a foot massage)〉 형태가 되어야 한다.

36 〈want+목적어+to부정사〉 형태가 되어야 한다.

37 ask의 직접목적어가 a question이므로 간접목적어 you 앞에 of를 쓴다.

38 cook은 간접목적어 앞에 for를 쓴다.

39 〈make+목적어+동사원형〉 형태로 쓴다.

40 〈help+목적어+(to) 동사원형〉 형태로 쓴다.

41 〈buy+간접목적어(me)+직접목적어(a new pair of shoes)〉 형태로 써야 한다.

42 〈make+목적어+동사원형〉 형태로 써야 한다.

43 〈make+목적어+동사원형〉 형태이므로 laugh가 알맞다.

44 〈let+목적어+동사원형〉 형태이므로 stay가 알맞다.

45 〈have+목적어+동사원형〉, 〈give+간접목적어(me)+직접목적어(some pocket money)〉 형태로 써야 한다.

46 수여동사 give는 간접목적어 앞에 to를 써야 한다.

47 수여동사 bake는 간접목적어 앞에 for를 써야 한다.

48 수여동사 write는 간접목적어 앞에 to를 써야 한다.

49 〈have+목적어+동사원형〉 형태로 써야 한다.

50 〈ask+목적어+to부정사〉 형태로 써야 한다.
after school 방과 후에

CHAPTER 11 to부정사와 동명사

Unit 01

p. 194

A

01 To learn
02 to see
03 To watch
04 To play
05 to swim
06 to tell
07 To ride
08 To take

B

01 It is good for your health to get up early.
02 It is not easy to do two jobs.
03 It was exciting to watch the soccer game.
04 It is important to make good friends.
05 It is difficult to understand others.
06 It can be dangerous to drive fast.

Unit 02

p. 195

A

01 to become
02 to leave
03 to collect
04 to play
05 to teach
06 to have
07 to become
08 to learn

B

01 His dream was to travel the world.
02 His work is to make desks and chairs.
03 Her dream is to become a great pianist.
04 Tom's hobby is to make a model car.
05 Our plan is to go to a concert.
06 Her hope is to study abroad.

Unit 03

pp. 196~197

A

01 S
02 C
03 O
04 O
05 S
06 O
07 O
08 C

B

01 hope to become
02 would like to play

03 plans to take
04 expects to pass
05 need to meet
06 decided to go

C
01 helped → help
02 are → is
03 be → to be
04 seeing → to see
05 go → to go
06 to cutting → to cut

D
01 ⓐ
02 ⓒ
03 ⓐ
04 ⓐ
05 ⓐ
06 ⓐ
07 ⓑ

내신기출 ②

Unit 04 p. 198

A
01 many things
02 something
03 a pen
04 cold water
05 something new
06 a coat
07 many places
08 nothing

B
01 a friend to help her
02 many books to read
03 a person to fix the TV
04 something important to tell
05 a place to work in
06 enough food to eat

Unit 05 p. 199

A
01 to meet
02 to help
03 to hear
04 to see
05 to watch
06 to buy
07 to study
08 to read

B
01 ⓑ
02 ⓐ
03 ⓐ
04 ⓑ
05 ⓐ
06 ⓐ
07 ⓑ
08 ⓐ
09 ⓑ

Unit 06 p. 200

A
01 ⓔ
02 ⓓ
03 ⓒ
04 ⓐ
05 ⓔ
06 ⓒ
07 ⓑ
08 ⓓ

B
01 His son grew up to be a great artist.
02 This new cell phone is easy to use.
03 She studied hard only to fail the exam.
04 This music is nice to listen to.
05 You are very wise to answer the question.

Unit 07 p. 201

A
01 Reading
02 going
03 Learning
04 becoming
05 Sending
06 Making
07 Taking
08 teaching

B
01 Keeping a diary in English is interesting.
02 Coming to class on time is very important.
03 His goal is saving a lot of money.
04 Swimming in the sea is not easy.
05 Driving at night is dangerous.
06 His dream is becoming a great soccer player.

Unit 08 p. 202

A
01 S
02 O
03 O
04 C
05 O
06 O
07 C
08 O
09 O
10 O
11 O
12 S

B
01 to taking → taking
02 learn → learning

03 rain → raining
04 to paint → painting
05 to dance → dancing
06 buy → buying
07 speak → speaking
08 to wash → washing

내신기출 ①

Unit 09

pp. 203～204

A

01 to go	05 singing
02 making	06 to come
03 to attend	07 to visit
04 going	

B

01 refused to answer
02 mind carrying
03 needs to practice
04 planning to study
05 enjoy playing
06 keep bothering

C

01 to swim	04 working
02 snowing	05 drawing
03 to cry	06 to watch

D

01 want to read
02 finished reading
03 started learning[to learn]
04 don't like talking[to talk]
05 decided to stay
06 enjoyed fishing
07 hope to visit
08 mind driving

내신기출 ②

Unit 10

p. 205

A

01 have → having	05 play → playing
02 to write → writing	06 to make → making
03 to shop → shopping	07 to hiking → hiking
04 to taking → taking	08 to buy → buying

B

01 is busy doing
02 goes climbing
03 were busy studying
04 spent a lot of time explaining
05 How about going
06 go swimming

중간고사 • 기말고사 실전문제

pp. 206～212

객관식 정답 [01～25]

01 ②	02 ④	03 ⑤	04 ①, ④	05 ②, ⑤
06 ④	07 ①	08 ④	09 ②, ③	10 ⑤
11 ④	12 ③	13 ③	14 ④	15 ⑤
16 ③	17 ④	18 ②	19 ③	20 ②
21 ③	22 ⑤	23 ⑤	24 ④	25 ③

주관식 정답 [26～50]

26 to visit
27 Climbing
28 to talk to
29 to meet
30 taking
31 warm something → something warm
32 take caring → taking care
33 That → It
34 to solve
35 give up losing

36 in order to make
37 go → going
38 traveling → travel
39 has a lot of friends to help him
40 has a dream to have her own company
41 After finishing the sixth grade
42 must be crazy to drive
43 to eat → eating
44 swim → swimming
45 being → to be
46 bring your jacket to wear
47 something to eat for lunch
48 some interesting things to do
49 It is dangerous to walk alone on the street at night.
50 Alex and Judy went to the market to buy some fruit, didn't they?

해설

01 to부정사는 문장에서 명사 역할을 할 수 있다.

02 동명사는 문장 내에서 보어로 쓸 수 있다.

03 〈be동사+busy+-ing〉 형태이므로 preparing이 알맞다.

04 start는 목적어로 to부정사와 동명사 둘 다 취할 수 있다.

05 like는 목적어로 to부정사와 동명사 둘 다 취할 수 있다.

06 ④는 감정의 원인을 나타내는 부사적 용법이고, 나머지는 앞의 명사를 수식하는 형용사적 용법이다.

07 ①은 보어로 쓰인 동명사이고, 나머지는 목적어로 쓰였다.

08 in order to는 '~하기 위해서'라는 의미로 to 다음에는 동사원형이 와야 한다. 따라서 becoming은 become이 되어야 한다.

09 ① expressing → to express, ④ aren't → isn't, ⑤ disturbed → disturb가 되어야 한다.

10 〈-thing+형용사+to부정사〉 형태로 의미상 '가지고 놀 재미있는 어떤 것'이므로 to play with가 알맞다.

11 so as to는 '~하기 위해서'라는 의미로 to 다음에 동사원형이 오므로 asking은 ask가 되어야 한다.

12 ③ asking은 형용사적 역할을 하는 to부정사를 이용해 to ask로 고쳐야 한다.

13 much time playing the computer games이므로 세 번째로 오는 단어는 playing이다.

14 continue to manage this website이므로 세 번째로 오는 단어는 manage이다.

15 〈-thing+형용사+to부정사〉 형태이므로 to부정사가 와야 한다.

16 〈go+-ing〉 형태이므로 skiing이, 〈be동사+busy+-ing〉 형태이므로 getting이 와야 한다.

17 주어진 문장에서 동명사 Keeping은 주어 역할을, to부정사 to become은 보어 역할을 하고 있다.
keep a diary 일기를 쓰다

18 감정의 원인을 나타내는 to부정사가 와야 한다.

19 앞의 형용사를 수식하는 to부정사가 와야 한다.

20 앞의 명사 the chairs를 수식하는 to부정사가 와야 한다. 이때, 전치사 on을 빠뜨리지 않도록 주의한다.

21 목적을 나타내는 to부정사는 '~하기 위해서'라는 의미로 쓰인다. keep 다음에는 형용사가 와야 한다.

22 주어진 문장과 ⑤에 쓰인 It은 가주어이다. ①, ③, ④ 비인칭주어 ② 대명사

23 (d), (e)는 목적어로 쓰였고, (a)는 현재진행형, (b)는 보어, (c)는 주어로 쓰였다.

24 앞의 명사를 수식하는 to부정사가 와야 한다. live in a big house, write in a notebook, talk about something interesting 형태이므로 전치사에 주의해야 한다.

25 ⓐ cleaning, ⓑ spent, ⓓ watching, ⓔ to go가 되어야 한다.

26 앞의 명사를 수식하는 to부정사가 와야 한다.

27 문장에서 주어 역할을 할 수 있는 동명사가 와야 한다.

28 앞의 명사를 수식하는 to부정사가 와야 한다. talk to someone이므로 전치사 to가 있어야 한다.

29 감정의 원인을 나타내는 to부정사가 와야 한다.

30 mind는 동명사를 목적어로 취한다.

31 〈-thing+형용사+to부정사〉 형태이므로 warm something이 아니라 something warm이 되어야 한다.

32 〈be동사+busy+-ing〉 형태이므로 taking이 되어야 한다.

take care of ~을 돌보다

33 가주어 It과 진주어 to부정사가 쓰인 문장이다.

34 형용사 hard를 수식하는 to부정사가 와야 한다.

35 give up은 '포기하다'라는 의미로 동명사를 목적어로 취한다.

36 in order to는 '~하기 위해서'라는 의미이다.

37 How about -ing ~?는 '~하는 게 어때?'라는 의미로 go는 going으로 고쳐야 한다.

38 would like는 목적어로 to부정사를 취한다.

39 a lot of friends를 수식하는 to부정사가 와야 한다.

40 a dream을 수식하는 to부정사가 와야 한다.

41 전치사 After 뒤에는 (동)명사가 와야 한다.

42 판단의 근거를 나타내는 to부정사로 쓰였다.

43 enjoy는 동명사를 목적어로 취한다.

44 〈go+-ing〉 형태이므로 swim은 동명사가 되어야 한다.

45 want는 to부정사를 목적어로 취한다.

46 your jacket 뒤에는 형용사적 용법의 to부정사가 와야 한다.

47 '점심으로 먹을 것'이라는 의미가 되어야 한다.

48 some interesting things를 수식하는 to부정사 to do가 와야 한다.

49 가주어 It으로 시작하고, 진주어 to walk alone on the street at night가 와야 한다.

50 목적을 나타내는 to부정사 to buy가 오고, Alex and Judy를 가리키는 대명사 they를 써서 부가의문문을 만든다.

CHAPTER 12 전치사

Unit 01

p. 214

A

01 at
02 in
03 at
04 on
05 in
06 on
07 at
08 in
09 at
10 on
11 in
12 in
13 on
14 at
15 in

B

01 at six o'clock
02 on November 5th
03 in the morning
04 at that moment
05 in summer
06 on Saturdays and Sundays

내신 기출 ②

Unit 02

p. 215

A

01 for
02 during
03 after
04 before
05 from, to
06 for
07 during

B

01 for two hours
02 before dinner
03 from eleven to eight
04 after a few hours
05 during the trip
06 for a week

Unit 03

p. 216

A

01 on
02 at
03 in
04 in
05 on
06 at

B

01 at
02 on
03 at
04 on
05 at

06 in
07 on
08 in
09 on, in

내신기출 ②

Unit 04

p. 217

A

01 near
02 between
03 over
04 behind

05 under
06 in front of
07 next to
08 across from

B

01 over
02 under
03 next to
04 in front of

05 between
06 across from
07 in front of
08 next to

Unit 05

p. 218

A

01 from
02 to
03 up

04 down
05 into
06 out of

B

01 to
02 out of
03 out of, into

04 up
05 from, to

Unit 06

p. 219

A

01 about
02 with
03 for
04 of

05 about
06 like
07 for
08 because of

B

01 for
02 with

03 of
04 about

05 because of
06 like

07 with
08 for

중간고사 • 기말고사 실전문제

pp. 220~226

객관식 정답 [01~25]

01 ①	**02** ④	**03** ⑤	**04** ②	**05** ③
06 ⑤	**07** ①	**08** ④	**09** ⑤	**10** ④
11 ③	**12** ④	**13** ⑤	**14** ④	**15** ②, ④
16 ③	**17** ①	**18** ②	**19** ①	**20** ⑤
21 ④	**22** ①	**23** ②, ④	**24** ③	**25** ③

주관식 정답 [26~50]

26 next to
27 on
28 during
29 in front of
30 before
31 during
32 during → for
33 behind → between
34 over → on
35 near
36 from, to
37 at, because of
38 at the end of this road
39 after finishing your homework
40 over the wall to escape from
41 sitting on the benches in the park
42 near the edge of the cliff
43 ⓐ at 7 p.m. on the 13th floor
ⓑ for five days from July
44 (b) at → on
45 (e) because → because of
46 on → at
47 with → on
48 into → in
49 He drove for five hours to get here.
50 Take the driving test after practicing a lot.

해설

01 '선반 위에'라는 의미이므로 on이 와야 한다.

02 from ~ to ...는 '~부터 …까지'라는 의미이다.

03 '~ 사이에'라는 의미의 between이 알맞다.

04 월 앞에는 in을 쓴다.

05 '~ 옆에'라는 의미의 next to가 와야 한다.

06 '한 시간 동안'이라는 의미이므로 구체적인 시간 an hour 앞에 for가 와야 한다.

07 도시 앞에는 in을 쓴다.

08 '~에 대해'라는 의미의 about이 와야 한다.

09 '영화를 보는 동안'이라는 의미이므로 during이 와야 한다. for 뒤에는 구체적인 기간이 온다.

10 an earthquake라는 명사가 왔으므로 '~ 때문에'라는 의미의 because of가 와야 한다.

11 in front of your bicycle이므로 네 번째로 오는 단어는 your이다.

12 because of a missing part이므로 네 번째로 오는 단어는 missing이다.

13 three days라는 구체적인 기간이 나오므로 during이 아니라 for가 되어야 한다.

14 '물속으로'라는 의미이므로 전치사 over는 into로 고쳐야 한다.

15 ① for → from, ③ in → on, ⑤ from → under가 되어야 한다.

16 '식사 중에, 회의 동안'이라는 의미이므로 during이 와야 한다.

17 to는 '~로'라는 의미이고, from ~ to …는 '~부터 …까지'라는 의미이다.

18 for는 뒤에 구체적인 기간이 나오면 '~ 동안'이라는 의미이고, '~을 위해'라는 의미도 가진다.

19 out of는 '~ 밖으로'라는 의미이다.

20 '구름 뒤로', '너와'라는 의미이므로 각각 behind와 with가 와야 한다.

21 '매 식사 전에', '입구 앞에'라는 의미이므로 before와 in front of가 와야 한다.

22 ①에는 with가, 나머지에는 about이 들어간다.

23 ① into → on, ③ next to → near, ⑤ down → up이 되어야 한다.

24 ⓐ에는 '~을 위해'라는 의미의 for가, ⓑ에는 좁은 장소에 쓰이는 at이, ⓒ에는 '~처럼, ~ 같은'이라는 의미의 like가 알맞다.

25 (a)에는 at이, (b)에는 on이, (c)에는 for가, (d)에는 because of가, (e)에는 on이 들어간다.

26 '네 옆에'라는 의미이므로 next to가 알맞다.

27 '탁자 위에'라는 의미이므로 on이 알맞다.

28 '그들의 점심시간 동안'이라는 의미이므로 during이 알맞다.

29 '~ 앞에'라는 의미의 in front of가 알맞다.

30 '~ 전에'라는 의미의 before가 알맞다.

31 '~ 동안'이라는 의미의 during은 특정기간 앞에 쓰인다.

32 ten years라는 구체적인 기간이 쓰였으므로 for가 와야 한다.

33 '손가락 두 개 사이에'라는 의미이므로 between이 와야 한다.

34 '계단 위에'라는 의미이므로 on이 와야 한다.

35 '우리 집 근처에'라는 의미이므로 near가 알맞다.

36 '금요일부터 일요일까지'라는 의미이므로 from ~ to ...가 알맞다.

37 정확한 시각 앞에는 at이, 명사구 앞에서 이유를 나타낼 때는 because of가 알맞다.

38 at은 '~에(서)'라는 의미이고, of는 '~의'라는 의미이다.

39 '~ 후에'라는 의미의 after 뒤에 동사가 올 경우에는 동명사 형태로 와야 한다.

40 climb over the wall은 '담을 넘다'라는 의미이고, from은 '~에서(부터)'라는 의미이다.

41 벤치 위에 앉아 있으므로 on이, 넓은 장소인 park 앞에는 in을 써야 한다.

42 near는 '~ 가까이'라는 의미이고, of는 '~의'라는 의미이다.

43 ⓐ 정확한 시각 7 p.m. 앞에는 at이, 장소를 나타내는 the 13th floor 앞에는 on이 와야 한다.
ⓑ 구체적인 기간 five days 앞에는 for를, '~부터 …까지'라는 의미는 from ~ to ...으로 쓴다.

44 '~날' 앞에는 on이 온다.

45 명사 앞에서 이유를 나타낼 때에는 because of가 알맞다.

46 an Italian restaurant라는 장소에는 on이 아니라 at을 써야 한다.

47 '대기자 명단 위에'라는 의미이므로 with가 아니라 on을 써야 한다.

48 '차 안에서'라는 의미이므로 into가 아니라 in을 써야 한다.

49 구체적인 기간 five hours 앞에는 for를 써야 한다.

50 '~후에'라는 의미의 after 뒤에 동사가 올 경우 동명사 형태가 되어야 한다.

CHAPTER 13 접속사

Unit 01

p. 228

A

01 and

02 but

03 but

04 and

05 but

06 and

B

01 These flowers look beautiful and (they) also smell good.

02 Mike bought a magazine, but (he) didn't read it.

03 The movie was good, but (it was) too long.

04 Mina and Junho went on a picnic.

05 My father usually drives to work, but (he) went by subway this morning.

Unit 02

p. 229

A

01 or

02 so

03 so

04 or

05 or

06 so

B

01 like better, summer or winter

02 so he went to the office by bus

03 go to the movies or stay at home

04 so I went to see a doctor

내신기출 or, and, but, so

Unit 03

p. 230

A

01 ⓔ

02 ⓕ

03 ⓓ

04 ⓑ

05 ⓗ

06 ⓒ

07 ⓐ

08 ⓖ

B

01 when I was young
02 before you go to work
03 after you finish eating
04 before your mom comes back
05 When I entered the room
06 after I bought some drinks and popcorn

Unit 04

p. 231

A

01 Because
02 If
03 because
04 if
05 If
06 Because

B

01 because I like skiing
02 If you are hungry
03 Because my English teacher is kind
04 because I was very busy today
05 if he gets up early

내신 기출 ③ fits

Unit 05

p. 232

A

01 S
02 C
03 O
04 C
05 O
06 S
07 O
08 O

B

01 that you did your best
02 that he will not be here in time
03 that you did not[didn't] make a mistake
04 that he does not[doesn't] know the answer
05 that the exam was very difficult
06 that she was learning yoga

중간고사 • 기말고사 실전문제

pp. 233~238

객관식 정답 [01~25]

01 ①	02 ②	03 ③	04 ④	05 ⑤
06 ⑤	07 ②	08 ⑤	09 ③	10 ②
11 ③	12 ①	13 ②	14 ③	15 ②
16 ④	17 ②	18 ③	19 ③	20 ⑤
21 ⑤	22 ④	23 ①	24 ②	25 ②, ④

주관식 정답 [26~50]

26 after
27 because
28 showed
29 gets up
30 playing
31 Because
32 that
33 and
34 call → will call
35 studied → (to) study
36 gets → got
37 but the sky is clear now
38 after I get out of the classroom
39 so he couldn't sleep well last night
40 (a) Fish → Fishing
41 (c) because of → because
42 (e) when → that
43 When you see the paintings in the museum
44 talk → will talk
45 will have → have
46 Mina and Tom went abroad to study medicine.
47 You should clean the bathroom after you take a shower.
48 I went to a traditional market, but I couldn't buy sweet potatoes.
49 Henry will go swimming or play soccer during this holiday.
50 When you go to the library, can you return this book?

해설

01 '~하면'이라는 의미의 if가 알맞다.

02 '그래서'라는 의미의 so가 알맞다.

03 '~할 때'라는 의미의 When이 알맞다.

04 '그리고'라는 의미의 and가 알맞다.

05 '~하기 때문에'라는 의미의 Because가 알맞다.

06 등위접속사 and의 앞, 뒤에 나오는 동사 형태가 동일해야 하므로 watching이 아니라 watch가 되어야 한다.

07 조건을 나타내는 if절에서는 현재시제가 미래시제를 대신하므로 will come이 아니라 come이 되어야 한다.

08 빈칸에는 행복을 느낄 때가 나와야 하는데, ⑤는 '시험 성적이 나쁠 때'라고 했으므로 알맞지 않다.

09 첫 번째에는 명사절 접속사 that이, 두 번째에는 '~이지만'이라는 의미의 but이 알맞다.

10 첫 번째에는 '~이거나'라는 의미의 or가, 두 번째에는 '~하기 전에'라는 의미의 before가 알맞다.

11 '~한 후에'라는 의미의 after를 써서 나타낸다.

12 ①은 의문사 When이고, 나머지는 접속사 When이다.

13 ②는 전치사 before이고, 나머지는 접속사 before이다.

14 '~이지만'이라는 의미의 but이 알맞다.

15 문장 내에서 주어와 보어 역할을 하는 명사절 접속사 that이 알맞다.

16 if절에서는 현재시제가 와야 하는데, 주어가 3인칭 단수이므로 invite가 아니라 invites가 되어야 한다.

17 when 뒤에는 〈주어+동사〉 순으로 와야 하므로 are you가 아니라 you are가 되어야 한다.

18 when he reads the newspaper가 되어야 하므로 세 번째로 오는 단어는 reads이다.

19 If you don't wear warm clothes가 되어야 하므로 세 번째로 오는 단어는 don't이다.

20 주어진 문장에서 that은 목적어로 쓰였다. ① 주어, ② 보어, ③ 진주어, ④ 보어

21 After you finish your homework 또는 After finishing your homework가 되어야 한다.

22 ④에는 and가 들어가고, 나머지에는 or가 들어간다.

23 ①에는 and가, ②에는 because가, ③에는 but이, ④에는 so가, ⑤에는 If가 들어간다.

24 (a), (e)에는 If가 들어가고, (b)에는 after가, (c)에는 When이, (d)에는 and가 들어간다.

25 ① watches → watched, ③ but → so, ⑤ After → If가 되어야 한다.

26 '~한 후에'라는 의미의 after가 알맞다.

27 '~하기 때문에'라는 의미의 because가 알맞다.

28 등위접속사 and의 앞, 뒤에 나오는 동사의 형태가 동일해야 하므로 과거형 showed가 되어야 한다.

29 if절에서는 현재시제가 미래시제를 대신하는데, 주어가 3인칭 단수이므로 gets up이 되어야 한다.

30 등위접속사 and의 앞, 뒤에 나오는 동사의 형태가 동일해야 하므로 동명사 형태인 playing이 되어야 한다.

31 이유를 나타내는 접속사 Because가 알맞다.

32 문장 내에서 목적어 역할을 하는 명사절 접속사 that이 알맞다.

33 '그리고'라는 의미의 접속사 and가 알맞다.

34 미래를 나타내는 부사 tomorrow가 있으므로 주절은 미래시제가 되어야 한다.

35 등위접속사 and의 앞, 뒤에 나오는 동사 형태가 동일해야 하므로 to부정사나 동사원형이 되어야 한다.

36 주절의 시제가 과거이므로 when절 역시 과거가 되어야 한다.

37 '~이지만'이라는 의미의 but을 쓴 후, 〈주어+동사〉 순으로 배열한다.

38 '~한 후에'라는 의미의 after를 쓴 후, 〈주어+동사〉 순으로 배열한다.
get out of ~에서 나오다

39 '그래서'라는 의미의 so를 쓴 후, 〈주어+동사〉 순으로 배열한다.

40 '낚시'라는 의미의 명사는 fishing이다.

41 이유를 나타내는 절 앞에는 접속사 because가 와야 한다. because of 뒤에는 명사(구)가 온다.

42 문장 내에서 보어 역할을 하는 명사절 접속사 that이 알맞다.

43 '~할 때'라는 의미의 when을 쓴 후, 〈주어+동사〉 순으로 배열한다.

44 미래를 나타내는 부사 tomorrow가 있으므로 주절은 미래시제가 되어야 한다.

45 조건을 나타내는 if절에서는 현재시제가 미래시제를 대신하므로 현재시제가 되어야 한다.

46 '~와'라는 의미의 and를 써서 한 문장으로 바꾼다.

47 '~한 후에'라는 의미의 after를 써서 한 문장으로 바꾼다.

48 '~이지만'이라는 의미의 but을 써서 한 문장으로 바꾼다.

49 '~이거나'라는 의미의 or를 써서 나타낸다.

50 '~할 때'라는 의미의 when을 써서 나타낸다.

내가 가장 취약한 부분에 대해
요점 정리를 해 보세요.

MY GRAMMAR COACH

내신기출 N제 중 1

Workbook

정답과 해설

CHAPTER 01 인칭대명사와 be동사

Unit 01 p. 4

01 We
02 you
03 it
04 We
05 You
06 It
07 They
08 He
09 She

Unit 02 p. 4

01 This book is very interesting.
02 My father is busy all the time.
03 Gina and Jack are tall and thin.
04 The man is a popular actor.
05 My friends are from Seoul.
06 That pretty girl is my daughter.
07 The boxes are big and heavy.
08 You and James are good baseball players.

Unit 03 p. 5

01 X
02 It's
03 They're
04 X
05 She's
06 X
07 You're
08 I'm
09 We're

Unit 04 p. 5

01 The movie was so sad.
02 Sally and Sam were close friends.
03 My bag was on the table.
04 The pictures were on the wall.
05 The store was closed.
06 He and I were the same age.
07 Kate and Jack were in the theater.
08 The weather was cool.
09 The cats were small.

Unit 05 p. 6

01 Bill and I are not[aren't] happy.
02 It is not[isn't] a new bicycle. / It's not a new bicycle.
03 My sisters are not[aren't] beautiful.
04 He and I were not[weren't] police officers.
05 My mom was not[wasn't] busy last night.
06 An apple is not[isn't] on the table.
07 The students were not[weren't] late for school.
08 The cat was not[wasn't] on the sofa this morning.

Unit 06 p. 6

01 Is his job interesting?
02 Was the shop open yesterday?
03 Was your father a good doctor?
04 Were you at home last night?
05 Is Mr. Kim his math teacher?
06 Are Jessica and her sister happy?
07 Were my brothers here yesterday?
08 Are the dirty shoes in the basket?
09 Was this your favorite book?

Unit 07 p. 7

01 Mina and Junsu are not[aren't] my cousins.
02 Mr. Johnson was your teacher.
03 Was the story short and interesting?
04 Minsu and I were in the same class.
05 They are[They're] in the kitchen now.
06 This apple pie is not[isn't] very delicious.
07 Is James your close friend?
08 Her watch was not[wasn't] in her bag.
09 Were Bill and his sister at the zoo on Sunday?

중간고사 • 기말고사 실전문제 pp. 8~12

객관식 정답 [01~15]

01 ③	**02** ⑤	**03** ④	**04** ③	**05** ①
06 ⑤	**07** ④	**08** ③	**09** ④	**10** ③
11 ③	**12** ②, ③	**13** ①	**14** ④	**15** ⑤

주관식 정답 [16~30]

16 are → is
17 are → were
18 Was → Were
19 Your phone was not here.
20 We were not late for class.
21 Mr. Brown is a firefighter.
22 (1) are (2) is, isn't
23 Was[was]
24 He, He, we
25 Were, wasn't
26 is, is
27 are, They
28 Are, I'm, not, I'm, Canada
29 Your birthday present is in my bag.
30 (1) No, they, weren't
(2) Jane was not[wasn't] at his birthday party.

해설

01 주어 your sister는 3인칭 단수이므로 be동사 is 또는 was가 올 수 있다. B의 대답에서 현재형 is로 답하고 있으므로 Is가 알맞다.

02 주어가 Jane and Tom으로 3인칭 복수이므로 B의 대답에서는 3인칭 복수 대명사인 they가 알맞다.

03 2인칭 대명사 you가 주어이므로 B에서는 1인칭 단수 또는 복수로 대답해야 하며, 시제가 과거이므로 대답의 시제도 과거형이 되어야 한다. B의 대답이 No로 시작하므로 1인칭 부정형 대답인 I wasn't가 알맞다.

04 be동사 is는 3인칭 단수 주어와 함께 쓰므로 3인칭 복수형 인칭대명사 They는 쓸 수 없다.

05 be동사 are는 2인칭 단수나 모든 인칭의 복수 주어와 함께 쓰므로 3인칭 단수 주어 He와 쓸 수 없다.

06 ①, ②, ③, ④의 be동사는 '(~에) 있다'라는 의미이고, ⑤는 '~이다'라는 의미이다.

07 ①, ②, ③, ⑤는 were가 들어가고, ④는 was가 들어간다.

08 Sarah and I는 1인칭 복수 주어이므로 was가 아닌 were가 되어야 한다.

09 The restaurant는 3인칭 단수 주어이므로 be동사는 단수형 동사가 와야 한다. 시제가 과거이므로 was가 오고, not을 써서 부정문으로 만들어 준다.

10 be동사의 부정은 be동사 다음에 not을 붙여준다.

11 Jisu and I는 1인칭 복수 주어이므로 They가 아닌 We가 알맞다.

12 ② B의 대답에서 주어가 they이므로 wasn't가 아닌 weren't가 되어야 한다.
③ B의 대답은 No, he isn't.나 Yes, he is.가 되어야 한다.

13 am not은 줄여서 쓰지 않는다.

14 ⓐ were → was, ⓒ is → are, ⓔ is → are가 되어야 한다.

15 Jimmy and Tom은 3인칭 복수 주어이므로 be동사는 Is가 아닌 Are가 와야 한다.

16 주어 This chocolate cake는 3인칭 단수이므로 be동사는 are가 아닌 is가 알맞다.

17 an hour ago(한 시간 전에)는 과거시제와 함께 쓰므로 be동사 are의 과거형 were가 알맞다.

18 주어 you and Andy는 2인칭 복수이므로 Was가 아닌 Were가 알맞다.

19 be동사의 부정은 be동사 다음에 not을 붙여 나타낸다.

20 be동사의 부정은 be동사 다음에 not을 붙여 나타낸다. be late for는 '~에 늦다'라는 의미의 표현이다.

21 주어가 Mr. Brown으로 바뀌면 3인칭 단수 주어가 되므로 be동사를 is로 바꿔 준다.

22 (1) Sharon과 Ryan은 둘 다 미용사이므로 Sharon and Ryan을 주어로 쓰면 be동사는 are가 와야 한다.
(2) Ryan은 홍콩에 있지만 Sharon은 그렇지 않으므로 Ryan 다음에는 is가 와야 하고, Sharon 다음에는 부정형 isn't가 와야 한다.

23 첫 번째 문장의 주어 Kate와 두 번째 문장의 주어 I는 과

거형 be동사인 was를 공통으로 쓸 수 있다.

24 첫 번째, 두 번째 빈칸에는 a little brother를 가리키는 3인칭 단수 대명사 He가 알맞고, 세 번째 빈칸에는 my little brother and I를 대신할 수 있는 1인칭 복수 주어 we가 알맞다.

25 첫 번째 빈칸에는 주어 you와 과거를 나타내는 부사 yesterday가 쓰였으므로 Were가 알맞고, 두 번째 빈칸에는 No로 시작하고 있으므로 부정형 wasn't가 알맞다.

26 Jisu와 She는 3인칭 단수 주어이므로 be동사 is가 알맞다.

27 Grace and Jisu는 3인칭 복수 주어이므로 be동사 are가 알맞고, Grace and Jisu를 대신할 수 있는 인칭대명사는 They이다.

28 Grace의 질문에서 주어가 2인칭 대명사 you이므로 be동사 Are로 물어봐야 하고, Irene은 이탈리아 출신이 아니라 캐나다 출신이므로 부정형으로 대답해야 한다.

29 주어 Your birthday present는 3인칭 단수이므로 be동사 is가 와야 한다. be동사는 '(~에) 있다'라는 뜻이 있다.

30 (1) Jane과 세민은 Mike의 생일파티가 아니라 민호의 생일파티에 갔으므로 부정형으로 대답해야 한다. Jane and Semin을 대신할 수 있는 3인칭 대명사는 they이고, be동사는 과거형 weren't가 알맞다.
(2) be동사의 부정은 be동사 다음에 not을 붙여 나타낸다.

CHAPTER 02 일반동사

Unit 01 p. 14

01 ride
02 rises
03 visit
04 makes
05 eats
06 learn
07 gets
08 clean
09 comes

Unit 02 p. 14

01 play
02 enjoys
03 carries
04 cries
05 brushes
06 go
07 has
08 flies
09 teaches

Unit 03 p. 15

01 wanted
02 stayed
03 cooked
04 called
05 talked
06 happened
07 missed
08 opened

Unit 04 p. 15

01 accepted
02 added
03 agreed
04 begged
05 believed
06 borrowed
07 collected
08 copied
09 covered
10 cried
11 decided
12 depended
13 dropped
14 enjoyed
15 failed
16 finished
17 hoped
18 hurried
19 laughed
20 learned
21 married
22 planned
23 played
24 raised
25 remembered
26 saved
27 smiled
28 stopped
29 studied
30 thanked

31 touched
32 tried
33 used
34 visited
35 waited
36 walked
37 watched
38 worried

Unit 05

p. 16

01 became
02 began
03 bet
04 bound
05 bit
06 bled
07 blew
08 broke
09 brought
10 built
11 bought
12 caught
13 chose
14 came
15 cut
16 did
17 drew
18 drank
19 drove
20 ate
21 fell
22 fed
23 felt
24 fought
25 found
26 flew
27 forgot
28 forgave
29 got
30 gave
31 went
32 grew
33 had
34 heard
35 hit
36 held
37 hurt
38 kept
39 knew
40 led
41 left
42 lent
43 let
44 lost
45 made
46 meant
47 met
48 paid
49 put
50 read
51 rode
52 rang
53 rose
54 ran
55 said
56 saw
57 sold
58 sent
59 set
60 shot
61 shut
62 sang
63 sat
64 slept
65 spoke
66 spent
67 spread
68 stood
69 stole
70 swam
71 took
72 taught
73 told
74 thought
75 threw
76 understood
77 woke
78 wore
79 won
80 wrote

Unit 06

p. 17

01 My father did not[didn't] watch TV after dinner.
02 We do not[don't] need a new computer.
03 He did not[didn't] call me last night.
04 The teacher does not[doesn't] play the guitar.
05 They do not[don't] go there every day.
06 My brother does not[doesn't] have a new camera.
07 I did not[didn't] do my homework yesterday.

Unit 07

p. 17

01 Did he play computer games yesterday? / he did
02 Does the woman live in this apartment? / she doesn't
03 Did you listen to the radio then? / I didn't
04 Do Tom and Jenny like their jobs? / they don't
05 Did she buy this magazine last week? / she did
06 Does Jason sleep late on weekends? / he does

Unit 08

p. 18

01 Kevin moved here five years ago.
02 She does her homework after dinner.
03 I did not[didn't] talk with my teacher after class.
04 Does he ride a bike on weekends?
05 The class began at nine o'clock.
06 Do the students ask questions in class?
07 They did not[didn't] arrive in Seoul at noon.
08 Did the girl lose her bag at school?
09 He does not[doesn't] wash his face before breakfast.

중간고사 • 기말고사 실전문제 pp. 19~23

객관식 정답 [01~15]

01 ①	**02** ②	**03** ②	**04** ④	**05** ③
06 ③	**07** ⑤	**08** ④	**09** ②	**10** ②
11 ⑤	**12** ④	**13** ④	**14** ①	**15** ①

주관식 정답 [16~30]

16 tastes

17 did not[didn't] drive

18 My coach does not[doesn't] drink coffee every day.

19 Did Jimmy go to bed before 9 last night?

20 (1) got (2) made

21 Yes, she, did

22 No, they, didn't

23 (1) grew (2) fought (3) forgot (4) spread

24 Did, they, go

25 He moved to Andong last year.

26 Grace stepped on something sticky.

27 watches TV after lunch

28 (1) Yes, he, did (2) No, she, didn't (3) Yes, they, did

29 (1) eat → eats (2) skiped → skipped

30 (1) ⓑ → ran (2) ⓔ → put

해설

01 eats는 3인칭 단수형 일반동사이므로 주어에는 3인칭 단수가 와야 한다.

02 일반동사의 부정문에서 don't는 주어가 1인칭, 2인칭, 3인칭 복수인 경우에 일반동사 앞에 붙여 쓴다.

03 일반동사의 현재형 의문문에서는 Do 또는 Does가 주어 앞에 쓰이는데, 주어가 3인칭 복수인 they이므로 Do가 알맞다.

04 Her uncle은 3인칭 단수이므로 일반동사 take가 아닌 takes를 써야 한다.

05 your mom은 3인칭 단수 주어이므로 의문문에서는 조동사 Do가 아닌 Does를 써야 한다.

06 일반동사의 현재형 의문문으로 주어가 3인칭 단수일 때에는 〈Yes, 주어+does.〉 또는 〈No, 주어+doesn't.〉로 대답한다.

07 2인칭 주어로 묻는 의문문에서는 1인칭 주어로 대답을 한다. 일반동사의 현재형 의문문이므로 Yes, I do. 또는 No, I don't.로 대답한다.

08 주어가 They로 3인칭 복수이므로 일반동사의 현재형 부정문을 쓸 때에는 doesn't가 아닌 don't를 써야 한다.

09 일반동사의 과거형 부정문을 쓸 때에는 didn't 다음에 동사원형을 써야 하므로 understood가 아닌 understand가 되어야 한다.

10 stop이 〈단모음+단자음〉으로 끝나는 동사이므로 과거형은 끝의 자음인 p를 한 번 더 쓰고 -ed를 써 준다. 따라서 stoped가 아닌 stopped가 되어야 한다.

11 일반동사의 의문문이나 부정문을 쓸 때에는 do/does/did를 주어 앞 또는 일반동사 앞에 쓴다. 두 문장의 주어가 Sangmin과 My friend로 3인칭 단수이므로 does를 써야 한다.

12 B의 대답이 Yes, they did.이므로 A의 질문은 일반동사의 과거형 의문문이 되어야 한다. 일반동사의 과거형 의문문은 〈Did+주어+동사원형 ~?〉의 어순으로 쓴다.

13 ⓐ droped → dropped, ⓒ finishd → finished, ⓔ helpped → helped가 되어야 한다.

14 주어가 Kate and Jenny로 3인칭 복수이므로 일반동사의 현재형 부정문을 쓸 때에는 동사원형 앞에 don't를 써야 한다.

15 take의 과거형은 taked가 아닌 took이다.

16 주어가 3인칭 단수이며 현재시제이므로 taste의 3인칭 단수 현재형인 tastes를 쓴다.

17 과거시제이고 부정문이므로 일반동사의 과거형 부정문의 어순에 따라 〈주어+did not[didn't]+동사원형〉으로 쓴다.

18 일반동사의 3인칭 단수 현재형이 쓰였고, 부정문으로 바꿀 때는 〈주어+does not[doesn't]+동사원형(drink)〉의 어순으로 써야 한다.

19 일반동사의 과거형 의문문으로 바꿀 때는 〈Did+주어+동사원형 ~?〉의 어순으로 써야 한다.

20 early this morning, were, made, tasted에서 과거시제임을 알 수 있으므로 과거형으로 바꿔 써야 한다.

21 일반동사의 과거형 의문문에서는 긍정의 대답일 경우 〈Yes, 주어+did.〉로 대답한다.

22 주어가 your classmates이므로 3인칭 복수형 인칭대명사인 they를 써야 한다. 일반동사의 과거형 의문문에서는 부정의 대답일 경우 〈No, 주어+didn't.〉로 대답한다.

23 (1)~(3)은 과거형이 불규칙적으로 변하는 동사이고, (4)는 현재형과 과거형이 같은 동사이다.

24 B의 대답이 No, they didn't.이므로 A는 일반동사의 과거형 의문문이 되어야 한다. 일반동사의 과거형 의문문은 〈Did+주어+동사원형 ~?〉의 어순으로 써야 한다.

25 과거시제이므로 일반동사 move의 과거형 moved를 쓴다.

26 step이 〈단모음+단자음〉으로 끝나는 동사이므로 과거형은 마지막 자음을 한 번 더 쓰고 -ed를 써 준다.
step on ~을 밟다

27 Jinsu는 3인칭 단수이므로 일반동사 watch의 3인칭 단수 현재형을 써야 한다. watch와 같이 -ch로 끝나는 일반동사의 현재형은 동사원형에 -es를 붙인다.

28 일반동사의 과거형 의문문은 〈Yes, 주어+did.〉 또는 〈No, 주어+didn't.〉로 대답한다. Minsu and Jane을 대신할 수 있는 대명사는 they이다.

29 (1) 반복되는 일은 현재시제로 써야 하며, 주어가 She로 3인칭 단수이므로 일반동사 eat을 eats로 바꿔 써야 한다.
(2) skip이 〈단모음+단자음〉으로 끝나는 동사이기 때문에 과거형은 마지막 자음을 한 번 더 쓰고 -ed를 써 준다.

30 run의 과거형은 ran이고, put의 과거형은 put이다.

CHAPTER 03 시제

Unit 01 p. 26

01 My mother drinks coffee in the morning.
02 They are late for class every time.
03 Kate goes to bed late at night.
04 My brother studies math every day.
05 Mike has a pen in his pocket.
06 My sister and I speak English every day.
07 We sleep 8 hours a day.
08 She exercises in the park every night.
09 He spends the weekends with his family.

Unit 02 p. 26

01 He took a shower in the morning.
02 I didn't play computer games last night.
03 My aunt arrived in New York last month.
04 Columbus discovered America in 1492.
05 Did the students break the window this morning?
06 She went camping with her friends last weekend.

Unit 03 p. 27

01 They'll get there by subway.
02 My sister will come to the party tonight.
03 I'll send an e-mail to you tomorrow.
04 My parents will stay at a hotel in Toronto.
05 He'll listen to music after dinner.
06 We'll play soccer after school.
07 They'll fly to London tomorrow morning.
08 The woman will meet her friends at the coffee shop.

Unit 04 p. 27

01 will not[won't] buy / Will Ms. Kim buy / she won't
02 will not[won't] wash / Will my father wash / he will
03 will not[won't] go / Will Mina and Jinho go / they will

Unit 05 p. 28

01 are not[aren't] going to have lunch / Are they going to have lunch / they are
02 is not[isn't] going to visit his grandmother / Is Jason going to visit his grandmother / he isn't
03 is not[isn't] going to buy a new cell phone / Is my sister going to buy a new cell phone / she is
04 are not[aren't] going to go there / Are we going to go there / we aren't

Unit 06 p. 28

01 My mother goes to church.
02 Did you get a haircut?
03 Mina did not[didn't] read the magazine.
04 We will[We'll] make cupcakes. / We are[We're] going to make cupcakes.
05 Does he work at the store?
06 Chris will not[won't] join the soccer club. / Chris is not[isn't] going to join the soccer club.
07 My family went to the museum.

Unit 07 p. 29

01 arriving
02 baking
03 beginning
04 believing
05 climbing
06 closing
07 coming
08 controlling
09 dancing
10 dying
11 flying
12 getting
13 giving
14 having
15 lying
16 loving
17 making
18 opening
19 putting
20 running
21 saving
22 shopping
23 sitting
24 smiling
25 stopping
26 studying
27 swimming
28 taking
29 winning
30 writing

Unit 08 p. 29

01 You are[You're] wearing a blue shirt.
02 I am[I'm] cutting the cake with my family.
03 She is[She's] sending an e-mail to James.
04 Bill and Seho are crossing the street now.
05 My father is cleaning the windows.
06 We are[We're] studying English now.
07 The girl is walking her dog in the park.
08 The students are waiting at the bus stop.
09 The children are playing soccer over there.

Unit 09 p. 30

01 are not[aren't] listening to the radio
02 is not[isn't] eating fruit
03 are not[aren't] making a toy car
04 is not[isn't] writing a letter to his friend
05 are not[aren't] watching a movie
06 not reading a newspaper

Unit 10 p. 30

01 Is he washing his hands? / he is
02 Are Tom and Bill playing games? / they are
03 Is she reading an interesting book? / she isn't [she's not]
04 Is your father watching TV? / he isn't[he's not]
05 Is Jenny studying at the library? / she is
06 Are the boys having pizza together? / they are
07 Is the girl running to the bus? / she isn't[she's not]
08 Are you cleaning your room? / I am
09 Are the students solving the problem? / they aren't[they're not]

Unit 11 p. 31

01 was taking
02 was talking
03 were waiting
04 was swimming
05 was living
06 were reading

Unit 12

p. 31

01 was not[wasn't] making / Was Sarah making / she was

02 were not[weren't] having / Were they having / they were

03 was not[wasn't] cleaning / Was he cleaning / he wasn't

04 was not[wasn't] playing / Was my sister playing / she wasn't

중간고사 • 기말고사 실전문제

pp. 32~36

객관식 정답 [01~15]

01 ①	**02** ③	**03** ④	**04** ③	**05** ④
06 ⑤	**07** ①	**08** ①	**09** ③	**10** ②
11 ②	**12** ②	**13** ①	**14** ③	**15** ④

주관식 정답 [16~30]

16 reads

17 wrote

18 is going to play the piano with Minho

19 I am[I'm] going to study at the library.

20 Is it going to rain this afternoon?

21 No, I, didn't, drank

22 He is going to have a date with Kate tonight.

23 Is she having a great weekend?

24 Mina's father was cleaning the living room 30 minutes ago.

25 went, met, going, to have

26 is riding a bike[bicycle]

27 No, she, isn't, sitting

28 She was watering flowers in the garden

29 He will[He'll] be six years old

30 they aren't[they're not] / washing their hands

해설

01 반복되는 습관은 현재시제로 나타내는데 주어가 3인칭 복수이므로 play가 알맞다.

02 last year(작년)에 일어난 일이므로 과거시제가 알맞다. buy의 과거형은 bought이다.

03 미래시제 will이 쓰였으므로 미래를 나타내는 부사 tomorrow가 알맞다.

04 be동사의 과거형인 was가 쓰였으므로 과거시제와 어울리는 부사구 last night이 알맞다.

05 미래를 나타내는 부사(구)인 tomorrow와 next year가 쓰였으므로 미래시제 will이 들어가야 한다.

06 '~하고 있다'라는 의미의 현재진행형은 〈be동사의 현재형+동사원형-ing〉로 나타낸다.

07 현재진행형의 의문문이므로 대답은 〈Yes, 주어+be동사의 현재형.〉 또는 〈No, 주어+be동사의 현재형+not.〉의 형태가 되어야 한다. the gardener는 3인칭 단수로 he 또는 she로 표현하면 된다.

08 동사원형에 -ing를 붙일 때, -ie로 끝나는 동사는 ie를 y로 바꾸고 -ing를 붙여주므로 tie의 -ing형은 tying이다.

09 첫 번째 문장에서는 be동사 is가 앞에 있으므로 동사는 -ing 형태가 되어야 한다. 두 번째 문장에서는 entering이 있으므로 진행형 시제로 be동사 Is 또는 Was가 들어가야 한다.

10 동사원형에 -ing를 붙일 때, lie와 같이 -ie로 끝나는 동사는 ie를 y로 바꾸고 -ing를 붙인다.

11 〈Do+주어+동사원형 ~?〉의 어순이므로 having이 아니라 have가 되어야 한다.

12 have가 소유(갖고 있다)의 의미로 사용될 때에는 진행시제로 쓸 수 없다.

13 '파리는 프랑스의 수도이다.'는 일반적 사실이므로 현재시제로 써야 한다. 따라서 was가 아니라 is가 알맞다.

14 B의 대답이 미래시제이므로 의문문도 미래시제로 써야 한다. B의 대답이 Yes나 No로 답하지 않으므로 의문사가 있는 의문문으로 나타내야 한다.

15 보기의 is going은 현재진행형으로 '가고 있는 중이다'라는 뜻이다. ④를 제외한 나머지 문장에서 is/are going은 뒤의 to와 함께 쓰이는 표현으로 '~할 예정이다'라는 의미로 미래시제를 나타낸다.

16 always는 반복되는 습관을 표현할 때 동반되는 부사로 동사의 형태는 현재형이 알맞다.

17 last Sunday는 과거시제와 함께 쓰이는 부사구이므로 동사의 형태는 과거형이 알맞다.

18 미래시제 will은 be going to로 바꿔 쓸 수 있는데, 주어가 3인칭 단수이므로 is going to를 써서 나타낸다.

19 be going to로 질문했으므로 〈주어+be going to+동사원형〉으로 대답해야 한다.

20 〈Be동사+주어+going to+동사원형 ~?〉의 어순으로 의문문을 나타낼 수 있다.

21 B의 대답에서 레몬에이드가 아닌 수박 주스를 마셨다고 했으므로 부정으로 대답해야 하며, A의 질문이 과거시제이므로 대답에는 didn't가 와야 한다. drink의 과거형은 drank이다.

22 〈주어+be going to+동사원형〉의 어순에 따라 배열한다.

23 현재진행형의 의문문이므로 〈Be동사의 현재형+주어+동사원형-ing ~?〉의 어순에 따라 배열한다.

24 과거진행형은 〈be동사의 과거형+동사원형-ing〉로 나타낸다.

25 첫 번째 빈칸에는 과거를 나타내는 부사구 an hour ago가 쓰였으므로 go의 과거형 went가, 두 번째 빈칸에도 과거를 나타내므로 meet의 과거형 met이, 세 번째 빈칸에는 현재를 나타내는 Now와 are가 있으므로 현재진행형이 되도록 going이, 네 번째 빈칸에는 are going 다음에는 〈to+동사원형〉이 와야 하므로 to have가 알맞다.

26 A의 질문이 현재진행형이므로 대답도 현재진행형으로 나타낸다. ride a bike[bicycle]는 '자전거를 타다'라는 의미이다.

27 Grace는 달리기를 하지 않고 벤치에 앉아 책을 읽고 있으므로 부정으로 대답해야 한다. Grace가 벤치에 앉아 책을 읽고 있으므로 현재진행형이 되도록 sitting을 써 준다.

28 과거진행형은 〈be동사의 과거형+동사원형-ing〉로 나타낸다.

29 Amy의 남동생은 올해 5살이므로 내년에는 6살이 된다. 따라서 미래시제를 나타내는 will을 써 준다.

30 Amy와 그녀의 남동생은 숨바꼭질을 하는 게 아니라 손을 씻고 있으므로 부정으로 대답한 후, 현재진행형을 써서 나타낸다.

CHAPTER 04 조동사

Unit 01 p. 38

01 can move
02 Can, swim, you can't
03 can sing
04 Can, borrow
05 can't go
06 can run
07 can't play
08 can't go
09 Can, lend, I can't

Unit 02 p. 38

01 I'm not able to sing
02 Are you able to read
03 He will[He'll] be able to get up
04 He could find
05 They are[They're] able to get
06 We were not[weren't] able to visit
07 Is Tony able to carry
08 The birds are able to fly
09 She was able to draw

Unit 03 p. 39

01 She may come to the meeting.
02 May I talk to your daughter?
03 He may be at work.
04 It may rain at night.
05 You may eat this bread.
06 May I borrow your bicycle?
07 You may not smoke here.
08 You may not like this movie.
09 May I go out with my friends?

Unit 04 p. 39

01 being → be
02 plays → play

03 are not → not be
04 taking → take
05 don't → am not
06 do take → take
07 reads → read
08 don't may → may not
09 is → be

Unit 05

p. 40

01 must drink
02 must be sick
03 must hurry
04 must clean
05 must not take
06 must read
07 must walk
08 must wash

Unit 06

p. 40

01 has → have
02 washing → wash
03 have → has
04 doesn't → don't
05 wears → wear
06 have → had
07 has not → doesn't have
08 Do → Does
09 have to walked → had to walk

Unit 07

p. 41

01 should wash
02 should not[shouldn't] drive
03 should go and see
04 should rest
05 should not[shouldn't] watch
06 Should I take, you should

중간고사 • 기말고사 실전문제

pp. 42~46

객관식 정답 [01~15]

01 ①	**02** ④	**03** ⑤	**04** ②	**05** ④
06 ⑤	**07** ④	**08** ②	**09** ②	**10** ④
11 ⑤	**12** ②	**13** ③	**14** ⑤	**15** ⑤

주관식 정답 [16~30]

16 Can you solve / Are you able to solve
17 didn't have to call
18 must not[should not/shouldn't] open
19 has, to
20 is, able, to
21 stays → stay
22 have → has
23 not may → may not
24 visited → visit
25 You should be nice to others.
26 Can you bring me some water?
27 We were able to arrive there in time.
28 Do the students have to clean the classroom?
29 You shouldn't watch too much TV. 또는 You shouldn't watch TV too much.
30 The machine must be useful for us.

해설

01 조동사 뒤에는 동사원형을 써야 하므로 dance가 알맞다.

02 조동사 뒤에는 동사원형을 써야 하므로 be가 알맞다.

03 '~할 수 있다'라는 능력을 나타낼 때는 조동사 can을 사용한다.

04 '~해도 된다'라는 허가를 나타낼 때는 조동사 may를 사용한다.

05 '~해야 한다'라는 의무를 나타낼 때는 조동사 must를 사용한다. 이는 have to로 바꾸어 쓸 수 있는데 주어가 3인칭 단수이므로 has to로 써야 하므로 ⑤는 답이 아니다.

06 '~하는 게 좋겠다, ~해야 한다'라는 뜻으로 충고나 제안을 할 때는 조동사 should를 사용한다.

07 ④의 can은 '~해도 될까?'라는 허가를 나타내고, 나머지는 모두 '~할 수 있니?'라는 뜻의 능력을 나타낸다.

08 ②의 may는 '~해도 된다'라는 허가를 나타내고, 나머지

는 모두 '~일지도 모른다'라는 추측을 나타낸다.

09 '~해서는 안 된다'라는 금지를 나타낼 때는 조동사 must의 부정인 must not을 사용한다. don't have to는 '~할 필요가 없다'라는 의미임에 주의한다.

10 '~일지도 모른다'라는 추측을 나타낼 때는 조동사 may를 사용한다. 조동사는 주어의 인칭과 수에 상관없이 같은 형태로 쓰며, 뒤에는 반드시 동사원형이 와야 한다.

11 가능을 나타내는 can의 미래시제는 will be able to로 써야 한다.

12 조동사 뒤에는 동사원형을 써야 하므로 following이 아닌 follow를 써야 한다.

13 have to의 의문문은 〈Do/Does+주어+have to ~?〉의 형태로 쓴다. 주어가 3인칭 단수이므로 Does she have to leave home early?가 되어야 한다.

14 사진을 찍어도 되냐는 질문에 '당신은 여기에서 사진을 찍을 수 없다.'고 대답했으므로 빈칸에는 '죄송하지만 안 된다.'라는 의미인 ⑤가 와야 한다.

15 '내가 너의 잃어버린 지갑을 찾아야 하니?'라고 묻는 질문에 '내가 이미 그것을 찾았어.'라고 대답했으므로 빈칸에는 '아니, 너는 그럴 필요가 없다.'라는 의미인 ⑤가 와야 한다.

16 '~할 수 있니?'라는 의미는 조동사 Can 또는 be able to의 의문문으로 써야 한다. be able to의 의문문은 〈Be동사+주어+able to+동사원형 ~?〉의 어순으로 써야 한다.

17 '~할 필요가 없다'는 don't have to로 나타낼 수 있으며, 과거시제이므로 didn't have to로 써야 한다.

18 '~해서는 안 된다'는 must 또는 should의 부정인 must not이나 should not으로 나타낼 수 있다.

19 must가 의무를 나타낼 때는 have to로 바꾸어 쓸 수 있는데, 주어가 3인칭 단수이므로 has to로 써야 한다.

20 can이 능력이나 가능을 나타낼 때는 be able to로 바꾸어 쓸 수 있으며, 주어가 3인칭 단수이므로 be동사는 is를 써야 한다.

21 조동사 뒤에는 반드시 동사원형을 써야 하므로 stays를 stay로 고쳐야 한다.

22 주어가 3인칭 단수이므로 have를 has로 고쳐야 한다.

23 may의 부정은 may 뒤에 not을 써서 나타내므로 not may를 may not으로 고쳐야 한다.

24 조동사 must 다음에는 동사원형이 와야 하므로 visited를 visit으로 고쳐야 한다.

25 '~하는 게 좋겠다, ~해야 한다'라는 뜻으로 충고나 제안을 할 때는 조동사 should를 사용한다.

26 상대방에게 요청을 할 때는 조동사 can을 사용하여 〈Can+주어+동사원형 ~?〉으로 나타낼 수 있다.

27 '~할 수 있었다'라는 의미는 can과 바꿔 쓸 수 있는 be able to로 나타낼 수 있으며, 주어가 복수이고 과거시제이므로 were able to로 써야 한다.

28 '~해야 하나요?'는 의무를 나타내는 have to의 의문문으로 나타낼 수 있다. 주어가 3인칭 복수이므로 〈Do+주어+have to+동사원형 ~?〉의 형태로 써야 한다.

29 '~하지 않는 게 좋겠다'라는 뜻으로 충고나 제안을 할 때는 조동사 should not으로 쓸 수 있는데 총 6단어로 써야 하므로 줄임말인 shouldn't로 쓴다.

30 '~임에 틀림없다'라는 강한 추측은 조동사 must를 사용한다.

CHAPTER 05 명사와 관사

Unit 01 p. 48

01 an expensive car
02 a hat, an umbrella
03 a day
04 a pen, an eraser
05 an uncle, an engineer
06 an apple, an orange

Unit 02 p. 48

01 dogs
02 books
03 cookie
04 Students
05 boys
06 chairs
07 eyes, tail
08 dolls, toys
09 forks, spoons

Unit 03 p. 49

01 pianos
02 stories
03 buses
04 churches
05 roofs
06 chefs
07 benches
08 dishes
09 tomatoes
10 boxes
11 leaves
12 radios
13 brushes
14 shelves
15 foxes
16 keys
17 knives
18 classes
19 cities
20 watches
21 potatoes
22 dresses
23 wolves
24 photos
25 heroes
26 fingers
27 babies
28 flies

Unit 04 p. 49

01 sheep
02 women
03 geese
04 children
05 oxen
06 feet
07 deer
08 mice
09 teeth
10 men
11 salmon
12 people

Unit 05 p. 50

01 breads → bread
02 a Canada → Canada
03 An English → English
04 moneys → money
05 juices → juice
06 new york → New York
07 cheeses → cheese
08 butters → butter
09 A spring → Spring

Unit 06 p. 50

01 a glass of milk
02 three pieces of pizza
03 a pair of shoes
04 a cup of coffee
05 ten glasses of water
06 five pieces of paper

Unit 07 p. 51

01 ⓑ
02 ⓒ
03 ⓐ
04 ⓒ
05 ⓐ
06 ⓑ
07 ⓓ
08 ⓒ
09 ⓐ

Unit 08 p. 51

01 the subway → subway
02 the work → work
03 the basketball → basketball
04 a math → math
05 the breakfast → breakfast
06 a car → car
07 a lunch → lunch
08 a soccer → soccer

Unit 09 p. 52

01 There is a car
02 There was some milk
03 There is a picture
04 There are many students
05 There was some food
06 There were many books

Unit 10 p. 52

01 There is not[isn't] a house
02 Are there 7 days / there are
03 Was there much water / there wasn't
04 There were not[weren't] two baseballs
05 There are a book and two pencils

중간고사 • 기말고사 실전문제 pp. 53~56

객관식 정답 [01~15]

01 ⑤	**02** ④	**03** ②	**04** ①	**05** ④
06 ②	**07** ②	**08** ⑤	**09** ③	**10** ⑤
11 ②	**12** ④	**13** ④	**14** ⑤	**15** ②

주관식 정답 [16~30]

16 knives
17 mice
18 pianos
19 England
20 information
21 the sky
22 a peace → peace
23 is → are 또는 dolls → doll
24 loaves of bread and a piece of cheese
25 houses have steep roofs
26 Are there two pairs of shoes
27 첫 번째 줄 the lunch → lunch
28 여덟 번째 줄 piece → pieces
29 아홉 번째 줄 waters → water
30 There are three geese in the yard.

해설

01 -x로 끝나는 명사는 끝에 -es를 붙여서 복수형을 만들므로 foxes가 되어야 한다.

02 ① apple, watch, ② eraser, ③ brush, ⑤ book은 셀 수 있는 명사이다.

03 빈칸 앞에 a가 있으므로 빈칸에는 첫 발음이 자음인 단수 명사만 들어갈 수 있다. 첫 발음이 모음인 단수 명사 앞에는 a가 아닌 an을 쓴다.

04 There are 다음에는 복수 명사를 써야 하므로 단수 명사 an orange는 빈칸에 들어갈 수 없다.

05 빈칸 앞에 '많은'이라는 의미의 Many가 있고, be동사 are가 있으므로 빈칸에는 명사의 복수형만 들어갈 수 있다. 따라서 단수 명사인 woman은 빈칸에 들어갈 수 없다.

06 셀 수 없는 명사를 셀 때는 용기나 단위를 이용하는데 rice는 bowl을 이용하여 세고, 나머지는 모두 piece를 이용하여 센다.

07 ②는 '~마다'라는 의미이고, 나머지는 모두 '하나의'라는 의미이다.

08 빈칸 앞에 a가 있으므로 빈칸에는 셀 수 있는 단수 명사만 들어갈 수 있다.

09 셀 수 없는 명사는 용기나 단위를 이용해서 셀 수 있는데, milk는 glass 또는 cup으로 셀 수 있으나 빈칸 앞에 a가 있으므로 용기나 단위를 단수형으로 써야 한다.

10 pants는 두 개가 한 쌍을 이루는 명사이므로 항상 복수로 써야 한다.

11 학생들이 학교에 가는 것은 본래의 목적이므로 관사를 쓰지 않는다. 따라서 ②는 the school이 아니라 school이 되어야 한다.

12 foot의 복수형은 feet이며, 복수 명사는 a와 함께 쓸 수 없다.

13 pizza와 juice는 둘 다 셀 수 없는 명사이므로 용기나 단위를 이용하여 세는데, 피자 두 조각은 two pieces of pizza로 쓰고, 주스 한 병은 a bottle of juice로 쓴다.

14 deer는 단수형과 복수형이 같은 명사이다.

15 interesting은 첫 발음이 모음이므로 a가 아닌 an을 써야 한다.

16 knife는 -fe를 v로 바꾸고 -es를 붙여 복수형을 만든다.

17 mouse는 불규칙 복수형을 가진 명사로 복수형은 mice 이다.

18 piano는 자음+o로 끝나는 명사이지만 복수형은 예외로 끝에 -s만 붙인다.

19 England는 국가명으로 고유명사이므로 부정관사를 붙이지 않는다.

20 information은 추상명사이므로 복수형으로 쓸 수 없다.

21 sky는 관용적으로 the를 붙이는 명사이다.

22 추상명사는 셀 수 없는 명사이므로 peace에 부정관사를 붙이지 않는다.

23 주어는 The dolls로 복수이므로 be동사는 is가 아니라 are가 되어야 한다. 또는 dolls를 단수 명사 doll로 고쳐도 된다.

24 bread와 cheese는 셀 수 없는 명사이므로 용기나 단위를 이용해서 개수를 세야 한다. loaf의 복수형은 loaves 이다.

25 house의 복수형은 houses이고, roof는 f로 끝나는 명사이지만 복수형은 예외로 끝에 -s만 붙인다.

26 '~가 있다'라는 의미로 There is/are를 쓸 수 있는데 뒤에 복수 명사가 나오므로 be동사는 are로 써야 하며, 의문문이므로 Are there ~?가 되어야 한다. shoes는 두 개가 한 쌍을 이루는 명사이므로 항상 복수로 쓰고, pair를 이용하여 개수를 센다.

27 식사명 앞에는 관사를 쓰지 않는다.

28 pizza는 셀 수 없는 명사이므로 piece를 이용해서 개수를 세어야 하므로 three pieces of pizza가 되어야 한다.

29 water는 셀 수 없는 명사이므로 복수형으로 쓸 수 없다.

30 '~가 있다'라는 의미로 There is/are를 쓸 수 있는데 뒤에 복수 명사가 나오므로 be동사는 are로 써야 하며, goose의 복수형은 geese이다.

CHAPTER 06 대명사

Unit 01 p. 58

01 Its → It is[It's]
02 it → them 또는 keys → key
03 we → our
04 me → my
05 her → hers
06 They → We
07 your → yours
08 he → him

Unit 02 p. 58

01 ⓐ
02 ⓐ
03 ⓑ
04 ⓑ
05 ⓑ
06 ⓐ
07 ⓑ

Unit 03 p. 59

01 These are your bags.
02 Is that his album?
03 This is a really big house.
04 That is not[isn't] Jessica's cat.
05 This is Mike's book.
06 Those are not[aren't] my brother's toys.
07 Are these your glasses?
08 That is Minsu's soccer ball.
09 These are Judy's new hats.

Unit 04 p. 59

01 that woman
02 these dishes
03 this bag
04 that picture
05 Those apples
06 this teddy bear
07 That man
08 This car
09 these students

Unit 05 p. 60

01 ⓐ
02 ⓑ
03 ⓐ
04 ⓐ
05 ⓐ
06 ⓑ
07 ⓐ
08 ⓐ

Unit 06 p. 60

01 it
02 one
03 one
04 ones
05 They
06 it
07 them
08 one
09 It

Unit 07 p. 61

01 One / the other
02 another
03 the other
04 One / the other
05 One / another / the other

Unit 08 p. 61

01 Some students went by bus, and others went by train.
02 Some are playing badminton, and the others are reading books.
03 Some are baseballs, and others are soccer balls.
04 Some of the boys are here, but where are the others?

중간고사 • 기말고사 실전문제 pp. 62~65

객관식 정답 [01~15]

01 ④	02 ④	03 ⑤	04 ⑤	05 ②
06 ③	07 ②	08 ④	09 ③	10 ③
11 ⑤	12 ①	13 ②	14 ④	15 ③

주관식 정답 [16~30]

16 She
17 Those
18 one
19 mine
20 theirs
21 hers
22 That → It
23 itself → herself
24 Paul → Paul's
25 Those cars are really nice
26 can protect themselves
27 세 번째 줄 other → the other
28 다섯 번째 줄 anothers → another
29 여섯 번째 줄 others → the other
30 How far is it from your house to school?

해설

01 his, your, its, their는 인칭대명사의 소유격이고, me는 목적격이다.

02 명사 앞에 쓰여 '~의'라는 의미를 나타내므로 인칭대명사의 소유격을 써야 한다.

03 동사 meet 뒤에서 '~을'이라는 의미를 나타내므로 인칭대명사의 목적격을 써야 한다.

04 첫 번째 빈칸에는 시간, 두 번째 빈칸에는 날짜를 나타내는 비인칭대명사 it이 들어가야 한다.

05 첫 번째 빈칸에는 앞에서 말한 umbrella와 같은 종류의 사물을 가리키므로 부정대명사 one이, 두 번째 빈칸에는 둘 중 하나는 one, 나머지 하나는 the other로 나타내므로 one이 들어가야 한다.

06 ③은 요일을 나타내는 비인칭대명사이고, 나머지는 모두 '그것'이라는 의미의 인칭대명사이다.

07 '이것은 Jane의 가방이니?'라는 말에 '아니, 그것은 ~의 것이야.'라고 대답해야 하므로 소유대명사가 들어가야 한다.

08 Brian and James는 복수이므로 '그들은'이라는 의미의 주격 인칭대명사 They를 써야 한다.

09 둘 중 하나를 말할 때는 부정대명사 one을, 나머지 하나를 말할 때는 the other를 쓴다.

10 '그녀의'라는 말은 she의 소유격인 her로 써야 한다.

11 '몇몇은 ~, 나머지 전부는 …'은 Some ~, the others ...로 나타낸다.

12 ①은 재귀대명사가 강조로 쓰였으므로 생략이 가능하고, 나머지는 모두 재귀로 쓰였으므로 생략할 수 없다.

13 뒤에 복수 명사인 sunglasses가 나왔으므로 this를 these로 고쳐야 한다.

14 명사 앞에 쓰여 '~의'라는 의미를 나타내는 인칭대명사의 소유격을 써야 하므로 It's를 Its로 고쳐야 한다.

15 ⓐ, ⓑ, ⓓ는 지시형용사이고, ⓒ, ⓔ는 지시대명사이다.

16 동사 앞에 쓰여 '~은/는'이라는 의미로 주어 역할을 하는 말이므로 인칭대명사의 주격인 She가 알맞다.

17 뒤에 복수 명사인 people이 나왔으므로 '저 ~들'이라는 의미의 지시형용사 Those가 알맞다.

18 정해지지 않은 불특정한 물건을 가리키는 것이므로 부정대명사 one이 알맞다.

19 〈소유격+명사〉는 소유대명사로 나타낼 수 있는데, mine이 '나의 것'이라는 의미이다.

20 〈소유격+명사〉는 소유대명사로 나타낼 수 있는데, theirs가 '그들의 것'이라는 의미이다.

21 〈소유격+명사〉는 소유대명사로 나타낼 수 있는데, hers가 '그녀의 것'이라는 의미이다.

22 날씨를 나타낼 때는 비인칭대명사 it을 써야 한다.

23 she의 재귀대명사는 herself이다.

24 명사의 소유격은 's로 나타낸다.

25 '저 ~들'이라는 의미의 지시형용사 those가 복수 명사 cars를 수식해야 하고, 주어가 복수이므로 be동사는 are가 와야 한다.

26 '~ 자신'이라는 의미의 재귀대명사로 써야 하며, they의 재귀대명사인 themselves라고 써야 한다.

27 둘 중 하나는 one, 나머지 하나는 the other로 쓴다.

28 셋 중 하나는 one, 또 다른 하나는 another로 쓴다.

29 셋 중 하나는 one, 또 다른 하나는 another, 나머지 하나는 the other로 쓴다.

30 거리를 묻고 있으므로 비인칭대명사 it을 사용한다. from ~ to ...는 '~에서 …까지'라는 의미의 표현이다.

CHAPTER 07 형용사와 부사의 비교 표현

Unit 01 p. 68

01 unable
02 bright
03 busy
04 dirty
05 dangerous
06 shallow
07 diligent
08 wet
09 difficult/hard
10 empty
11 expensive
12 fat
13 good
14 unhappy
15 healthy
16 heavy
17 low
18 hungry
19 unkind
20 long
21 young
22 closed
23 polite
24 ugly
25 poor
26 foolish
27 strong
28 short
29 thick
30 unwise

Unit 02 p. 68

01 ⓐ
02 ⓑ
03 ⓑ
04 ⓐ
05 ⓐ
06 ⓑ
07 ⓐ

Unit 03 p. 69

01 some
02 any
03 some
04 any
05 some
06 any
07 some
08 any

Unit 04 p. 69

01 many[a lot of/lots of] cars
02 many[a lot of/lots of] flowers
03 much money
04 many hours
05 many[a lot of/lots of] friends
06 much[a lot of/lots of] interest

Unit 05

p. 70

01 few students

02 a little milk

03 little food

04 a few candies

05 a little time

06 A few children

Unit 06

p. 70

01 This game is very exciting.

02 She arrived early this morning.

03 Mike plays basketball very well.

04 Don't drink too much coffee.

05 The doctor was very kind to everyone.

Unit 07

p. 71

01 carefully

02 safely

03 really

04 usually

05 sadly

06 happily

Unit 08

p. 71

01 late

02 near

03 near

04 high

05 hard

06 late

Unit 09

p. 72

01 usually play basketball

02 sometimes gets up early / gets up early sometimes

03 never comes

04 often go swimming

05 is always clean

06 will never go

Unit 10

p. 72

01 didn't pass the math test, either

02 is too expensive, too

03 can't speak English, either

04 doesn't like apples, either

05 must finish his homework today, too

06 don't like watching TV, either

Unit 11

p. 73

01 angrier / angriest

02 worse / worst

03 more beautiful / most beautiful

04 bigger / biggest

05 more careful / most careful

06 more carefully / most carefully

07 more comfortable / most comfortable

08 more dangerous / most dangerous

09 more delicious / most delicious

10 more difficult / most difficult

11 more diligent / most diligent

12 dirtier / dirtiest

13 easier / easiest

14 more easily / most easily

15 more expensive / most expensive

16 fatter / fattest

17 friendlier / friendliest

18 better / best

19 heavier / heaviest

20 hotter / hottest

21 worse / worst

22 more important / most important

23 lazier / laziest

24 less / least

25 lovelier / loveliest

26 more / most

27 more popular / most popular

28 prettier / prettiest

29 quieter / quietest

30 sadder / saddest

31 more serious / most serious

32 more terrible / most terrible

33 thinner / thinnest

34 uglier / ugliest

35 better / best

Unit 12

p. 74

01 as well as

02 as exciting as
03 as smart as
04 is not[isn't] as[so] pretty as
05 is not[isn't] as[so] expensive as

Unit 13 p. 74

01 ⓐ faster than ⓑ slower than
02 ⓐ longer than ⓑ shorter than
03 ⓐ taller than ⓑ shorter than
04 ⓐ longer than ⓑ shorter than

Unit 14 p. 75

01 the shortest student
02 the biggest city
03 the kindest teacher
04 the highest mountain
05 the worst scores
06 the oldest buildings

Unit 15 p. 75

01 as interesting as
02 larger than
03 the most popular
04 the fastest
05 sweeter than
06 not as[so] fat as

중간고사 • 기말고사 실전문제 pp. 76~79

객관식 정답 [01~15]

01 ④	02 ③	03 ②	04 ①	05 ②
06 ②	07 ①	08 ③	09 ⑤	10 ④
11 ⑤	12 ③	13 ②	14 ③	15 ④

주관식 정답 [16~30]

16 happily
17 younger
18 best
19 dangerous
20 much
21 late
22 too → either
23 terriblest → most terrible
24 he eats too quickly
25 My son seldom watches TV
26 Honesty is one of the most important things
27 John, heavier
28 Sam, is, tallest
29 Eddy, as, old
30 Spaghetti was much more delicious than pizza.

해설

01 ④는 '명사 : 형용사' 관계이고, 나머지는 모두 '형용사 : 부사' 관계이다.

02 빈칸에는 명사 girl을 꾸며 주는 역할을 하는 형용사가 들어가야 하므로 부사는 들어갈 수 없다.

03 셀 수 있는 명사의 복수형인 people이 있으므로 셀 수 없는 명사 앞에 쓰이는 수량형용사 much는 들어갈 수 없다.

04 ①은 '시기적절한'이라는 의미의 형용사이고, 나머지는 모두 빈도부사이다.

05 ① hot – hotter – hottest
③ lucky – luckier – luckiest
④ serious – more serious – most serious
⑤ large – larger – largest

06 '거의 없는'이라는 의미의 수량형용사 중 뒤에 복수 명사가 올 수 있는 것은 few이다.

07 always는 빈도부사이므로 일반동사 앞에 써야 한다.

08 문장 전체를 수식하여 그 뜻을 분명하게 하는 역할을 하는 것은 부사이다.

09 sisters는 셀 수 있는 명사의 복수형이므로 수량형용사 many를 써야 한다.

10 '~만큼 …한/하게'라는 의미의 〈as+형용사/부사의 원급+as〉 문장이므로 빈칸에 비교급과 최상급은 올 수 없으며, 보어로 쓰였으므로 부사 또한 올 수 없다.

11 fast는 형용사와 부사의 형태가 같은 단어이므로 fastly가 아닌 fast가 되어야 한다.

12 interesting은 3음절 이상의 형용사이므로 비교급은 more interesting이 되어야 한다.

13 '~만큼 …하지 않다'라는 말은 ⟨not+as[so]+형용사/부사의 원급+as⟩로 쓸 수 있다.

14 picture는 셀 수 있는 명사이므로 '많은'이라는 표현은 many, a lot of, lots of로 쓸 수 있으며, 뒤에는 복수형인 pictures로 써야 한다.

15 money는 셀 수 없는 명사이므로 a few가 아닌 a little을 써야 한다.

16 동사구 are playing을 수식하므로 부사의 형태가 되어야 한다. happy의 부사는 y를 i로 바꾸고 -ly를 붙여준다.

17 '~보다'라는 의미의 than이 있으므로 비교급으로 써야 한다.

18 빈칸 앞에 the가 있고 앞에 Out of the three ways가 있으므로 최상급으로 써야 한다. good의 최상급은 best이다.

19 명사 situation을 꾸며 주므로 형용사가 알맞다.

20 time은 셀 수 없는 명사이므로 '많은'이라는 의미의 수량 형용사는 much로 써야 한다.

21 late는 형용사와 부사의 형태가 같은 단어이고, lately는 '최근에'라는 의미의 부사이다.

22 '또한, 역시'라는 의미의 동의를 나타낼 때, 부정문에서는 too가 아닌 either를 써야 한다.

23 terrible은 앞에 most를 붙여 최상급을 만든다.

24 부사는 문장 뒤에서 동사를 수식하거나 다른 부사 바로 앞에 쓰여 그 부사를 수식한다.

25 빈도부사는 일반동사 앞에 써야 한다.

26 '가장 ~한 것들 중 하나'라는 표현은 ⟨one of the+최상급+복수 명사⟩로 쓰며, important는 앞에 most를 붙여 최상급을 만든다.

27 Sam보다 몸무게가 더 많이 나가는 사람은 John이다. heavy의 비교급은 heavier이다.

28 넷 중 키가 가장 큰 사람은 Sam이다. tall의 최상급은 tallest이다.

29 Peter와 나이가 같은 사람은 Eddy이다. 원급 표현은 ⟨as+형용사/부사의 원급+as⟩로 나타낸다.

30 delicious는 앞에 more를 써서 비교급을 만들고, '훨씬'이라는 의미의 much를 비교급 앞에 써 준다.

CHAPTER 08 의문사 의문문

Unit 01

p. 82

01 Who sings the song?
02 Who saw James?
03 Who(m) did he invite?
04 Who is making the cake?
05 Who is your favorite singer?
06 Who is playing in the park now?
07 Who uses this cell phone?
08 Who cooked this food?
09 Who(m) is she talking to?

Unit 02

p. 82

01 What do you want?
02 What did she do yesterday?
03 What is in this box?
04 What is Jason interested in?
05 What is your favorite subject?
06 What is he looking for?

Unit 03

p. 83

01 When did you meet her?
02 When do you go on a picnic?
03 When do you do your homework?
04 Where was he this morning?
05 Where do they go on Sundays?
06 What time do you go to bed?
07 Where did she put the box?
08 Where did you buy the dress?
09 Where do they play soccer?

Unit 04

p. 83

01 ⓐ
02 ⓒ
03 ⓓ
04 ⓑ
05 ⓔ
06 ⓐ
07 ⓑ
08 ⓓ
09 ⓒ

Unit 05 p. 84

01 How often
02 How long
03 How far
04 How many
05 How tall
06 How long
07 How often
08 How many
09 How much

Unit 06 p. 85

01 Whose gloves are these?
02 Which movie does he want to see?
03 What time is your birthday party?
04 Whose cell phone did you borrow?
05 Which pet do you want, a cat[dog] or a dog[cat]?
06 What subject are they studying now?

중간고사 • 기말고사 실전문제 pp. 86~90

객관식 정답 [01~15]

01 ①	02 ②	03 ⑤	04 ④	05 ③
06 ②	07 ①	08 ③	09 ②	10 ⑤
11 ④	12 ③	13 ⑤	14 ⑤	15 ③

주관식 정답 [16~30]

16 Where
17 How long
18 What
19 do → does
20 When → What 또는 time 삭제
21 Why
22 How often
23 Who
24 Which color do you like
25 time does your plane leave
26 How can I get to the airport
27 ⓐ Who → Whose
28 ⓒ leaving → leave
29 when did you send the e-mail to me
30 How long does it take from here to City Hall

해설

01 '너의 새로운 선생님은 누구시니?'라는 의미이므로 '누구'라는 의미의 의문사 Who가 알맞다.

02 '너는 어제 집에서 무엇을 했니?'라는 의미이므로 '무엇을'이라는 의미의 의문사 What이 알맞다.

03 '너는 과학과 수학 중에서 어느 과목을 더 좋아하니?'라는 의미이므로 '어느'라는 의미의 의문사 Which가 알맞다.

04 두 문장의 빈칸에는 '언제'라는 의미의 의문사 When이 들어가야 한다.

05 '얼마나 자주'와 '얼마나 많이'라는 의미의 의문사는 How often과 〈How many+셀 수 있는 명사〉이다.

06 Kevin이 학교에 결석한 이유를 말하고 있으므로 '왜'라는 의미의 의문사 Why가 알맞다.

07 인터뷰가 어땠는지를 묻고 있으므로 '어떤'이라는 의미의 의문사 How가 알맞다.

08 일반동사가 있는 경우에는 〈What+do동사+주어+동사원형 ~?〉의 형태이므로 saw가 아니라 see가 되어야 한다.

09 주어가 you이므로 do동사는 does가 아니라 do가 되어야 한다.

10 '어디서'라는 의미의 의문사는 where이고, 과거시제이므로 〈Where+did+주어+동사원형 ~?〉의 형태가 되어야 한다.

11 books가 셀 수 있는 명사이므로 much가 아니라 many가 되어야 한다.

12 일반동사가 있는 경우에는 〈What+do동사+주어+동사원형 ~?〉의 형태이므로 your brother did가 아니라 did your brother가 되어야 한다.

13 첫 번째 빈칸에는 '어디에'라는 의미의 의문사 Where가, 두 번째 빈칸에는 '언제'라는 의미의 의문사 When이, 세 번째 빈칸에는 '어느'라는 의미의 의문사 Which가 알맞다.

14 ⑤에는 What이 들어가고, 나머지에는 How가 들어간다.

15 ⓑ 주어가 Jane's umbrella로 단수이므로 are가 아니라 is가, ⓓ '어느 채소'라는 의미가 되어야 하므로 What이 아니라 Which가 되어야 한다.

16 '어디서'라는 의미의 의문사 Where가 알맞다.

17 '얼마나'라는 의미의 의문사 How long이 알맞다.

18 빈칸 뒤의 명사를 수식하면서 '무슨'이라는 의미의 의문사 What이 알맞다.

19 주어 Julia가 3인칭 단수이므로 do동사는 do가 아니라 does가 되어야 한다.

20 시간을 물을 때는 When 또는 What time으로 묻는다.

21 이유를 물을 때는 '왜'라는 의미의 의문사 Why를 써야 한다.

22 '얼마나 자주'라는 의미의 의문사는 How often이다.

23 '누가'라는 의미의 의문사는 Who이다.

24 which color는 '어떤 색깔'이라는 의미의 의문사로 일반동사 like가 있으므로 Which color 다음에 do가 나오도록 배열한다.

25 what time은 '몇 시'라는 의미의 의문사로 일반동사 leave가 있으므로 What time 다음에 does가 나오도록 배열한다.

26 how는 '어떻게'라는 의미의 의문사로 How로 시작하도록 배열한다.

27 명사 brother를 수식하면서 '누구의'라는 의미의 의문사는 Whose이다.

28 일반동사가 있는 경우에는 〈의문사+do동사+주어+동사원형 ~?〉의 형태이므로 leave가 되어야 한다.

29 '언제'라는 의미의 의문사 when을 써서 〈when+do동사+주어+동사원형 ~?〉의 형태로 써야 한다. 과거시제이므로 do동사는 did가 되어야 한다.

30 '얼마나 걸립니까?'라는 의미의 표현은 How long does it take이고, '~에서 …까지'라는 의미의 표현은 from ~ to ...이다.

CHAPTER 09 문장의 종류

Unit 01 p. 92

01 Don't sit on the desk.
02 Don't eat too much.
03 Open the box.
04 Sing a song together.
05 Never swim in this river.
06 Carry this bag for me.
07 Don't watch TV after dinner.
08 Don't use this computer.

Unit 02 p. 92

01 goes → go
02 eating → eat
03 don't → not
04 Lets → Let's
05 to go → go
06 to leave → leave
07 has → have
08 will go → go
09 do not → not do

Unit 03 p. 93

01 isn't she / she is
02 isn't he / he isn't
03 don't you / I do
04 did he / he did
05 weren't you / I wasn't
06 do you / I don't
07 doesn't she / she does
08 is it / it isn't
09 aren't they / they aren't

Unit 04 p. 93

01 will you
02 will you
03 won't they
04 can she
05 shall we
06 can't he
07 will it
08 shall we

Unit 05 p. 94

01 Isn't she reading

02 Won't you go
03 Isn't he interested
04 Didn't you use

Unit 06
p. 94

01 Do you want to return or stay here?
02 Who runs faster, you or Jason?
03 Which sports do you prefer, soccer or baseball?
04 Will he come to the office today or tomorrow?
05 Which would you like for lunch, a sandwich or a hamburger?
06 Which desk is bigger, this one or that one?

Unit 07
p. 95

01 What a smart girl she is!
02 What an exciting game baseball is!
03 What nice people they are!
04 What delicious apples these are!
05 What an old museum it is!
06 What a lovely house you have!

Unit 08
p. 95

01 How delicious this cake is!
02 How happy she looks!
03 How polite the man is!
04 How slowly she walks!
05 How interesting the story is!
06 How boring the movie was!

중간고사 • 기말고사 실전문제
pp. 96~100

객관식 정답 [01~15]

01 ④	**02** ③	**03** ①	**04** ⑤	**05** ②
06 ③	**07** ③	**08** ①	**09** ⑤	**10** ②
11 ①, ④	**12** ③	**13** ②	**14** ⑤	**15** ③

주관식 정답 [16~30]

16 Which, or
17 isn't he
18 we did
19 they are → it is 또는
an interesting story → interesting stories
20 should we → will he
21 not → don't
22 Yes, it, is
23 No, he, doesn't
24 What a wonderful world
25 How fast she swims
26 Let's not open the door, shall we
27 How → What
28 doesn't → isn't
29 No, I don't. I'm an only child.
30 Let's not have fish for dinner.

해설

01 be동사가 있는 긍정문 뒤에 나오는 부가의문문은 be동사가 있는 부정형이 되어야 하므로 isn't가 알맞다.

02 〈What+a(n)+형용사+단수 명사+(주어+동사)!〉이므로 What이 알맞다.

03 둘 중에 하나를 고르는 선택의문문이므로 or가 알맞다.

04 '~하자', '~하지 말자'라는 의미로 제안을 나타내고 있으므로 Let's가 공통으로 알맞다.

05 ②에는 doesn't가 들어가지만, 나머지에는 aren't가 들어간다.

06 How로 시작하는 감탄문은 How 다음에 형용사나 부사가 오므로 How delicious the ice cream is!가 되어야 한다.

07 앞 문장에 조동사 will이 있으므로 can't가 아니라 won't가 되어야 한다.

08 뒤의 명사 color를 수식하며, '어느 색깔'이라는 의미이므로 선택의문문에서 쓰이는 의문사 Which가 알맞다.

09 앞 문장에 주어 Mina와 일반동사의 과거형 invited가 쓰였으므로 부가의문문은 did의 부정형 didn't와 주격 인칭대명사 she가 알맞다.

10 조동사가 쓰인 부정의문문으로 '~할 수 없다'라는 의미의 Can't로 시작해야 한다.

11 일반동사의 현재형 go가 쓰였으므로 긍정으로 대답할 경

우에는 〈Yes, 주어+do.〉가 되고, 부정으로 대답할 경우에는 〈No, 주어+don't.〉가 되어야 한다.

12 〈What+a(n)+형용사+단수 명사+(주어+동사)!〉의 어순이 되어야 한다.

13 첫 번째 빈칸에는 〈What+a(n)+형용사+단수 명사+주어+동사!〉의 형태이므로 What이, 두 번째 빈칸에는 선택의문문이므로 or가, 세 번째 빈칸에는 〈How+형용사!〉의 형태이므로 How가 알맞다.

14 청유문의 부가의문문은 shall we가 되어야 한다.

15 첫 번째 make not → not make, 세 번째 Looks → Look, 네 번째 were she → was she가 되어야 한다.

16 선택의문문으로 '어느 영화'라는 의미이므로 의문사 Which와 접속사 or가 알맞다.

17 be동사가 있는 긍정문이므로 is의 부정형 isn't와 Mr. Jones를 가리키는 주격 인칭대명사 he가 알맞다.

18 질문에서 you and your sister는 대답에서는 we가 된다. 긍정으로 대답하고 있으므로 we did가 알맞다.

19 an interesting story가 단수이므로 it is가 알맞다. 또는 they are가 복수이므로 interesting stories로 고쳐도 된다.

20 앞 문장에서 조동사 won't가 쓰였으므로 will과 My brother를 가리키는 주격 인칭대명사 he가 알맞다.

21 부정명령문은 〈Don't+동사원형 ~.〉으로 나타낸다.

22 빈칸 뒤에 누가 물고기를 가장 많이 잡는지 내기하자는 내용이 나오므로 긍정의 대답이 알맞다.

23 빈칸 뒤에 드라마 보는 것을 좋아한다는 내용이 나오므로 부정의 대답이 알맞다.

24 〈What+a(n)+형용사+단수 명사!〉 어순이 되어야 한다.

25 〈How+부사+주어+동사!〉 어순이 되어야 한다.

26 〈Let's not+동사원형 ~, shall we?〉 어순이 되어야 한다.

27 How 뒤에 a와 형용사 그리고 단수 명사가 나왔으므로 What으로 시작하는 감탄문이 되어야 한다.

28 앞 문장에 be동사 is가 나왔으므로 is의 부정형 isn't가 되어야 한다.

29 형제가 없다고 했으므로 부정으로 대답해야 하고, '외동'의 표현은 an only child이다.

30 '~하지 말자'는 〈Let's not+동사원형 ~.〉의 형태로 쓴다.

CHAPTER 10 문장의 형식

Unit 01

p. 102

01 Today is Sunday.
S V C

02 Mr. Smith bought his son a new car.
S V O O

03 I met my friends in the park.
S V O M

04 My brother is very smart.
S V M C

05 You get up early every morning.
S V M

06 She studies English every day.
S V O M

07 They called their baby Star.
S V O C

08 They are swimming in the sea.
S V M

Unit 02

p. 102

01 Mike runs very fast. / 1
S V M

02 She looks young. / 2
S V C

03 Sally's backpack is blue. / 2
S V C

04 Judy dances very well. / 1
S V M

05 The teacher is tall and handsome. / 2
S V C

06 She walks to school every morning. / 1
S V M

07 My father is a famous cook. / 2
S V C

08 We went to the library every day. / 1
S V M

09 The leaves turn red in autumn. / 2
S V C M

10 Our family lived in America for two years. / 1
S V M

Unit 03 p. 103

01 It smells bad.
02 This pie tastes good.
03 He looks so kind.
04 This soap smells good.
05 It feels very soft.
06 She looks like a boy.

Unit 04 p. 103

01 She plays the violin very well.
02 He is wearing a blue shirt.
03 I met Tom at the party last night.
04 My sister and I take a walk every morning.
05 She usually eats a salad for breakfast.
06 They study English together on weekends.

Unit 05 p. 104

01 will make his daughter a chair
02 teaches us swimming on weekends
03 bought my sister a new dress
04 made his son a toy box
05 will send my friend a birthday card
06 told her parents the news

Unit 06 p. 104

01 a new bicycle for me
02 a lot of presents to her
03 some cookies for us
04 his son some money
05 my mother a pretty bag
06 a message to me

Unit 07 p. 105

01 They named the baby Lisa.
02 My brother kept his room clean.
03 The story made us happy.
04 We found the computer game interesting.
05 Don't make the man angry.
06 The news made her famous.

Unit 08 p. 105

01 wants me to be
02 asked him to bring
03 told her to take
04 allowed her to play
05 advised me to go
06 encouraged him to solve

Unit 09 p. 106

01 He had me carry these bags.
02 Let me help you.
03 I'll have him do it.
04 She made me do my homework.
05 Let me introduce my friend to you.
06 He helps his sister study English.

중간고사 • 기말고사 실전문제 pp. 107~111

객관식 정답 [01~15]

01 ③	**02** ①	**03** ①	**04** ②	**05** ⑤
06 ③	**07** ①	**08** ⑤	**09** ④	**10** ④
11 ②	**12** ④	**13** ②	**14** ①, ③	**15** ③

주관식 정답 [16~30]

16 to
17 for
18 happily → happy
19 choosing → (to) choose
20 explain → to explain
21 looks, comfortable
22 keep, their, garden, beautiful
23 bring, a, cup, of, water, to, me
24 Mr. Jacob teaches English to us. /
Mr. Jacob teaches us English.
25 She bought a pair of gloves for her brother. /
She bought her brother a pair of gloves.

26 Alex[him] borrow her textbook
27 Jian[her] to wear his sunglasses
28 me wash my hands
29 going me → me go
30 to study → study

해설

01 taste는 '맛이 나다'라는 의미로 감각을 나타내는 2형식 동사이다.

02 5형식 동사 help는 ⟨help+목적어+(to) 동사원형⟩의 형태로 쓰이므로 동사원형 lose가 알맞다.

03 5형식 동사 let은 ⟨let+목적어+원형부정사⟩의 형태로 쓰이므로 동사원형 go가 알맞다.

04 감각동사 feel 다음에는 보어로 형용사가 와야 한다.

05 수여동사 buy는 간접목적어 앞에 전치사 for를 쓰고, 5형식 동사 ask는 ⟨ask+목적어+to부정사⟩의 형태로 쓰이므로 lend 앞에 to가 와야 한다.

06 ⟨make+목적어+목적격보어⟩ 형태의 5형식 문장으로 목적격보어에 형용사가 와야 하므로 angry가 되어야 한다.

07 5형식 동사 want는 ⟨want+목적어+to부정사⟩의 형태로 쓰이므로 do가 아니라 to do가 되어야 한다.

08 ⑤는 3형식 동사로 쓰인 make이고, 나머지는 모두 5형식 동사로 쓰인 make이다.

09 look like는 '~처럼 보이다'라는 의미로 뒤에 명사가 나온다. 주어가 3인칭 단수이고, 현재시제이므로 looks like가 되어야 한다.

10 5형식 동사 tell은 ⟨tell+목적어+to부정사⟩의 형태로 쓰는데, 과거시제이므로 told가 되어야 한다.

11 3형식 문장을 4형식으로 바꿀 때, of 뒤의 me가 간접목적어 자리로 오고, a hard question이 직접목적어 자리로 와야 한다.

12 사역동사 make는 ⟨make+목적어+원형부정사⟩의 형태이므로 ⓓ는 fix가 되어야 한다.

13 보기에서 look은 감각을 나타내는 2형식 동사로 look 다음에는 형용사가 나온다.

14 ② cleanly → clean, ④ has → had, ⑤ to return → return이 되어야 한다.

15 ⓐ strangely → strange, ⓒ a letter my dad → my dad a letter 또는 my dad → to my dad가 되어야 한다.

16 수여동사 send는 간접목적어 앞에 전치사 to를 쓴다.

17 수여동사 make는 간접목적어 앞에 전치사 for를 쓴다.

18 감각동사 look 다음에는 보어로 형용사가 와야 한다.

19 준사역동사 help는 ⟨help+목적어+(to) 동사원형⟩의 형태이므로 choose 또는 to choose가 되어야 한다.

20 5형식 동사 ask는 ⟨ask+목적어+to부정사⟩의 형태이므로 to explain이 되어야 한다.

21 look은 '~해 보이다'라는 의미의 감각동사로 look 다음에 형용사가 와야 한다. 주어가 3인칭 단수이므로 looks가 되어야 한다.

22 5형식 동사 keep은 ⟨keep+목적어+형용사⟩의 형태로 써야 한다. do one's best 최선을 다하다

23 수여동사 bring은 간접목적어 앞에 전치사 to를 쓴다. a cup of water 물 한 컵

24 3형식 문장은 ⟨teach+직접목적어+to+간접목적어⟩의 형태로, 4형식 문장은 ⟨teach+간접목적어+직접목적어⟩의 형태로 쓴다.

25 3형식 문장은 ⟨buy+직접목적어+for+간접목적어⟩의 형태로, 4형식 문장은 ⟨buy+간접목적어+직접목적어⟩의 형태로 쓴다.

26 사역동사 let은 ⟨let+목적어+원형부정사⟩의 형태로 써야 한다.

27 5형식 동사 allow는 ⟨allow+목적어+to부정사⟩의 형태로 써야 한다.

28 사역동사 make는 ⟨make+목적어+원형부정사⟩의 형태로 써야 한다.

29 사역동사 let은 ⟨let+목적어+원형부정사⟩의 형태이므로 목적어 me가 먼저 오고, 동사원형 go가 되어야 한다.

30 사역동사 make는 ⟨make+목적어+원형부정사⟩의 형태이므로 study가 되어야 한다.

CHAPTER 11 to부정사와 동명사

Unit 01
p. 114

01 It is very hard to get a job.
02 It is bad to eat a lot.
03 It is very exciting to learn swimming.
04 It is not easy to solve this problem.
05 It is very useful to read books.

Unit 02
p. 114

01 My hobby is to read English books.
02 My father's plan is to buy a new car.
03 Sally's job is to design clothes.
04 Mike's hobby is to draw pictures.
05 My homework is to keep a diary.

Unit 03
p. 115

01 plans to go
02 decided not to do
03 want to swim
04 promised not to say
05 hope to meet
06 agreed to take

Unit 04
p. 115

01 a lot of friends to meet
02 some fruit to eat
03 something hot to drink
04 no chance to talk
05 a lot of homework to do
06 something to eat

Unit 05
p. 116

01 ⓐ
02 ⓑ
03 ⓐ
04 ⓐ
05 ⓑ
06 ⓐ
07 ⓑ

Unit 06
p. 116

01 She grew up to be a famous dancer.
02 Sam must be a fool to believe it.
03 The question was hard to answer.
04 She must be angry to say so.
05 Your phone number is easy to remember.
06 English is not difficult to learn.

Unit 07
p. 117

01 Teaching English is interesting.
02 My favorite hobby is climbing mountains.
03 Her good habit is getting up early in the morning.
04 Playing computer games makes children excited.
05 My plan is watching a movie tonight.

Unit 08
p. 117

01 made → making
02 to write → writing
03 listen → listening
04 shout → shouting
05 to write → writing
06 do → doing
07 close → closing
08 to eat → eating
09 to smoking → smoking

Unit 09
p. 118

01 decided to sell
02 Avoid wasting
03 hopes to enter
04 finished cleaning
05 promised to join
06 expect to see
07 denied stealing
08 enjoyed watching
09 agreed to study
10 quit working
11 refused to answer
12 mind opening

Unit 10
p. 119

01 was busy doing
02 spent a week finishing
03 How about having
04 go shopping
05 What about writing
06 spend every Sunday playing
07 is so busy finishing

중간고사 • 기말고사 실전문제 pp. 120~124

객관식 정답 [01~15]

01 ④	**02** ③	**03** ①	**04** ③	**05** ⑤
06 ④	**07** ④	**08** ③	**09** ②	**10** ⑤
11 ③	**12** ④	**13** ⑤	**14** ②	**15** ②

주관식 정답 [16~30]

16 close → closing
17 seen → see
18 recycle → recycling
19 smoking
20 to hear
21 to, turn
22 to, see
23 anything cold to drink
24 in order to get a good seat
25 going hike → go hiking
26 visiting → to visit
27 Mike wants to buy a house to live in.
28 Suji has a lot of homework to finish by tomorrow.
29 finished reading a book / enjoyed taking pictures
30 enjoys playing soccer / to be a soccer player in the future

해설

01 love는 to부정사와 동명사 둘 다 목적어로 취하는 동사이다.

02 동명사(동사원형+-ing)는 문장의 주어 역할을 할 수 있다.

03 〈It is+형용사+to부정사 ~〉 구문으로 It은 가주어이고, to부정사 이하가 진주어이다.

04 enjoy는 동명사를 목적어로 취하는 동사이고, 나머지는 to부정사를 목적어로 취하는 동사이다.

05 decide는 to부정사를 목적어로 취하는 동사이고, 나머지는 동명사를 목적어로 취하는 동사이다.

06 '더 많은 정보를 얻기 위해서'라는 의미이므로 목적을 나타내는 부사적 용법의 to부정사가 알맞다.

07 sandwiches and *gimbap*을 수식하는 형용사적 용법의 to부정사가 되도록 to eat이 되어야 한다.

08 〈be busy -ing〉의 형태이므로 was busy answering이 되어야 한다.

09 〈-thing/-one/-body+형용사+to부정사〉의 형태이므로 warm anything은 anything warm이 되어야 한다.

10 동명사 주어는 단수 취급하므로 are가 아니라 is가 되어야 한다.

11 첫 번째 빈칸에는 〈be busy -ing〉의 형태가 되어야 하므로 studying이, 두 번째 빈칸에는 동명사가 문장에서 보어로 쓰일 수 있으므로 making이 알맞다.

12 첫 번째 빈칸에는 a hotel을 수식하는 형용사적 용법의 to부정사 to stay in이, 두 번째 빈칸에는 〈It is+명사+to부정사 ~〉의 형태가 되어야 하므로 to부정사 to ask가 알맞다.

13 앞의 명사를 수식하는 to부정사의 형용사적 용법을 고른다. ①, ②는 주어와 목적어로 쓰인 명사적 용법이고, ③, ④는 결과와 목적으로 쓰인 부사적 용법이다.

14 감정의 원인을 나타내는 to부정사의 부사적 용법을 고른다. ①, ③은 보어와 목적어로 쓰인 명사적 용법이고, ④는 판단의 근거로 쓰인 부사적 용법이며, ⑤는 앞의 명사를 수식하는 형용사적 용법이다.

15 두 번째 문장에서 listen은 listening(전치사의 목적어)이, 다섯 번째 문장에서 living은 to live(진주어)가 되어야 한다.

16 mind는 동명사를 목적어로 취하는 동사이므로 close가 아닌 closing이 되어야 한다.

17 '배웅하기 위해서'라는 의미로 to부정사의 목적을 나타내고 있으므로 to 다음에는 동사원형 see가 와야 한다.

18 전치사의 목적어로 동명사가 와야 하므로 recycle이 아니라 recycling이 되어야 한다.

19 '~하는 것을 멈추다'라는 의미이므로 stopped 뒤에 동명사가 와야 한다.

20 '그 소식을 들어서 행복했다'라는 의미이므로 감정의 원인을 나타내는 to부정사가 와야 한다.

21 '제출하기 위해서'라는 목적을 나타내므로 to부정사가 되어야 한다. turn in ~을 제출하다

22 '보기 위해서'라는 목적을 나타내므로 to부정사가 되어야 한다.

23 ⟨-thing+형용사+to부정사⟩의 어순으로 배열해야 한다.

24 ⟨in order to+동사원형⟩의 형태로 배열해야 한다.

25 want는 to부정사를 목적어로 취하는 동사로 to 다음에는 동사원형인 go가 와야 하고, ⟨go -ing⟩는 '~하러 가다'라는 의미의 관용 표현이므로 hiking이 되어야 한다.

26 plan은 to부정사를 목적어로 취하는 동사이므로 visiting이 아니라 to visit이 되어야 한다.

27 to부정사가 앞의 명사 a house를 수식하는 문장이 되어야 한다.

28 to부정사가 앞의 명사 a lot of homework를 수식하는 문장이 되어야 한다.

29 finish와 enjoy는 동명사를 목적어로 취하는 동사이다.

30 enjoy는 동명사를 목적어로 취하고, want는 to부정사를 목적어로 취한다. in the future 장래에, 미래에

CHAPTER 12 전치사

Unit 01 p. 126

01 at noon
02 in December
03 at 8
04 in the evening
05 on Sunday
06 in 2012

Unit 02 p. 126

01 from Monday to Friday
02 for three[3] hours
03 after work
04 before sunrise
05 during the day
06 for a week

Unit 03 p. 127

01 at
02 in
03 on
04 at
05 in
06 on
07 in
08 at

Unit 04 p. 127

01 between
02 behind
03 in front of
04 next to
05 over
06 under
07 behind
08 between

Unit 05 p. 128

01 down
02 into
03 up
04 to
05 into
06 from, to
07 out of
08 up
09 to
10 down
11 out of
12 from

Unit 06 p. 129

01 for
02 with
03 like
04 of

05 with
06 for
07 about
08 like
09 because of / with
10 of
11 about
12 because of

중간고사 • 기말고사 실전문제 pp. 130~134

객관식 정답 [01~15]

01 ①	02 ⑤	03 ③	04 ④	05 ②
06 ①	07 ②	08 ④	09 ①	10 ④
11 ④	12 ①	13 ③	14 ③	15 ①

주관식 정답 [16~30]

16 in → from
17 at → in
18 because → because of
19 behind
20 like
21 for
22 on, in
23 from
24 like
25 at ABC Tower on December 31st
26 this plant in front of the window
27 front → in front of
28 in → at
29 at the airport at 9 o'clock
30 walking under a ladder brings bad luck

해설

01 for는 '~ 동안'이라는 의미로 뒤에 구체적인 시간이 온다.

02 '~ 앞에'라는 의미의 전치사 in front of가 와야 한다.

03 공간이 없는 장소나 하나의 지점을 나타낼 때는 전치사 at이 와야 한다.

04 '~을 위해'라는 의미의 전치사 for가 와야 한다.

05 '~ 위로'라는 의미의 전치사 up이 와야 한다.

06 정확한 시각 앞에는 at이, 연도 앞에는 in이 와야 한다.

07 '~와'라는 의미의 전치사 with가, '~에 대해'라는 의미의 전치사 about이 와야 한다.

08 because of는 '~ 때문에'라는 의미로 이유를 나타내는 명사구인 the heavy rain(폭우) 앞에 와야 한다.

09 ①에는 near, behind, in front of 등이 들어가고, 나머지에는 of가 들어간다.

10 정확한 시각 앞이므로 during이 아니라 at이 알맞다.

11 '~부터 …까지'라는 의미의 전치사 from ~ to ...가 쓰여야 하므로 두 번째 in은 to가 되어야 한다.

12 '박스 안에'라는 의미이므로 at이 아니라 in이 알맞다.

13 '~ 안에, 안으로'라는 의미의 전치사 into를 써야 한다.

14 from이 아니라 on, under, behind 등이 되어야 한다.

15 two weeks라는 구체적인 시간이 왔으므로 during이 아니라 for가 되어야 한다.

16 '~부터 …까지'라는 의미의 전치사 from ~ to ...를 써야 하므로 in이 아니라 from이 되어야 한다.

17 '아침에'라는 의미로 at이 아니라 in이 되어야 한다.

18 '~ 때문에'라는 의미의 because of는 뒤에 명사(구)가 온다. because는 접속사로 because 뒤에는 〈주어+동사〉가 온다.

19 '우체국 뒤에'라는 의미이므로 '~ 뒤에'라는 의미의 전치사 behind가 와야 한다.

20 '~처럼, ~ 같은'이라는 의미의 전치사 like가 와야 한다.

21 '한 시간 반 동안'이라는 의미로 구체적인 시간이 나오므로 for가 알맞다.

22 '저녁에 침대 위에서'라는 의미이므로 on the bed와 in the evening이 되어야 한다.

23 from은 '~에서부터'라는 의미이고, across from은 '~ 맞은편에'라는 의미이다.

24 like는 '~처럼, ~ 같은'이라는 의미이다.

25 장소와 시간이 함께 나올 경우에는 장소를 먼저 써 주는데, ABC Tower 앞에는 at이, 날짜 앞에는 on을 써 준다.

26 in front of는 '~ 앞에'라는 의미이다.

27 '~ 앞에'라는 의미의 전치사는 front가 아니라 in front of이다.

28 하나의 지점을 나타낼 때는 at을 써야 한다.

29 〈장소+시간〉 순으로 써야 하는데, the airport 앞에는 at이, 정확한 시각 앞에도 at을 써 준다.

30 동명사 walking이 주어이고, '사다리 아래'는 under a ladder이다. 동명사가 주어이므로 brings가 되었다.

CHAPTER 13 접속사

Unit 01 p. 136

01 She likes cats, but she doesn't pet them.
02 I stayed at home and (I) played computer games.
03 He can play the guitar, but he can't play the piano.
04 She went to the window and (she) looked out.
05 Jake wants to drink some milk, but he doesn't have any money.

Unit 02 p. 136

01 so everyone likes him
02 on the desk or in the drawer
03 or go shopping with me
04 so I can't buy the book
05 washes the dishes or cleans her room
06 so I can't hear you well

Unit 03 p. 137

01 before you go out
02 when I was waiting for the bus
03 before you moved here
04 when you ride a bicycle
05 before she goes to bed
06 after his brother comes home

Unit 04 p. 137

01 Because the water was cold
02 if you meet her
03 because it was going to rain
04 Because the car is too expensive
05 if it is nice outside

Unit 05 p. 138

01 that she will be a famous movie star
02 that her father is ill in bed
03 that you will come back soon
04 that you are waiting for him
05 that she will leave tomorrow
06 that the summer vacation is coming

중간고사 • 기말고사 실전문제 pp. 139~143

객관식 정답 [01~15]

01 ③	**02** ①	**03** ④	**04** ②	**05** ①
06 ④	**07** ②	**08** ④	**09** ②	**10** ⑤
11 ⑤	**12** ④	**13** ③	**14** ②	**15** ⑤

주관식 정답 [16~30]

16 but
17 before
18 that
19 will exercise → exercise
20 to play → playing
21 think, that
22 and, become[be]
23 ⓒ after → when
24 ⓔ or → so
25 when you won the award in 2018
26 Because I lived in Rome for 7 years
27 you take this medicine, you will[you'll] get better
28 is certain that my uncle will come to my house tonight
29 We couldn't play tennis because it was raining. / Because it was raining, we couldn't play tennis.
30 Raise your right hand when you have a question. / When you have a question, raise your right hand.

해설

01 '너와 나'라는 의미로 '~와'라는 의미의 등위접속사 and가 알맞다.

02 문장 내에서 목적어 역할을 하는 명사절 접속사 that이 알맞다.

03 '너는 네 숙제를 끝마친 후에'라는 의미로 '~한 후에'라는 의미의 접속사 after가 알맞다.

04 '~이지만'이라는 의미의 등위접속사 but이 알맞다.

05 '~한다면'이라는 의미로 조건을 나타내는 접속사 if가 알맞다.

06 이유를 나타내는 접속사 because는 치통이 있다는 이유 앞에 들어가야 한다.

07 '또는, ~이거나'라는 의미의 등위접속사 or가 알맞다.

08 조건을 나타내는 if절에서는 현재시제가 미래시제를 대신하므로 (A)에는 현재시제인 take가, (B)에는 미래시제인 will take가 와야 한다.

09 ②는 '언제'라는 의미의 의문사 when이고, 나머지는 접속사 when이다.

10 ⑤는 '저'라는 의미의 지시형용사 that이고, 나머지는 명사절 접속사 that이다.

11 등위접속사 and의 앞, 뒤에 나오는 동사 형태가 동일해야 하므로 shouted가 아니라 (is) shouting이 되어야 한다.

12 ④에는 because가 들어가는 반면, 나머지에는 if가 들어간다.

13 (A)에는 '그래서'라는 의미의 접속사 so가, (B)에는 '~할 때'라는 의미의 접속사 When이, (C)에는 '~하기 전에'라는 의미의 접속사 before가 알맞다.

14 ⓑ에는 문장 내에서 보어 역할을 하는 명사절 접속사 that이 알맞다.

15 오늘 아침에 아무것도 먹지 못했기 때문에 배가 고프다는 의미이므로 이유를 나타내는 접속사 because로 연결해야 한다.

16 '소고기는 좋아하지만 돼지고기는 좋아하지 않는다'라는 의미로 '~이지만'이라는 의미의 but이 알맞다.

17 '나가기 전에'라는 의미로 '~하기 전에'라는 의미의 before가 알맞다.

18 문장 내에서 진주어 역할을 하는 명사절 접속사 that이 알맞다.

19 조건을 나타내는 if절에서는 현재시제가 미래시제를 대신하므로 will exercise가 아니라 exercise가 되어야 한다.

20 등위접속사 and의 앞, 뒤에 나오는 동사 형태가 동일해야 하고, enjoy 뒤에는 동명사가 와야 하므로 to play가 아니라 playing이 되어야 한다.

21 문장 내에서 목적어 역할을 하는 명사절 접속사 that을 써야 한다.

22 등위접속사 and의 앞, 뒤에 나오는 동사 형태가 동일해야 하므로 동사원형인 become 또는 be를 써야 한다.

23 '울고 싶을 때'라는 의미로 '~할 때'라는 의미의 when이 알맞다.

24 '내 친구가 병원에 있어서'라는 의미로 '그래서'라는 의미의 so가 알맞다.

25 '~할 때'라는 의미의 when 뒤에 〈주어+동사〉 순으로 배열한다.

26 '~하기 때문에'라는 의미의 Because 뒤에 〈주어+동사〉 순으로 배열한다.

27 조건을 나타내는 if절에서는 현재시제가 미래시제를 대신하므로 take로 쓰고, 주절에서는 미래시제 will을 써서 나타낸다.

28 가주어 It과 진주어 that절 형태가 되어야 한다. It is certain that ~.은 '~라는 것은 확실하다.'라는 의미이다.

29 '비가 내리고 있었기 때문에'라는 의미가 되도록 because를 it was raining 앞에 쓴다. 또한 because절은 문장 앞으로 나올 수 있다.

30 '질문이 있을 때'라는 의미가 되도록 when을 you have a question 앞에 쓴다. 또한 when절은 문장 앞으로 나올 수 있다.

EBS

MY GRAMMAR COACH

내신기출 N제 중1

중학도 EBS!

EBS중학의 무료강좌와 프리미엄강좌로 완벽 내신대비!

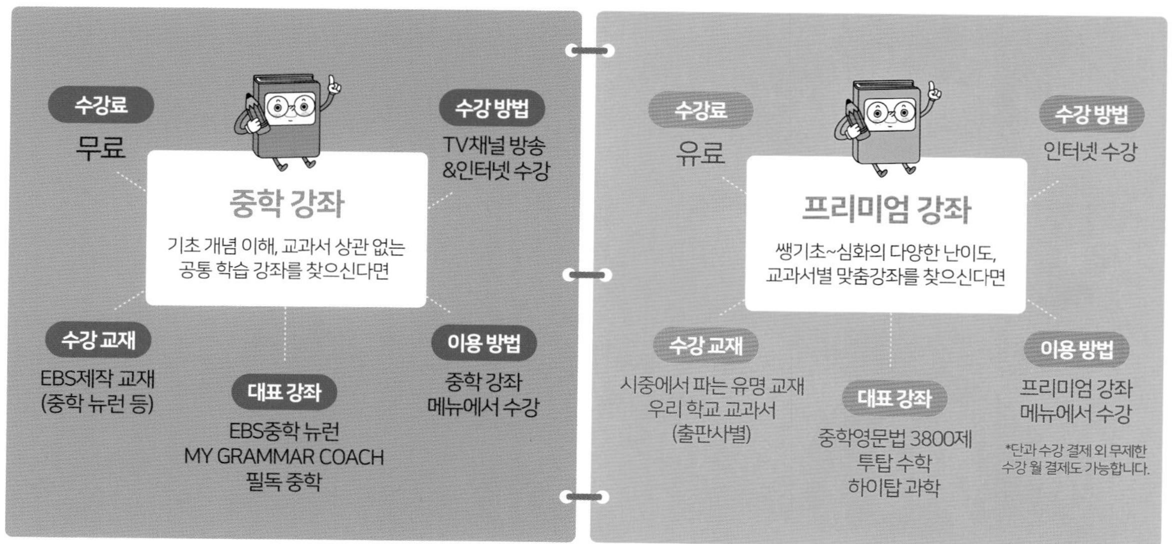

프리패스 하나면 EBS중학프리미엄 전 강좌 무제한 수강

내신 대비 진도 강좌

- 국어/영어: 출판사별 국어7종/ 영어9종
  우리학교 교과서 맞춤강좌
- 수학/과학: 시중 유명 교재 강좌
  모든 출판사 내신 공통 강좌
- 사회/역사: 개념 및 핵심 강좌
  자유학기제 대비 강좌

영어 수학 수준별 강좌

- 영어: 영역별 다양한 레벨의 강좌
  문법 5종/독해 1종/듣기 1종
  어휘 3종/회화 3종/쓰기 1종
- 수학: 실력에 딱 맞춘 수준별 강좌
  기초개념 3종/ 문제적용 4종
  유형훈련 3종/ 최고심화 3종

시험 대비 / 예비 강좌

- 중간, 기말고사 대비 특강
- 서술형 대비 특강
- 수행평가 대비 특강
- 반배치 고사 대비 강좌
- 예비 중1 선행 강좌
- 예비 고1 선행 강좌

왜 EBS중학프리미엄 프리패스를 선택해야 할까요?

현직 교사들이 직접 참여하는 강의

타사 대비 60% 수준의 합리적 수강료

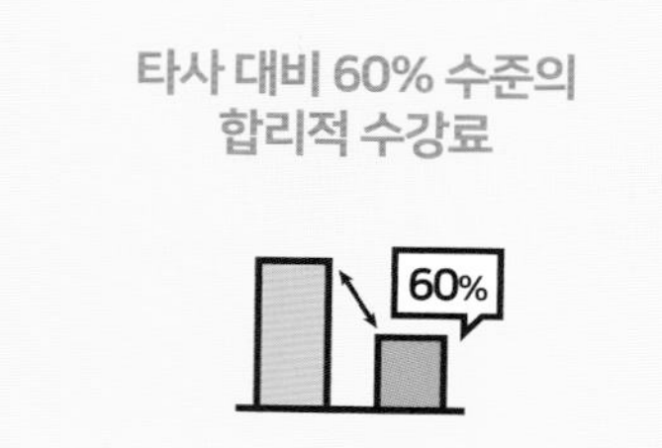

프리패스 회원만을 위한 특별한 혜택

자세한 내용은 EBS중학 > 프리미엄 강좌 > 무한수강 프리패스(http://mid.ebs.co.kr/premium/middle/index) 에서 확인할 수 있습니다.

*사정상 개설강좌, 가격정책은 변경될 수 있습니다.

중학도 EBS! 최고의 강의, 합리적인 가격

프리패스 구매 문의 : 1588-1580 / 연중무휴 EBS중학프리미엄